THE BUDDHA
and
HIS TEACHINGS

NARADA

Buddhist Missionary Society
Malaysia.

Publication of the Buddhist Missionary Society
123, Jalan Berhala,
50470 Kuala Lumpur, Malaysia.

First Edition 2508-1964
Second Edition 2517-1973
Third Edition 2521-1977

Fourth Edition 2532-1988
Printed by Syarikat Chip Seng Trading Sdn. Bhd.,
Kuala Lumpur, Malaysia.

ISBN: 967-9920-44-5 (1988)

CONTENTS

Chapter		Page.

INTRODUCTION

Many valuable books have been written by Eastern and Western scholars, Buddhists and non-Buddhists alike, to present the life and teachings of the Buddha to those who are interested in Buddhism.

Amongst them one of the most popular works is still *The Light of Asia* by Sir Edwin Arnold. Many Western truth-seekers were attracted to Buddhism by this world-famous poem.

Congratulations of Eastern and Western Buddhists are due to the learned writers on their laudable efforts to enlighten the readers on the Buddha-Dhamma.

This new treatise is another humble attempt made by a member of the Order of the Sangha, based on the Páli Texts, commentaries, and traditions prevailing in Buddhist countries, especially in Ceylon.

The first part of the book deals with the Life of the Buddha, the second with the Dhamma, the Páli term for His Doctrine.

●

The Buddha-Dhamma is a moral and philosophical system which expounds a unique path of Enlightenment, and is not a subject to be studied from a mere academic standpoint.

The Doctrine is certainly to be studied, more to be practised, and above all to be realized by oneself.

Mere learning is of no avail without actual practice. The learned man who does not practise the Dhamma, the Buddha says, is like a colourful flower without scent.

He who does not study the Dhamma is like a blind man. But, he who does not practise the Dhamma is comparable to a library.

●

There are some hasty critics who denounce Buddhism as a passive and inactive religion. This unwarranted criticism is far from the truth.

The Buddha was the first most active missionary in the world. He wandered from place to place for forty-five years preaching His doctrine to the masses and the intelligentsia. Till His last moment, He served humanity both by example and by precept. His distinguished disciples followed suit. Penniless, they even travelled to distant lands to propagate the Dhamma, expecting nothing in return.

"Strive on with diligence", were the last words of the Buddha. No emancipation or purification can be gained without personal striving. As such petitional or intercessory prayers are denounced in Buddhism and in their stead is meditation which leads to self-control, purification, and enlightenment. Both meditation and service form salient characteristics of Buddhism. In fact, all Buddhist nations grew up in the cradle of Buddhism.

"Do no evil", that is, be not a curse to oneself and others, was the Buddha's first advice. This was followed by His second admonition—"Do good", that is, be a blessing to oneself and others. His final exhortation was—"Purify one's mind"—which was the most important and the most essential.

Can such a religion be termed inactive and passive?

It may be mentioned that, amongst the thirty-seven factors that lead to enlightenment (*Bodhipakkhiya-Dhamma*), *viriya* or energy occurs nine times.

Clarifying His relationship with His followers, the Buddha states:

"You yourselves should make the exertion.

The Tathāgatas are mere teachers."

The Buddhas indicate the path and it is left for us to follow that path to obtain our purification. Self-exertion plays an important part in Buddhism.

"By oneself is one purified; by oneself is one defiled."

●

Bound by rules and regulations, Bhikkhus can be active in their own fields without trespassing their limits, while lay followers can serve their religion, country and the world in their own way, guided by their Buddhist principles.

Buddhism offers one way of life to Bhikkhus and another to lay followers.

x

In one sense all Buddhists are courageous warriors. They do fight, but not with weapons and bombs. They do kill, but not innocent men, women and children.

With whom and with what do they fight? Whom do they mercilessly kill?

They fight with themselves, for man is the worst enemy of man. Mind is his worst foe and best friend. Ruthlessly they kill the passions of lust, hatred and ignorance that reside in this mind by morality, concentration and wisdom.

Those who prefer to battle with passions alone in solitude are perfectly free to do so. Bhikkhus who live in seclusion are noteworthy examples. To those contended ones, solitude is happiness. Those who seek delight in battling with life's problems living in the world and thus make a happy world where men can live as ideal citizens in perfect peace and harmony, can adopt that responsibility and that arduous course.

Man is not meant for Buddhism. But Buddhism is meant for man.

●

According to Buddhism, it should be stated that neither wealth nor poverty, if rightly viewed, can be an obstacle towards being an ideal Buddhist. Anāthapindika, the Buddha's best supporter, was a millionaire. Ghatikāra, who was regarded even better than a king, was a penniless potter.

As Buddhism appeals to both the rich and the poor it appeals equally to the masses and the intelligentsia.

The common folk are attracted by the devotional side of Buddhism and its simpler ethics while the intellectuals are fascinated by the deeper teachings and mental culture.

A casual visitor to a Buddhist country, who enters a Buddhist temple for the first time, might get the wrong impression that Buddhism is confined to rites and ceremonies and is a superstitious religion which countenances worship of images and trees.

Buddhism, being tolerant, does not totally denounce such external forms of reverence as they are necessary for the masses. One can see with what devotion they perform such religious ceremonies. Their faith is increased thereby. Buddhists kneel before the image and pay their respects to what that image represents. Understanding Buddhists reflect on the virtues of the Buddha. They seek not wordly or spiritual favours from the image. The Bodhi-tree, on the other hand, is the symbol of enlightenment.

What the Buddha expects from His adherents are not these forms of obeisance but the actual observance of His Teachings. "He who practises my teaching best, reveres me most", is the advice of the Buddha.

An understanding Buddhist can practise the Dhamma without external forms of homage. To follow the Noble Eightfold Path neither temples nor images are absolutely necessary.

●

Is it correct to say that Buddhism is absolutely other-worldly although Buddhism posits a series of past and future lives and an indefinite number of habitable planes?

The object of the Buddha's mission was to deliver beings from suffering by eradicating its cause and to teach a way to put an end to both birth and death if one wishes to do so. Incidentally, however, the Buddha has expounded discourses which tend to worldly progress. Both material and spiritual progress are essential for the development of a nation. One should not be separated from the other, nor should material progress be achieved by sacrificing spiritual progress as is to be witnessed today amongst materialistic-minded nations in the world. It is the duty of respective Governments and philanthropic bodies to cater for the material development of the people and provide congenial conditions, while religions like Buddhism, in particular, cater for the moral advancement to make people ideal citizens.

●

Buddhism goes counter to most religions in striking the Middle Way and in making its Teaching homo-centric in contradistinction to theo-centric creeds. As such Buddhism is introvert and is concerned with individual emancipation. The Dhamma has to be realized by oneself (*sandiṭṭhiko*)

●

As a rule, the expected ultimate goal of the majority of mankind is either nihilism or eternalism. Materialists believe in complete annihilation after death. According to some religions the goal is to be achieved in an after-life, in eternal union either with an Almighty Being or an inexplicable force which, in other words, is one form of eternalism.

Buddhism advocates the middle path. Its goal is neither nihilism, for there is nothing permanent to annihilate nor eternalism, for there is no permanent soul to eternalise. The Buddhist goal can be achieved in this life itself.

●

What happens to the Arahant after death? This is a subtle and difficult question to be answered as Nibbána is a supramundane state that cannot be expressed by words and is beyond space and time. Strictly speaking, there exists a Nibbāna but no person to attain Nibbāna. The Buddha says it is not right to state that an Arahant exists nor does not exist after death. If, for instance, a fire burns and is extinguished, one cannot say that it went to any of the four directions. When no more fuel is added, it ceases to burn. The Buddha cites this illustration of fire and adds that the question is wrongly put. One may be confused. But, it is not surprising.

Here is an appropriate illustration by a modern scientist.

Robert Oppenheimer writes:

"If we ask, for instance, whether the position of the electron remains the same, we must say 'no'; if we ask whether the electron's position changes with time, we must say 'no'; if we ask whether the electron is at rest, we must say 'no'; if we ask whether it is in action, we must say 'no'.

"The Buddha had given such answers when interrogated as to the condition of man's self after death, but they are not familiar answers from the tradition of the 17th and 18th century science."

Evidently the learned writer is referring to the state of an Arahant after death.

●

What is the use of attaining such a state? Why should we negate existence? Should we not affirm existence for life is full of joy?

These are not unexpected questions. They are the typical questions of persons who either desire to enjoy life or to work for humanity, facing responsibilities and undergoing suffering.

To the former, a Buddhist would say—you may if you like, but be not slaves to worldly pleasures which are fleeting and illusory; whether you like it or not, you will have to reap what you sow. To the latter a Buddhist might say—by all means work for the weal of humanity and seek pleasure in altruistic service.

Buddhism offers the goal of Nibbána to those who need it, and is not forced on any. "Come and see", advises the Buddha.

●

Till the ultimate goal is achieved a Buddhist is expected to lead a noble and useful life.

Buddhism possesses an excellent code of morals suitable to both advanced and unadvanced types of individuals.

They are:

(a) The five precepts–not to kill, not to steal, not to commit adultery, not to lie, and not to take intoxicating liquor.

(b) The four Sublime States (*Brahma-Vihāra*):
Loving-kindness, compassion, appreciative joy and equanimity.

(c) The ten transcendental virtues (*Pāramitā*):—generosity, morality, renunciation, wisdom, energy, patience, truthfulness, resolution, loving-kindness, and equanimity.

(d) The Noble Eightfold Path:

Right understanding, right thoughts, right speech, right action, right livelihood, right effort, right mindfulness and right concentration.

Those who aspire to attain Arahantship at the earliest possible opportunity may contemplate on the exhortation given to Venerable Rāhula by the Buddha—namely.

"This body is not mine; this am I not; this is not my soul."

(*N'etaṁ mama, n'eso' hamasmi, na me so attā*).

●

It should be humbly stated that this book is not intended for scholars but students who wish to understand the life of the Buddha and His fundamental teachings.

The original edition of this book first appeared in 1942. The second one, a revised and enlarged edition with many additions and modifications, was published in Saigon in 1964 with voluntary contributions from my devout Vietnamese supporters. In the present one I have added two more chapters and an appendix with some important Suttas.

It gives me pleasure to state that a Vietnamese translation of this book by Mr. Pham Kim Kanh (Sunanda) was also published in Saigon.

In preparing this volume I have made use of the translations of the Pāli Text Society and several works written by Buddhists and non-Buddhists. At times I may have merely echoed their authentic views and even used their appropriate wording. Wherever possible I have acknowledged the source.

I am extremely grateful to the late Mr. V. F. Gunaratna who, amidst his multifarious duties as Public Trustee of Ceylon, very carefully revised and edited the whole manuscript with utmost precision and great faith. Though an onerous task, it was a labour of love to him since he was an ideal practising Buddhist, well versed in the Buddha-Dhamma.

My thanks are due to generous devotees for their voluntary contributions, to Mrs. Coralie La Brooy and Miss Ranjani Goonetilleke for correcting the proofs and also to the Associated Newspapers of Ceylon Ltd. for printing the book with great care.

NĀRADA.

14th July,2522—1980.

Vajirārāma,

Colombo 5.

THE BUDDHA
AND
HIS TEACHINGS

Namo tassa Bhagavato Arahato
Sammā-Sambuddhassa!
Homage to Him, the Exalted, the Worthy,
the Fully Enlightened One!

CHAPTER I
THE BUDDHA

FROM BIRTH TO RENUNCIATION

*"A unique Being, an extraordinary Man arises in
this world for the benefit of the many, for the happiness of the many, out of compassion for the world,
for the good, benefit, and happiness of gods and
men. Who is this Unique Being? It is the Tathāgata, the Exalted, Fully Enlightened One."*

Anguttara Nikāya Pt. I, XIII P. 22.

Birth

On the full moon day of May,[1] in the year
623 B.C.[2] there was born in the *Lumbini Park*[3] at

---

1. Corresponding to Pāli *Vesākha*, Saṁskrit—*Vaisākha*,
    and Siṁhala—*Vesak*.

2. Unlike the Christian Era the Buddha Era is reckoned
    from the death of the Buddha, which occurred in 543
    B.C. (in His 80th year), and not from His birth.

3. A pillar, erected at this sacred spot by King Asoka, still
    stands to this day to commemorate the event.

Kapilavatthu,[1] on the Indian borders of present *Nepal,* a noble prince who was destined to be the greatest religious teacher of the world.

His father[2] was *King Suddhodana* of the aristocratic *Sākya*[3] clan and his mother was *Queen Mahā Māyā.* As the beloved mother died seven days after his birth, *Mahā Pajāpati Gotamī,* her younger sister, who was also married to the King, adopted the child, entrusting her own son, *Nanda,* to the care of the nurses.

Great were the rejoicings of the people over the birth of this illustrious prince. An ascetic of

---

1. The site of *Kapilavatthu* has been identified with Bhuila (Bhulya) in the Basti district, three miles from the Bengal and N. W. Railway station of Babuan.
2. See the genealogical table.
3. *Gotama* is the family name, and *Sākya* is the name of the race to which the Buddha belonged.

Tradition holds that the sons of *King Okkāka* of the *Mahāsammata* line, were exiled through the plotting of their step-mother. These princes, in the course of their wanderings, arrived at the foothills of the Himalayas. Here they met the sage *Kapila,* on whose advice, and after whom, they founded the city of Kapilavatthu, the site of *Kapila. King Okkāka,* hearing of the enterprise of the princes, exclaimed—"*Sakyā vata bho rāja-kumārā*-Capable, indeed, are the noble princes." Hence the race and the kingdom they originated were known by the name *Sākya.*

The Sākya kingdom was situated in South Nepal and extended over much of modern Oudh.

See E. J. Thomas, *Life of Buddha,* p. 6.

high spiritual attainments, named *Asita*, also known as *Kāladevala*, was particularly pleased to hear this happy news, and being a tutor of the King, visited the palace to see the Royal babe. The King, who felt honoured by his unexpected visit, carried the child up to him in order to make the child pay him due reverence, but, to the surprise of all, the child's legs turned and rested on the matted locks of the ascetic. Instantly, the ascetic rose from his seat and, foreseeing with his supernormal vision the child's future greatness, saluted him with clasped hands.[1] The Royal father did likewise.

The great ascetic smiled at first and then was sad. Questioned regarding his mingled feelings, he answered that he smiled because the prince would eventually become a Buddha, an Enlightened One, and he was sad because he would not be able to benefit by the superior wisdom of the Enlightened One owing to his prior death and rebirth in a Formless Plane (*Arūpaloka*).[2]

---

1. See Warren, *Buddhism in Translations*, p. 49 and Jātaka Commentary.

   On *Asita's* advice his nephew *Nālaka* renounced the world and when the prince, as expected, attained Buddhahood, he heard His teaching and became an Arahant.

   See Nālaka Sutta, Sutta Nipāta, p. 131.

2. *Arūpalokas* are immaterial planes where those who have developed the Arūpa Jhānas (Absorptions or Ecstasies) are born.

Naming Ceremony

On the fifth day after the prince's birth he was named *Siddhattha* which means "wish fulfilled". His family name was *Gotama*.[1]

In accordance with the ancient Indian custom many learned brahmins were invited to the palace for the naming ceremony. Amongst them there were eight distinguished men. Examining the characteristic marks of the child, seven of them raised two fingers each, indicative of two alternative possibilities, and said that he would either become a Universal Monarch or a Buddha. But the youngest, *Kondañña*,[2] who excelled others in wisdom, noticing the hair on the forehead turned to the right, raised only one finger and convincingly declared that the prince would definitely retire from the world and become a Buddha.

Ploughing Festival

A very remarkable incident took place in his childhood. It was an unprecedented spiritual

1. Saṁskrit—*Siddhārtha Gautama*.

2. Hearing that Prince *Siddhattha* renounced the world, this *Kondañña* and four sons of the other seven brahmins retired from the world and joined him as his followers. These were the first five Chief Disciples of the Buddha See Ch. VI.

experience which, later, during his search after truth, served as a key to his Enlightenment.[1]

To promote agriculture, the King arranged for a ploughing festival. It was indeed a festive occasion for all, as both nobles and commoners decked in their best attire, participated in the ceremony. On the appointed day, the King, accompanied by his courtiers, went to the field, taking with him the young prince together with the nurses. Placing the child on a screened and canopied couch under the cool shade of a solitary roseapple tree to be watched by the nurses, the King participated in the ploughing festival. When the festival was at its height of gaiety the nurses too stole away from the prince's presence to catch a glimpse of the wonderful spectacle.

In striking contrast to the mirth and merriment of the festival it was all calm and quiet under the rose-apple tree. All the conditions conducive to quiet meditation being there, the pensive child, young in years but old in wisdom, sat cross-legged and seized the opportunity to commence that all-important practice of intent concentration on the breath—on exhalations and inhalations—which gained for him then and there that one pointedness of mind known as Samādhi and he thus

1. See Majjhima Nikāya, Mahā Saccaka Sutta—No. 36.

developed the First *Jhāna*[1] (Ecstasy). The child's
nurses, who had abandoned their precious charge
to enjoy themselves at the festival, suddenly
realizing their duty, hastened to the child and were
amazed to see him sitting cross-legged plunged in
deep meditation. The King hearing of it, hurried
to the spot and, seeing the child in meditative
posture, saluted him, saying—"This, dear child,
is my second obeisance".

Education

As a Royal child, Prince *Siddhattha* must have
received an education that became a prince
although no details are given about it. As a scion
of the warrior race he received special training
in the art of warfare.

Married Life

At the early age of sixteen, he married his
beautiful cousin Princess *Yasodharā*[2] who was
of equal age. For nearly thirteen years, after his
happy marriage, he led a luxurious life, blissfully
ignorant of the vicissitudes of life outside the
palace gates. Of his luxurious life as prince, he
states:

---

1. *Jhāna* — a developed state of consciousness gained by
   concentration.
2. Also known as *Bhaddakaccānā, Bimbā, Rāhulamātā.*

"I was delicate, excessively delicate. In my father's dwelling three lotus-ponds were made purposely for me. Blue lotuses bloomed in one, red in another, and white in another. I used no sandal-wood that was not of Kāsi.[1] My turban, tunic, dress and cloak, were all from Kāsi.

"Night and day a white parasol was held over me so that I might not be touched by heat or cold, dust, leaves or dew.

"There were three palaces built for me—one for the cold season, one for the hot season, and one for the rainy season. During the four rainy months, I lived in the palace for the rainy season without ever coming down from it, entertained all the while by female musicians. Just as, in the houses of others, food from the husks of rice together with sour gruel is given to the slaves and workmen, even so, in my father's dwelling, food with rice and meat was given to the slaves and workmen."[2]

With the march of time, truth gradually dawned upon him. His contemplative nature and boundless compassion did not permit him to spend

1. A province in Central India noted for silk. Modern Benares was its capital.
2. Anguttara Nikāya, part I, p. 145; *Gradual Sayings,* part 1 p. 128.

his time in the mere enjoyment of the fleeting
pleasures of the Royal palace. He knew no personal grief but he felt a deep pity for suffering
humanity. Amidst comfort and prosperity, he
realized the universality of sorrow.

Renunciation

Prince *Siddhattha* reflected thus:

"Why do I, being subject to birth, decay,
disease, death, sorrow and impurities, thus search
after things of like nature. How, if I, who am
subject to things of such nature, realize their
disadvantages and seek after the unattained, unsurpassed, perfect security which is Nibbāna!"[1]
"Cramped and confined is household life, a den
of dust, but the life of the homeless one is as
the open air of heaven! Hard is it for him who
bides at home to live out as it should be lived
the Holy Life in all its perfection, in all its purity."[2]

One glorious day as he went out of the palace
to the pleasure park to see the world outside, he came in direct contact with the stark
realities of life. Within the narrow confines of

1. Majjhima Nikāya. Part 1, Ariyapariyesana Sutta No.
   26, p. 163.
2. Majjhima Nikāya, Part 1, Mahāsaccaka Sutta, No. 36.

the palace he saw only the rosy side of life, but the dark side, the common lot of mankind, was purposely veiled from him. What was mentally conceived, he, for the first time, vividly saw in reality. On his way to the park his observant eyes met the strange sights of a decrepit old man, a diseased person, a corpse and a dignified hermit.[1] The first three sights convincingly proved to him, the inexorable nature of life, and the universal ailment of humanity. The fourth signified the means to overcome the ills of life and to attain calm and peace. These four unexpected sights served to increase the urge in him to loathe and renounce the world.

Realizing the worthlessness of sensual pleasures, so highly prized by the worldling, and appreciating the value of renunciation in which the wise seek delight, he decided to leave the world in search of Truth and Eternal Peace.

When this final decision was taken after much deliberation, the news of the birth of a son was conveyed to him while he was about to leave the park. Contrary to expectations, he was not overjoyed, but regarded his first and only offspring as an impediment. An ordinary father would have welcomed the joyful tidings, but

---

1. "Seeing the four signs, I set out on horse-back...." Buddhavaṁsa, XXVI, p. 65.

Prince *Siddhattha*, the extraordinary father as he
was, exclaimed—"An impediment (*rāhu*) has been
born; a fetter has arisen". The infant son was
accordingly named Rāhula[1] by his grandfather.

The palace was no longer a congenial place to
the contemplative Prince *Siddhattha*. Neither his
charming young wife nor his lovable infant son
could deter him from altering the decision he had
taken to renounce the world. He was destined to
play an infinitely more important and beneficial
role than a dutiful husband and father or even as
a king of kings. The allurements of the palace
were no more cherished objects of delight to
him. Time was ripe to depart.

He ordered his favourite charioteer *Channa*
to saddle the horse *Kanthaka*, and went to the
suite of apartments occupied by the princess.
Opening the door of the chamber, he stood on the
threshold and cast his dispassionate glance on the
wife and child who were fast asleep. Great was
his compassion for the two dear ones at this
parting moment. Greater was his compassion for
suffering humanity. He was not worried about the
future worldly happiness and comfort of the
mother and child as they had everything in abundance and were well protected. It was not that he
loved them the less, but he loved humanity more.

---

1. Lit., bound or seized (*la*) by a fetter (*rāhu*).

Leaving all behind, he stole away with a light heart from the palace at midnight, and rode into the dark, attended only by his loyal charioteer. Alone and penniless he set out in search of Truth and Peace. Thus did he renounce the world. It was not the renunciation of an old man who has had his fill of worldly life. It was not the renunciation of a poor man who had nothing to leave behind. It was the renunciation of a prince in the full bloom of youth and in the plenitude of wealth and prosperity—a renunciation unparalleled in history.

It was in his twenty-ninth year that Prince *Siddhattha* made this historic journey.

He journeyed far and, crossing the river *Anomā*, rested on its banks. Here he shaved his hair and beard and handing over his garments and ornaments to *Channa* with instructions to return to the palace, assumed the simple yellow garb of an ascetic and led a life of voluntary poverty.

The ascetic *Siddhattha*, who once lived in the lap of luxury, now became a penniless wanderer, living on what little the charitably-minded gave of their own accord.

He had no permanent abode. A shady tree or a lonely cave sheltered him by day or night. Bare-footed and bare-headed, he walked in the scorching sun and in the piercing cold. With no possessions to call his own, but a bowl to collect his food and robes just sufficient to cover the body, he concentrated all his energies on the quest of Truth.

Search

Thus as a wanderer, a seeker after what is good, searching for the unsurpassed Peace, he approached *Ālāra Kālāma*, a distinguished ascetic, and said: "I desire, friend *Kālāma* to lead the Holy Life in this Dispensation of yours." Thereupon *Ālāra Kālāma* told him: "You may stay with me, O Venerable One. Of such sort is this teaching that an intelligent man before long may realize by his own intuitive wisdom his master's doctrine, and abide in the attainment thereof."

Before long, he learnt his doctrine, but it brought him no realization of the highest Truth.

Then there came to him the thought: When *Ālāra Kālāma* declared: "Having myself realized by intuitive knowledge the doctrine, I—'abide in the attainment thereof—' it could not have been a mere profession of faith; surely *Ālāra Kālāma* lives having understood and perceived this doctrine."

So he went to him and said "How far, friend *Kālāma*, does this doctrine extend which you yourself have with intuitive wisdom realized and attained?"

Upon this *Āḷāra Kālāma* made known to him the Realm of Nothingness (*Ākiñcaññāyatana*)[1], an advanced stage of Concentration.

Then it occurred to him: "Not only in *Āḷāra Kālāma* are to be found faith, energy, mindfulness, concentration, and wisdom. I too possess these virtues. How now if I strive to realize that doctrine whereof *Āḷāra Kālāma* says that he himself has realized and abides in the attainment thereof!"

So, before long, he realized by his own intuitive wisdom that doctrine and attained to that state, but it brought him no realization of the highest Truth.

Then he approached *Āḷāra Kālāma* and said; "Is this the full extent, friend *Kālāma*, of this doctrine of which you say that you yourself have realized by your wisdom and abide in the attainment thereof?"

"But I also, friend, have realized thus far in this doctrine, and abide in the attainment thereof."

The unenvious teacher was delighted to hear of the success of his distinguished pupil. He honoured him by placing him on a perfect level with himself and admiringly said:

---

1. The third *Arūpa Jhāna*.

"Happy, friend, are we, extremely happy; in that we look upon such a venerable fellow-ascetic like you! That same doctrine which I myself have realized by my wisdom and proclaim, having attained thereunto, have you yourself realized by your wisdom and abide in the attainment thereof; and that doctrine you yourself have realized by your wisdom and abide in the attainment thereof, that have I myself realized by my wisdom and proclaim, having attained thereunto. Thus the doctrine which I know, and also do you know; and the doctrine which you know, that I know also. As I am, so are you; as you are, so am I. Come, friend, let both of us lead the company of ascetics."

The ascetic *Gotama* was not satisfied with a discipline and a doctrine which only led to a high degree of mental concentration, but did not lead to "disgust, detachment, cessation (of suffering), tranquillity; intuition, enlightenment, and Nibbāna." Nor was he anxious to lead a company of ascetics even with the co-operation of another generous teacher of equal spiritual attainment, without first perfecting himself. It was, he felt, a case of the blind leading the blind. Dissatisfied with his teaching, he politely took his leave from him.

In those happy days when there were no political disturbances the intellectuals of India were preoccupied with the study and exposition of some religious system or other. All facilities were provided for those more spiritually inclined to lead

holy lives in solitude in accordance with their temperaments and most of these teachers had large
followings of disciples. So it was not difficult for
the ascetic *Gotama* to find another religious teacher who was more competent than the former.

On this occasion he approached one *Uddaka
Rāmaputta* and expressed his desire to lead the
Holy Life in his Dispensation. He was readily
admitted as a pupil.

Before long the intelligent ascetic *Gotama*,
mastered his doctrine and attained the final stage
of mental concentration, the Realm of Neither
Perception nor Non-Perception (*"N'eva saññā
N'āsaññāyatana*),[1] revealed by his teacher. This
was the highest stage in worldly concentration
when consciousness becomes so subtle and refined
that it cannot be said that a consciousness either
exists or not. Ancient Indian sages could not
proceed further in spiritual development.

The noble teacher was delighted to hear of the
success of his illustrious royal pupil. Unlike his
former teacher the present one honoured him by
inviting him to take full charge of all the disciples
as their teacher. He said: "Happy friend, are
we; yea, extremely happy, in that we see such
a venerable fellow-ascetic as you! The doctrine

---

1. The fourth *Arūpa Jhāna*.

which *Rāma* knew, you know; the doctrine which you know, *Rāma* knew. As was *Rāma* so are you; as you are, so was *Rāma*. Come, friend, henceforth you shall lead this company of ascetics."

Still he felt that his quest of the highest Truth was not achieved. He had gained complete mastery of his mind, but his ultimate goal was far ahead. He was seeking for the Highest, the Nibbāna, the complete cessation of suffering, the total eradication of all forms of craving. "Dissatisfied with this doctrine too, he departed thence, content therewith no longer."

He realized that his spiritual aspirations were far higher than those under whom he chose to learn. He realized that there was none capable enough to teach him what he yearned for—the highest Truth. He also realized that the highest Truth is to be found within oneself and ceased to seek external aid.

PRINCE SIDDHATTHA'S GENEALOGICAL TABLE

Father's Side

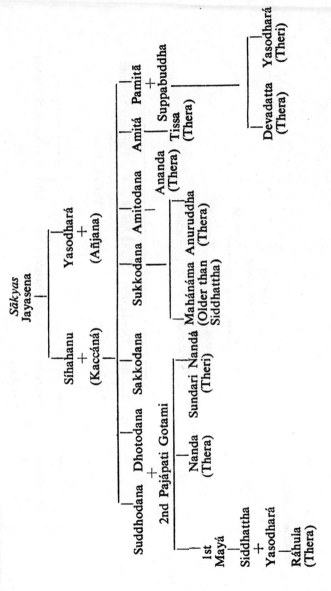

Mother's Side

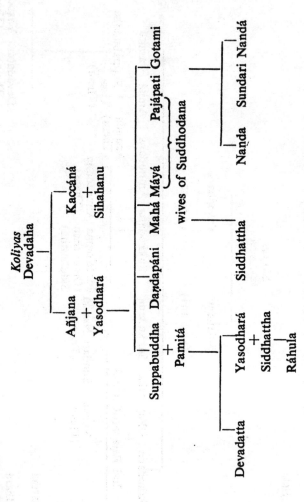

CHAPTER 2

HIS STRUGGLE FOR ENLIGHTENMENT

"Easy to do are things that are bad and not beneficial to self;
But very, very hard to do indeed is that which is beneficial and good".

DHAMMAPADA

Struggle

Meeting with disappointment, but not discouraged, the ascetic *Gotama* seeking for the incomparable Peace, the highest Truth, wandered through the district of Magadha, and arrived in due course at *Uruvelā*, the market town of *Senāni*. There he spied a lovely spot of ground, a charming forest grove, a flowing river with pleasant sandy fords, and hard by was a village where he could obtain his food. Then he thought thus:

"Lovely, indeed, O Venerable One, is this spot of ground, charming is the forest grove, pleasant is the flowing river with sandy fords, and hard by is the village where I could obtain food. Suitable indeed is this place for spiritual exertion for those noble scions who desire to strive."[1]

---

1. Majjhima Nikāya, Ariya-Pariyesana Sutta—No. 26, Vol. 1, p. 166.

The place was congenial for his meditation. The atmosphere was peaceful. The surroundings were pleasant. The scenery was charming. Alone, he resolved to settle down there to achieve his desired object.

Hearing of his renunciation, *Koṇḍañña*, the youngest brahmin who predicted his future, and four sons of the other sages—*Bhaddiya*, *Vappa*, *Mahānāma*, and *Assaji*—also renounced the world and joined his company.

In the ancient days in India, great importance was attached to rites, ceremonies, penances and sacrifices. It was then a popular belief that no Deliverance could be gained unless one leads a life of strict asceticism. Accordingly, for six long years the ascetic *Gotama* made a superhuman struggle practising all forms of severest austerity. His delicate body was reduced to almost a skeleton. The more he tormented his body the farther his goal receded from him.

How strenuously he struggled, the various methods he employed, and how he eventually succeeded are graphically described in his own words in various Suttas.

Mahā Saccaka[1] *Sutta* describes his preliminary efforts thus:

"Then the following thought occurred to me:

"How if I were to clench my teeth, press my tongue against the palate, and with (moral) thoughts hold down, subdue and destroy my (immoral) thoughts!

"So I clenched my teeth, pressed my tongue against the palate and strove to hold down, subdue, destroy my (immoral) thoughts with (moral) thoughts. As I struggled thus, perspiration streamed forth from my armpits.

"Like unto a strong man who might seize a weaker man by head or shoulders and hold him down, force him down, and bring into subjection, even so did I struggle.

"Strenuous and indomitable was my energy. My mindfulness was established and unperturbed. My body was, however, fatigued and was not calmed as a result of that painful endeavour— being overpowered by exertion. Even though such painful sensations arose in me, they did not at all affect my mind.

---

1. Majjhima Nikāya No. 36, Vol. 1, p. 242.

"Then I thought thus: How if I were to cultivate the non-breathing ecstasy!

"Accordingly, I checked inhalation and exhalation from my mouth and nostrils. As I checked inhalation and exhalation from mouth and nostrils, the air issuing from my ears created an exceedingly great noise. Just as a blacksmith's bellows being blown make an exceedingly great noise, even so was the noise created by the air issuing from my ears when I stopped breathing.

"Nevertheless, my energy was strenuous and indomitable. Established and unperturbed was my mindfulness. Yet my body was fatigued and was not calmed as a result of that painful endeavour—being over-powered by exertion. Even though such painful sensations arose in me, they did not at all affect my mind.

"Then I thought to myself: How if I were to cultivate that non-breathing exercise!

"Accordingly, I checked inhalation and exhalation from mouth, nostrils, and ears. And as I stopped breathing from mouth, nostrils and ears, the (imprisoned) airs beat upon my skull with great violence. Just as if a strong man were to bore one's skull with a sharp drill, even so did the airs beat my skull with great violence as I stopped breathing. Even, though such painful sensations arose in me, they did not at all affect my mind.

"Then I thought to myself: How if I were to cultivate that non-breathing ecstasy again!

"Accordingly, I checked inhalation and exhalation from mouth, nostrils, and ears. And as I stopped breathing thus, terrible pains arose in my head. As would be the pains if a strong man were to bind one's head tightly with a hard leathern thong, even so were the terrible pains that arose in my head.

"Nevertheless, my energy was strenuous. Such painful sensations did not affect my mind.

"Then I thought to myself: How if I were to cultivate that non-breathing ecstasy again!

"Accordingly, I stopped breathing from mouth, nostrils, and ears. As I checked breathing thus, plentiful airs pierced my belly. Just as if a skilful butcher or a butcher's apprentice were to rip up the belly with a sharp butcher's knife, even so plentiful airs pierced my belly.

"Nevertheless, my energy was strenuous. Such painful sensations did not affect my mind.

"Again I thought to myself: How if I were to cultivate that non-breathing ecstasy again!

"Accordingly, I checked inhalation and exhalation from mouth, nostrils, and ears. As I suppressed my breathing thus, a tremendous burning pervaded my body. Just as if two strong men were each to seize a weaker man by his arms and scorch and thoroughly burn him in a pit of glowing charcoal, even so did a severe burning pervade my body.

"Nevertheless, my energy was strenuous. Such painful sensations did not affect my mind.

"Thereupon the deities who saw me thus said: 'The ascetic *Gotama* is dead.' Some remarked: 'The ascetic *Gotama* is not dead yet, but is dying'. While some others said: 'The ascetic *Gotama* is neither dead nor is dying but an Arahant is the ascetic *Gotama*. Such is the way in which an Arahant abides."

Change of Method: Abstinence from Food

"Then I thought to myself: How if I were to practise complete abstinence from food!

"Then deities approached me and said: 'Do not, good sir, practise total abstinence from food. If you do practise it, we will pour celestial essence through your body's pores; with that you will be sustained."

"And I thought: 'If I claim to be practising starvation, and if these deities pour celestial essence. through my body's pores and I am sustained thereby, it would be a fraud on my part'. So I refused them, saying 'There is no need'.

"Then the following thought occurred to me: How if I take food little by little, a small quantity of the juice of green gram, or vetch, or lentils, or peas!

"As I took such small quantity of solid and liquid food, my body became extremely emaciated. Just as are the joints of knot-grasses or bulrushes, even so were the major and minor parts of my body owing to lack of food. Just as is the camel's hoof, even so were my hips for want of food. Just as is a string of beads, even so did my backbone stand out and bend in, for lack of food. Just as the rafters of a dilapidated hall fall this way and that, even so appeared my ribs through lack of sustenance. Just as in a deep well may be seen stars sunk deep in the water, even so did my eye-balls appear deep sunk in their sockets, being devoid of food. Just as a bitter pumpkin, when cut while raw, will by wind and sun get shrivelled and withered, even so did the skin of my head get shrivelled and withered, due to lack of sustenance.

"And I, intending to touch my belly's skin, would instead seize my backbone. When I intended to touch my backbone, I would seize my belly's skin. So was I that, owing to lack of sufficient food, my belly's skin clung to the backbone, and I, on going to pass excreta or urine, would in that very spot stumble and fall down, for want of food. And I stroked my limbs in order to revive my body. Lo, as I did so, the rotten roots of my body's hairs fell from my body owing to lack of sustenance. The people who saw me said: "The ascetic *Gotama* is black.' Some said, 'The ascetic

Gotama is not black but blue.' Some others said: 'The ascetic *Gotama* is neither black nor blue but tawny.' To such an extent was the pure colour of my skin impaired owing to lack of food.

"Then the following thought occurred to me: Whatsoever ascetics or brahmins of the past have experienced acute, painful, sharp and piercing sensations, they must have experienced them to such a high degree as this and not beyond. Whatsoever ascetics and brahmins of the future will experience acute, painful, sharp and piercing sensations they too will experience them to such a high degree and not beyond. Yet by all these bitter and difficult austerities I shall not attain to excellence, worthy of supreme knowledge and insight, transcending those of human states. Might there be another path for Enlightenment!"

Temptation of Māra the Evil One

His prolonged painful austerities proved utterly futile. They only resulted in the exhaustion of his valuable energy. Though physically a superman his delicately nurtured body could not possibly stand the great strain. His graceful form completely faded almost beyond recognition. His golden coloured skin turned pale, his blood dried up, his sinews and muscles shrivelled up, his eyes were sunk and blurred. To all appearance he was a living skeleton. He was almost on the verge of death.

At this critical stage, while he was still intent on the Highest (*Padhāna*), abiding on the banks of the *Nerañjarā* river, striving and contemplating in order to attain to that state of Perfect Security, came *Namuci*,[1] uttering kind words thus:

[2]"You are lean and deformed. Near to you is death.

"A thousand parts (of you belong) to death; to life (there remains) but one. Live, O good sir! Life is better. Living, you could perform merit.

"By leading a life of celibacy and making fire sacrifices, much merit could be acquired. What will you do with this striving? Hard is the path of striving, difficult and not easily accomplished."

Māra reciting these words stood in the presence of the Exalted One.

To Māra who spoke thus, the Exalted One replied:

"O Evil One, kinsman of the heedless! You have come here for your own sake.

"Even an iota of merit is of no avail. To them

---

1. Another name for Māra. According to the Books there are five kinds of Māras—namely, i. Deity Māra (*Devaputta*), ii. Passion (*Kilesa*), iii. Kammic Activities (*Abhisamkhāra*), iv. Aggregates (*Khandha*) and v. Death (*Maccu*).
2. Sutta Nipāta—*Padhāna Sutta*, p. 74.

who are in need of merit it behoves you, Māra, to speak thus.

"Confidence (*Saddhā*), self-control (*Tapo*),[1] perseverence (*Viriya*), and wisdom (*Paññā*) are mine. Me who am thus intent, why do you question about life?

"Even the streams of rivers will this wind dry up. Why should not the blood of me who am thus striving dry up?

"When blood dries up, the bile and phlegm also dry up. When my flesh wastes away, more and more does my mind get clarified. Still more do my mindfulness, wisdom, and concentration become firm.

"While I live thus, experiencing the utmost pain, my mind does not long for lust! Behold the purity of a being!

"Sense-desires (*Kāmā*), are your first army. The second is called Aversion for the Holy Life (*Arati*). The third is Hunger and Thirst[2] (*Khuppipāsā*.) The fourth is Craving (*Tanhā*). The fifth is Sloth and Torpor (*Thīna-Middha*). The sixth is called Fear (*Bhīru*). The seventh is Doubt[3] (*Vici-kicchā*), and the eighth is Detraction and Obstinacy (*Makkha-Thambha*). The ninth is Gain (*Lābha*),

---

1. *Tato*—Pali Text Society's edition.
2. Resulting from voluntary poverty.
3. That is, indecision as to the certainty of the Goal.

Praise (*Siloka*) and Honour (*Sakkāra*), and that ill-gotten Fame (*Yasa*). The tenth is the extolling of oneself and contempt for others (*Attukkaṁsanaparavambhana*).

"This, Namuci, is your army, the opposing host of the Evil One. That army the coward does not overcome, but he who overcomes obtains happiness.

"This Muñja[1] do I display! What boots life in this world! Better for me is death in the battle than that one should live on, vanquished![2]

"Some ascetics and brahmins are not seen plunged in this battle. They know not nor do they tread the path of the virtuous.

"Seeing the army on all sides with Mara arrayed on elephant, I go forward to battle. Mara shall not drive me from my position. That army of yours, which the world together with gods conquers not, by my wisdom I go to destroy as I would an unbaked bowl with a stone.

"Controlling my thoughts, and with mindfulness well-established, I shall wander from country to country, training many a disciple.

---

1. Warriors wear Muñja grass crest on their heads or on their banners to indicate that they will not retreat from the battle-field.

2. *Sangāme me matam seyyo—Yañ ce jive parājito.*

"Diligent, intent, and practising my teaching, they, disregarding you, will go where having gone they grieve not."

The Middle Path

The ascetic *Gotama* was now fully convinced from personal experience of the utter futility of self-mortification which, though considered indispensable for Deliverance by the ascetic philosophers of the day, actually weakened one's intellect, and resulted in lassitude of spirit. He abandoned for ever this painful extreme as did he the other extreme of self-indulgence which tends to retard moral progress. He conceived the idea of adopting the Golden Mean which later became one of the salient features of his teaching.

He recalled how when his father was engaged in ploughing, he sat in the cool shade of the rose-apple tree, absorbed in the contemplation of his own breath, which resulted in the attainment of the First *Jhāna* (Ecstasy)[1]. Thereupon he thought: "Well, this is the path to Enlightenment."

He realized that Enlightenment could not be gained with such an utterly exhausted body: Physical fitness was essential for spiritual progress. So he decided to nourish the body sparingly and took some coarse food both hard and soft.

---

1. See Ch.I.

The five favourite disciples who were attending
on him with great hopes thinking that whatever
truth the ascetic *Gotama* would comprehend, that
would he impart to them, felt disappointed at this
unexpected change of method. and leaving him
and the place too, went to Isipatana, saying that
"the ascetic *Gotama* had become luxurious, had
ceased from striving, and had returned to a life of
comfort."

At a crucial time when help was most welcome
his companions deserted him leaving him alone.
He was not discouraged, but their voluntary separation was advantageous to him though their
presence during his great struggle was helpful
to him. Alone, in sylvan solitudes, great men often
realize deep truths and solve intricate problems.

Dawn of Truth

Regaining his lost strength with some coarse
food, he easily developed the First *Jhāna* which
he gained in his youth.   By degrees he developed
the second, third and fourth *Jhānas* as well.

By developing the *Jhānas* he gained perfect
one-pointedness of the mind. His mind was now
like a polished mirror where everything is reflected
in its true perspective.

Thus with thoughts tranquillized, purified,
cleansed, free from lust and impurity, pliable,
alert, steady, and unshakable, he directed his mind

to the knowledge as regards "The Reminiscence
of Past Births" (*Pubbe-nivāsānussati Nāṇa*). He
recalled his varied lots in former existences as
follows: first one life, then two lives, then three,
four, five, ten, twenty, up to fifty lives; then a
hundred, a thousand, a hundred thousand; then
the dissolution of many world cycles, then the
evolution of many world cycles, then both the
dissolution and evolution of many world cycles.
In that place he was of such a name, such a family,
such a caste, such a dietary, such the pleasure and
pain he experienced, such his life's end.   Departing
from there, he came into existence elsewhere, Then
such was his name, such his family, such his caste,
such his dietary, such the pleasure and pain he
did experience, such life's end.   Thence departing,
he came into existence here.

Thus he recalled the mode and details of his
varied lots in his former births.

*This, indeed, was the First Knowledge that he
realized in the first watch of the night.*

Dispelling thus the ignorance with regard to
the past, he directed his purified mind to "The
Perception of the Disappearing and Reappearing
of Beings" (*Cutùpapāta Nāṇa*). With clairvoyant
vision, purified and supernormal, he perceived
beings disappearing from one state of existence
and reappearing in another; he beheld the base
and the noble, the beautiful and the ugly, the

happy and the miserable, all passing according to their deeds. He knew that these good individuals, by evil deeds, words, and thoughts, by reviling the Noble Ones, by being misbelievers, and by conforming themselves to the actions of the misbelievers, after the dissolution of their bodies and after death, had been born in sorrowful states. He knew that these good individuals, by good deeds, words, and thoughts, by not reviling the Noble Ones, by being right believers, and by conforming themselves to the actions of the right believers, after the dissolution of their bodies and after death, had been born in happy celestial worlds.

Thus with clairvoyant supernormal vision he beheld the disappearing and the reappearing of beings.

This, indeed, was the Second Knowledge that he realized in the middle watch of the night.

Dispelling thus the ignorance with regard to the future, he directed his purified mind to "The Comprehension of the Cessation of Corruptions"[1] (*Āsavakkhaya Nāna*).

---

1.   *Āsavas* (*Defilements*)—are those which flow right up to the top-most plane of existence with respect to spheres, or right up to the *Gotrabhū* state, with respect to mind-flux.   There are four Āsavas, viz: Sense-desires (*Kāma*), Becoming (*Bhava*), False Views (*Ditthi*) and Ignorance (*Avijjā*). In this particular text only three are mentioned. Here Bhava means the desire to be born in the realms of form and formless realms (*Rūpa* and *Arūpa Bhava*).

He realized in accordance with· fact: "This is Sorrow", "This, the Arising of Sorrow", "This, the Cessation of Sorrow", "This, the Path leading to the Cessation of Sorrow". Likewise in accordance with fact he realized: "These are the Corruptions", "This, the Arising of Corruptions", "This, the Cessation of Corruptions", "This, the Path leading to the Cessation of Corruptions". Thus cognizing, thus perceiving, his mind was delivered from the Corruption of Sensual Craving; from the Corruption of Craving for Existence; from the Corruption of Ignorance.

Being delivered, He knew, *"Delivered am I"*[1] and He realized, *"Rebirth is ended; fulfilled the Holy Life; done what was to be done; there is no more of this state again."*[2]

This was the Third Knowledge that He Realized in the last watch of the night.

Ignorance was dispelled, and wisdom arose; darkness vanished, and light arose.

---

1. *Vimutto'smi.*
2. *Khīṇā jāti, vusitaṁ brahmacariyaṁ, kataṁ karaṇīyaṁ. nāparam itthattaya.*

CHAPTER 3

THE BUDDHAHOOD

"The Tathāgatas are only teachers".

DHAMMAPADA

Characteristics of the Buddha

After a stupendous struggle of six strenuous years, in His 35th year the ascetic *Gotama,* unaided and unguided by any supernatural agency, and solely relying on His own efforts and wisdom, eradicated all defilements, ended the process of grasping, and, realizing things as they truly are by His own intuitive knowledge, became a *Buddha*— an Enlightened or Awakened One.

Thereafter he was known as Buddha *Gotama*[1],

---

1. His disciples addressed Him as *Buddha, Bhagavā* (Exalted One), *Sugata* (Well-gone One) etc, while alien followers addressed Him as *Bho Gotama,* (Venerable Gotama), *Samana Gotama* (Ascetic Gotama), etc., Referring to Himself the Buddha used the term *"Tathāgata"* meaning "He who hath thus come", "He who hath thus gone."

one of a long series of Buddhas that appeared in the past and will appear in the future.

He was not born a Buddha, but became a Buddha by His own efforts.

The Pāli term Buddha is derived from *"budh"*, to understand, or to be awakened. As He fully comprehended the four Noble Truths and as He arose from the slumbers of ignorance He is called a Buddha. Since He not only comprehends but also expounds the doctrine and enlightens others, He is called a *Sammā Sambuddha*—a Fully Enlightened One—to distinguish Him from *Pacceka* (Individual) Buddhas who only comprehend the doctrine but are incapable of enlightening others.

Before His Enlightenment He was called Bodhisatta[1] which means one who is aspiring to attain Buddhahood.

Every aspirant to Buddhahood passes through the Bodhisatta Period—a period of intensive exercise and development of the qualities of generosity, discipline, renunciation, wisdom, energy, endurance, truthfulness, determination, benevolence and perfect equanimity.

In a particular era there arises only one Sammā Sambuddha. Just as certain plants and trees can bear only one flower even so one world-system (*lokadhātu*) can bear only one Sammā Sambuddha.

---

1.   Samskrit—Bodhisattva.

The Buddha was a unique being. Such a being arises but rarely in this world, and is born out of compassion for the world, for the good, benefit, and happiness of gods and men. The Buddha is called "*acchariya manussa*" as He was a wonderful man. He is called "*amatassa dātā*" as He is the giver of Deathlessness. He is called "*varado*" as He is the Giver of the purest love, the profoundest wisdom, and the Highest Truth. He is also called *Dhammassāmi* as He is the Lord of the Dhamma (Doctrine).

As the Buddha Himself says, "He is the Accomplished One(*Tathāgata*), the Worthy One(*Arahaṁ*), the Fully Enlightened One (*Sammā Sambuddha*), the creator of the unarisen way, the producer of the unproduced way, the proclaimer of the unproclaimed way, the knower of the way, the beholder of the way, the cognizer of the way."[1]

The Buddha had no teacher for His Enlightenment. "*Na me ācariyo atthi*"[2]--A teacher have I not—are His own words. He did receive His mundane knowledge from His lay teachers,[3] but teachers He had none for His supramundane knowledge which He himself realized by His own intuitive wisdom.

---

1. Samyutta Nikāya part iii, p. 66; *Kindred Sayings,* part iii p. 58.
2. Majjhima Nikāya, *Ariyapariyesana Sutta* N. 26.
3. Such as Kondañña, Ālāra Kālāma, Uddakka Rāmaputta etc.

If He had received His knowledge from another
teacher or from another religious system such as
Hinduism in which He was nurtured, He could not
have said of Himself as being the incomparable
teacher (*aham satthā anuttaro*).[1] In His first discourse He declared that light arose in things not
heard before.

During the early period of His renunciation
He sought the advice of the distinguished religious
teachers of the day, but He could not find what
He sought in their teachings. Circumstances
compelled Him to think for Himself and seek the
Truth. He sought the Truth within Himself.
He plunged into the deepest profundities of
thought, and He realized the ultimate Truth which
He had not heard or known before. Illumination
came from within and shed light on things which
He had never seen before.

As He knew everything that ought to be known
and as He obtained the key to all knowledge,
He is called *Sabbaññū*—the Omniscient One. This
supernormal knowledge He acquired by His own
efforts continued through a countless series of
births.

Who is the Buddha?

Once a certain brahmin named *Dona*, noticing

1. Majjhima Nikāya, *Ariyapariyesana Sutta,* N. 26.

the characteristic marks of the footprint of the Buddha, approached Him and questioned Him.

"Your Reverence will be a Deva?[1]"

"No, indeed, brahmin, a Deva am I not,"replied the Buddha.

"Then Your Reverence will be a Gandhabba?[2]"
"No, indeed, brahmin, a Gandhabba am I not."
"A Yakkha then?[3]"
"No, indeed, brahmin, not a Yakkha."
"Then Your Reverence will be a human being?"
"No indeed, brahmin, a human being am I not."

"Who, then, pray, will Your Reverence be?"

The Buddha replied that He had destroyed Defilements which condition rebirth as a Deva, Gandhabba, Yakkha, or a human being and added:

"*As a lotus, fair and lovely,*
By the water is not soiled,
By the world am I not soiled;
Therefore, brahmin, am I Buddha."[4]

---

1. A celestial being who resides in heavenly planes.
2. A heavenly musician.
3. A demon.
4. *Gradual Sayings*, Pt. ii, pp. 44-45, Anguttara *Nikāya* Pt. ii—p.37.

The Buddha does not claim to be an incarnation (*Avatāra*) of Hindu God Vishnu, who, as the Bhagavadgitā[1] charmingly sings, is born again and again in different periods to protect the righteous, to destroy the wicked, and to establish the Dharma (right).

According to the Buddha countless are the gods (*Devas*) who are also a class of beings subject to birth and death; but there is no one Supreme God, who controls the destinies of human beings and who possesses a divine power to appear on earth at different intervals, employing a human form as a vehicle[2].

Nor does the Buddha call Himself a "Saviour" who freely saves others by his personal salvation. The Buddha exhorts His followers to depend on themselves for their deliverance, since both defilement and purity depend on oneself. One cannot directly purify or defile another.[3] Clarifying His relationship with His followers and emphasizing the importance of self-reliance and individual striving, the Buddha plainly states:

---

1. *Paritrānāya sādhūnām vināsāya ca duskrtām.*
    Dharmsamsthāpanārthāya sambhavāmi yuge yuge.

2. Hindu teachers, however, with the object of bringing within the fold of Hinduism the increasing adherents of Buddhism, have unjustly called the Buddha God's incarnation (*Avatāra*)—an idea which He repudiated in His own time.

3. *Suddhi asuddhi paccattam n'añño aññam visodhaye*
    Dhammapada v. 165.

"You yourselves should make an exertion. *The Tathāgatas are only teachers.*"[1]

The Buddha only indicates the path and method whereby He delivered Himself from suffering and death and achieved His ultimate goal. It is left for His faithful adherents who wish their release from the ills of life to follow the path.

"To depend on others for salvation is negative, but to depend on oneself is positive." Dependence on others means a surrender of one's effort.

"Be ye isles unto yourselves; be ye a refuge unto yourselves; seek no refuge in others."[2]

These significant words uttered by the Buddha in His last days are very striking and inspiring. They reveal how vital is self-exertion to accomplish one's ends, and how superficial and futile it is to seek redemption through benignant saviours, and crave for illusory happiness in an afterlife through the propitiation of imaginary gods by fruitless prayers and meaningless sacrifices.

The Buddha was a human being. As a man He was born, as a Buddha He lived, and as a Buddha His life came to an end. Though human,

---

1. *Tumhehi kiccaṁ ātappaṁ akkhātāro tathāgatā.* Dhammapada v. 276.
2. *Attadipā viharatha, attapatisaranā, anaññasaranā.* Digha Nikāya,Mahāparinibbána Sutta Vol. 2, p. 100.

He became an extraordinary man owing to His unique characteristics. The Buddha laid stress on this important point, and left no room for any one to fall into the error of thinking that He was an immortal being. It has been said of Him that there was no religious teacher who was "ever so godless as the Buddha, yet none was so god-like."[1] In His own time the Buddha was no doubt highly venerated by His followers, but He never arrogated to Himself any divinity.

The Buddha's Greatness

Born a man, living as a mortal, by His own exertion He attained that supreme state of perfection called Buddhahood, and without keeping His Enlightenment to Himself, He proclaimed to the world the latent possibilities and the invincible power of the human mind. Instead of placing an unseen Almighty God over man, and giving man a subservient position in relation to such a conception of divine power, He demonstrated how man could attain the highest knowledge and Supreme Enlightenment by his own efforts. He thus raised the worth of man. He taught that man can gain his deliverance from the ills of life and realize the eternal bliss of Nibbāna without depending on an external God or mediating priests. He taught the egocentric, power-seeking world the noble ideal of

---

1. Dwight Goddard—*Buddhist Bible*, p. 20.

selfless service. He protested against the evils of caste-system that hampered the progress of mankind and advocated equal opportunities for all. He declared that the gates of deliverance were open to all, in every condition of life, high or low, saint or sinner, who would care to turn a new leaf and aspire to perfection. He raised the status of down-trodden women, and not only brought them to a realization of their importance to society but also founded the first religious order for women. For the first time in the history of the world He attempted to abolish slavery. He banned the sacrifice of unfortunate animals and brought them within His compass of loving kindness. He did not force His followers to be slaves either to His teachings or to Himself, but granted complete freedom of thought and admonished His followers to accept His words not merely out of regard for Him but after subjecting them to a thorough examination "even as the wise would test gold by burning, cutting, and rubbing it on a piece of touchstone." He comforted the bereaved mothers like Patācārā and Kisāgotami by His consoling words. He ministered to the deserted sick like Putigatta Tissa Thera with His own hands. He helped the poor and the neglected like Rajjumālā and Sopāka and saved them from an untimely and tragic death. He ennobled the lives of criminals like Angulimala and courtesans like Ambapāli. He encouraged the feeble, united the divided, enlightened the ignorant, clarified the mystic, guided the deluded, elevated the base, and dignified the noble. The rich and the poor, the saint and the criminal, loved Him alike. His noble example was a source of inspiration to all. He was the most compassionate and tolerant of teachers.

His will, wisdom, compassion, service, renunciation, perfect purity, exemplary personal life, the blameless methods that were employed to propagate the Dhamma and His final success—all these factors have compelled about one fifth of the population of the world to hail the Buddha as the greatest religious teacher that ever lived on earth.

Paying a glowing tribute to the Buddha, Sri Radhakrishnan writes:

"In Gautama the Buddha we have a master mind from the East second to none so far as the influence on the thought and life of the human race is concerned, and sacred to all as the founder of a religious tradition whose hold is hardly less wide and deep than any other. He belongs to the history of the world's thought, to the general inheritance of all cultivated men, for, judged by intellectual integrity, moral earnestness, and spiritual insight, he is undoubtedly one of the greatest figures in history."[1]

---

1. *Gautama the Buddha*, p. 1.

In the *Three Greatest Men in History* H. G. Wells states:

"In the Buddha you see clearly a man, simple, devout, lonely, battling for light, a vivid human personality, not a myth. He too gave a message to mankind universal in character.   Many of our best modern ideas are in closest harmony with it. All the miseries and discontents of life are due, he taught, to selfishness. Before a man can become serene he must cease to live for his senses or himself.   Then he merges into a greater being. Buddhism in different language called men to self-forgetfulness 500 years before Christ.   In some ways he was nearer to us and our needs. He was more lucid upon our individual importance in service than Christ and less ambiguous upon the question of personal immortality."

The Poet Tagore calls Him the Greatest Man ever born.

In admiration of the Buddha, Fausboll, a Danish scholar says—"The more I know Him, the more I love Him."

A humble follower of the Buddha would modestly say: The more I know Him, the more I love Him; the more I love Him, the more I know Him.

CHAPTER 4

AFTER THE ENLIGHTENMENT

"Happy in this world is non-attachment".

UDĀNA

In the memorable forenoon, immediately preceding the morn of His Enlightenment, as the Bodhisatta was seated under the *Ajapāla* banyan tree in close proximity to the Bodhi tree[1], a generous lady, named *Sujātā*, unexpectedly offered Him some rich milkrice, specially prepared by her with great care. This substantial meal He ate, and after His Enlightenment the Buddha fasted for seven weeks, and spent a quiet time, in deep contemplation, under the Bodhi tree and in its neighbourhood.

The Seven Weeks
First Week

Throughout the first week the Buddha sat under the Bodhi tree in one posture, experiencing the Bliss of Emancipation (*Vimutti Sukha*).[2]

After those seven days had elapsed, the Buddha emerged from the state of concentration, and in the first watch of the night, thoroughly reflected on "The Dependent Arising" (*Paṭicca Samuppāda*) in

---

1. The famous Pipal tree at Buddha Gayā in northern India which sheltered Him during His struggle for Enlightenment.
2. I.e., The Fruit of Arahantship.

direct order thus: "When this (cause) exists, this (effect) is; with the arising of this (cause), this effect arises."

Dependent on Ignorance (*avijjā*) arise moral and immoral Conditioning Activities (*saṁkhārā*).

Dependent on Conditioning Activities arises (Relinking) Consciousness (*viññāṇa*).

Dependent on (Relinking) Consciousness arise Mind and Matter (*nāma-rupa*).

Dependent on Mind and Matter arise the Six Spheres of Sense (*salāyatana*).

Dependent on the Six Spheres of Sense arises Contact (*phassa*).

Dependent on Contact arises Feeling (*vedanā*).

Dependent on Feeling arises Craving (*tanhā*)

Dependent on Craving arises Grasping (*upādāna*).

Dependent on Grasping arises Becoming (*bhava*)

Dependent on Becoming arises Birth (*jāti*)

Dependent on Birth arise Decay (*jarā*), Death (*marana*), Sorrow (*soka*), Lamentation (*parideva*), Pain (*dukkha*) Grief (*domanassa*), and Despair (*upāyāsa*).

Thus does this whole mass of suffering originate.

---

1. See chapter 25.

Thereupon the Exalted One, knowing the meaning of this, uttered, at that time, this paean of joy:

"When, indeed, the Truths become manifest unto the strenuous, meditative Brahmana[1], then do all his doubts vanish away, since he knows the truth together with its cause."

In the middle watch of the night the Exalted One thoroughly reflected on "The Dependent Arising" in reverse order thus: "When this cause does not exist, this effect is not; with the cessation of this cause, this effect ceases.

With the cessation of Ignorance, Conditioning Activities cease.

With the cessation of Conditioning Activities (Relinking) Consciousness ceases.

With the cessation of (Relinking) Consciousness, Mind and Matter cease.

With the cessation of Mind and Matter, the six Spheres of Sense cease.

With the cessation of the Six Spheres of Sense, Contact ceases.

---

1. Brahmin is a racial term which means "one who studies the Vedas", generally applied to the priestly caste. Sometimes the Buddha uses this term in the sense of "one who has discarded evil"—a Saint.

   In this book "Brahmana" is used to denote a Saint, and "brahmin", to denote a member of that particular caste.

With the cessation of Contact, Feeling ceases.

With the cessation of Feeling, Craving ceases.

With the cessation of Craving, Grasping ceases.

With the cessation of Grasping, Becoming ceases.

With the cessation of Becoming, Birth ceases.

With the cessation of Birth, Decay, Death, Sorrow, Lamentation, Pain, Grief, and Despair cease.

Thus does this whole mass of usffering cease.

Thereupon the Exalted One, knowing the meaning of this, uttered, at that time, this paean of joy:

"When, indeed, the Truths become manifest unto the strenuous and meditative Brahmana, then all his doubts vanish away since he has understood the destruction of the causes."

In the third watch of the night, the Exalted One reflected on "The Dependent Arising" in direct and reverse order thus. "When this cause exists, this effect is; with the arising of this cause, this effect arises. When this cause does not exist, this effect is not; with the cessation of this cause, this effect ceases.

Dependent on Ignorance arise Conditioning Activities....and so forth.

Thus does this whole mass of suffering arise.

With the cessation of Ignorance, Conditioning Activities cease....and so forth.

Thus does this whole mass of suffering cease.

Thereupon the Blessed One, knowing the meaning of this, uttered, at that time, this paean of joy:

"When indeed the Truths become manifest unto the strenuous and meditative Brahmana, then he stands routing the hosts of the Evil One even as the sun illumines the sky."

Second Week

The second week was uneventful, but He silently taught a great moral lesson to the world. As a mark of profound gratitude to the inanimate Bodhi tree that sheltered him during His struggle for Enlightenment, He stood at a certain distance gazing at the tree with motionless eyes for one whole week.[1]

Following His noble example, His followers, in memory of His Enlightenment, still venerate not only the original Bodhi tree but also its descendants.[2]

---

1. On the spot where the Buddha stood, a Cetiya has been erected by King Asoka. This was named Animisalocana Cetiya and is still to be seen.

2. The right-hand branch of the original Bodhi tree which was brought to Ceylon by Sanghamittā Theri and planted by King Devánampiyatissa at Anuradhapura, the ancient capital of Ceylon, still exists in a flourishing condition, though more than 2200 years old.

Third week

As the Buddha had not given up His temporary residence at the Bodhi tree the Devas doubted His attainment to Buddhahood. The Buddha read their thoughts, and in order to clear their doubts He created by His psychic powers a jewelled ambulatory (*ratana caṁkamana*) and paced up and down for another week.

Fourth Week

The fourth week He spent in a jewelled chamber (*ratanaghara*)[1] contemplating the intricacies of the Abhidhamma (Higher Teaching). Books state that His mind and body were so purified when He pondered on the Book of Relations (*Paṭṭhāna*), the seventh treatise of the Abhidhamma, that six coloured rays emitted from His body.[2]

Fifth week

During the fifth week too the Buddha enjoyed the Bliss of Emancipation (*Vimuttisukha*), seated in one posture 'under the famous *Ajapāla* banyan tree in the vicinity of the Bodhi tree. When He arose from that transcendental state a conceited (*huhunkajātika*) brahmin approached Him and after the customary salutations and friendly, greetings, questioned Him thus: "In what respect,

---

1. So called because the Buddha reflected on the jewels of the Abhidhamma.
2. Namely, blue (*nīla*), yellow (*pīta*), red (*lohita*), white (*odāta*), orange (*mañjettha*) and a mixture of these five colours (*pabhassara*).

O Venerable Gotama, does one become a Brahmana and what are the conditions that make a Brahmana?"

The Buddha uttered this paean of joy in reply:

"That brahmin who has discarded evil, without conceit (*huhuṁka*), free from Defilements, self-controlled, versed in knowledge and who has led the Holy Life rightly, would call himself a Brahmana.   For him there is no elation anywhere in this world."[1]

According to the Jātaka commentary it was during this week that the daughters of Māra-*Tanhā, Arati* and *Ragā*[2] —made a vain attempt to tempt the Buddha by their charms.

Sixth week

From the *Ajapāla* banyan tree the Buddha proceeded to the *Mucalinda* tree, where he spent the sixth week, again enjoying the Bliss of Emancipation.   At that time there arose an unexpected great shower.   Rain clouds and gloomy weather with cold winds prevailed for several days.

Thereupon *Mucalinda*, the serpent-king,[3] came out of his abode, and coiling round the body of

---

1. Udāna, p. i.
2. These three cannot be personified passions as the incident took place after the Enlightenment.
3. This Nāga King cannot be a human being.   The Vinaya texts also cite an interesting story of a serpent who, assuming the form of a human being, lived for some time as a Bhikkhu in robes.

the Buddha seven times, remained keeping his large hood over the head of the Buddha so that He may not be affected by the elements.

At the close of seven days *Mucalinda*, seeing the clear, cloudless sky, uncoiled himself from around the body of the Buddha, and, leaving his own form, took the guise of a young man, and stood in front of the Exalted One with clasped hands.

Thereupon the Buddha uttered this paean of joy:

"Happy is seclusion to him who is contented, to him who has heard the truth, and to him who sees. Happy is goodwill in this world, and so is restraint towards all beings. Happy in this world is non-attachment, the passing beyond of sense-desires. The suppression of the 'I am' conceit is indeed the highest happiness."[1]

Seventh week

The seventh week the Buddha peacefully passed at the *Rājāyatana* tree, experiencing the Bliss of Emancipation.

---

1. *Sukho viveko tutthassa sutadhammassa passato*
   Abyāpajjhaṁ sukhaṁ loke pāṇabhūtesu saṁyamo
   Sukhā virāgatā loke kāmānaṁ samatikkamo
   Asmimānassa yo vinayo etaṁ ve paramaṁ sukhaṁ
   Udāna p. 10.

One of the First Utterances of the Buddha

'*Thro' many a birth in existence wandered I,*

Seeking, but not finding, the builder of this house.

Sorrowful is repeated birth.

O housebuilder,[2] thou art seen. Thou shalt build no house[3] again.

All thy rafters[4] are broken. Thy ridge-pole[5] is shattered.

Mind attains the Unconditioned.[6]

Achieved is the End of Craving.

At dawn on the very day of His Enlightenment the Buddha uttered this paean of joy (*Udāna*) which vividly describes His transcendental moral victory and His inner spiritual experience.

The Buddha admits His past wanderings in

---

1. This famous Paean of joy appears only in the Dhammapada—vv. 153, 154.
    Anekajāti saṁsāraṁ sandhāvissaṁ anibbisaṁ
    Gahakārakaṁ gavesanto dukkhā jāti punappunaṁ
    Gahakāraka, diṭṭho' si puna gehaṁ na kāhasi
    Sabbā te phāsukā bhaggā gahakūtaṁ visamkhitaṁ
    Visaṁkhāragataṁ cittaṁ tanhānaṁ khayaṁ' ajjhagā.
2. I.e., Craving (*tanhā*).
3. Body.
4. Passions (*kilesa*)
5. Ignorance (*avijjā*).
6. Nibbána.

existence which entailed suffering, a fact that
evidently proves the belief in rebirth. He was
compelled to wander and consequently to suffer,
as He could not discover the architect that built
this house, the body. In His final birth, while
engaged in solitary meditation which He had
highly developed in the course of His wanderings,
after a relentless search He discovered by His own
intuitive wisdom the elusive architect, residing not
outside but within the recesses of His own heart.
It was craving or attachment, a self-creation,
a mental element latent in all. How and when
this craving originated is incomprehensible. What
is created by oneself can be destroyed by oneself.
The discovery of the architect is the eradication of
craving by attaining Arhantship, which in these
verses is alluded to as "end of craving."

The rafters of this self-created house are the
passions (*kilesa*) such as attachment (*lobha*)
aversion (*dosa*), illusion (*moha*), conceit (*māna*),
false views (*diṭṭhi*), doubt (*vicikicchā*), sloth (*thīna*),
restlessness (*uddhacca*), moral shamelessness (*ahi-
rika*), moral fearlessness (*anottappa*). The ridge-
pole that supports the rafters represents ignorance,
the root cause of all passions. The shattering
of the ridge-pole of ignorance by wisdom results
in the complete demolition of the house. The
ridge-pole and rafters are the material with
which the architect builds this undesired house.

With their destruction the architect is deprived of the material to rebuild the house which is not wanted.

With the demolition of the house the mind, for which there is no place in the analogy, attains the unconditioned state, which is Nibbāna. Whatever that is mundane is left behind, and only the Supramundane State, Nibbāna, remains.

CHAPTER 5

THE INVITATION TO EXPOUND THE DHAMMA

"He who imbibes the Dhamma abides in happiness with mind pacified. The wise man ever delights in the Dhamma revealed by the Ariyas".

DHAMMAPADA

The Dhamma as the Teacher

On one occasion soon after the Enlightenment, the Buddha was dwelling at the foot of the *Ajapāla* banyan tree by the bank of the *Nerañjarā* river. As He was engaged in solitary meditation the following thought arose in His mind:

"Painful indeed is it to live without someone to pay reverence and show deference. How if I should live near an ascetic or brahmin respecting and reverencing him?"[1]

Then it occurred to Him:

"Should I live near another ascetic or brahmin, respecting and reverencing him, in order to bring morality (*sīlakkhandha*) to perfection? But I do not see in this world including gods, Māras, and Brahmas, and amongst beings including ascetics, brahmins, gods and men, another ascetic or brah-

---

1. Anguttara Nikāya: part ii, p. 20; *Gradual Sayings*, part ii, p. 20.

min who is superior to me in morality and with whom I could associate, respecting and reverencing him.

"Should I live near another ascetic or brahmin, respecting and reverencing him, in order to bring concentration (*samādhikkhandha*) to perfection? But I do not see in this world any ascetic or brahmin who is superior to me in concentration and with whom I should associate, respecting and reverencing him.

"Should I live near another ascetic or brahmin, respecting and reverencing him, in order to bring wisdom (*paññākkandha*) to perfection? But I do not see in this world any ascetic or brahmin who is superior to me in wisdom and with whom I should associate, respecting and reverencing him.

"Should I live near another ascetic or brahmin, respecting and reverencing him, in order to bring emancipation (*vimuttikkhandha*) to perfection? But I do not see in this world any ascetic or brahmin who is superior to me in emancipation and with whom I should associate, respecting and reverencing him.

Then it occurred to Him: "How if I should live respecting and reverencing this very Dhamma which I myself have realized?"

Thereupon Brahmā *Sahampati*, understanding with his own mind the Buddha's thought, just as a strong man would stretch his bent arm or bend his stretched arm even so did he vanish from the Brahma realm and appeared before the Buddha. And, covering one shoulder with his upper robe and placing his right knee on the ground, he saluted the Buddha with clasped hands and said thus:

"It is so, O Exalted One! It is so, O Accomplished One! O Lord, the worthy, supremely Enlightened Ones, who were in the past, did live respecting and reverencing this very Dhamma.

"The worthy, supremely Enlightened Ones, who will be in the future, will also live respecting and reverencing this very Dhamma.

"O Lord, may the Exalted One, the worthy, supremely Enlightened One of the present age also live respecting and reverencing this very Dhamma!"

This the Brahmā *Sahampati* said, and uttering which, furthermore he spoke as follows:

"Those Enlightened Ones of the past, those of the future, and those of the present age, who dispel the grief of many—all of them lived, will live, and are living respecting the noble Dhamma. This is the characteristic of the Buddhas.

"Therefore he who desires his welfare and expects his greatness should certainly respect the noble Dhamma, remembering the message of the Buddhas."

This the Brahmā *Sahampati* said, and after which, he respectfully saluted the Buddha and passing round Him to the right, disappeared immediately.

As the Sangha is also endowed with greatness there is also His reverence towards the Sangha.[1]

The Invitation to Expound the Dhamma

From the foot of the *Rājāyatana* tree the Buddha proceeded to the *Ajapāla* banyan tree and as He was absorbed in solitary meditation the following thought occurred to Him.

"This Dhamma which I have realized is indeed profound, difficult to perceive, difficult to comprehend, tranquil, exalted, not within the sphere of logic, subtle, and is to be understood by the wise. These beings are attached to material pleasures. This causally connected 'Dependent Arising' is a subject which is difficult to comprehend. And this Nibbāna—the cessation of the conditioned, the abandoning of all passions, the destruction of craving, the non-attachment, and the cessation—is also a matter not easily comprehensible. If I too were to teach this Dhamma, the others would not understand me. That will be wearisome to me, that will be tiresome to me."

---

1. This discourse was delivered by the Buddha while residing at Jetavana, Sāvatthi, long after the establishment of the Order of the Sangha. He showed His reverence towards the Sangha by requesting the Queen Mahā Pajāpati Gotami to offer to the Sangha the robe specially prepared for Him.

Then these wonderful verses unheard of before occurred to the Buddha:

"With difficulty have I comprehended the Dhamma.   There is no need to proclaim it now. This Dhamma is not easily understood by those who are dominated by lust and hatred. The lust-ridden, shrouded in darkness, do not see this Dhamma, which goes against the stream, which is abstruse, profound, difficult to perceive and subtle."

As the Buddha reflected thus, he was not disposed to expound the Dhamma.

Thereupon Brahmā *Sahampati* read the thoughts of the Buddha, and, fearing that the world might perish through not hearing the Dhamma, approached Him and invited Him to teach the Dhamma thus:

"O Lord, may the Exalted One expound the Dhamma! May the Accomplished One expound the Dhamma! There are beings with little dust in their eyes, who, not hearing the Dhamma, will fall away.   There will be those who understand the Dhamma."

Furthermore he remarked:

"In ancient times there arose in Magadha a Dhamma, impure, thought out by the corrupted. Open this door to the Deathless State.   May they hear the Dhamma understood by the Stainless One! Just as one standing on the summit of a rocky mountain would behold the people around, even so may the All-Seeing, Wise One ascend this palace of Dhamma! May the Sorrowless One look upon the people who are plunged in grief and are overcome by birth and decay!

"Rise, O Hero, victor in battle, caravan leader, debt-free One, and wander in the World! May the Exalted One teach the Dhamma! There will be those who will understand the Dhamma."

When he said so the Exalted One spoke to him thus:

"The following thought, O Brahma, occurred to me—'This Dhamma which I have comprehended is not easily understood by those who are dominated by lust and hatred. The lust-ridden, shrouded in darkness, do not see this Dhamma, which goes against the stream, which is abstruse, profound, difficult to perceive, and subtle'. As I reflected thus, my mind turned into inaction and not to the teaching of the Dhamma."

Brahmā Sahampati appealed to the Buddha for the second time and He made the same reply.

When he appealed to the Buddha for the third time, the Exalted One, out of pity for beings, surveyed the world with His Buddha-Vision.

As He surveyed thus He saw beings wtih little and much dust in their eyes, with keen and dull intellect, with good and bad characteristics, beings who are easy and beings who are difficult to be taught, and few others who, with fear, view evil and a life beyond.[1]

"As in the case of a blue, red or white lotus pond, some lotuses are born in the water, grow in the water, remain immersed in the water, and thrive plunged in the water; some are born in the water, grow in the water and remain on the surface of the water; some others are born in the water, grow in the water and remain emerging out of the water, unstained by the water. Even so, as the Exalted One surveyed the world with His Buddha-Vision, He saw beings with little and much dust in their eyes, with keen and dull intellect, with good and bad characteristics, beings who are easy and difficult to be taught, and few others who, with fear, view evil and a life beyond. And He addressed the Brahmā *Sahampati* in a verse thus:

"Opened to them are the Doors to the Deathless State. Let those who have ears repose confidence.[2] Being aware of the weariness, O Brahma, I did not teach amongst men this glorious and excellent Dhamma."

The delighted Brahma, thinking that he made himself the occasion for the Exalted One to ex-

---

1. *Paralokavajjabhayadassāvino.*

2. *Apārutā tesaṁ amatassa dvārā—ye sotavantā pamuñcantu saddham.*

pound the Dhamma respectfully saluted- Him and, passing round Him to the right, disappeared immediately.[1]

The First Two Converts

After His memorable fast for forty-nine days, as the Buddha sat under the *Rājāyatana* tree, two merchants, *Tapassu* and *Bhallika*, from *Ukkala* (Orissa) happened to pass that way. Then a certain deity[2], who was a blood relative of theirs in a past birth, spoke to them as follows:

"The Exalted One, good sirs, is dwelling at the foot of the *Rājāyatana* tree, soon after His Enlightenment. Go and serve the Exalted One with flour and honey-comb.[3] It will conduce to your well-being and happiness for a long time."

Availing themselves of this golden opportunity, the two delighted merchants went to the Exalted One, and, respectfully saluting Him, implored Him to accept their humble alms so that it may resound to their happiness andwell-being.

---

1. See Majjhima Nikāya, *Ariyapariyesana Sutta,* No. 26.

2. *Devatās* (Pāli) are terrestrial or celestial deities, a class of beings, who, as a rule, are invisible to the physical eye. This particular feminine deity had been related to the merchants in a previous birth. It is interesting to note the non-human element appearing in various places connected with the life of the Buddha.

3. *Sattu,* fried flour, and *Madhu,* honey, were a regular diet of travellers in India in the ancient days.

Then it occurred to the Exalted One:

"The Tathāgatas do not accept food with their hands. How shall I accept this flour and honey-comb?"

Forthwith the four Great Kings[1] understood the thoughts of the Exalted One with their minds and from the four directions offered Him four granite bowls,[2] saying—"O Lord, may the Exalted One accept herewith this flour and honey-comb!"

The Buddha graciously accepted the timely gift with which He received the humble offering of the merchants, and ate His food after His long fast.

After the meal was over the merchants prostrated themselves before the feet of the Buddha and said:

"We, O Lord, seek refuge in the Exalted One and the Dhamma. May the Exalted One treat us as lay disciples who have sought refuge from today till death."[3]

---

1. *Cātummahārājikas*, the Guardian Deities of the four quarters.
2. The commentary states that the Buddha wished that the four bowls be amalgamated into one.
3. *Buddhaṁ saraṇaṁ gacchāmi* (I seek refuge in the Buddha), *Dhammaṁ saraṇaṁ gacchāmi* (I seek refuge in the Dhamma), is the twofold formula. As the Sangha or the Noble Order was not in existence then they did not recite the third formula—*Saṅghaṁ saraṇaṁ gacchāmi* (I seek refuge in the Sangha). One becomes a Buddhist by intelligently reciting the Three Refuges.

These were the first lay disciples[1] of the Buddha who embraced Buddhism by seeking refuge in the Buddha and the Dhamma, reciting the twofold formula.

On the Way to Benares to Teach the Dhamma

On accepting the invitation to teach the Dhamma, the first thought that occurred to the Buddha before He embarked on His great mission was— "To whom shall I teach the Dhamma first? Who will understand the Dhamma quickly? Well, there is *Ālāra Kālāma*[2] who is learned, clever, wise and has for long been with little dust in his eyes. How if I were to teach the Dhamma to him first? He will understand the Dhamma quickly."

Then a deity appeared before the Buddha and said: "Lord! *Ālāra Kālāma* died a week ago."

With His supernormal vision He perceived that it was so.

---

1. The Jātaka commentary relates that when these two first converts begged of the Buddha to give them an object of worship the Buddha touched His head and presented them some hair relics.
   It is believed that these relics have been enshrined in the modern Swe Dagon Pagoda in Rangoon, the pride and glory of Burmese Buddhists. This bell-shaped massive Cetiya appears like a golden mountain from a distance.
2. The first religious teacher who taught the Bodhisatta the Jhānas extending up to the Realm of Nothingness (*Akiñcaññáyatana*).

Then He thought of *Uddaka Rāmaputta*[1]. Instantly a deity informed Him that he died the evening before.

With His supernormal vision He perceived this to be so.

Ultimately the Buddha thought of the five energetic ascetics who attended on Him during His struggle for Enlightenment. With His supernormal vision He perceived that they were residing in the Deer Park at Isipatana near Benares. So the Buddha stayed at Uruvela till such time as He was pleased to set out for Benares.

The Buddha was travelling on the highway, when between Gayā and the Bodhi tree, beneath whose shade He attained Enlightenment, a wandering ascetic named *Upaka* saw Him and addressed Him thus: "Extremely clear are your senses, friend! Pure and clean is your complexion. On account of whom has your renunciation been made, friend? Who is your teacher? Whose doctrine do you profess?"

The Buddha replied:

"All have I overcome, all do I know.

From all am I detached, all have I renounced.

---

1. The second religious teacher who taught the Bodhisatta the highest state of mundane mental development— The Realm of Neither Perception nor Non-perception (*N'eva saññā n' āsaññāyatana*).

*Wholly absorbed am I in the destruction of
craving (Arahantship).*

*Having comprehended all by myself whom shall
I call my teacher?*

No teacher have I.[1] An equal to me there is not.

*In the world including gods there is no rival
to me.*

Indeed an Arahant am I in this world.

An unsurpassed teacher am I;

Alone am I the All-Enlightened.

Cool and appeased am I.

*To establish the wheel of Dhamma to the city of
Kāsi I go.*

*In this blind world I shall beat the drum of
Deathlessness."[2]*

"Then, friend, do you admit that you are an
Arahant, a limitless Conqueror?" queried *Upaka*.

"Like me are conquerors who have attained
to the destruction of defilements. All the evil
conditions have I conquered. Hence, *Upaka*,
I am called a conqueror," replied the Buddha.

---

1. The Buddha uttered these words because He attained
   Enlightenment by Himself without the aid of a teacher.
   He had teachers before His Enlightenment, but nobody
   taught Him the way to attain Buddhahood. It is therefore not correct to say that Buddhism is a natural outgrowth of Hinduism.
2. Majjhima Nikāya, Ariyapariyesana Sutta, N, 26.

"It may be so, friend!" *Upaka* curtly remarked, and, nodding his head, turned into a by-road and departed.

Unperturbed by the first rebuff, the Buddha journeyed from place to place, and arrived in due course at the Deer Park in Benares.

Meeting the Five Monks

The five ascetics who saw Him coming from afar decided not to pay Him due respect as they misconstrued His discontinuance of rigid ascetic practices which proved absolutely futile during His struggle for Enlightenment.

They remarked:

"Friends, this ascetic *Gotama* is coming. He is luxurious. He has given up striving and has turned into a life of abundance. He should not be greeted and waited upon. His bowl and robe should not be taken. Nevertheless, a seat should be prepared. If he wishes, let him sit down."

However, as the Buddha continued to draw near, His august personality was such that they were compelled to receive Him with due honour. One came forward and took His bowl and robe, another prepared a seat, and yet another kept water for His feet. Nevertheless, they addressed Him by name and called Him friend (*āvuso*), a form of address applied generally to juniors and equals.

At this the Buddha addressed them thus:

"Do not, O Bhikkhus, address the *Tathāgata*
by name or by the title '*āvuso*'. An Exalted One,
O Bhikkhus, is the *Tathāgata*. A Fully Enlightened One is He. Give ear, O Bhikkhus! Deathlessness
(*Amata*) has been attained. I shall instruct and
teach the Dhamma. If you act according to my
instructions, you will before long realize, by your
own intuitive wisdom, and live, attaining in this
life itself, that supreme consummation of the Holy
Life, for the sake of which sons of noble families
rightly leave the household for homelessness."

Thereupon the five ascetics replied.:

"By that demeanour of yours, *āvuso Gotama*,
by that discipline, by those painful austerities,
you did not attain to any superhuman specific
knowledge and insight worthy of an Ariya. How
will you, when you have become luxurious, have
given up striving, and have turned into a life of
abundance, gain any such superhuman specific
knowledge and insight worthy of an Ariya?"

In explanation the Buddha said:

"The *Tāthagata*, O Bhikkhus, is not luxurious,
has not given up striving, and has not turned into
a life of abundance. An Exalted One is the *Tathāgata*. A Fully Enlightened One is He. Give ear,
O Bhikkhus! Deathlessness has been attained. I
shall instruct and teach the Dhamma. If you act

according to my instructions, you will before long realize, by your own intuitive wisdom, and live, attaining in this life itself, that supreme consummation of the Holy Life, for the sake of which sons of noble families rightly leave the household for homelessness."

For the second time the prejudiced ascetics expressed their disappointment in the same manner.

For the second time the Buddha reassured them of His attainment to Enlightenment.

When the adamant ascetics refusing to believe Him, expressed their view for the third time, the Buddha questioned them thus: "Do you know, O Bhikkhus, of an occasion when I ever spoke to you thus before?"

"Nay, indeed, Lord!"

The Buddha repeated for the third time that He had gained Enlightenment and that they also could realize the Truth if they would act according to His instructions.

It was indeed a frank utterance, issuing from the sacred lips of the Buddha. The cultured ascetics, though adamant in their views, were then fully convinced of the great achievement of the Buddha and of His competence to act as their moral guide and teacher.

They believed His word and sat in silence to listen to His Noble Teaching.

Two of the ascetics the Buddha instructed, while three went out for alms. With what the three ascetics brought from their alms-round the six maintained themselves. Three of the ascetics He instructed, while two ascetics went out for alms. With what the two brought six sustained themselves.

And those five ascetics thus admonished and instructed by the Buddha, being themselves subject to birth, decay, death, sorrow, and passions, realized the real nature of life and, seeking out the birthless, decayless, diseaseless, deathless, sorrowless, passionless, incomparable Supreme Peace, Nibbāna, attained the incomparable Security, Nibbāna, which is free from birth, decay, disease, death, sorrow, and passions, The knowledge arose in them that their Deliverance was unshakable, that it was their last birth and that there would be no more of this state again.

Dhammacakkappavattana Sutta,[1] which deals, with the four Noble Truths, was the first discourse delivered by the Buddha to them. Hearing it, *Kondañña*, the eldest, attained the first stage of Sainthood. After receiving further instructions, the other four attained *Sotāpatti*[2] later. On hearing the *Anattalakkhana Sutta*,[3] which deals with soul-

1. See ch. 6.
2. Lit.—Stream-Winner.
3. See ch. 6.

lessness, all the five attained Arahantship,[1] the
final stage of Sainthood.

The first Five Disciples

The five learned monks who thus attained
Arahantship and became the Buddha's first disciples were *Kondañña, Bhaddiya, Vappa, Mahānāma*, and *Assaji* of the brahmin clan.

Kondañña was the youngest and the cleverest
of the eight brahmins who were summoned by
King *Suddhodana* to name the infant prince. The
other four were the sons of those older brahmins.
All these five retired to the forest as ascetics in
anticipation of the Bodhisatta while he was endea-
vouring to attain Buddhahood. When he gave up
his useless penances and severe austerities and
began to nourish the body sparingly to regain
his lost strength, these favourite followers, disappointed at his change of method, deserted him
and went to Isipatana. Soon after their departure
the Bodhisatta attained Buddhahood.

The venerable *Kondañña* became the first Arahant and the most senior member of the Sangha.
It was *Assaji*, one of the five, who converted the
great *Sāriputta*, the chief disciple of the Buddha.

---

1. Lit.—The Worthy One.

CHAPTER 6

DHAMMACAKKAPPAVATTANA SUTTA
THE FIRST DISCOURSE

"The best of paths is the Eightfold Path. The best of Truths are the four Sayings. Non-attachment is the best of states. The best of bipeds is the Seeing One."

DHAMMAPADA

Introduction

Ancient India was noted for distinguished philosophers and religious teachers who held diverse views with regard to life and its goal. Brahmajāla Sutta of the Dīgha Nikāya mentions sixty-two varieties of philosophical theories that prevailed in the time of the Buddha.

One extreme view that was diametrically opposed to all current religious beliefs was the nihilistic teaching of the materialists who were also termed *Cārvākas* after the name of the founder.

According to ancient materialism which, in Pāli and Saṃskrit, was known as Lokāyata, man is annihilated after death, leaving behind him whatever force generated by him. In their opinion death is the end of all. This present world alone is real. "Eat, drink, and be merry, for death comes to all," appears to be the ideal of their system. "Virtue", they say, "is a delusion and enjoyment is the only reality. Religion is a foolish aberration, a mental disease. There was a distrust of everything good, high, pure and compassionate. Their theory stands for sensualism and selfishness and the gross affirmation of the loud will. There is no need to control passion and instinct, since they are the nature's legacy to men."[1]

Another extreme view was that emancipation was possible only by leading a life of strict asceticism. This was purely a religious doctrine firmly held by the ascetics of the highest order. The five monks that attended on the Bodhisatta, during His struggle for Enlightenment, tenaciously adhered to this belief.

In accordance with this view the Buddha, too, before His Enlightenment subjected Himself to all forms of austerity. After an extraordinary struggle for six years He realized the utter futility of self-mortification. Consequently, He changed His unsuccessful hard course and adopted a middle way. His favourite disciples thus lost confidence in Him and deserted Him, saying—"The ascetic *Gotama* had become luxurious, had ceased from striving, and had returned to a life of comfort."

Their unexpected desertion was definitely a material loss to Him as they ministered to all His

1. Sri Radhakrishnan, *Indian Philosophy*, vol. 1, pp. 281-282.

needs. Nevertheless, He was not discouraged. The iron-willed Bodhisatta must have probably felt happy for being left alone. With unabated enthusiasm and with restored energy He persistently strove until He attained Enlightenment, the object of His life.

Precisely two months after His Enlightenment on the *Āsāḷha* (July) full moon day the Buddha delivered His first discourse to the five monks that attended on Him.

The first Discourse of the Buddha

Dhammacakka is the name given to this first discourse of the Buddha. It is frequently represented as meaning "The Kingdom of Truth." "The Kingdom of Righteousness." "The Wheel of Truth." According to the commentators *Dhamma* here means wisdom or knowledge, and *Cakka* means founding or establishment. *Dhammacakka* therefore means the founding or establishment of wisdom. *Dhammacakkappavattana* means The Expositon of the Establishment of Wisdom. *Dhamma* may also be interpreted as Truth, and *cakka* as wheel. *Dhammacakkappavattana* would therefore mean—The Turning or The Establishment of the Wheel of Truth.

In this most important discourse the Buddha expounds the Middle Path which He Himself discovered and which forms the essence of His new teaching. He opened the discourse by exhorting the five monks who believed in strict asceticism to avoid the extremes of self-indulgence and self-mortification as both do not lead to perfect Peace and Enlightenment. The former retards one's spiritual progress, the latter weakens one's intellect. He criticized both views as He realized by personal experience their futility and enunciated the most practicable, rational and beneficial path, which alone leads to perfect purity and absolute Deliverance.

This discourse was expounded by the Buddha while He was residing at the Deer Park in Isipatana near Benares.

The intellectual five monks who were closely associated with the Buddha for six years were the only human beings that were present to hear the sermon. Books state that many invisible beings such as Devas and Brahmas also took advantage of the golden opportunity of listening to the sermon. As Buddhists believe in the existence of realms other than this world, inhabited by beings with subtle bodies imperceptible to the physical eye, possibly many Devas and Brahmas were also present on this great occasion. Nevertheless, it is clear that the Buddha was directly addressing the five monks and the discourse was intended mainly for them.

At the outset the Buddha cautioned them to avoid the two extremes. His actual words were:— "There are two extremes (*antā*) which should not be resorted to by a recluse (*pabbajitena*)." Special emphasis was laid on the two terms "*anta*" which means end or extreme and "*pabbajita*" which means one who has renounced the world.

One extreme, in the Buddha's own words, was the constant attachment to sensual pleasures (*kāmasukhallikānuyoga*). The Buddha described this extreme as base, vulgar, worldly, ignoble, and profitless.

This should not be misunderstood to mean that the Buddha expects all His followers to give up material pleasures and retire to a forest without enjoying this life. The Buddha was not so narrow-minded.

Whatever the deluded sensualist may feel about it, to the dispassionate thinker the enjoyment of sensual pleasures is distinctly short-lived, never completely satisfying, and results in unpleasant reactions. Speaking of worldly happiness, the Buddha says that the acquisition of wealth and the enjoyment of possessions are two sources of pleasure for a layman. An understanding recluse would not however seek delight in the pursuit of these fleeting pleasures. To the surprise of the average man he might shun them. What constitutes pleasure to the former is a source of alarm to the latter to whom renunciation alone is pleasure.

The other extreme is the constant addiction to self-mortification (*attakilamathānuyoga*). Commenting on this extreme, which is not practised by the ordinary man, the Buddha remarks that it is painful, ignoble, and profitless. Unlike the first extreme this is not described as base, worldly, and vulgar. The selection of these three terms is very striking. As a rule it is the sincere recluse who has renounced his attachment to sensual pleasures that resorts to this painful method, mainly with the object of gaining his deliverance from the ills of life. The Buddha, who has had painful experience of this profitless course, describes it as useless. It only multiplies suffering instead of diminishing it.

The Buddhas and Arahants are described as *Ariyas* meaning Nobles. *Anariya* (ignoble) may therefore be construed as not characteristic of the Buddha and Arahants who are free from passions. *Attha* means the ultimate Good, which for a Buddhist is Nibbāna, the complete emancipation from suffering. Therefore *anatthasaṁhitā* may be construed as not conducive to ultimate Good.

The Buddha at first cleared the issues and removed the false notions of His hearers. When their troubled minds became pliable and receptive the Buddha related His personal experience with regard to these two extremes.

The Buddha says that He (the Tathāgata), realizing the error of both these two extremes, followed a middle path. This new path or way was discovered by Himself. The Buddha termed His new system *Majjhimā Paṭipadā*—the Middle Way. To persuade His disciples to give heed to His new path He spoke of its various blessings. Unlike the two diametrically opposite extremes this middle path produces spiritual insight and intellectual wisdom to see things as they truly are. When the insight is clarified and the intellect is sharpened everything is seen in its true perspective.

Furthermore, unlike the first extreme which stimulates passions, this Middle Way leads to the subjugation of passions which results in Peace. Above all it leads to the attainment of the four supramundane Paths of Sainthood, to the understanding of the four Noble Truths, and finally to the realization of the ultimate Goal, Nibbāna.

Now, what is the Middle Way? The Buddha replies: It is the Noble Eightfold Path. The eight factors are then enumerated in the discourse.

The first factor is Right Understanding, the keynote of Buddhism. The Buddha started with Right Understanding in order to clear the doubts of the monks and guide them on the right way

Right Understanding deals with the knowledge of oneself as one really is; it leads to Right Thoughts of non-attachment or renunciation (*nekkhamma-samkappa*), loving-kindness (*avyāpāda samkappa*), and harmlessness (*avihimsā samkappa*), whioh are opposed to selfishness, illwill, and cruelty respectively. Right Thoughts result in Right Speech, Right Action, and Right Livelihood, which three factors perfect one's morality. The sixth factor is Right Effort which deals with the elimination of evil states and the development of good states in oneself. This self-purification is best done by a careful introspection, for which Right Mindfulness, the seventh factor, is essential. Effort, combined with Mindfulness, produces Right Concentration or one-pointedness of the mind, the eighth factor. A one-pointed mind resembles a polished mirror where everything is clearly reflected with no distortion.

Prefacing the discourse with the two extremes and His newly discovered Middle Way, the Buddha expounded the Four Noble Truths in detail.

Sacca is the Pali term for Truth which means *that which is*. Its Samskrit equivalent is *satya* which denotes an incontrovertible fact. The Buddha enunciates four such Truths, the foundations of His teaching, which are associated with the so-called being. Hence His doctrine is homo-centric, opposed to theo-centric religions. It is introvert and not extrovert. Whether the Buddha arises or not these Truths exist, and it is a Buddha that reveals them to the deluded world. They do not and cannot change with time, because they are eternal truths. The Buddha was not indebted to anyone for His realization of them, as He Himself remarked in this discourse thus: "With regard to things unheard before, there arose in me the eye, the knowledge, the wisdom, the insight and the light." These words are very significant because they testify to the originality of His new Teaching. Hence there is no justification in the statement that Buddhism is a natural outgrowth of Hinduism, although it is true that there are some fundamental doctrines common to both systems.

These Truths are in Pali termed *Ariya Saccāni.* They are so called because they were discovered by the Greatest Ariya, that is, one who is far removed from passions.

The First Noble Truth deals with *dukkha* which, for need of a better English equivalent, is inappropriately rendered by suffering or sorrow. As a feeling *dukkha* means that which is difficult to be endured. As an abstract truth *dukkha* is used in the sense of contemptible (*du*) emptiness (*kha*). The world rests on suffering—hence it is contemptible. It is devoid of any reality—hence it is empty or void. *Dukkha* therefore means contemptible void.

Average men are only surface-seers. An Ariya sees things as they truly are.

To an Ariya all life is suffering and he finds
no real happiness in this world which deceives
mankind with illusory pleasures. Material happiness is merely the gratification of some desire.

All are subject to birth (*jāti*) and consequently
to decay (*jarā*), disease (*vyādhi*) and finally to
death (*maraṅa*). No one is exempt from these four
causes of suffering.

Wish unfulfilled is also suffering. As a rule one
does not wish to be associated with things or
persons one detests nor does one wish to be separated from things or persons one likes. One's
cherished desires are not however always gratified.
At times what one least expects or what one least
desires is thrust on oneself. Such unexpected
unpleasant circumstances become so intolerable
and painful that weak ignorant people are compelled to commit suicide as if such an act would
solve the problem.

Real happiness is found within, and is not to
be defined in terms of wealth, power, honours or
conquests. If such worldly possessions are forcibly
or unjustly obtained, or are misdirected or even
viewed with attachment, they become a source of
pain and sorrow for the possessors.

Normally the enjoyment of sensual pleasures
is the highest and only happiness of the average
person. There is no doubt some momentary happiness in the anticipation, gratification, and retros-

pection of such fleeting material pleasures, but
they are illusory and temporary. According to the
Buddha non-attachment (*virāgatā*) or the transcending of material pleasures is a greater bliss.

In brief this composite body (*pañcupādanak-
khandha*) itself is a cause of suffering.

There are three kinds of craving. The first
is the grossest form of craving, which is simple
attachment to all sensual pleasures (*kāmataṇhā*)
The second is attachment to existence (*bhavataṇhā*).
The third is attachment to non-existence (*vibhavataṇhā*). According to the commentaries the last
two kinds of craving are attachment to sensual
pleasures connected with the belief of Eternalism
(*sassatadiṭṭhi*) and that wthch is connected with
the belief of Nihilism (*ucchedadiṭṭhi*). *Bhavataṇhā*
may also be interpreted as attachment to Realms
of Form and *vibhavataṇhā*, as attachment to
Formless Realms since *Rūparāga* and *Arūparāga*
are treated as two Fetters (*saṁyojanas*).

This craving is a powerful mental force latent
in all, and is the chief cause of most of the ills of
life. It is this craving, gross or subtle, that leads to
repeated births in Saṁsāra and that which makes
one cling to all forms of life.

The grossest forms of craving are attenuated
on attaining *Sakadāgāmi*, the second stage of Sainthood, and are eradicated on attaining *Anāgāmi*,

the third stage of Sainthood. The subtle forms of craving are eradicated on attaining *Arahantship*.

Right Understanding of the First Noble Truth leads to the eradication (*pahātabba*) of craving. The Second Noble Truth thus deals with the mental attitude of the ordinary man towards the external objects of sense.

The Third Noble Truth is that there is a complete cessation of suffering which is Nibbāna, the ultimate goal of Buddhists. It can be achieved in this life itself by the total eradication of all forms of craving.

This Nibbāna is to be comprehended (*sacchikātabba*) by the mental eye by renouncing all attachment to the external world.

This First Truth of suffering which depends on this so-called being and various aspects of life, is to be carefully perceived, analysed and examined (*pariññeyya*). This examination leads to a proper understanding of oneself as one really is.

The cause of this suffering is craving or attachment (*taṇhā*). This is the Second Noble Truth.

The Dhammapada states:

"From craving springs grief, from craving springs fear;

For him who is wholly free from craving, there is no grief, much less fear." (V 216).

Craving, the Buddha says, leads to repeated births (*ponobhavikā*). This Pali term is very noteworthy as there are some scholars who state that the Buddha did not teach the doctrine of rebirth. This Second Truth indirectly deals with the past, present and future births.

This Third Noble Truth has to be realized by developing (*bhāvetabba*) the Noble Eightfold Path (*ariyaṭṭhaṅgika magga*). This unique path is the only straight way to Nibbāna. This is the Fourth Noble Truth.

Expounding the Four Truths in various ways, the Buddha concluded the discourse with the forcible words:

"As long, O Bhikkhus, as the absolute true intuitive knowledge regarding these Four Noble Truths under their three aspects and twelve modes was not perfectly clear to me, so long I did not acknowledge that I had gained the incomparable Supreme Enlightenment.

"When the absolute true intuitive knowledge regarding these Truths became perfectly clear to me, then only did I acknowledge that I had gained the incomparable Supreme Enlightenment (*anuttara sammāsambodhi*).

"And there arose in me the knowledge and insight: Unshakable is the deliverance of my mind, this is my last birth, and now there is no existence again."

At the end of the discourse *Koṇḍañña*, the senior of the five disciples, understood the Dhamma and, attaining the first stage of Sainthood, realized that whatever is subject to origination all that is subject to cessation—*Yaṁ kiñci samudayadhammaṁ sabbaṁ taṁ nirodhadhammaṁ.*

When the Buddha expounded the discourse of the *Dhammacakka*, the earth-bound deities exclaimed: "This excellent *Dhammacakka*, which could not be expounded by any ascetic, priest, god, Māra or Brahma in this world, has been expounded by the Exalted One at the Deer Park, in Isipatana, near Benares."

Hearing this, Devas and Brahmas of all the other planes also raised the same joyous cry.

A radiant light, surpassing the effulgence of the gods, appeared in the world.

The light of the Dhamma illumined the whole world, and brought peace and happiness to all beings.

THE FIRST DISCOURSE OF THE BUDDHA

DHAMMACAKKAPPAVATTANA SUTTA

Thus have I heard:

On one occasion the Exalted One was residing at the Deer Park,[1] in Isipatana,[2] near Benares. Thereupon the Exalted One addressed the group of five Bhikkhus as follows:

"There are these two extremes (*antā*), O Bhikkhus, which should be avoided by one who has renounced (*pabbajitena*)—

(i) Indulgence in sensual pleasures[3]—this is base, vulgar, worldly, ignoble and profitless; and,

(ii) Addiction to self-mortification[4]—this is painful, ignoble and profitless.

Abandoning both these extremes the Tathāgata[5] has comprehended the Middle Path (*Majjhimā Paṭipadā*) which promotes sight (*cakkhu*) and knowledge (*ñāṇa*), and which tends to peace

---

1. Mahāvagga p. 10, Samyutta Nikāya Vol. V, p. 420.
2. Modern Saranath where, in a former existence, the Master sacrificed His life to save a helpless doe and her unborn little one. The locality takes its modern name from the Bodhisatta who, in that ancient birth, was Sāranganātha, protector of the deer.
3. *Kāmasukhallikānuyoga.*
4. *Attakilamathānuyoga.*
5. Lit.—'Thus who hath come' or 'Thus who hath gone.' When the Buddha refers to Himself He usually uses this epithet.

(*vupasamāya*),[1] higher wisdom (*abhiññāya*,),[2] enlightenment (*sambodhāya*),[3] and Nibbāna.

What, O Bhikkhus, is that Middle Path the Tathāgata has comprehended which promotes sight and knowledge, and which tends to peace, higher wisdom, enlightenment, and Nibbāna?

The very Noble Eightfold Path—namely, Right Understanding (*sammā diṭṭhi*), Right Thoughts (*sammā saṁkappa*), Right Speech (*sammā vācā*), Right Action (*sammā-kammanta*), Right Livelihood (*sammā ājīva*), Right Effort (*sammā vāyāma*), Right Mindfulness (*sammā sati*), and Right Concentration (*sammā samādhi*),—This, O Bhikkhus is the Middle Path which the Tathāgata has comprehended." (The Buddha continued):

Now, this, O Bhikkhus, is the Noble Truth of Suffering (*dukkha-ariya-sacca*)!

Birth is suffering, decay is suffering, disease is suffering, death is suffering, to be united with the unpleasant is suffering, to be separated from the pleasant is suffering, not to get what one desires

---

1. Subjugation of passions.
2. Realization of the Four Noble Truths
3. Attainment of the four Paths and four Fruits of Saintship.

is suffering. In brief the five aggregates[1] of attachment are suffering.

Now, this, O Bhikkhus, is the Noble Truth of the Cause of Suffering (*dukkha-samudaya-ariya-sacca*):

It is this craving which produces rebirth (*pono-bhavikā*), accompanied by passionate clinging, welcoming this and that (life). It is the craving for sensual pleasures (*kāmataṇhā*), craving for existence (*bhavataṇhā*) and craving for non-existence (*vibhavataṇhā*).

Now, this, O Bhikkhus, is the Noble Truth of the Cessation of Suffering (*dukkha - nirodha- ariya-sacca*:)

It is the complete separation from, and destruction of, this very craving, its forsaking, renunciation, the liberation therefrom, and non-attachment thereto.

Now, this, O Bhikkhus, is the Noble Truth of the Path leading to the Cessation of Suffering (*dukkha-nirodha-gāminī-paṭipadā-ariya-sacca*).

---

1. *Pañcūpādānakkhandha*—According to Buddhism this so-called being is composed of five groups, viz: *Rūpa,* matter, *Vedanā,* feeling, *Saññā* perception, *Samkhārā,* mental states and *Viññāna,* consciousness. These are the five psycho-physical component parts that constitute an individual. Matter is composed of forces and qualities. Mind too is composed of mental states (*cetasikas*). They are fifty-two in number. Of them *Vedanā,* and *Saññā* are treated as two distinct groups. The remaining fifty are collectively called *Samkhārā.*

It is this Noble Eightfold Path—namely, Right Understanding, Right Thoughts, Right Speech, Right Action, Right Livelihood, Right Effort, Right Mindfulness and Right Concentration.

1. (i) "This is the Noble Truth of Suffering."

Thus, O Bhikkhus, with respect to things unheard before, there arose in me the eye, the knowledge, the wisdom, the insight, and the light.

(ii) "This Noble Truth of Suffering should be perceived (*pariññeyya*)."

Thus, O Bhikkhus, with respect to things unheard before, there arose in me the eye, the knowledge, the wisdom, the insight, and the light.

(iii) "This Noble Truth of Suffering has been perceived (*pariññāta*)."

Thus, O Bhikkhus, with respect to things unheard before, there arose in me the eye, the knowledge, the wisdom, the insight, and the light.

2. (i) "This is the Noble Truth of the Cause of Suffering."

Thus, O Bhikkhus, with respect to things unheard before, there arose in me the eye, the knowledge, the wisdom, the insight, and the light.

(ii) "This Noble Truth of the Cause of Suffering should be eradicated (*pahātabba*)."

Thus, O Bhikkhus, with respect to things unheard before, there arose in me the eye, the knowledge, the wisdom, the insight, and the light.

(iii) "This Noble Truth of the Cause of Suffering has been eradicated (*pahīnaṁ*)."

Thus, O Bhikkhus, with respect to things unheard before, there arose in me the eye, the knowledge, the wisdom, the insight, and the light.

3. (i) "This is the Noble Truth of Cessation of Suffering."

Thus, O Bhikkhus, with respect to things unheard before, there arose in me the eye, the knowledge, the wisdom, the insight, and the light.

(ii) "This Noble Truth of the Cessation of Suffering should be realized (*sacchikātabba*)."

Thus, O Bhikkhus, with respect to things unheard before, there arose in me the eye, the knowledge, the wisdom, the insight, and the light.

(iii) "This Noble Truth of the Cessation of Suffering has been realized (*sacchikataṁ*)."

Thus, O Bhikkhus, with respect to things unheard before, there arose in me the eye, the knowledge, the wisdom, the insight, and the light.

4. (i) "This is the Noble Truth of the Path leading to the Cessation of Suffering."

Thus, O Bhikkhus, with respect to things, unheard before, there arose in me the eye, the knowledge, the wisdom, the insight, and the light.

(ii) "This Noble Truth of the Path leading to the Cessation of Suffering should be developed (*bhāvetabbaṁ*)."

Thus, O Bhikkhus, with respect to things, unheard before, there arose in me the eye, the knowledge, the wisdom, the insight, and the light.

(iii) "This Noble Truth of the Path leading to the Cessation of Suffering has been developed (*bhāvitaṁ*)."

Thus, O Bhikkhus, with respect to things, unheard before, there arose in me the eye, the knowledge, the wisdom, the insight, and the light.

(Concluding His discourse the Buddha said):

As long, O bhikkhus, as the absolute true intuitive knowledge regarding these Four Noble Truths under their three aspects[1] and twelve modes[2] was not perfectly clear to me, so long I did not acknowledge in this world inclusive of gods, Māras and Brahmas and amongst the hosts of

---

1. They are (i) the knowledge of the Four Truths (*sacca-nāna*) (ii) the knowledge as regards the respective function of the Four Truths (*kiccanāna*). (iii) and the knowledge that the respective function of each Truth has been accomplished (*kata nāna*).
2. Each Truth consists of three aspects. Thus four Truths consist of twelve modes.

ascetics and priests, gods and men, that I had gained the Incomparable Supreme Enlightenment (*anuttaraṁ sammā-sambodhiṁ*).

When, O Bhikkhus, the absolute true intuitive knowledge regarding these Four Noble Truths under their three aspects and twelve modes, became perfectly clear to me, then only did I acknowledge in this world inclusive of gods, Māras, Brahmas, amongst the hosts of ascetics and priests, gods and men, that I had gained the Incomparable Supreme Enlightenment.

And there arose in me the knowledge and insight (*ñāṇadassana*)—"Unshakable is the deliverance of my mind.[1] This is my last birth, and now there is no existence again."

Thus the Exalted One discoursed, and the delighted Bhikkhus applauded the words of the Exalted One.

When this doctrine was being expounded there arose in the Venerable *Koṇḍañña* the dustless, stainless, Truth-seeing Eye (*Dhammacakkhu*)[2] and he saw that "whatever is subject to origination all that is subject to cessation."[3]

---

1. The reference is to the Fruit of Arahantship (*Arahattaphala*).
2. *Dhammacakkhu* signifies any of the lower three Paths—*Sotāpatti, Sakadāgāmi,* and *Anāgāmi.* Koṇḍañña attained the first stage of Sainthood (*Sotāpatti*). The other Bhikkhus attained *Sotāpatti* later.
3. *Yam kiñci samudayadhammam sabbam tam nirodhadhammam.*

When the Buddha expounded the discourse of the Dhammacakka, the earth-bound deities exclaimed:—"This excellent Dhammacakka which could not be expounded by any ascetic, priest, god, Māra or Brahma in this world has been expounded by the Exalted One at the Deer Park, in Isipatana, near Benares."

Hearing this, the Devas[1] *Cātummahārājika, Tāvatimsa, Yāma, Tusita, Nimmānarati, Paranimmitavasavatti,* and the *Brahmas* of *Brahma Pārisajja, Brahma Purohita, Maha Brahma, Parittābhā, Appamānābhā, Ābhassara, Parittasubha, Appamānasubha, Subhakinna, Vehapphala, Aviha, Atappa, Sudassa, Sudassi,* and *Akaniṭṭha,* also raised the same joyous cry.

Thus at that very moment, at that very instant, this cry extended as far as the Brahma realm. These ten thousand world systems quaked, tottered and trembled violently.

A radiant light, surpassing the effulgence of the gods, appeared in the world. Then the Exalted One said, "Friends, *Kondañña* has indeed understood. Friends, *Kondañña* has indeed understood."

Therefore the Venerable *Kondañña* was named *Aññāta Koṇḍañña.*

---

1. Celestial beings of Deva and Brahma planes.

SOME REFLECTIONS ON THE DHAMMACAKKA SUTTA

1. Buddhism is based on personal experience. As such it is rational and not speculative.

2. The Buddha discarded all authority and evolved a Golden Mean which was purely His own.

3. Buddhism is a way or a Path—*Magga*.

4. Rational understanding is the keynote of Buddhism.

5. Blind beliefs are dethroned.

6. Instead of beliefs and dogmas the importance of practice is emphasized.

Mere beliefs and dogmas cannot emancipate a person.

7. Rites and ceremonies so greatly emphasized in the Vedas play no part in Buddhism.

8. There are no gods to be propitiated.

9. There is no priestly class to mediate.

10. Morality (*sīla*) Concentration (*samādhi*), and Wisdom (*paññā*), are essential to achieve the goal—Nibbāna.

11. The foundations of Buddhism are the Four Truths that can be verified by experience.

12. The Four Truths are associated with one's person—Hence Buddhism is homo-centric and introvert.

13. They were discovered by the Buddha and He is not indebted to anyone for them. In His own words—"They were unheard of before."

14. Being truths, they cannot change with time.

15. The first Truth of suffering, which deals with the constituents of self or so-called individuality and the different phases of life, is to be analysed, scrutinised and examined. This examination leads to a proper understanding of oneself.

16. Rational understanding of the first Truth leads to the eradication of the cause of suffering —the second Truth which deals with the psychological attitude of the ordinary man towards the external objects of sense.

17. The second Truth of suffering is concerned with a powerful force latent in us all.

18. It is this powerful invisible mental force— craving—the cause of the ills of life.

19. The second Truth indirectly deals with the past, present and future births.

20. The existence of a series of births is therefore advocated by the Buddha.

21. The doctrine of Kamma, its corollary, is thereby implied.

22.   The third Truth of the destruction of suffering, though dependent on oneself, is beyond logical reasoning and supramundane (*lokuttara*) unlike the first two which are mundane (*lokiya*).

23.   The third Truth is purely a self-realization —a Dhamma to be comprehended by the mental eye (*sacchikātabba*).

24.   This Truth is to be realized by complete renunciation. It is not a case of renouncing external objects but internal attachment to the external world.

25.   With the complete eradication of this attachment is the third Truth realized. It should be noted that mere complete destruction of this force is not the third Truth—Nibbāna. Then it would be tantamount to annihilation. Nibbāna has to be realized by eradicating this force which binds oneself to the mundane.

26.   It should also be understood that Nibbāna is not produced (*uppādetabba*) but is attained (*pattabba*). It could be attained in this life itself. It therefore follows that though rebirth is one of the chief doctrines of Buddhism the goal of Buddhism does not depend on a future birth.

27.   The third Truth has to be realized by developing the fourth Truth.

28.   To eradicate one mighty force eight powerful factors have to be developed.

29.   All these eight factors are purely mental.

30.   Eight powerful good mental forces are summoned to attack one latent evil force.

31.   Absolute purity, a complete deliverance from all repeated births, a mind released from all passions, immortality (*amata*) are the attendant blessings of this great victory.

32.   Is this deliverance a perfection or absolute purity?

The latter is preferable.

33.   In each case one might raise the question—

What is being perfected?   What is being purified?

There is no being or permanent entity in Buddhism, but there is a stream of consciousness.

It is more correct to say that this stream of consciousness is purified by overthrowing all defilements.

ANATTALAKKHANA SUTTA[1]

On one occasion the Exalted One was dwelling at the Deer Park, in Isipatana, near Benares. Then the Exalted One addressed the Band of five Bhikkhus, saying, "O Bhikkhus!"

"Lord," they replied.

Thereupon the Exalted One spoke as follows:

"The body (rūpa), O Bhikkhus, is soulless (anattā). If, O Bhikkhus, there were in this a soul[2] then this body would not be subject to suffering. "Let this body be thus, let this body be not thus," such possibilities would also exist. But inasmuch as this body is soulless, it is subject to suffering, and no possibility exists for (ordering): 'Let this be so, let this be not so."

In like manner feelings (vedanā), perceptions (saññā), mental states (samkhārā), and consciousness (viññāna),[3] are soulless.[4]

"What think ye, O Bhikkhus, is this body permanent or impermanent?"

"Impermanent (anicca), Lord."

---

1. Mahāvagga, p. 13; Samyutta Nikāya pt. iii, p. 66.
2. A Permanent unchanging entity, created by a God or emanating from a Paramātma (Divine Essence).
3. The so-called being is composed of these five aggregates. Outside these five there is no being. If one removes the aggregates, nothing remains. A soul abides neither in any one group or aggregate nor in all of them nor outside them.
4. The Buddha makes the same assertion as above in connection with each of the remaining four component parts of the so-called being. The Buddha raises similar queries with regard to each of the other constituents of being. The translation is abridged here.

"Is that which is impermanent happy or pain-ful?"

"It is painful (*dukkha*), Lord."

"Is it justifiable, then, to think of that which is impermanent, painful and transitory: "This is mine; this am I; this is my soul?""

"Certainly not, Lord."

Similarly, O Bhikkhus, feelings, perceptions, mental states and consciousness are impermanent and painful.

"Is it justifiable to think of these which are impermanent, painful and transitory:—"This is mine; this am I; this is my soul?""[1]

"Certainly not, Lord."

"Then, O Bhikkhus, all body, whether past, present or future, personal or external, coarse or subtle, low or high, far or near, should be under-stood by right knowledge in its real nature—"This is not mine (*n'etaṁ mama*); this am I not; (*n'eso h'amasmi*); this is not my soul (*na me so attā*).""

"All feelings, perceptions, mental states and consciousness whether past, present or future, personal or external, coarse or subtle, low or high, far or near, should be understood by right know-

---

1. With craving (*taṇhā*) one erroneously thinks—This is mine. With pride (*māna*) one thinks—This am I. With false view one thinks—This is my soul. These are the three misconceptions (*maññanā*).

ledge in their real nature as: "These are not mine; these am I not; these are not my soul."

"The learned Ariyan disciple who sees thus gets a disgust for body, for feelings, for perceptions, for mental states, for consciousness; is detached from the abhorrent thing and is emancipated through detachment. Then dawns on him the knowledge- 'Emancipated am I'. He understands that rebirth is ended, lived is the Holy Life, done what should be done, there is no more of this state again."

"This the Exalted One said, and the delighted Bhikkhus applauded the words of the Exalted One."

When the Buddha expounded this teaching the minds of the Group of five Bhikkhus were freed of defilements without any attachment.[1]

---

1. That is, they all attained Arahantship.

CHAPTER 7

THE TEACHING OF THE DHAMMA

"Happy is the birth of Buddhas. Happy is the teaching of the sublime Dhamma. Happy is the unity of the Sangha. Happy is the discipline of the united ones."

DHAMMAPADA

The Conversion of Yasa and His Friends

In Benares there was a millionaire's son, named *Yasa*, who led a luxurious life. One morning he rose early and, to his utter disgust, saw his female attendants and musicians asleep in repulsive attitudes. The whole spectacle was so disgusting that the palace presented the gloomy appearance of a charnel house. Realizing the vanities of worldly life, he stole away from home, saying—"Distressed am I, oppressed am I", and went in the direction of Isipatana where the Buddha was temporarily residing after having made the five Bhikkhus attain Arahantship.[1]

At that particular time the Buddha, as usual, was pacing up and down in an open space. Seeing him coming from afar, the Buddha came out of His ambulatory and sat on a prepared seat. Not

---

1. This event took place on the fifth day after the delivery of the first sermon when all the five Bhikkhus had attained Arahantship.

far from Him stood *Yasa*, crying—"O distressed
am I! Oppressed am I!"

Thereupon the Buddha said—"Here there is
no distress, O *Yasa!* Here there is no oppression,
O *Yasa!* Come hither, *Yasa!* Take a seat. I shall
expound the Dhamma to you."

The distressed *Yasa* was pleased to hear the
encouraging words of the Buddha. Removing his
golden sandals, he approached the Buddha, respectfully saluted Him and sat on one side.

The Buddha expounded the doctrine to him,
and he attained the first stage of Sainthood
(*Sotāpatti*).

At first the Buddha spoke to him on genero-
sity (*dāna*), morality (*sīla*), celestial states (*sagga*),
the evils of sensual pleasures (*kāmādīnava*), the
blessings of renunciation (*nekkhammānisaṁsa*).
When He found that his mind was pliable and was
ready to appreciate the deeper teaching He taught
the Four Noble Truths.

Yasa's mother was the first to notice the absence
of her son and she reported the matter to her
husband. The millionaire immediately dispatched
horsemen in four directions and he himself went
towards Isipatana, following the imprint of the
golden slippers. The Buddha saw him coming
from afar and, by His psychic powers, willed that
he should not be able to see his son.

The millionaire approached the Buddha and respectfully inquired whether He had seen his son *Yasa*.

"Well, then, sit down here please. You would be able to see your son," said the Buddha.

Pleased with the happy news, he sat down. The Buddha delivered a discourse to him, and he was so delighted that he exclaimed:

"Excellent, O Lord, excellent! It is as if, Lord, a man were to set upright that which was over-turned, or were to reveal that which was hidden, or were to point out the way to one who had gone astray, or were to hold a lamp amidst the darkness, so that those who have eyes may see! Even so has the doctrine been expounded in various ways by the Exalted One.

"I, Lord, take refuge in the Buddha, the Doctrine and the Order. May the Lord receive me as a follower, who has taken refuge from this very day to life's end!"

He was the first lay follower to seek refuge with the threefold formula.

On hearing the discourse delivered to his father, *Yasa* attained Arahantship. Thereupon the Buddha withdrew His will-power so that *Yasa's* father may be able to see his son. The millionaire beheld his son and invited the Buddha and His disciples for alms on the following day. The Buddha expressed His acceptance of the invitation by His silence.

After the departure of the millionaire *Yasa* begged the Buddha to grant him the Lesser[1] and the Higher Ordination.

"Come, O Bhikkhus! Well taught is the Doctrine. Lead the Holy Life to make a complete end of suffering." With these words the Buddha conferred on him the Higher Ordination.[2]

With the Venerable *Yasa* the number of Arahants increased to six.

As invited, the Buddha visited the millionaire's house with His six disciples.

Venerable *Yasa's* mother and his former wife heard the doctrine expounded by the Buddha and, having attained the first stage of Sainthood, became His first two lay female followers.[3]

---

1. By *Pabbajjā*, lit., going forth or renunciation, is meant the mere admission into the Holy Order by seeking refuge in the Buddha, Dhamma and the Sangha.
2. In the early days of the Order the Higher Ordination—*Upasampadā* —lit., replete with a higher morality, was granted with these words. See ch. 14.
3. *Upāsaka* (m.) *Upāsikā* (f.) lit., one who closely associates with the Triple Gem. These two terms are applied to male and female lay followers of the Buddha. One becomes an *Upāsaka* or *Upāsikā* immediately after taking the three Refuges, viz:
   Buddhaṁ saranaṁ gacchāmi—

   I seek refuge in the Buddha.
   Dhammam saranaṁ gacchāmi—

   I seek refuge in the Doctrine.
   Sanghaṁ saranaṁ gacchāmi—

   I seek refuge in the Order.
   This is the threefold formula (*Tevācika*).

Venerable *Yasa* had four distinguished friends named *Vimala, Subāhu, Punnaji* and *Gavampati.* When they heard that their noble friend shaved his hair and beard, and, donning the yellow robe, entered the homeless life, they approached Venerable *Yasa* and expressed their desire to follow his example. Venerable *Yasa* introduced them to the Buddha, and, on hearing the Dhamma, they also attained Arahantship.

Fifty more worthy friends of Venerable *Yasa,* who belonged to leading families of various districts, also receiving instructions from the Buddha, attained Arahantship and entered the Holy Order.

Hardly two months had elapsed since His Enlightenment when the number of Arahants gradually rose to sixty. All of them came from distinguished families and were worthy sons of worthy fathers.

The First Messengers of Truth (*Dhammadūta*)

The Buddha who, before long, succeeded in enlightening sixty disciples, decided to send them as messengers of Truth to teach His new Dhamma to all without any distinction. Before dispatching them in various directions He exhorted them as follows:

"Freed am I, O Bhikkhus, from all bonds, whether divine or human.

---

1.   Mahāvagga, pp.19,20

"You, too, O Bhikkhus, are freed from all bonds, whether divine or human.

"Go forth, O Bhikkhus, for the good of the many, for the happiness of the many, out of compassion for the world, for the good, benefit, and happiness of gods[1] and men. Let not two go by one way: Preach, O Bhikkhus, the Dhamma, excellent in the beginning, excellent in the middle, excellent in the end, both in the spirit and in the letter. Proclaim the Holy Life,[2] altogether perfect and pure.

"There are beings with little dust in their eyes, who, not hearing the Dhamma, will fall away. There will be those who understand the Dhamma."

"I too, O Bhikkhus, will go to Uruvelā in Senānigāma, in order to preach the Dhamma."

"Hoist the Flag of the Sage. Preach the Sublime Dhamma, Work for the good of others, you who have done your duties."[3]

The Buddha was thus the first religious teacher to send His enlightened ordained disciples to propagate the doctrine out of compassion for others. With no permanent abode, alone and

---

1. Note the reference to gods (Devas).

2. The Pāli term *Brahmacariya* has no connection whatever with a God or Brahma. It is used in the sense of noble or holy.

3. *Samussayatha   saddhammam—desayantā   isiddhajam Katakattabbakammantā—parattham   patipajjatha.*

penniless, these first missioners were expected to
wander from place to place to teach the sublime
Dhamma. They had no other material possessions but their robes to cover themselves and an
alms-bowl to collect food. As the field was ex-
tensive and the workers were comparatively few
they were advised to undertake their missionary
journeys alone. As they were Arahants who were
freed from all sensual bonds their chief and
only object was to teach the Dhamma and proclaim the Holy Life (*Brahmacariya*). The original
role of Arahants, who achieved their life's goal,
was to work for the moral upliftment of the
people both by example and by precept. Material
development, though essential, was not their
concern.

Founding of the Order of the Sangha

At that time there were sixty Arahant disciples
in the world. With these Pure Ones as the nucleus
the Buddha founded a celibate Order which "was
democratic in constitution and communistic in
distribution." The original members were drawn
from the highest status of society and were all
educated and rich men, but the Order was open to
all worthy ones, irrespective of caste, class or rank.
Both young and old, belonging to all the castes,
were freely admitted into the Order and lived like
brothers of the same family without any distinction. This Noble Order of Bhikkhus, which stands
to this day, is the oldest historic body of celibates
in the world.

All were not expected to leave the household and enter the homeless life. As lay followers, too, they were able to lead a good life in accordance with the Dhamma and attain Sainthood. Venerable *Yasa's* parents and his former wife, for instance, were the foremost lay followers of the Buddha. All the three were sufficiently spiritually advanced to attain the first stage of Sainthood.

With the sixty Arahants, as ideal messengers of Truth, the Buddha decided to propagate His sublime Dhamma, purely by expounding the doctrine to those who wish to hear.

Conversion of Thirty Young Men

The Buddha resided at Isipatana in Benares as long as He liked and went towards Uruvelā. On the way He sat at the foot of a tree in a grove.

At that time thirty happy young men went with their wives to this particular grove to amuse themselves. As one of them had no wife he took with him a courtesan. While they were enjoying themselves this woman absconded with their valuables. The young men searched for her in the forest, and, seeing the Buddha, inquired of Him whether He saw a woman passing that way.

"Which do you think, young men, is better; seeking a woman or seeking oneself?"[1] questioned the Buddha.

"Seeking oneself is better, O Lord!" replied the young men.

"Well, then, sit down. I shall preach the doctrine to you," said the Buddha.

"Very well, Lord," they replied, and respectfully saluting the Exalted One, sat expectantly by.

They attentively listened to Him and obtained "The Eye of Truth."[2]

After this they entered the Order and received the Higher Ordination.

Conversion of the Three Kassapa Brothers

Wandering from place to place, in due course, the Buddha arrived at Uruvelā. Here lived three (*Jatila*) ascetics with matted hair known as *Uruvela*

---

1. Seeking oneself. This phrase is very significant. *Attā-nam* is the accusative of *atta* which means self. Here the Buddha was not referring to any soul or spirit latent in man as some scholars attempt to show. How could the Buddha affirm the existence of a soul when He had clearly denied its existence in His second discourse? The Buddha has used this phrase exactly in the sense of "seek thyself" or "look within."

2. *Dhammacakkhu*—This refers to any of the three lower Paths—*Sotāpatti, Sakadāgāmi*, and *Anāgāmi*.

Kassapa, Nadī Kassapa, and *Gayā Kassapa.* They were all brothers living separately with 500, 300 and 200 disciples respectively. The eldest was infatuated by his own spiritual attainments and was labouring under a misconception that he was an Arahant. The Buddha approached him first and sought his permission to spend the night in his fire-chamber where dwelt a fierce serpent-king. By His psychic powers the Buddha subdued the serpent. This pleased *Uruvela Kassapa* and he invited the Buddha to stay there as his guest. The Buddha was compelled to exhibit His psychic powers on several other occasions to impress the ascetic, but still he adhered to the belief, that the Buddha was not an Arahant as he was. Finally the Buddha was able to convince him that He was an Arahant. Thereupon he and his followers entered the Order and obtained the Higher Ordination.

His brothers and their followers also followed his example. Accompanied by the three *Kassapa* brothers and their thousand followers, the Buddha repaired to Gayā Sīsa, not far from Uruvelā. Here He preached the *Ādittapariyāya Sutta,* hearing which all attained Arahantship.

Āditta-Pariyaya Sutta—Discourse on "All in Flames"

"All in flames, O Bhikkhus! What, O Bhikkhus, is all in flames?

Eye is in flames. Forms are in flames. Eye-consciousness is in flames. Eye-contact is in flames. Feeling which is pleasurable or painful, or neither pleasurable nor painful, arising from eye-contact is in flames. By what is it kindled? By the flames of lust, hatred, ignorance, birth, decay, death, sorrow, lamentation, pain, grief, and despair is it kindled, I declare.

Reflecting thus, O Bhikkhus, the learned Ariya disciple gets disgusted with the eye, the forms, the eye-consciousness, the eye-contact, whatever feeling—pleasurable, painful, or neither pleasureable nor painful—that arises from contact with the eye. He gets disgusted with the ear, sounds, nose, odours, tongue, tastes, body, contact, mind, mental objects, mind-consciousness, mind contacts, whatever feeling—pleasurable, painful or neither pleasurable nor painful—that arises from contact with the mind. With disgust he gets detached; with detachment he is delivered. He understands that birth is ended, lived the Holy Life, done what should be done, and that there is no more of this state again."

When the Buddha concluded this discourse all the Bhikkhus attained Arahantship, eradicating all Defilements.

Conversion of Sāriputta and Moggallāna, the two Chief Disciples

Not far from Rājagaha in the village Upatissa, also known as Nālaka, there lived a very intelligent youth named *Sārīputta* (—son of Sāri).

Since he belonged to the leading family of the village, he was also called *Upatissa.*

Though nurtured in Brahmanism, his broad outlook on life and matured wisdom compelled him to renounce his ancestral religion for the more tolerant and scientific teachings of the Buddha Gotama. His brothers and sisters followed his noble example. His father, *Vanganta,* apparently adhered to the Brahmin faith. His mother, who was displeased with the son for having become a Buddhist, was converted to Buddhism by himself at the moment of his death.

Upatissa was brought up in the lap of luxury. He found a very intimate friend in Kolita, also known as Moggallāna, with whom he was closely associated from a remote past. One day as both of them were enjoying a hill-top festival they realized how vain, how transient, were all sensual pleasures. Instantly they decided to leave the world and seek the Path of Release. They wandered from place to place in quest of Peace.

The two young seekers went at first to *Sañjaya*, who had a large following, and sought ordination under him. Before long they acquired the meagre knowledge which their master imparted to them, but dissatisfied with his teachings—as they could not find a remedy for that universal ailment with which humanity is assailed—they left him and wandered hither and thither in search of Peace. They approached many a famous brahmin and ascetic, but disappointment met them everywhere. Ultimately they returned to their own village and agreed amongst themselves that whoever would first discover the Path should inform the other.

It was at that time that the Buddha dispatched His first sixty disciples to proclaim the sublime Dhamma to the world. The Buddha Himself proceeded towards Uruvelā, and the Venerable *Assaji*, one of the first five disciples, went in the direction of Rajagaha.

The good Kamma of the seekers now intervened, as if watching with sympathetic eyes their spiritual progress. For *Upatissa*, while wandering in the city of Rajagaha, casually met an ascetic whose venerable appearance and saintly deportment at once arrested his attention. This ascetic's eyes were lowly fixed a yoke's distance from him, and his calm face betokened deep peace within him. With body well composed, robes neatly arranged, this venerable figure passed with measured steps from door to door, accepting the morsels of food which the charitable placed in his bowl. Never before have I seen, he thought to himself, an ascetic like this. Surely he must be one of those

who have attained Arahantship or one who is
practising the path leading to Arahantship.   How
if I were to approach him and question, "For whose
sake, Sire, have you retired from the world? Who
is your teacher? Whose doctrine do you profess?"

Upatissa, however, refrained from questioning
him as he thought he would thereby interfere with
his silent begging tour.

The Arahant *Assaji*, having obtained what little
he needed, was seeking a suitable place to eat his
meal. *Upatissa* seeing this, gladly availed himself
of the opportunity to offer him his own stool and
water from his own pot. Fulfilling thus the preliminary duties of a pupil, he exchanged pleasant
greetings with him and reverently inquired:—

"Venerable Sir, calm and serene are your
organs of sense, clean and clear is the hue of your
skin.   For whose sake have you retired from the
world? Who is your teacher? Whose doctrine do
you profess?"

The unassuming Arahant *Assaji* modestly replied, as is the characteristic of all great men—
"I am still young in the Order, brother, and I am
not able to expound the Dhamma to you at
length."

"I am *Upatissa*, Venerable Sir. Say much or
little according to your ability, and it is left to me
to understand it in a hundred or thousand ways".

"Say little or much," *Upatissa* continued, "tell me just the substance. The substance only do I require. A mere jumble of words is of no avail."

The Venerable *Assaji* uttered a four line stanza, thus skilfully summing up the profound philosophy of the Master, on the truth of the law of cause and effect.

Ye dhammā hetuppabhavā —
           tesaṁ hetuṁ tathāgato
Āha tesañ ca yo nirodho —
           evaṁ vādī mahā samano.

Of things that proceed from a cause,
Their cause the Tathāgata has told,
And also their cessation:
Thus teaches the Great Ascetic.

Upatissa was sufficiently enlightened to comprehend such a lofty teaching though succintly expressed. He was only in need of a slight indication to discover the truth. So well did the Venerable *Assaji* guide him on his upward path that immediately on hearing the first two lines, he attained the first stage of Sainthood, *Sotāpatti.*

The new convert *Upatissa* must have been, no doubt, destitute of words to thank to his heart's content his venerable teacher for introducing him to the sublime teachings of the Buddha. He expressed his deep indebtedness for his brilliant exposition of the truth, and obtaining from him the necessary particulars with regard to the Master, took his leave.

Later, the devotion he showed towards his teacher was such that since he heard the Dhamma from the Venerable *Assaji*, in whatever quarter he heard that his teacher was residing, in that direction he would extend his clasped hands in an attitude of reverent obeisance and in that direction he would turn his head when he lay down to sleep.

Now, in accordance with the agreement, he returned to his companion *Kolita* to convey the joyful tidings. *Kolita*, who was as enlightened as his friend, also attained the first stage of Sainthood on hearing the whole stanza. Overwhelmed with joy at their successful search after Peace, as in duty bound, they went to meet their teacher *Sañjaya* with the object of converting him to the new doctrine. Frustrated in their attempt *Upatissa* and *Kolita*, accompanied by many followers of *Sañjaya*, who readily joined them, repaired to the Veluvana monastery to visit their illustrious Teacher, the Buddha.

In compliance with their request, the Buddha admitted both of them into the Order by the mere utterance of the words—*Etha Bhikkhave!* (Come, O Bhikkhus!).

A fortnight later, the Venerable *Sāriputta*, attained Arahantship on hearing the Buddha expound the Vedanā Pariggaha Sutta to the wandering ascetic *Dīghanakha*. On the very same day in the evening the Buddha gathered round Him His disciples and the exalted positions of the first and second disciples in the Sangha were respectively conferred upon the Theras *Upatissa* (*Sāriputta*) and *Kolita* (*Moggallāna*), who also had attained Arahantship a week earlier.

CHAPTER 8

THE BUDDHA AND HIS RELATIVES

"Service to relatives is a blessing."

MANGALA SUTTA

King Suddhodana desires to see the Buddha

News that the Buddha was residing at Rajagaha and was preaching His Dhamma reached the ears of the aged King *Suddhodana*, and his anxiety to see his enlightened son grew stronger and stronger. On nine successive occasions he sent nine courtiers, each with a large following, to invite the Buddha to Kapilavatthu. Contrary to his expectations, they all heard the Dhamma and, attaining Arahantship, entered the Order. Since Arahants were indifferent to worldly things they did not convey the message to the Buddha.

The disappointed King finally dispatched another faithful courtier, *Kāludāyī*, who was a playmate of the Buddha. He agreed to go as he was granted permission to enter the Order.

Like the rest he also had the fortune to attain Arahantship and join the Order. But, unlike the others, he conveyed the message to the Buddha, and persuaded Him to visit His aged royal father. As the season was most suitable for travelling, the Buddha, attended by a large retinue of His disciples, journeyed the whole distance by slow stages preaching the Dhamma on the way, and in due course arrived at Kapilavatthu in two months.

Arrangements were made for Him to reside at the Park of Nigrodha, a Sākya. The conceited elderly Sākyas, thinking within themselves, "He is our younger brother, our nephew, our grandson," said to the young princes—"You do him obeisance; we will sit behind you." As they sat without paying Him due reverence He subdued their pride by rising into the air and exhibiting the "Twin Wonder".[1] The King, seeing this wonderful phenomenon, saluted Him immediately, saying that it was his third salutation.[2] All Sākyas were then compelled to pay Him due reverence. Thereupon the Buddha came down from the sky and sat on the seat prepared for Him. The humbled relatives took their seats eager to listen to His Teaching.

---

1. *Yamaka Pāṭihāriya*, often translated as "The Twin Miracle" is a psychic phenomenon which only a Buddha could perform. By his psychic powers He makes fire and water issue from the pores of the body simultaneously. *Paṭisambhidāmagga* commentary states that by fire and water are meant red and blue rays.

2. He saluted Him for the first time when he saw the infant prince's feet rest on the head of Ascetic Asita whom he wanted the child to revere. His second salutation took place at the Ploughing Festival when he saw the infant prince seated cross-legged on the couch, absorbed in meditation.

At this moment an unexpected shower of rain fell upon the Sākya kinsfolk. The occurrence of this strange phenomenon resulted in a discussion amongst themselves. Then the Buddha preached the Vessantara Jātaka[1] to show that a similar incident took place in the presence of His relatives in a previous birth.

The Sākyas were delighted with the discourse, and they departed, not knowing that it was their duty to invite the Buddha and His disciples for the noon meal. It did not occur to the King too to invite the Buddha, although he thought to himself—"If my son does not come to my house, where will he go?" Reaching home, he, however, made ready several kinds of food expecting their arrival in the palace.

The Buddha goes round for Alms
King Suddhodana's Conversion

As there was no special invitation for the noon meal on the following day, the Buddha and His disciples got ready to seek alms from the houses of the citizens of Kapilavatthu. Before proceeding He considered within Himself—"Did the Buddhas of the past, upon entering the city of their kinsfolk, straightway enter the houses of the

---

1. See Jātaka Vol. vi, p. 479—No. 547, Dhammapadaṭṭha-kathā, vol. iii, pp. 163-164. This interesting story, which is the longest in the Jātaka commentary, illustrates his unrivalled generosity.

relatives, or did they go from house to house in regular order receiving alms?" Perceiving that they did so from house to house, the Buddha went in the streets of Kapilavatthu seeking alms.

On hearing of this seemingly disgraceful conduct of the Buddha from his daughter-in-law, *Yasodharā*, the King, greatly perturbed in mind, hurried to the scene, and saluting Him, said—"Son, why do you ruin me? I am overwhelmed with shame to see you begging alms. Is it proper for you, who used to travel in a golden palanquin, to seek alms in this very city? Why do you put me to shame?"

"I am not putting you to shame, O great King! I am following the custom of my lineage," replied the Buddha, to the King's astonishment.

"But, dear son, is it the custom of my lineage to gain a livelihood by seeking alms? Surely, Lord. ours is the warrior lineage of Mahāsammata, and not a single warrior has gone seeking alms."

"O great King, that is not the custom of your royal lineage. But it is the custom of my Buddha lineage. Several thousands of Buddhas have lived by seeking alms."

Standing on the street, the Buddha then advised the King thus:

---

1. See Dhammapadaṭṭhakathā, vol, iii, p. 164, *Buddhist Legends,* vol. 3 p. 3.

"Be not heedless in standing (at doors for alms) Lead a righteous life. The righteous live happily both in this world and in the next.[1]"

Hearing it, the King realized the Truth and attained the first stage of Sainthood. Immediately after, he took the Buddha's bowl and, conducting Him and His disciples to the palace, served them with choice food. At the close of the meal the Buddha again exhorted him thus:

"Lead a righteous life, and not one that is corrupt. The righteous live happily both in this world and in the next."[2]

Thereupon the King attained the second stage of Sainthood (*Sakadāgāmi*) and Pajāpati Gotami attained the first stage of Sainthood (*Sotāpatti*)

On a later occasion when it was related to the Buddha that the King refused to believe that his son had died owing to his severe austerities without achieving his goal, the Buddha preached the Dhammapāla Jātaka[3] to show that in a previous birth too he refused to believe that his son had died although he was shown a heap of bones. This time he attained the third stage of Sainthood (*Anāgāmi*).

On his death-bed, the King heard the Dhamma from the Buddha for the last time and attained

---

1. Dhammapada, v. 168.
2. Ibid v. 169.
3. No. 447.

Arahantship. After experiencing the bliss of
Emancipation for seven days, he passed away as
a lay Arahant when the Buddha was about forty
years old.

The Buddha and Yasodharā

Princess *Yasodharā*, also known as *Rāhulamātā*,
Bimbā and *Bhaddakaccānā*, was the daughter of
King *Suppabuddha*, who reigned over the Koliya
race, and *Pamitā*, sister of King *Suddhodana*. She
was of the same age as Prince *Siddhattha*, whom she
married at the age of sixteen. It was by exhibiting
his military prowess that he won her hand.
She led an extremely happy and luxurious life.
In her 29th year, on the very day she gave birth
to her only son, *Rāhula*, her wise and contemplative husband, whom she loved with all her heart,
resolved to renounce the world to seek deliverence
from the ills of life. Without even bidding fare-
well to his faithful and charming wife, he left the
palace at night, leaving young *Yasodharā* to look
after the child by herself. She awoke as usual to
greet her beloved husband, but, to her surprise,
she found him missing. When she realized that her
ideal Prince had left her and the new-born babe,
she was overcome with indescribable grief. Her
dearest possession was lost for ever. The palace
with all its allurements was now a dungeon to her.
The whole world appeared to be blank. Her only
consolation was her infant son.

Though several Kshatriya princes sought her hand, she rejected all those proposals, and lived ever faithful to her beloved husband. Hearing that her husband was leading a hermit's life, she removed all her jewellery and wore a plain yellow garb. Throughout the six years during which the ascetic *Gotama* struggled for Enlightenment Princess *Yasodharā* watched his actions closely and did likewise.

When the Buddha visited Kapilavatthu after His Enlightenment and was being entertained by the King in the palace on the following day all but the Princess *Yasodharā* came to pay their reverence to Him. She thought:

"Certainly if there is any virtue in me, the noble Lord Himself will come to my presence. Then will I reverence Him."

After the meal was over the Buddha handed over the bowl to the King, and accompanied by His two chief disciples, entered the chamber of *Yasodharā* and sat on a seat prepared for Him, saying: "Let the King's daughter reverence me as she likes. Say nothing."

Hearing of the Buddha's visit, she bade the ladies in the court wear yellow garments. When the Buddha took His seat, *Yasodharā* came swiftly to Him and clasping His ankles, placed her head on His feet and reverenced Him as she liked.

Demonstrating her affection and respect thus, she sat down with due reverence.   Then the King praised her virtues and, commenting on her love and loyalty, said:

"Lord, when my daughter heard that you were wearing yellow robes, she also robed herself in yellow; when she heard that you were taking one meal a day, she also did the same; when she heard that you had given up lofty couches, she lay on a low couch; when she heard that you had given up garlands and scents, she also gave them up; when her relatives sent messages to say that they would maintain her, she did not even look at a single one.   So virtuous was my daughter."

"Not only in this last birth, O King, but in a previous birth, too, she protected me and was devoted and faithful to me," remarked the Buddha and cited the Candakinnara Jataka.[1]

Recalling this past association with her, He consoled her and left the palace.

After the death of King *Suddhodana*, when *Pajā- pati Gotami* became a nun (Bhikkhuni) *Yasodharā* also entered the Order and attained Arahantship.

Amongst women disciples she was the chief of those who attained great supernormal powers

---

1.   Jātaka Translation Vol. IV. p. 179 (No. 485).

(*Maha Abhiññā*)[1]. At the age of 78 she passed away.

Her name does not appear in the Therigatha but her interesting verses are found in the Apadana[2].

The Buddha and Rāhula

Rāhula was the only son of Prince *Siddhattha* and Princess *Yasodharā*. He was born on the day when Prince *Siddhattha* decided to renounce the world. The happy news of the birth of his infant son was conveyed to him when he was in the park in a contemplative mood. Contrary to ordinary expectations, instead of rejoicing over the news, he exclaimed '*Rāhu jāto, bandhanaṁ jātaṁ-*A Rahu is born, a fetter has arisen!' Accordingly the child was named *Rāhula*[3] by King *Suddhodana*, his grandfather.

Rāhula was brought up as a fatherless child by his mother and grandfather. When he was seven years old, the Buddha visited Kapilavatthu

1.   *Anguttara Nikāya* commentary states: "Of one Buddha four disciples only have great supenormal powers: The rest can recall 100,000 Kalpas, not beyond that; but those recall incalculable eras. Under our Teacher's Order the two great disciples and the elder Bakkula and Bhadda Kaccānā, just these four, had this power." *Gradual Sayings,* Vol. 1, p. 22.

2.   PP. 584-599. Here she relates her association with the Bodhisatta when he met the Buddha Dipamkara and resolved to become a Buddha.

3.   Lit., bound or seized (*la*) by a fetter (*rāhu*).

for the first time after His Enlightenment. On the seventh day after His arrival Princess *Yasodharā* gaily dressed up young *Rāhula* and pointing to the Buddha, said—"Behold, son, that golden coloured ascetic, looking like Brahmā, surrounded by twenty thousand ascetics! He is your father, and He had great treasures. Since His renunciation we do not see them. Go up to him and ask for your inheritance, and say—"Father, I am the prince. After my consecration I will be a universal monarch. I am in need of wealth. Please give me wealth, for the son is the owner of what belongs to the father."

Innocent *Rāhula* came to the Buddha's presence, and asking for his inheritance, as advised by his mother, very affectionately said: "O ascetic, even your shadow is pleasing to me."[1]

After the meal the Buddha left the palace and *Rāhula* followed Him, saying—"Give me my inheritance" and uttering much else that was becoming. Nobody attempted to stop him. Nor did the Buddha prevent him from following Him. Reaching the park the Buddha thought: "He desires his father's wealth, but it goes with the world and is full of trouble. I shall give him the sevenfold noble wealth which I received at the foot of the Bodhi tree, and make him an owner of a transcendental inheritance. He called Venerable *Sāriputta* and asked him to ordain little *Rāhula*.

---

1. *Sukhā vata te chāyā, samana,*

Rāhula, who was then only seven years of age, was admitted into the Noble Order.

King *Suddhodana* was deeply grieved to hear of the unexpected ordination of his beloved grandson. He approached the Buddha and, in humbly requesting Him not to ordain any one without the prior consent of the parents, said— "When the Lord renounced the world it was a cause of great pain to me. It was so when *Nanda* renounced and especially so in the case of *Rāhula*. The love of a father towards a son cuts through the skin, (the hide), the flesh, the sinew, the bone and the marrow. Grant, Lord, the request that the Noble Ones may not confer ordination on a son without the permission of his parents."[1]

The Buddha readily granted the request, and made it a Vinaya rule.

How a young boy of seven years could lead the Holy Life is almost inconceivable. But Sāmanera (Novice) *Rāhula*, cultured, exceptionally obedient and well-disciplined as he was, was very eager to accept instruction from his superiors. It is stated that he would rise early in the morning and taking a handful of sand throw it up, saying— "Today may I receive from my instructors as much counsel as these grains of sand."

---

1. See *Buddhist Legends*, part 1, p. 219.

One of the earliest discourses preached to him, immediately after his ordination, was the *Amba-laṭṭhika-rāhulovāda Sutta* in which He emphasized the importance of Truthfulness.

One day the Buddha visited the Venerable *Rāhula* who, seeing Him coming from afar, arranged a seat and supplied water for washing the feet. The Buddha washed His feet and leaving a small quantity of water in the vessel, said: "Do you see, *Rāhula*, this small quantity of water left in the vessel?"

"Yes, Lord."

"Similarly, *Rāhula*, insignificant, indeed, is the Samanaship (monkhood) of those who are not ashamed of uttering deliberate lies."

Then the Buddha threw away that small quantity of water, and said;

"Discarded, indeed, is the Samanaship of those who are not ashamed of deliberate lying."

The Buddha turned the vessel upside down, and said— "Overturned, indeed, is the Samanaship of those who are not ashamed of uttering deliberate lies."

Finally the Buddha set the vessel upright and said—"Empty and void, indeed, is the Samanaship of those who are not ashamed of deliberate lying."

---

1.   Majjhima Nikāya No. 61. See *The Blessing*, p. 173.

"I say of anyone who is not ashamed of uttering deliberate lies, that there is no evil that could not be done by him. Accordingly, *Rāhula*, thus should you train yourself.—"Not even in play will I tell a lie."

Emphasizing the importance of truthfulness with such homely illustrations, the Buddha explained to him the value of reflection and the criterion of morality in such a way as a child could understand.

"*Rāhula*, for what purpose is a mirror?" questioned the Buddha.

"For the purpose of reflecting, Lord."

"Similarly, *Rāhula*, after reflecting and reflecting should bodily action be done; after reflecting should verbal action be done; after reflecting should mental action be done.

"Whatever action you desire to do with the body, of that particular bodily action you should reflect: 'Now, this action that I desire to perform with the body—would this, my bodily action be conducive to my own harm, or to the harm of others, or to that of both myself and others?' Then, unskilful is this bodily action, entailing suffering and producing pain.

"If, when reflecting, you should realize: 'Now, this bodily action of mine that I am desirous of performing, would be conducive to my own harm or to the harm of others, or to that of both myself and others." Then unskilful is this bodily action, entailing suffering and producing pain. Such an action with the body, you must on no account perform.

"If, on the other hand, when reflecting you realize: 'Now, this bodily action that I am desirous of performing, would conduce neither to the harm of myself, nor to that of others, nor to that of both myself and others.' Then skilful is this bodily action, entailing pleasure and producing happiness. Such bodily action you should perform."

Exhorting the Sāmanera *Rāhula* to use reflection during and after one's actions, the Buddha said:

"While you are doing an action with the body, of that particular action should you reflect: 'Now, is this action that I am doing with my body conducive to my own harm, or to the harm of others or to that of both myself and others?' Then unskilful is this bodily action, entailing suffering and producing pain."

"If, when reflecting, you realize: 'Now, this action that I am doing with my body is conducive to my own harm, to the harm of others, and to that of both myself and others.' Then unskilful is this bodily action, entailing suffering and producing pain. From such a bodily action *you must desist*".

"If when reflecting, you should realize: 'Now, this action of mine that I am doing with the body is conducive neither to my own harm, nor to the harm of others, nor to that of both myself and others.' Then skilful is this bodily action, entailing pleasure and happiness. Such a bodily action *you should do again and again*."

The Buddha adds "If, when reflecting, you should realize: 'Now, this action that I have done is unskilful.' Such an action should be confessed, revealed, and made manifest to the Teacher, or to the learned, or to your brethren of the Holy Life. Having confessed, you should acquire restraint in the future."

The admonition with regard to skilful and unskilful verbal and mental actions was treated in the same way.

Stating that constant reflection was essential for purification, the Buddha ended the discourse as follows:

"Thus must you train yourself—By constantly reflecting shall we purify our bodily actions, by constantly reflecting shall we purify our verbal actions, by constantly reflecting shall we purify our mental actions."

In the Samyutta Nikāya there is a special chapter where the Buddha explains to Sāmanera *Rāhula* the transitoriness of nature.[1]

---

1. Samyutta Nikāya ii, pp. 244-253, *Kindred Sayings*, ii, pp. 164-168.

As Venerable *Rāhula* entered the Order in his boyhood the Buddha availed Himself of every opportunity to advise and guide him on the right path. The Sutta Nipāta[1] states that the Buddha repeatedly admonished him with the following stanzas:

"*Give up five-fold sensual pleasures—so sweet, so charming. Going forth from home, with faith, be one who has put an end to suffering.*

Seek a remote lodging, secluded and noiseless. Be moderate in food.

Have no attachment to robes, alms, requisites and lodging.

Come not to this world again.

Practise restraint with regard to the Fundamental Code and the five senses.

Cultivate mindfulness as regards the body and be full of dispassionateness.

Avoid alluring, lust-provoking objects (of sense). Develop your one-pointed, composed mind towards loathsomeness. Think not of the outward appearance of sense. Give up latent pride. Thus eradicating pride, you shall fare on in perfect peace."[1]

In his eighteenth year the Buddha preached a profound discourse on mind-culture, the occasion for it being a sense-desire that arose in Venerable

---

1. Sutta Nipāta, Rāhula Sutta. Chalmers—*Buddha's Teachings*, p. 81.

Rāhula's mind on account of his beautiful appearance. One day the Venerable *Rāhula* was following the Buddha in quest of alms. As the Buddha went along, followed by *Rāhula*, it seems that the pair was like an auspicious royal elephant and his noble offspring, a royal swan with its beauteous cygnet, a regal lion with its stately cub. Both were golden in complexion, almost equal in beauty; both were of the warrior caste; both had renounced a throne. *Rāhula*, admiring the Teacher, thought: 'I too am handsome like my parent the Exalted One. Beautiful is the Buddha's form, and mine is similar.'"[1]

The Buddha instantly read his evil thought, and looking back addressed him thus:

"Whatsoever form there be should be regarded thus:

'This is not mine (*N etam mama*); this am I not (*N'eso'ham' asmi*); this is not my soul (*Na me so attā*).' "[2]

Rāhula submissively inquired of Him whether he should regard only form as such.

The Buddha replied that he should regard all the five aggregates (*Khandhas*)[3] as such.

---

1. Majjhima Nikāya No. 62. See *The Blessing*, p. 182.
2. See *Anattalakkhana Sutta*, Ch. 6.
3. See p. 90, N. 1.

The Venerable *Rāhula*, having been thus edified by the Buddha Himself, preferred not to enter the village for alms. He turned back and sat at the foot of a tree, with legs crossed, the body held erect, intent on mindfulness.

Venerable *Sariputta* noting the suggestive posture of *Rāhula* Sāmanera, advised him to concentrate on inhaling and exhaling, not knowing that he was practising another object of meditation on the instruction of the Buddha.

Venerable *Rāhula* was perplexed because he was given two different objects of meditation—one by the Buddha and the other by his own teacher. In obedience to his teacher he concentrated on "breathing" and went to the Buddha to get His own instruction on the subject. As a wise physician would give the needed medicine, ignoring the patient's desires, the Buddha first expanded His brief instruction on meditation on form and other aggregates and then briefly enumerated certain subjects of meditation with the specific evil conditions temporarily eliminated by each and then explained the meditation on "respiration" (*Ānā-pāna Sati*).

Acting according to the Buddha's instructions, he succeeded in his meditations, and, before long, hearing the Cūla Rāhulovāda Sutta,[1] he attained Arahantship.

---

1. Majjhima Nikāya No. 147.

In the fourteenth year after the Enlightenment of the Buddha, Sāmanera *Rāhula* received his Higher Ordination

He predeceased the Buddha and Venerable *Sariputta*.

Venerable *Rāhula* was distinguished for his high standard of discipline. The following four verses are attributed to him in the *Theragāthā*:

"Being fortunate from both sides, they call me "Lucky Rāhula". I was the son of the Buddha and that of the Seer of Truths.

Destroyed are all my Corruptions. There is no more rebirth to me.

An Arahant am I, worthy of offering.

Possessed of threefold knowledge and a seer of Deathless am I,"[1]

"Blinded by sense-desires, spread over by a net, covered by a cloak of craving, bound by the 'kinsman of heedlessness' was I like a fish caught in the mouth of a funnel-net.

That sense-desire have I burnt. The bond of Mara have I cut.

Eradicating craving, from its root, cool am I, peaceful am I now."[1]

---

1. vv. 297, 298. *Psalms of the Brethren*, p. 183.

CHAPTER 9

THE BUDDHA AND HIS RELATIVES
(Continued)

"Trustful are the best of relatives".

DHAMMAPADA

The Buddha and His step-brother Nanda

On the third day after the arrival of the Buddha at Kapilavatthu, Prince *Nanda*, the son of Queen *Maha Pajāpati Gotami*, was celebrating his consecration ceremony, marriage ceremony, and the house-warming ceremony. It was on the occasion of these three festivals when congratulations were being offered to the prince that the Buddha visited the palace. After the meal the Buddha handed the bowl to the prince, and uttering a Blessing, rose to go without taking the bowl.

The prince followed Him thinking that the Buddha would take the bowl from him at any moment. But the Buddha would not take it, and the prince out of reverence for Him continued to follow the Teacher.

Janapada Kalyāni, to whom he was betrothed, hearing that the prince was following the Buddha with bowl in hand, with tears streaming down her cheeks and hair half-combed, ran after Prince *Nanda* as fast as she could and said to him: "Return quickly, O noble Lord"! These affectionate words penetrated his heart and he was deeply moved, but with deference to the Buddha he could not possibly return the bowl to Him. So he accompanied the Buddha to the park, His temporary residence. On arrival there the Buddha questioned *Nanda* whether he would become a monk. So great was his reverence for Him as the Buddha and as an elder brother of his, that, with reluctance, he agreed to be admitted into the Order.

But *Nanda* Bhikkhu enjoyed no spiritual happiness resulting from renunciation. He was greatly depressed, and was constantly thinking of his bride. He related his mental troubles to the Bhikkhus, saying: "Brethren, I am dissatisfied. I am now living the Religious Life, but I cannot endure to lead the Holy Life any longer. I intend to abandon the higher precepts and return to the lower life, the life of a layman".

Hearing this, the Buddha questioned Venerable *Nanda* whether such report was true. He admitted his weakness, and stated that He was worried about his bride.

The Buddha devised a means to set him on the right path. With the object of showing him celestial nymphs the Buddha, using His psychic powers, took him to the Tavatimsa Heaven. On the way the Venerable *Nanda* was shown a singed she-monkey who had lost her ears, nose, and tail in a fire, clinging to a burnt-up stump in a scorched field. Reaching heaven, the Buddha pointed to him celestial nymphs and asked him: "*Nanda*, which do you regard as being the more beautiful and fair to look upon and handsome—your noble wife *Janapada Kalyāni* or the celestial nymphs?"

"Venerable Sir, *Janapada Kalyani* is like the singed monkey when compared to those celestial nymphs, who are infinitely more beautiful and fair."

"Cheer up, *Nanda*. I guarantee that you will possess them if you persevere as I bid you."

"In that case I shall take the greatest pleasure in living the Holy Life," said Venerable *Nanda* childishly.

Hearing that Venerable *Nanda* was living the Holy Life with the object of winning celestial nymphs, the Bhikkhus ridiculed him calling him "hireling." Eventually he became ashamed of his base motive, and striving diligently, attained Arahantship.

He thereupon approached the Buddha and said: "Venerable Sir, I release the Exalted One from the promise that He made when He guaranteed that I should win celestial nymphs."

The Buddha replied: "When, *Nanda*, you ceased to cling to the things of the world, and your heart was released from the Corruptions, at that moment I was released from that promise."

He then uttered the following paean of joy:

"He that has crossed over the mud and crushed the thorn of lust;

"He that has destroyed delusion, such a man is unmoved whether in pleasure or in pain."

When some monks doubted his attainment of Arahantship the Buddha in explanation uttered the following stanzas:

"Even as rain penetrates an ill-thatched house, so does lust penetrate an undeveloped mind."

"Even as rain does not penetrate a well-thatched house, so does lust not penetrate a well-developed mind."

Enjoying the bliss of Emancipation, he praised the Teacher, saying: "O excellent is the method of the Master, whereby I was drawn out of the mire of rebirth and set on Nibbāna's strand!"

Theragāthā attributes the following verses to him:

Through not reflecting rightly I was attached to outward show. Overcome by passionate love, I was restless and fickle.

Because of the skilful means devised by the Buddha, the "kinsman of the sun", rightly I acted and drew out my mind from existence.

1. Dhammapada vs. 13-14.
2. *Psalms of the Brethren*, p. 127 vs. 157, 158.

Venerable *Nanda* Thera was placed chief amongst disciples in respect of self-control.

The Buddha and Ānanda

Ānanda, a cousin of Prince *Siddhattha*, was the son of *Amitodana*, a younger brother of King *Suddhodana*. As he was born bringing happiness to all his kinsfolk, he was named Ānanda.

In the second year of the Buddha's ministry *Ānanda* entered the Order together with the Sakya Nobles—*Anuruddha*, *Bhaddiya*, *Bhagu*, *Kimbila*, and *Devadatta*. Not long after, hearing a sermon from Venerable *Punna Mantāniputta*, he attained the first stage of Sainthood (*Sotāpatti*).

When the Buddha was fifty-five years old Venerable *Ānanda* became His chief attendant.

During the first twenty years after His Enlightenment the Buddha had no permanent attendant. The few temporary attendants were not very dutiful and their behaviour was not highly commendable. One day while residing at Jetavana the Buddha addressed the Bhikkhus and said: "Now I am old, O Bhikkhus. When I say: Let us go this way some go by another way; some drop my bowl and robe on the ground. Choose out one disciple to attend always upon me."[1]

---

1.   Jātaka No. 456, Jātaka Translation, vol. iv. p. 61.

Forthwith all the Bhikkhus, from Venerable *Sariputta* downwards, volunteered their services. But the Buddha declined their kind offer. As the Venerable *Ānanda* was silent, he was advised by the Bhikkhus to offer his services. He consented on condition the Buddha would grant the following eight boons:

i. The Buddha should not give him robes which He Himself had received.

ii. The Buddha should not give him food which He had received.

iii. The Buddha should not allow him to dwell in the same Fragrant Chamber.

iv. The Buddha should not take him with Him wherever the Buddha is invited.

v. The Buddha should kindly go with him wherever He is invited.

vi. The Buddha should kindly give him permission to introduce visitors that come from afar to see the Buddha.

vii. The Buddha should kindly grant him permission to approach Him whenever any doubt should arise.

viii. The Buddha should kindly repeat to him the discourses that were declared in his absence.

The Buddha granted these four negative and
positive boons. Thenceforth the Venerable
Ānanda acted as His favourite attendant for twenty-five years till the Buddha's last moment. Like a
shadow he followed Him everywhere, attending to
all His needs with great love and care. Both during
day and night his services were always at the disposal of his Master. At night it is stated that he
used to go round the Fragrant Chamber nine
times with staff and torch in hand to keep him
awake and to prevent the Buddha's sleep from
being disturbed.

Ānanda Bodhi Tree

It was Venerable *Ānanda* who was responsible
for the planting of the Ānanda Bodhi Tree. In the
absence of the Buddha devout followers, who used
to bring flowers and garlands, lay them at the
entrance to the Fragrant Chamber and depart with
much rejoicing. *Anāthapindika* came to hear of it
and requested Venerable *Ānanda* to inquire of the
Buddha whether there was a possibility of finding
a place where his devotees might pay obeisance to
the Buddha when He was away on His preaching
tours. Venerable *Ānanda* approached the Buddha
and asked:

[1]"Lord, how many objects of reverence (*Ceti-
yani*) are there, may it please you?"

---

1. Kālingabodhi Jātaka, No. 479, Jātaka, vol. iv, p. 228,
   Jātaka Translation, vol. iv, p. 142.

"There are three, *Ānanda*. They are objects of reverence appertaining to the body (*Sāririka*),[1] objects of reverence appertaining to personal use (*Pāribhogika*) and objects of reverence reminiscent of the Buddha (*Uddesika*)."

"Is it proper, Lord, to construct a Cetiya while you are alive?"

"No, not an object of reverence appertaining to the body which it is proper to erect after the passing away of the Buddha. An object of reverence reminiscent of the Buddha has no physical basis; it is purely mental. But the great Bodhi tree, used by the Buddha, whether He is alive or dead, is an object of reverence (*Cetiya*)."

"Lord, when you go on your preaching tours, the great monastery of Jetavana is without refuge, and people find no place of reverence. Lord, may I bring a seed from the great Bodhi tree and plant it at the entrance to Jetavana.?"

"Very well, *Ānanda*, plant it. It will then be as if I constantly abide in Jetavana."

Venerable *Ānanda* mentioned this matter to Buddha's principal lay attendants—*Anāthapiṇḍika, Visākhā*, and King *Kosala*—and requested the Venerable *Moggallāna* to secure a fruit from the great Bodhi tree. Readily he consented and obtained a fruit that was falling from the tree and delivered it to Venerable *Ānanda*.

---

1. Such as bodily relics of the Buddha.

This he presented to the King who in turn
handed it to *Anāthapiṇḍika*. Then he stirred up
the fragrant soil and dropped it in the hole that
was dug. The tree that sprang up in that place
was known as the *Ānanda-Bodhi*.[1]

Ānanda and Women

It was also Venerable *Ānanda* who persuaded
the Buddha to admit women into the Order. Had
it not been for his intervention *Maha Pajāpati
Gotami* would not have succeeded in becoming a
Bhikkhuni (Nun). Bhikkhunis held him in high
esteem, and his sermons were greatly appreciated
by them.

On one occasion he approached the Buddha
and asked Him:

"How are we to conduct ourselves, Lord, with
regard to womankind?"

"As not seeing them, *Ānanda*."

"But if we should see them, Lord, what are
we to do?"

"Do not talk to them *Ānanda*."

"But if they should speak to us, Lord, what
are we to do?"

"Be watchful, *Ānanda*."

---

1. This oldest historic sacred tree is still to be seen at
    modern Sahet Mahet (Sāvatthi) in India.

This general exhortation was given to Bhikkhus so that they may constantly be watchful in their dealings with women.

As he possessed a powerfully retentive memory, and as he had the rare privilege of listening to all the discourses of the Buddha owing to his close association with Him, he was later appointed the Custodian of the Dhamma (*Dhamma-bhaṇḍā-gārika*).

Referring to his own knowledge of the Dhamma, in reply to a question put by a brahmin, Venerable Ānanda said:

"Eighty-two thousand from the Buddha and two thousand from the Bhikkhus I received.

There exist eighty-four thousand texts in all. "[1]

The Buddha ranked him foremost amongst His disciples in five respects: erudition (*bahussutā-nam*), retentive memory (*satimantānam*) good, behaviour (*gatimantānam*), steadfastness (*dhitiman tānam*) and ministering care (*upaṭṭhakānam*).[2]

Though a distinguished disciple, well-versed in the Dhamma, he lived as a "learner" (*sekha*), till the death of the Buddha. The Buddha's final

---

1. *Psalms of the Brethren*, p. 354. Theragāthā vs. 1424.
2. Anguttara Nikāya, Vol. i, p. 24. *Gradual Sayings*, part I. p. 19

exhortation to him was—"You have done merit in the past, Ānanda. Quickly be free from Corruptions."[1]

It was only after the passing away of the Buddha that he attained Arahantship. As he was expected to take a leading part in the First Council, which was composed only of Arahants, he made a strenuous effort and attained Arahantship on the night preceding the Convocation while he was about to lie down on his couch. It is stated that he was the only disciple who attained Arahantship free from the postures of sitting, standing, walking or sleeping.[2]

Venerable *Ānanda* passed away at the age of one hundred and twenty. The Dhammapada commentary states that as people of both the sides of the river Rohini were equally serviceable to him and as both sides vied with each other to possess his relics, he sat cross-legged in the air over the middle of the river, preached the Dhamma to the multitude and wished that his body would split in two and that one portion would fall on the near side and the other on the farther side. He then entered into the ecstatic meditation on the element of fire (*Tejokasina samāpatti*). Instantly flames of fire issued from his body, and, as willed, one portion of the body fell on the near side and the other on the farther side.

---

1. Dīgha Nikāya, Parinibbāna Sutta.
2. *Buddhist Legends*, vol. iii, p. 160.

The Theragāthā gives several stanzas uttered by him on various occasions. The following verses which deal with the frailty of this so-called beautiful body are particularly interesting:

"Behold this adorned body, a mass of sores, a lump infirm, much thought of, whereof nothing lasts, nothing persists."[1]

The Buddha and Mahā Pajāpati Gotami

Maha Pajāpati Gotamī, was the youngest sister of King *Suppabuddha*. Her elder sister was Queen *Maha Maya*. Both were married to King *Suddhodana*. She had a daughter named *Nandā* and a son named *Nanda*. Later, both of them entered the Order. When *Maha Maya* died she adopted her sister's son, Prince *Siddhattha*, entrusting her own son *Nanda* to the charge of nurses.

Her family name was *Gotamī*, and she was named *Mahā Pajāpati* because soothsayers predicted that she would be the head of a large following.

When the Buddha visited the palace and preached the Dhammapāla Jātaka to His father she attained the first stage of Sainthood.

After the death of King *Suddhodana*, as both Princes *Siddhattha* and *Nanda* had renounced the world, she also decided to enter the Noble Order

---

1.   *Psalms of the Brethren*, p. 353. Theragāthā, v. 1020, Dhammapada v. 147.

and lead the Holy Life. When the Buddha visited Kapilavatthu to settle a dispute between the Sakyas and Koliyas with regard to the irrigation of channels from the river Rohini and was residing at the Nigrodha park, *Mahā Pajāpti Gotamī* approached the Buddha and begging Him to grant permission for women to enter the Order, pleaded thus:[1]

"It would be well, Lord, if women should be allowed to renounce their homes and enter the homeless state under the doctrine and discipline proclaimed by the Tathāgata."

Without stating His reasons, the Buddha straightway refused, saying:

"Enough, O *Gotami*, let it not please you that women should be allowed to do so.

For the second and third time *Maha Pajāpati Gotamī* repeated her request, and the Buddha gave the same reply.

Later, the Buddha having stayed at Kapilavatthu as long as He liked journeyed to Vesali, and arriving there in due course, resided at the Mahāvana in the Kūtāgāra Hall.

---

1. Vinaya Texts, part iii, p. 320. Anguttara Nikāya, Part iv, 274.

Resolute *Pajāpati Gotamī*, without being discouraged by her disappointment, got her hair cut off, donned yellow garments, and surrounded by a great number of Sakya ladies, walked from Kapilavatthu to Vesali, a distance of about 150 miles, experiencing many a hardship. With swollen feet, her body covered with dust, she arrived at Vesali and stood outside the porch of the Pinnacled Hall. Venerable *Ānanda* found her weeping and learning the cause of her grief, approached the Buddha and said:

"Behold, Lord, *Mahā Pajāptī Gotamī* is standing outside the porch, with swollen feet, body covered with dust, and sad. Please permit women to renounce home and enter the homeless state under the doctrine and discipline proclaimed by the Exalted One. It were well, Lord, if women should be allowed to renounce their homes and enter the homeless state."

"Enough, *Ānanda*, let it not please you that women should be allowed to do so!" was the Buddha's reply.

For the second and third time he interceded on their behalf, but the Buddha would not yield.

So Venerable *Ānanda* made a different approach and respectfully questioned the Buddha: "Are women, Lord, capable of realizing the state of a Stream-Winner (*Sotāpanna*), Once-Returner (*Sakadāgāmi*,) Never-Returner (*Anāgāmi*) and an

Arahant, when they have gone forth from home
to the homeless state under the doctrine and
discipline proclaimed by the Exalted one?"

The Buddha replied that they were capable of
realizing Saintship.

Encouraged by this favourable reply, Venerable
Ānanda appealed again, saying: "If then, Lord,
they are capable of attaining Saintship, since *Mahā*
Pajāpati Gotamī had been of great service to the
Exalted One, when as aunt and nurse she nourished Him and gave Him milk, and on the death of
His mother suckled the Exalted One at her own
breast, it were well, Lord, that women should be
given permission to renounce the world and enter
the homeless state under the doctrine and discipline
proclaimed by the Tathāgata."

"If, *Ānanda*, *Mahā Pajāpati Gotamī* accepts
the Eight Chief Rules, let that be reckoned to her
as the form of her ordination," said the Buddha,
finally yielding to the entreaties of Venerable
Ānanda.

The Eight Chief Rules[1] are as follows:

1—A Bhikkhuni, even of a hundred years'
standing by Upasampadā,[2]   should   salute   a

---

1.   Some of these rules will not be intelligible to the lay
      readers as they pertain to Vinaya Discipline.
2.   The Higher Ordination.

Bhikkhu, rise up before him, reverence him, and perform all proper duties towards him though he had received the Higher Ordination that very day.

2—A Bhikkhunī should not spend a Retreat (*Vassa*) in a place where there is no Bhikkhu.

3—Every fortnight a Bhikkhuni should ask from the Order of Bhikkhus the time of Uposatha[1] meeting and when a Bhikkhu would come to admonish them.

4—The *Pavāraṇa*[2] ceremony after the Retreat should be held by a Bhikkhunī in the presence of both Bhikkhus and Bhikkhunīs (to inquire whether through any of the three ways of seeing, hearing, or suspicion a wrong has been done.)

5—A Bhikkhunī who has committed a major offence should undergo *Mānatta*[3] discipline in the presence of the Order of both Bhikkhus and Bhikkhunīs.

6—A female novice (*Sikkamānā*), who is trained in the Six Rules for two years, should receive the Higher Ordination from the Order of both Bhikkhus and Bhikkhunis.

7—A Bhikkhunī should on no account rebuke or abuse a Bhikkhu.

---

1. The full moon and new moon days when Bhikkhus assemble to recite their Fundamental Rules.
2. The formal termination of the rainy season.
3. A form of disciplinary action.

8—Henceforth Bhikkhunīs should not give admonition to Bhikkhus, but Bhikkhus should admonish Bhikkhunis.

These rules are to be revered, reverenced, honoured and respected as long as life lasts and should not be transgressed.

When Venerable *Ānanda* mentioned them to *Mahā Pajāpati Gotamī* she gladly agreed to abide by those eight Chief Rules. By their acceptance she automatically received the Higher Ordination.

In founding this Order of Bhikkhunīs the Buddha, foreseeing the future repercussions, remarked: "If, *Ānanda*, women had not received permission to renounce the world and enter the homeless state under the doctrine and discipline proclaimed by the Tathāgata, the Holy Life would have lasted long and the Sublime Dhamma would have survived for thousand years. But since women have entered this homeless state, the Holy Life would not last long and the Sublime Dhamma would now remain only for five hundred years."[1]

The Buddha added—"Just as, *Ānanda*, houses in which there are many women and but few men are easily violated by burglars, even so, under whatsoever doctrine and discipline women are permitted to renounce the world and enter the homeless state, that Holy Life will not last long.

"And just as a man would in anticipation build an embankment to a great reservoir beyond which

1.   See *Gradual Sayings*, iv, p. 184.

the water should not overpass, even so have I in anticipation laid down these eight Chief Rules for the Bhikkhunis, not to be transgressed throughout their lives."[1]

In making these comments, which may not generally be very palatable to womankind, the Buddha was not in any way making a wholesale condemnation of women but was only reckoning with the weaknesses of their sex.

Although for several valid reasons the Buddha reluctantly permitted women to enter the Order, it should be stated that it was the Buddha who, for the first time in the history of the world, founded an Order for women with rules and regulations. Just as He appointed two chief disciples, Venerable *Sāriputta* and *Mogallāna* for the Order of monks, two chief female disciples—Venerable *Khemā* and *Uppalavannā*—were appointed for the Order of nuns as well.

One day Bhikkhunī *Mahā Pajāpatī Gotamī* approached the Buddha and invited him to deliver a discourse so that she may strive alone and achieve her goal.

The Buddha declared—"Of whatsoever doctrine thou shalt be conscious, *Gotamī*, that these things conduce to passion and not to peace, to pride and not to veneration, to wishing for much and not to wishing for little, to love of society and

---

1.   See *Gradual Sayings*, iv, p. 185

not to seclusion, to sloth and not to the exercise
of zeal, to being hard to satisfy and not to contentment, verily mayest thou then, *Gotamī*, bear in
mind: that is not Dhamma, that is not Vinaya,
that is not the teaching of the Master. But of
whatsoever doctrine thou shalt be conscious,
Gotamī, that these things conduce to peace and
not to passion, to veneration and not to pride,
to wishing for little and not to wishing for much,
to seclusion and not to love of society, to the
exercise of zeal and not to sloth, to contentment
and not to querulousness, verily mayest thou
then bear in mind: that is Dhamma, and that is
Vinaya, and that is the teaching of the Master."[1]

Before long she attained Arahantship, accompanied by intuitive and analytical knowledge
(*Paṭisambhidā*).[2]

The other Sakya ladies, who received their
ordination with her, also attained Arahantship.

Amongst the female disciples *Mahā Pajāpati
Gotamī* was assigned the foremost place in senio-
rity and experience (*Rattaññu*).

In the Therigāthā appear several verses uttered
by her after attaining Arahantship.

1. Vinaya Texts part III, pp. 329-330. See *Gradual Sayings*,
   iv, pp. 186, 187.
2. Analytical Knowledge with regard to the meaning
   (*Attha*), Texts (*Dhamma*) Etymology (*Nirutti*), and the
   Understanding of these three (*Paṭibhāna*).

CHAPTER 10

THE BUDDHA'S CHIEF OPPONENTS AND SUPPORTERS

"*As a solid rock is not shaken by the wind
Even so the wise are not ruffled by praise or
blame.*"

DHAMMAPADA

The Buddha worked disinterestedly for the weal of mankind, making no distinction between the rich and the poor, the high and the low. His followers and supporters were drawn both from the highest and lowest rungs of the social ladder. So spontaneous was the love and so profound was the veneration of the people, that kings and nobles, millionaires and paupers, pious folk and courtesans, men and women of all ranks, vied with one another to be of service to Him and make His noble mission a success. The wealthy spent lavishly to erect suitable monasteries for Him, while the poor, full of faith, demonstrated their piety in their humble way. With perfect equanimity He accepted the gifts of the rich and the poor, but showed no partiality to any. Nevertheless, He showed more compassion to the poor and the lowly. Like a bee that extracts honey from a flower without hurting it, He lived amongst His followers and supporters without causing the slightest inconvenience to any. Offerings of diverse kinds were showered on Him, and He accepted them all with perfect non-attachment.

Though absolutely pure in motive and perfectly
selfless in His service to humanity, yet, in preaching and spreading His teaching, the Buddha had to
contend against strong opposition. He was severely criticised, roundly abused, insulted and ruthlessly attacked, as no other religious teacher had
been. His chief opponents were ordinary teachers
of rival sects and followers of heretical schools
whose traditional teachings and superstitious rites
and ceremonies He justly criticised. His greatest
personal enemy, who made a vain attempt to kill
Him, was His own brother-in-law and an erstwhile
disciple—Devadatta.

The Buddha and Devadatta

Devadatta was the son of King *Suppabuddha*
and *Pamitā*, an aunt of the Buddha. *Yasodharā*
was his sister. He was thus a cousin and brother-
in-law of the Buddha. He entered the Order in the
early part of the Buddha's ministry together with
Ānanda and other Sakya princes. He could not
attain any of the stages of Sainthood, but was
distinguished for worldly psychic powers (*pothujja-
nika-iddhi*). One of his chief supporters was
King *Ajātasattu* who built a monastery for him.

During the early part of his career he led such
an exemplary life that even Venerable *Sāriputta*
went about *Rājagaha* extolling him. Later, overcome by worldly gain and honour, and growing
jealous of the Buddha, *Devadatta* became so radi-

cally changed in his character that he proved to be the greatest personal enemy of the Buddha. Simultaneous with the arising of ill-will in his heart towards the Buddha his psychic powers automatically ceased.

Despite his evil ways and corrupt life, he had a large following and many admirers, and some even preferred him to Venerable *Sāriputta.*

On one occasion he approached the Buddha and requested Him to hand over the leadership of the Sangha to him as the Buddha was advanced in age. The Buddha straightway refused, saying; "Not even to *Sāriputta* or *Moggallāna* would I hand over the Sangha. Would I then hand it over to thee?" He was enraged at this refusal and vowed vengeance. To safeguard and maintain the dignity of the Sangha the Buddha caused a proclamation to be made that *Devadatta* alone was responsible for anything done by him in the name of the Buddha, the Dhamma, or the Sangha.

He, therefore, conspired with King *Ajātasattu* to kill the Buddha. *Ajātasattu* was advised to kill his father and usurp the throne. while he himself decided to kill the Buddha and lead the Sangha. Ungrateful *Ajātasattu* succeeded in killing his devout father, and *Devadatta* hired bowmen to murder the Buddha but, contrary to his expectations, all the hirelings became the Buddha's followers. Foiled in his attempt, he himself resolved to kill the Buddha. When the Buddha was walking on the slopes of Gijjhakūta he climbed the Peak and mercilessly hurled a rock at the Buddha. Fortunately it struck another piece of rock and a splinter slightly wounded His foot, causing the blood to flow. *Jīvaka* the physician attended on Him and cured Him.

Devadatta made another unsuccessful attempt to kill the Buddha by dispatching the elephant *Nālāgiri*, after infuriating him with liquor, against the Teacher. When the ferocious elephant approached the Buddha the Venerable *Ānanda* stepped forward to sacrifice his life for the sake of his Master, but the Buddha subdued the beast by His loving-kindness (*Mettā*).

By this last wicked act *Devadatta* became extremely unpopular, and public opinion was so much against him that the King was compelled to withdraw his patronage. *Devadatta* fell into disrepute and all his favours decreased.

He now decided to live by deceit. His fertile brain devised another seemingly peaceful plan. With the help of equally evil-minded Bhikkhus like *Kokālika*, he thought of causing a schism in the Order.

He requested the Buddha to enforce the following five rules among the Bhikkhus:

i. That monks should dwell all their lives in the forest.

ii. That they should live on alms begged.

iii. That they should wear Paṁsakūla robes (i.e., robes made from rags collected from the dust-heap and cemeteries.)

iv. That they should live at the foot of a tree.

v. That they should not eat fish or flesh throughout life.

This he did, knowing fully well that the Buddha would not assent thereto. He desired to make Buddha's refusal a pretext for disparaging the Buddha, and thereby winning the support of the ignorant masses.

When this request was made the compassionate and tolerant Buddha declared that His disciples were free to adopt these rules or not, but would not make them compulsory for all.

Devadatta made this refusal a cause for a schism in the Order. He appealed to the Bhikkhus, saying: "Brethren, whose words are the nobler, the words of the Tathāgata or the words which I myself have uttered? Whoever desires release from suffering, let him come with me."

Newly ordained monks, who were not conversant with the Dhamma, apparently approved of his demands and went over to him. Accompanied by them, he went to Gayāsisa. But Venerable *Sāriputta* and *Mogallāna*, on the advice of the Buddha, went there and succeeded in winning them back after explaining the Dhamma to them.

Thereafter evil days fell upon *Devadatta*. He fell grievously ill, and before his death he sincerely repented and desired to see the Buddha. But his bad Kamma interfered and he had to die a miserable death without seeing the Buddha. However, he sought refuge in the Buddha at the last moment.

Although he suffers in a woeful state for his heinous crimes, yet as a result of the Holy Life he led during the early part of his career, it is stated that he would become a Pacceka Buddha named *Aṭṭhissara* in the distant future.

ANĀTHAPINDIKA

The chief supporter of the Buddha was *Anātha-pindika* the millionaire. Amongst His lay-follo-wers he was regarded as the foremost alms–giver (*dāyaka*).

The original name of *Anāthapindika*, which means the "Feeder of the Helpless", was *Sudatta*. Owing to his unparallelled generosity he was latterly known by his new name. His birthplace was Sāvatthi.

One day he visited his brother-in-law in Rāja-gaha to transact some business. He did not come forward as usual to welcome him but *Suddatta* found him in the backyard making preparations for a feast. On inquiry, to his indescribable joy, he understood that those arrangements were being made to entertain the Buddha on the following day. The utterance of the mere word "Buddha" roused his interest and he longed to see Him. As he was told that the Buddha was living in the Sītavana forest in the neighbourhood and that he could see Him on the following morning, he went to sleep. His desire to visit the Buddha was so intense that he had a sleepless night and he arose at an unusual hour in the morning to start for the Sītavana. It appears that, owing to his great faith in the Buddha, a light emanated from his body. He proceeded to the spot passing through a cemetery. It was pitch dark and a fear arose in him. He thought of turning back. Then Sīvaka, a Yakkha, himself invisible, encouraged him, saying:

"A hundred elephants and horses too,
Ay, and a hundred chariots drawn by mules,
A hundred thousand maidens, in their ears
Bejewelled rings:—all are not worth
The sixteenth fraction of a single stride.
Advance, O citizen, go forward thou!
Advance for thee is better than retreat"[1]

His fear vanished and faith in the Buddha arose in its place. Light appeared again, and he courageously sped forward. Nevertheless, all this happened a second time and yet a third time. Ultimately He reached Sītavana where the Buddha was pacing up and down in the open air anticipating his visit. The Buddha addressed him by his family name, *Sudatta,* and called him to His presence.

Anāthapiṇḍika was pleased to hear the Buddha address him thus and respectfully inquired whether the Buddha rested happily.

The Buddha replied:

"Surely at all times happily doth rest
The Arahant in whom all fire's extinct.
Who cleaveth not to sensuous desires,
Cool all his being, rid of all the germs
That bring new life, all cumbrances cut out,
Subdued the pain and pining of the heart,
Calm and serene he resteth happily
For in his mind he hath attained to Peace"[2]

---

1. *Kindred Sayings*, Part, 1, p. 272.
2. *Kindred Sayings*, Part, 1, p. 273.

Hearing the Dhamma, he became a *Sotāpanna* (Stream-Winner), and invited the Buddha to spend the rainy season at Sāvatthi. The Buddha accepted the invitation suggesting that Buddhas take pleasure in solitude. *Anāthapiṇḍika* returning to Sāvatthi, bought the park belonging to Prince *Jeta* at a price determined by covering, so the story goes, the whole site with gold coins, and erected the famous Jetavana Monastery at a great cost. Here the Buddha spent nineteen rainy seasons. This monastery where the Buddha spent the major part of His life was the place where He delivered many of His sermons.

Several discourses which were of particular interest to laymen were delivered to *Anāthapiṇḍika*, although he refrained from asking any question from the Buddha, lest he should weary Him.

Once the Buddha discoursing on generosity reminded *Anāthapiṇḍika* that alms given to the Order of monks together with the Buddha is very meritorious; but more meritorious than such alms is the building of a monastery for the use of the Order; more meritorious than such monasteries is seeking refuge in the Buddha, the Dhamma, and the Sangha; more meritorious than seeking refuge in the Buddha, the Dhamma and

the Sangha is the observance of the five precepts;
more meritorious than such observance is meditation on loving-kindness (*Mettā*) for a moment;
and most meritorious of all is the development of
Insight as to the fleeting nature of things (*Vipassanā*),[1]

It is evident from this discourse that generosity
is the first stage on the way of Buddhist life. More
important than generosity is the observance of at
least the five rules of regulated behaviour which
tend to the disciplining of words and deeds. Still
more important and more beneficial is the cultivation of such ennobling virtues like loving-
kindness which lead to self-development. Most
important and most beneficial of all self-discipline
is the sincere effort to understand things as they
truly are.

Commenting on the four kinds of bliss a layman may enjoy, the Buddha declared:

[2]"There are these four kinds of bliss to be
won by the householder who enjoys the pleasures
of sense from time to time and when occasion
offers —the bliss of ownership (*atthisukha*), the
bliss of wealth (*bhogasukha*), the bliss of debtless
ness (*ananasukha*), and the bliss of blamelessness
(*anavajjasukha*).

---

1. See *Gradual Sayings*, vol. iv, pp. 264-265
2. *Gradual Sayings*, vol. ii, pp. 77-78, Anguttara Nikāya ii,
   pp. 67-68.

"What is the bliss of ownership?"

Herein a clansman has wealth acquired by energetic striving, amassed by strength of arm, won
by sweat, lawful, and lawfully gotten. At the
thought, wealth is mine, acquired by energetic
striving, lawfully gotten, bliss comes to him, satisfaction comes to him. This is called the bliss of
ownership.

"What is the bliss of wealth?"

Herein a clansman by means of wealth acquired
by energetic striving, both enjoys his wealth and
does meritorious deeds therewith. At the thought,
by means of wealth acquired, I both enjoy my
wealth and do meritorious deeds, bliss comes to
him, satisfaction comes to him. This is called the
bliss of wealth.

"What is the bliss of debtlessness?"

Herein a clansman owes no debt, great or
small, to anyone. At the thought, I owe no debt,
great or small, to anyone, bliss comes to him,
satisfaction comes to him. This is called the bliss
of debtlessness.

"What is the bliss of blamelessness?"

Herein the Aryan disciple is blessed with
blameless action of body, blameless action of
speech, blameless action of mind. At the thought,

I am blessed with blameless action of body, speech and mind, bliss comes to him, satisfaction comes to him.   This is called the bliss of blamelessness."

"Winning the bliss of debtlessness a man
May then recall the bliss of really having.
When he enjoys the bliss of wealth, he sees
'Tis such by wisdom.   When he sees he knows.
Thus is he wise indeed in both respects.
But these have not one-sixteenth of the bliss
(That cometh to a man) of blamelessness."

On another occasion when the Buddha visited the house of *Anāthapiṇḍika*, he heard an unusual uproar inside the house and inquired what it was.

"Lord, it is *Sujātā*, my daughter-in-law, who lives with us.   She is rich and has been brought here from a wealthy family.   She pays no heed to her mother-in-law, nor to her father-in-law, nor to her husband; neither does she venerate, honour, reverence nor respect the Exalted One," replied *Anāthapiṇḍika.*

The Buddha called her to His presence and preached an illuminative discourse on seven kinds of wives that exist even in modern society as it was in the days of old.

'*Whoso is wicked in mind, ill-disposed, pitiless, fond of other (men) neglecting husband, a prostitute, bent on harassing—*
such a one is called "a troublesome wife."

(**Vadhakabhariyā**)

Whoso wishes to squander whatever profits, though little, that the husband gains whether by crafts, trade, or plough—
such a one is called "a thievish wife."

(**Corabhariyā**)

Whoso is not inclined to do anything, lazy, gluttonous, harsh, cruel, fond of bad speech, lives domineering the industrious—
such a one is called "a lordly wife."

(**Ayyabhariyā**)

Whoso is ever kind and compassionate, protects her husband like a mother, her son, guards the accumulated wealth of her husband—
such a one is called "a motherly wife."

(**Mātubhariyā**)

---

1. *Gradual Sayings*, vol. iv, pp. 56-58. Anguttara Nikāya, vol. iv, pp. 92–93.

*Whoso is respectful towards her husband just
as a younger sister towards her elder brother,
modest, lives in accordance with her husband's
wishes—*
such a one is called "a sisterly wife."

(Bhaginibhariyā)

*Whoso rejoices at the sight of her husband even
as a friend on seeing a companion who has
come after a long time, is of noble birth, virtuous
and chaste—*
such a one is called "a friendly wife."

(Sakhībhariyā)

*Whoso, when threatened with harm and punish-
ment, is not angry but calm, endures all things
of her husband with no wicked heart, free from.
hatred, lives in accordance with her husband's
wishes—*
such a one is called "a handmaid wife."

(Dāsibhariyā)

The Buddha describing the characteristics of
the seven kinds of wives remarked that of them
the troublesome wife (*vadhakabhariyā*), the thievish
wife (*corabhariyā*), and the lordly wife (*ayyabhariyā*), are bad and undesirable ones, while the
motherly wife (*mātubhariyā*), sisterly wife (*bha-*

ginibhariyā), friendly wife (*sakhībhariyā*), and handmaid wife (*dāsibhariyā*), are good and praiseworthy ones.

"These *Sujātā*, are the seven kinds of wives a man may have: and which of them are you?"

"Lord, let the Exalted One think of me as a handmaid wife (*dāsibhariyā*) from this day forth."

Anāthapiṇḍika used to visit the Buddha daily and, finding that people go disappointed in the absence of the Buddha, wished to know from the Venerable *Ānanda* whether there was a possibility for the devout followers to pay their respects when the Buddha goes out on His preaching tours. This matter was reported to the Buddha with the result that the *Ānanda-Bodhi* Tree,[1] which stands to this day, was planted at the entrance to the monastery.

Puṇṇalakkhaṇā, a very virtuous lady, was his wife. *Mahā Subhaddā, Cuṭa Subhaddā*, and *Sumanā* were his three devout daughters. The elder two had attained Sotāpatti, while the youngest was a Sakadāgāmi. His only son Kāla, who was at first irreligious, later became a Sotāpanna by the skilfullness of the father.

Anāthapiṇḍika breathed his last after hearing a profound discourse from Venerable *Sāriputta*.[2]

---

1. See p. 145.
2. Majjhima Nikāya iii, 262; *Further Dialogues of the Buddha*, vol. ii, pp. 302-305.

As he was about to die he sent a messenger to inform the Buddha that he was seriously ill and that he paid His homage to Him and then to request the Venerable *Sāriputta* to have compassion on him and visit him in his house. As invited, the Venerable *Sāriputta*, accompanied by Venerable *Ānanda*, proceeded to his house and inquired about his health. He replied that he was suffering from an acute pain and that he saw no signs of progress.

The Venerable *Sāriputta* then preached a profound discourse. Tears came to his eyes at the close of the sermon. Venerable *Ānanda* seeing him in tears asked him whether he was sinking, *Anāthapindika* answered: "Not at all, Venerable Sir. Though I have long attended on the Master and His disciples, never did I hear such a discourse."

"Such profound discourses are not taught to the white-robed laymen as they cannot comprehend their meaning but are reserved for advanced disciples," replied Venerable *Sāriputta*.

But *Anāthapindika* begged Venerable *Sāriputta* to expound such intricate Dhamma to the laity as well for there would be some who could understand.

Not long before the departure of these two great disciples *Anāthapindika* passed away and was immediately reborn in Tusita heaven.

At night Deva *Anāthapiṇḍika*, illuminating, the whole Jeta Grove, came up to the Buddha, saluted Him, and extolling the virtues of Venerable *Sāriputta*, expressed his pleasure on seeing the Buddha and His disciples residing in his monastery, and said:

"Goodwill and wisdom, mind by method trained,
The highest conduct on good morals based,
This maketh mortals pure, not rank nor wealth."[1]

---

1. *Kindred Sayings*, Part i, p. 80.

VISĀKHĀ

Visākhā was the devout and generous daughter of millionaire *Dhanañjaya*. Her mother was *Sumanā Devi*, and her beloved grand-father was millionaire *Meṇḍaka*.

When she was only seven years old, the Buddha happened to visit her birth place, Bhaddiya, in the kingdom of Anga. Her grand-father, hearing of Buddha's visit, said to her: "Dear girl, this is a happy day for you and a happy day for me. Summon the five hundred maidens who are your attendants, mount five hundred chariots, and accompanied by your five hundred slave-maidens, go forth to welcome the Buddha."

Readily she agreed and, as advised, went up to the Buddha, saluted Him and sat respectfully at a side. The Buddha was pleased with her refined manners and He preached the Dhamma to her and others. Though young in age, she was comparatively far advanced from a moral standpoint. As such, immediately after hearing the Dhamma, she attained the first stage of Sainthood (*Sotāpatti*) in her early age.

Books state that even in the prime of her youth she possessed masculine strength and was gifted with all womanly charms.[1] Her hair was like a peacock's tail and when loosened it reached the hem of her skirt and then the ends of the hair

---

1. *Kesakalyāna, maṁsakalyāna, aṭṭhikalyāna, chavikalyāna* and *vayakalyāna.*

curled and turned upwards. Her lips were of a bright red colour and were smooth and soft to the touch. Her teeth were white and were evenly set without interstices and shone like a row of diamonds. Her skin, without the use of any cosmetic, was as smooth as a blue lotus-wreath and was of a golden colour. She retained her youthful appearance although she bore several children.

Endowed with these five kinds of feminine beauty—hair, flesh, bone, skin and youth—young *Visākhā* excelled both in worldly wisdom and spiritual insight.

When she was about fifteen or sixteen years old, on a certain Festival Day, she went on foot with her retinue in a holiday spirit to the river to bathe. Suddenly there arose an unexpected shower, and all but young *Visākhā* ungraciously ran as fast as they could and entered a hall where there were some brahmins who had come in search of a suitable maiden possessed of the five kinds of beauty for their young master. Cultured *Visākhā*, without any particular haste, gracefully proceeded at her usual gait and entered the hall with garments and ornaments all wet. The inquisitive brahmins criticised her for not quickening up her pace as others had done and thus escaping being drenched in the rain.

Talented *Visākhā* rose to the occasion and gave an extempore discourse on deportment according to her view. She said that she could have run

even faster but she refrained from doing so
purposely. Then she explained that it was not
becoming for a King, adorned with all jewels,
to gird up his loins and run in the palace-court.
Likewise it is not becoming for a fully capa-
risoned state elephant to run; it should move
about with the natural grace of an elephant.
Monks also incur criticism when they run about
like ordinary laymen. Likewise it is not a dignified
spectacle to see a woman running about like a man.

Brahmins were pleased with her instructive
talk and thought that she was an ideal wife for
their master. Accordingly, arrangements were
made to give her in marriage to their master,
Punnavaddhana, himself the son of a millionaire
named *Migāra*, who was not a follower of the
Buddha.

The marriage festival was conducted on an
elaborate scale. On the wedding day, in addition
to a large dowry and an exquisitely rich ornament
(*mahālatāpilandhana*), her wise father gave her
the following admonitions:

1.—Do not carry outside the indoor fire.[1]

2.—Do not take inside the outdoor fire.

3.—Give only to those that give.

4.—Do not give to those that do not give.

---

1. Here fire signifies slandering.

5.—Give both to those that give and do not give.

6.—Sit happily.

7. Eat happily.

8.—Sleep happily.

9.—Tend the fire.

10.—Honour the household divinities.

Their implied meaning is as follows.

1. The wife should not speak ill of her husband and parents-in-law to others. Neither should their shortcomings nor household quarrels be reported elsewhere.

2. A wife should not listen to the reports and stories, of other households.

3. Things should be lent to those who do return them.

4. No article should be lent to those who do not return them.

5. Poor kinsfolk and friends should be helped even if they do not repay.

6. A wife should sit in a becoming way. On seeing her parents-in-law or her husband, she should keep standing and not sit.

7. Before partaking of her meals, a wife should first see that her parents-in-law and husband are served. She should also see that her servants are well cared for.

8. Before sleep a wife should see that all doors are closed, furniture is safe, servants have performed their duties, and that parents-in-law have retired. As a rule a wife should rise early in the morning and, unless unwell, she should not sleep during the day.

9. Parents-in-law and husband should be regarded as fire. One should deal carefully with them as one would deal with fire.

10. Parents-in-law and husband should be regarded as divinities. It is noteworthy that the Buddha Himself refers to parents-in-law as divinities (*sassudevā*).

On the day she arrived in Sāvatthi, the city of her husband, she was showered with various presents sent from people of all ranks according to their status and ability. But so kind and generous was she that she distributed them amongst the donors themselves with a kind message, and treated all the residents of the city as her own kinsfolk. By this noble gesture on the very first day she came to her husband's home, she became endeared to all the people of the city.

There is an incident in her life which reveals
her dutiful kindness even towards animals. Hearing that her well-bred mare gave birth to a foal
in the middle of the night, immediately she
repaired to the stable with her female attendants
bearing torches in their hands, and attended to all
the mare's needs with the greatest care and attention.

As her father-in-law was a staunch follower
of *Nigaṇṭha Nātaputta,* he invited a large number
of naked ascetics to his house for alms. On their
arrival *Visākhā* was requested to come and render
homage to these so-called Arahants. She was
delighted to hear the word Arahant and hurried to
the hall only to see naked ascetics devoid of all
modesty. The sight was too unbearable for a
refined lady like *Visākhā.* She reproached her
father-in-law and retired to her quarters without
entertaining them. The naked ascetics took
offence and found fault with the millionaire for
having brought a female follower of the Ascetic
Gotama to his house. They asked him to expel her
from the house immediately.

The millionaire pacified them. One day he sat
on a costly seat and began to eat some sweet rice-
porridge from a golden bowl. At that moment a
Bhikkhu entered the house for alms. *Visākhā* was
fanning her father-in-law and without informing
him of his presence she moved aside so that he
might see him. Although he saw him he continued
eating as if he had not seen him.

Visākhā politely told the Bhikkhu: "Pass on, Venerable Sir, my father-in-law is eating stale fare (*purāṇaṁ*)."

The ignorant millionaire, misconstruing her words, was so provoked that he ordered the bowl to be removed and *Visākhā* to be expelled from the house.

Visākhā was the favourite of all the inmates of the house, and so nobody dared to touch her.

But *Visākhā*, disciplined as she was, would not accept without protest such treatment even from her father-in-law. She politely said: "Father, this is no sufficient reason why I should leave your house.   I was not brought here by you like a slave girl from some ford. Daughters, whose parents are alive, do not leave like this. It is for this very reason that my father, when I set out to come here, summoned eight clansmen and entrusted me to them, saying: 'If there be any fault in my daughter, investigate it.'   Send word to them and let them investigate my guilt or innocence."

The millionaire agreed to her reasonable proposal and summoning them said: "At a time of festivity, while I was sitting and eating sweet milk rice-porridge from a golden bowl, this girl said that I was eating what was unclean.   Convict her of this fault and expel her from the house."

Visākhā proved her innocence stating—"That is not precisely what I said. When a certain Bhikkhu was standing at the door for alms, my father-in-law was eating sweet milk rice-porridge, ignoring him. Thinking to myself that my father, without performing any good deed in this life, is only consuming the merits of past deeds, I told the Bhikkhu: 'Pass on, Venerable Sir, my father-in-law is eating stale fare.' What fault of mine is there in this?"

She was acquitted of the charge, and the father-in-law himself agreed she was not guilty.

But the spiteful millionaire charged her again for having gone behind the house with male and female attendants in the middle watch of the night.

When she explained that she actually did so in order to attend on a mare in travail, the clansmen remarked that their noble daughter had done an exemplary act which even a slave-girl would not do. She was thus acquitted of the second charge too.

But the revengeful millionaire would not rest until she was found guilty. Next time he found fault with her for no wrong of hers. He said that before her departure from home her father gave her ten admonitions. For instance, he said to her: "The indoor fire is not to be taken out of doors. Is it really possible to live without giving fire even to our neighbours on both sides of us?" questioned the millionaire.

She availed herself of the opportunity to explain all the ten admonitions in detail to his entire satisfaction.

The millionaire was silenced and he had no other charges to make.

Having proved her innocence, self-respecting *Visākhā* now desired to leave the house as she was ordered to do so at first.

The millionaire's attitude towards *Visākhā* was completely changed, and he was compelled to seek pardon from her daughter-in law for what he had uttered through ignorance.

Forbearing *Visākhā*, in accordance with her true Buddhist spirit, granted him pardon on condition that he would give complete freedom to her to carry on her religious activities as she desired. Her father-in law readily agreed to this and granted her full freedom to perform her religious activites.

Now *Visākhā*, lost no time in inviting the Buddha to the house for alms. The Buddha came and had His meal. After the meal was over the Buddha expounded a sermon. The millionaire sat behind a curtain and listened to the sermon. At the end of the discourse he became *Sotāpanna* and acknowledged his boundless gratitude to his daughter-in law for having initiated him into the True Path of Deliverance and emotionally remarked that he would hereafter regard *Visākhā* as his mother.

Later on when she bore a son she called him *Migāra*.

On the following day the Buddha visited her house, and on that occasion her mother-in-law heard the Dhamma and became a *Sotāpanna* (Stream-winner).

By her tact, wisdom, and patience she gradually succeeded in converting her husband's household to a happy Buddhist home.

Daily *Visākhā* used to give alms to the Sangha at her own house. Both in the forenoon and afternoon she used to visit the monastery to minister to the needs of the Sangha and hear sermons from the Buddha. *Suppiyā*, another devout Buddhist lady, usually accompanied her during her visits.

Visākhā was so generous and so serviceable to the Sangha that once she approached the Buddha and asked for the following eight boons:

1. To give robes to the Sangha during the rainy season as long as she lived.

2. To provide alms for the Bhikkhus coming to Sāvatthi.

3. To provide alms for those going out of Sāvatthi.

4. To give food for sick Bhikkhus.

5. To give food for those who attend on the sick.

6. To give medicine for the sick Bhikkhus.

7. To give rice-gruel for Bhikkhus.

8. To give bathing garments for nuns.

The Buddha granted these boons to her.

One day *Visākhā* happened to visit the monastery, decked in her best garment, presented to her by her father as a dowry. But as she thought it was unseemly to see the Buddha, so gaily decked, she made a bundle of it gave it to the slave-girl and went to the Buddha, dressed in another garment given to her by her father-in-law. After the sermon she left the monastery accompanied by the slave-girl who forgot to take the bundle which was placed in her custody. Venerable *Ānanda* saw it and, as instructed by the Buddha, kept it in a safe place to be returned to the owner. *Visākhā*, on hearing that the bundle was inadvertently left by the maid, asked her to bring it back unless Venerable *Ānanda* had touched it. When what had happened was reported to *Visākhā*, she went to the Buddha and expressed her desire to do something beneficial with the money, realized by selling the garment. The Buddha advised her to erect a monastery at the East gate for the use of the Sangha As no one had the means to buy the costly garment, she herself, bought it back and erected a monastery at a great cost and named it *Pubbārāma*. As invited by *Visākhā*, the Buddha and His disciples spent

the Vassāna period in this new spacious monastery.
Great was *Visākhā 's* joy when the Buddha spent
six rainy seasons there.

Books state that the kind *Visākhā*, instead of
chastising the slave-girl for her apparent negli-
gence, transferred to her a share of the merit
acquired by erecting the monastery, because the
slave-girl had given the occasion for this good deed.

On various occasions several discourses were
delivered to *Visākhā* by the Buddha. In one discourse the Buddha spoke on the observance of the
Eight Precepts by laymen on Uposatha Days,[1]
which observance prevails in almost all Buddhist
countries in Asia up to this day.

Dealing with the eight qualities that make
a woman seek birth in happy states, the Buddha
said:

---

1.   Usually the 1st, 8th, 15th, and 23rd of the lunar month
     are regarded as the Uposatha or Holy Days when lay
     followers observe the following Eight Precepts (*aṭṭha-
     sīla*)—namely, abstinence from 1. killing, 2. stealing,
     3. incelibacy, 4. lying, 5. liquor, 6. eating food after
     midday, 7. dancing, singing, music, unseemly shows,
     using garlands, perfumes, unguents, ornaments, and
     8. using high and luxurious seats.

     Though, as a rule, they are sometimes observed on
     Uposatha Days, there is no objection to practising
     them on any convenient day–the object being to control
     deeds, words, and five senses.

"Active, alert to cherish him alway,
Not to that man who brings her every joy
She offers slight, nor will a good wife move
To wrath her husband by some spiteful word;
And she reveres all whom her lord doth honour
For she is wise. Deft, nimble, up betimes,
She minds his wealth amid his folk at work
And sweetly orders all. A wife like this,
Who with her husband's wish and will complies
Is born again where lovely devas dwell."[1]

In another discourse the Buddha referring to the eight qualities in a woman that tend to weal and happiness in this world and in the next spoke as follows:

"Herein, *Visākhā*, a woman is capable at her work, she manages the servants, in her ways she is lovely to her lord, she guards his wealth.

"Herein, *Visākhā*, a woman is accomplished in trustful confidence (*Saddhā*), virtue (*Sīla*), charity (*Cāga*) and wisdom (*Paññā*).[2]

Being a lady of many parts, she played an important role in various activities connected with the Sāsana. At times she was deputed by the Buddha to settle disputes that arose amongst Bhihkkunis. Some Vinaya rules were also laid down for Bhikkhus owing to her intervention.

---

1. *Gradual Sayings*, iv. pp. 178–179.
2. Ibid, iv. pp. 177-178.

Owing to her magnanimity she was regarded as the chief benefactress of the Sāsana and the greatest female supporter of the Buddha.

By her dignified conduct, graceful deportment, refined manners, courteous speech, obedience and reverence to elders, compassion to those who are less fortunate, kind hospitality, and religious zeal, she won the hearts of all who knew her.

Books state that she had the good fortune to be the happy mother of ten fortunate sons and ten fortunate daughters. She died at the ripe age of one hundred and twenty.

JĪVAKA THE FOSTERLING

Jīvaka was the celebrated physician of the Buddha.

Immediately after his birth he was placed in a casket and was cast away by his mother, a courtesan, on a dust heap by the road side.

Prince *Abhaya*, a son of King *Bimbisāra*, who happened to pass that way, saw the helpless infant surrounded by crows, and discovering that he was alive (*Jīvati*), caused him to be given to the care of the nurses.

As he was found alive he was named *Jīvaka*. Being adopted by a prince, he was called *Komāra-bhacca*.

Growing up, he became a skilful physician and surgeon. Books state that he made two successful operations on a millionaire who was suffering from a severe headache.

He used to attend on the Buddha three times a day.

When the Buddha's foot was wounded by a splinter caused by the hurling of a rock by Devadatta, it was Jīvaka who attended on Him and healed Him.[1]

Realizing the manifold advantages of having a monastery close to his residence, he erected one in his mango park. After the consecration ceremony of this monastery, he became a Stream-Winner (*Sotāpanna*).

Jīvaka Sutta,[2] which deals with the question of eating flesh, was delivered by the Buddha to *Jīvaka*.

It was *Jīvaka* who induced King *Ajātasattu* to visit the Buddha after his parricide.

At his request the Buddha enjoined upon His disciples to take physical exercise such as sweeping etc.

1.   See p. 161.
2.   Majjhima Nikāya No. 55.

CHAPTER 11

THE BUDDHA'S ROYAL PATRONS

————

"A treacherous bog it is, this patronage
Of bows and gifts and treats from wealthy folk.
'Tis like a fine dart, bedded in the flesh.
For erring human hard to extricate."
MAHĀKASSAPA THERA GĀTHĀ (1053)

King Bimbisāra

King *Bimbisāra*, who ruled in Magadha with its capital at Rājagaha, was the Buddha's first royal patron. Ascending the throne at the age of fifteen, he reigned for fifty-two years.

When Prince *Siddhattha* renounced the world and was seeking alms in the streets of Rājagaha as a humble ascetic, the King saw him from his palace and was highly impressed by his majestic appearance and dignified deportment. Immediately he sent messengers to ascertain who he was. On learning that he was resting after his meal under the Pandavapabbata, the King, accompanied by his retinue, went up to the royal ascetic and inquired about his birthplace and ancestry. The ascetic *Gotama* replied:

"Just straight, O King, upon the Himalaya, there is, in the district of Kosala of ancient families, a country endowed with wealth and energy. I am sprung from that family which by clan belongs to the Solar dynasty, by birth to the Sākyas. I crave not for pleasures of the senses. Realizing the evil of sensual pleasures and seeing renunciation as safe, I proceeded to seek the Highest, for in that my mind rejoices."[1]

Thereupon the King invited him to visit his kingdom after his Enlightenment.

The Buddha meets King Bimbisāra

In accordance with the promise the Buddha made to King *Bimbisāra* before His Enlightenment, He, with His large retinue of Arahant disciples, went from Gayā to Rājagaha, the capital of the district of Magadha. Here He stayed at the Suppatittha Shrine in a Palm Grove.

This happy news of the Buddha's arrival in the kingdom and His high reputation as an unparalleled religious teacher soon spread in the city. The King, hearing of His arrival, came with a large number of his subjects to welcome the Buddha. He approached the Buddha, respectfully saluted Him and sat at a side. Of his subjects some respectfully saluted Him, some looked towards him with expression of friendly greetings, some saluted Him with clasped hands, some introduced themselves, while others in perfect silence took their seats. As both the Buddha *Gotama* and Venerable *Kassapa* were held in high esteem by the multitude they were not certain whether the Buddha was leading the Holy Life under Venerable *Kassapa*

---

1. Sutta Nipāta, Pabbajjā, Sutta.

or the latter under the former. The Buddha read their thoughts and questioned Venerable *Kassapa* as to why he had given up his fire-sacrifice. Understanding the motive of the Buddha's question, he explained that he abandoned fire-sacrifice because he preferred the passionless and peaceful state of Nibbāna to worthless sensual pleasures. After this he fell at the feet of the Buddha and acknowledging his superiority said: "My teacher, Lord, is the Exalted One: I am the disciple. My teacher, Lord, is the Exalted One: I am the disciple."

The devout people were delighted to hear of the conversion.[1] The Buddha thereupon preached the Mahā Nārada Kassapa Jātaka[2] to show how in a previous birth when He was born as *Nārada*, still subject to passion, He converted *Kassapa* in a similar way.

Hearing the Dhamma expounded by the Buddha, the "Eye of Truth[3]" arose in them all. King *Bimbisāra* attained Sotāpatti, and seeking refuge in the Buddha, the Dhamma, and the Sangha, invited the Buddha and His disciples to his palace for the meal on the following day. After the meal the King wished to know where the Buddha

---

1.   See chapter 7.
2.   No. 544.
3.   See p. 111, note 2.

would reside.   The Buddha replied that a secluded place, neither too far nor too close to the city, accessible to those who desire to visit Him, pleasant, not crowded during the day, not too noisy at night, with as few sounds as possible, airy and fit for the privacy of men, would be suitable.

The King thought that his Bamboo Grove would meet all such requirements.   Therefore in return for the transcendental gift the Buddha had bestowed upon him, he gifted for the use of the Buddha and the Sangha the park with this ideally secluded bamboo grove, also known as 'The Sanctuary of the Squirrels.' It would appear that this park had no building for the use of Bhikkhus but was filled with many shady trees and secluded spots.   However, this was the first gift of a place of residence for the Buddha and His disciples. The Buddha spent three successive rainy seasons and three other rainy seasons in this quiet Veluvanārāma.[1]

After his conversion the King led the life of an exemplary monarch observing Uposatha regularly on six days of the month.

1.   The Pāli Ārāma means a mere park. There were no buildings when the Buddha accepted this generous gift. At present the term Ārāma is used in the sense of a monastery with necessary buildings for monks.

Kosala Devi, daughter of King *Mahā Kosala*, and sister of King *Pasenadi Kosala*, was his chief loyal queen. *Ajātasattu* was her son. *Khemā* who, through the ingenuity of the King, became a follower of the Buddha and who later rose to the position of the first female disciple of the Order of Nuns, was another queen.

Though he was a pious monarch, yet, due to his past evil Kamma, he had a very sad and pathetic end.

Prince *Ajātasattu*, successor to the throne, instigated by wicked *Devadatta* Thera, attempted to kill him and usurp the throne. The unfortunate prince was caught red-handed, and the compassionate father, instead of punishing him for his brutal act, rewarded him with the coveted Crown.

The ungrateful son showed his gratitude to his father by casting him into prison in order to starve him to death. His mother alone had free access to the King daily. The loyal queen carried food concealed in her waist-pouch. To this the prince objected. Then she carried food concealed in her hair-knot. The prince resented this too. Later she bathed herself in scented water and besmeared her body with a mixture of honey, butter, ghee, and molasses. The King licked her body and sustained himself. The over-vigilant prince detected this and ordered his mother not to visit his father.

King *Bimbisāra* was without any means of sustenance, but he paced up and down enjoying spiritual happiness as he was a Sotāpanna. Ultimately the wicked son decided to put an end to the life of his noble father. Ruthlessly he ordered his barber to cut open his soles and put salt and oil thereon and make him walk on burning charcoal.

The King, who saw the barber approaching, thought that the son, realizing his folly, was sending the barber to shave his grown beard and hair and release him from prison. Contrary to his expectations, he had to meet an untimely sad end. The barber mercilessly executed the inhuman orders of the barbarous prince. The good King died in great agony. On that very day a son was born unto *Ajātasattu*. Letters conveying the news of birth and death reached the palace at the same time.

The letter conveying the happy news was first read. Lo, the love he cherished towards his first-born son was indescribable! His body was thrilled with joy and the paternal love penetrated upto the very marrow of his bones.

Immediately he rushed to his beloved mother and questioned: "Mother dear, did my father love me when I was a child?"

"What say you, son! When you were conceived in my womb, I developed a craving to sip some blood from the right hand of your father. This I dare not say. Consequently I grew pale and thin. I was finally persuaded to disclose my inhuman desire. Joyfully your father fulfilled my wish, and I drank that abhorrent potion. The soothsayers predicted that you would be an enemy of your father. Accordingly you were named *Ajātasattu* (*unborn enemy*). I attempted to effect a miscarriage, but your father prevented it. After you were born, again I wanted to kill you. Again your father interfered. On one occasion you were suffering from a boil in your finger, and nobody was able to lull you into sleep. But your father, who was administering justice in his royal court, took you into his lap and caressing you sucked the boil. Lo, inside the mouth it burst open. O, my dear son, that pus and blood! Yes, your affectionate father swallowed it out of love for you."

Instantly he cried, "Run and release, release my beloved father quickly!"

His father had closed his eyes for ever.

The other letter was then placed in his hand.

Ajātasattu shed hot tears. He realized what paternal love was only after he became a father himself.

King *Bimbisāra* died and was immediately after born as a *Deva* named *Janavasabha* in the Cātummahārājika Heaven.

Later, *Ajātasattu*, met the Buddha and became one of His distinguished lay followers and took a leading part in the holding of the first Convocation.

King Pasenadi Kosala

King *Pasenadi Kosala*, the son of King *Mahā Kosala*, who reigned in the kingdom of Kosala with its capital at Sāvatthi, was another royal patron of the Buddha. He was a contemporary of the Buddha, and owing to his proficiency in various arts, he had the good fortune to be made King by his father while he was alive.

His conversion must probably have taken place during the very early part of the Buddha's ministry. In the Saṁyutta Nikāya it is stated that once he approached the Buddha and questioning Him about His perfect Enlightenment referred to Him as being young in years and young in ordination.[1]

The Buddha replied—"There are four objects, O Mahārāja, that should not be disregarded or despised. They are a Khattiya (*a warrior prince*), a snake, fire, and a Bhikkhu (*mendicant monk*).[2]

---

1. Samyutta Nikāya. 1.64: *Kindred Sayings*, 1, p. 94.
2. An enraged warrior prince, though young, may ruthlessly cause harm to others. The bite of even a small snake may prove fatal. A little fire may produce a conflagration. Even a young monk may be a Saint or a Dhamma scholar.

Then He delivered an interesting sermon on this subject to the King. At the close of the sermon the King expressed his great pleasure and instantly became a follower of the Buddha. Since then till his death he was deeply attached to the Buddha. It is said that on one occasion the King prostrated himself before the Buddha and stroked His feet covering them with kisses.[1]

His chief queen, *Mallikā* a very devout and wise lady, well versed in the Dhamma, was greatly responsible for his religious enthusiasm. Like a true friend, she had to act as his religious guide on several occasions.

One day the King dreamt sixteen unusual dreams and was greatly perturbed in mind, not knowing their true significance. His brahmin advisers interpreted them to be dreams portending evil and instructed him to make an elaborate animal sacrifice to ward off the dangers resulting therefrom. As advised he made all necessary arrangements for this inhuman sacrifice which would have resulted in the loss of thousands of helpless creatures. Queen *Mallikā*, hearing of this barbarous act about to be perpetrated, persuaded the King to get the dreams interpreted by the Buddha whose understanding infinitely surpassed that of those worldly brahmins. The King approached the Buddha and mentioned the object of

1. Majjhima Nikāya ii, No. 120

his visit. Relating the sixteen dreams[1] he wished
to know their significance, and the Buddha
explained their significance fully to him.

Unlike King *Bimbisāra* King *Kosala* had the
good fortune to hear several edifying and instructive discourses from the Buddha. In the Samyutta
Nikāya there appears a special section called the
Kosala Samyutta[2] in which are recorded most of
the discourses and talks given by the Buddha to
the King.

Once while the King was seated in the company
of the Buddha, he saw some ascetics with hairy
bodies and long nails passing by, and rising from
his seat respectfully saluted them calling out his
name to them: "I am the King, your reverences,
the *Kosala*, *Pasenadi*," When they had gone he
came back to the Buddha and wished to know
whether they were Arahants or those who were
striving for Arahantship. The Buddha explained
that it was difficult for ordinary laymen enjoying
material pleasures to judge whether others are
Arahants or not and made the following interesting
observations:

"It is by association (*samvāsena*) that one's
conduct (*sīla*) is to be understood, and that, too,

1, See Mahā Supina Jātaka. Jātaka Translation—Book I,
   pp. 188-192 No. 77.

2. Samyutta Nikāya 1, 68, *Kindred Sayings, i*, p. 94.

after a long time and not in a short time, by one
who is watchful and not by a heedless person, by
an intelligent person and not by an unintelligent
one. It is by converse (*saṁvohārena*) that one's
purity (*soceyyaṁ*) is to be understood. It is in
time of trouble that one's fortitude is to be understood. It is by discussion that one's wisdom is to
be understood, and that, too, after a long time
and not in a short time, by one who is watchful
and not by a heedless person, by an intelligent
person and not by an unintelligent one."

Summing up the above, the Buddha uttered
the following verses:

"Not by his outward guise is man well known.
In fleeting glance let none place confidence.
In garb of decent well-conducted folk
The unrestrained live in the world at large.
As a clay earring made to counterfeit.
Or bronze half penny coated over with gold,
Some fare at large hidden beneath disguise,
Without, comely and fair; within, impure."[1]

King *Kosala*, as ruler of a great kingdom,
could not possibly have avoided warfare, especially with Kings of neighbouring countries.
Once he was compelled to fight with his own nephew, King *Ajātasattu*, and was defeated. Hearing
it, the Buddha remarked:

---

1. *Kindred Sayings*, pt. 1, pp. 104-106.

"Victory breeds hatred. The defeated live in pain. Happily the peaceful live, giving up victory and defeat.[1]"

On another occasion King *Kosala* was victorious and he confiscated the whole army of King *Ajātasattu*, saving only him. When the Buddha heard about this new victory, He uttered the following verse, the truth of which applies with equal force to this modern war-weary world as well:

"A man may spoil another, just so far
As it may serve his ends, but when he's spoiled
By others he, despoiled, spoils yet again.
So long as evil's fruit is not matured,
The fool doth fancy 'now's the hour, the chance!'
But when the deed bears fruit, he fareth ill.
The slayer gets a slayer in his turn;
The conqueror gets one who conquers him;
Th'abuser wins abuse, th'annoyer, fret.
Thus by the evolution of the deed,
A man who spoils is spoiled in his turn.[2]

What the Buddha has said to King *Kosala* about women is equally interesting and extremely encouraging to womankind. Once while the King

---

1. *Kindred Sayings*, part 1, pp. 109, 110. Dhammapada v. 201.
2. Ibid p. 110.

was engaged in a pious conversation with the
Buddha, a messenger came and whispered into his
ear that Queen *Mallikā* had given birth to a daughter. The King was not pleased at this unwelcome
news. In ancient India, as it is to a great extent
today, a daughter is not considered a happy
addition to a family for several selfish reasons as,
for instance, the problem of providing a dowry:
The Buddha, unlike any other religious teacher,
paid a glowing tribute to women and mentioned
four chief characteristics that adorn a woman in
the following words:

"*Some women are indeed better* (*than men*).
Bring her up, O Lord of men.
*There are women who are wise, virtuous, who
regard mother-in-law as a goddess, and who are
chaste.*
*To such a noble wife may be born a valiant son,
a lord of realms, who would rule a kingdom*".[1]

Some women are even better than men. "*Itthi
hi pi ekacciyā seyyā*" were the actual words used
by the Buddha. No religious teacher has made
such a bold and noble utterance especially in India,
where women were not held in high esteem.

Deeply grieved over the death of his old grandmother, aged one hundred and twenty years,

1. *Kindred Sayings,* part 1, p. 111.
   Samyutta Nikāya, part I, p.86.

King *Kosala* approached the Buddha and said
that he would have given everything within his
means to save his grandmother who had been
as a mother to him. The Buddha consoled him,
saying: "All beings are mortal; they end with
death, they have death in prospect. All the ves-
sels wrought by the potter, whether they are
baked or unbaked, are breakable; they finish
broken, they have breakage in prospect."[1]

The King was so desirous of hearing the Dhamma
that even if affairs of state demanded his presence in other parts of the kingdom, he would
avail himself of every possible opportunity to
visit the Buddha and engage in a pious conversation. The Dhammacetiya[2] and Kannakatthala[3]
Suttas were preached on such occasions.

King *Kosala's* chief consort, the daughter of a
garland-maker, predeceased him. A sister of
King *Bimbisāra* was one of his wives. One of his
sisters was married to King *Bimbisāra* and *Ajātasattu* was her son.

King *Kosala* had a son named *Viḍūḍabha* who
revolted against him in his old age. This son's
mother was the daughter of Mahānāma the *Sakya*,
who was related to the Buddha, and his grandmother was a slave-girl. This fact the King did

---

1. See *Kindred Sayings*, part I, p. 122.
2. Majjhima Nikāya No. 89.
3. Ibid. No. 90.

not know when he took her as one of his consorts. Hearing a derogatory remark made by Sākyas about his ignoble lineage, *Viḍūḍabha* took vengeance by attempting to destroy the Sākya race. Unfortunately it was due to *Viḍūḍabha* that the King had to die a pathetic death in a hall outside the city with only a servant as his companion. King *Kosala* predeceased the Buddha.

CHAPTER 12

THE BUDDHA'S MINISTRY

"Freed am I from all bonds, whether divine or human.
"You, too, O Bhikkhus, are freed from all bonds."

MAHĀVAGGA

The Buddha's beneficent and successful ministry lasted forty-five years. From His 35th year, the year of His Enlightenment, till His death in His 80th year, He served humanity both by example and by precept. Throughout the year He wandered from place to place, at times alone, sometimes accompanied by His disciples, expounding the Dhamma to the people and liberating them from the bonds of Saṁsāra. During the rainy season (*vassāna*) from July to November, owing to incessant rains, He lived in retirement. as was customary with all ascetics in India in His time.

In ancient times, as today, three regular seasons prevailed in India, namely, *vassāna*, (rainy) *hemanta* (winter) and *gimhāna* (hot). The *vassāna* or rainy season starts in *Āsālha* and extends up to *Assayuga*, that is, approximately from the middle of July to the middle of November.

During the *vassāna* period, due to torrential rains, rivers and streams usually get flooded, roads get inundated, communications get interrupted and people as a rule are confined to their homes and villages and live on what provisions they have collected during the previous seasons. During this time the ascetics find it difficult to engage in their preaching tours, wandering from place to place. An infinite variety of vegetable and animal life also appears to such an extent that people could not move about without unconsciously destroying them. Accordingly all ascetics including the disciples of the Buddha, used to suspend their itinerant activities and live in retirement in solitary places. As a rule the Buddha and His disciples were invited to spend their rainy seasons either in a monastery or in a secluded park. Sometimes, however, they used to retire to forests. During these rainy seasons people flocked to the Buddha to hear the Dhamma and thus availed themselves of His presence in their vicinity to their best advantage.

The First Twenty Years

1st Year at Benares.

After expounding the *Dhammacakka Sutta* to His first five disciples on the Āsālha full moon day, He spent the first rainy season in the Deer Park at Isipatana, near Benares. Here there was no special building where he could reside. Yasa's conversion took place during this Retreat.

2nd, 3rd, 4th Years at Rājagaha.

Rājagaha was the capital of the Kingdom of Magadha where ruled King *Bimbisāra*. When the Buddha visited the King, in accordance with a promise made by Him before His Enlightenment, he offered his Bamboo Grove (*Veluvana*) to the Buddha and His disciples. This was an ideal solitary place for monks as it was neither too far nor too near to the city. Three rainy seasons were spent by the Buddha in this quiet grove.

5th Year at Vesāli.

During this year while He was residing in the Pinnacle Hall at Mahāvana near Vesāli, He heard of the impending death of King *Suddhodana* and, repairing to his death chamber, preached the Dhamma to him. Immediately the King attained Arahantship. For seven days thereafter he experienced the bliss of Emancipation and passed away.

It was in this year that the Bhikkhunī Order was founded at the request of Mahā *Pajāpati Gotamī*.

After the cremation of the King, when the Buddha was temporarily residing at Nigrodhārāma, *Mahā Pajāpati Gotamī* approached the Buddha and begged permission for women to enter

the Order.   But the Buddha refused and returned
to the Pinnacle Hall at Rājagaha. *Mahā Prajā-
pati Gotamī* was so intent on renouncing the world
that she, accompanied by many Sākya and Koliya
ladies, walked all the way from Kapilavatthu to
Rājagaha and, through the intervention of Venerable *Ānanda*, succeeded in entering the Order.[1]

6th Year at Mankula Hill in Kosambi near
Allahabad.

Just as He performed the "Twin Wonder"
(*Yamaka Pāṭihāriya*)[2] to overcome the pride of
His relatives at Kapilavatthu, even so did He
perform it for the second time at Mankula Hill to
convert His alien followers.

7th Year at Tāvatiṁsa Heaven.

A few days after the birth of Prince *Siddhattha*
Queen *Mahā Māyā* died and was born as a Deva
(*god*) in the Tusita Heaven,   In this seventh year,
during the three rainy months, the Buddha preached the Abhidhamma[3] to the Devas of the Tāvatiṁsa
Heaven where the mother-Deva   repaired to
hear him.   Daily He came to earth and gave a
summary of His sermon to the Venerable *Sāriputta* who in turn expounded the same doctrine in

---

1. See chapter 9.
2. See p. 120.
3. Abhidhamma is the Higher Doctrine which deals with
    Buddhist Philosophy. See chapter 15.

detail to his disciples. What is embodied in the present Abhidhamma Pitaka is supposed to be this detailed exposition of the Dhamma by him.

It is stated that, on hearing these discourses, the Deva who was His mother attained the first stage of Sainthood.

8th Year at Bhesakalā Forest, near Su*m*sumāra Rock, in the Bhagga District.

9th Year at Kosambi.

It was in this year that *Māgandiyā* harboured a grudge against the Buddha and sought an opportunity to dishonour him.

Māgandiyā was a beautiful maiden. Her parents would not give her in marriage as the prospective suitors, in their opinion, were not worthy of their daughter. One day as the Buddha was surveying the world, He perceived the spiritual development of the parents. Out of compassion for them He visited the place where the father of the girl was tending the sacred fire. The brahmin, fascinated by His physical beauty, thought that He was the best person to whom he could give his daughter in marriage and requesting Him to stay there until his arrival, hurried home to bring his daughter. The Buddha in the meantime stamped His footprint on that spot and moved to a different place. The brahmin and his wife, accompanied by their daughter who was dressed in her

best garments, came to that spot and observed the
footprint. The wife who was conversant with
signs said that it was not the footprint of an ordinary man but of a pure person who had eradicated
all passions. The Brahmin ridiculed the idea, and,
noticing the Buddha at a distance offered his
daughter unto Him. The Buddha describing how
He overcame His passions said:

"*Having seen Taṇhā, Aratī and Ragā*,[1]
I had no pleasure for the pleasures of love.
What is this body, filled with urine and dung?
I should not be willing to touch it, even with
my foot".[2]

Hearing His Dhamma, the brahmin and his
wife attained Anāgāmi, the third stage of Sainthood. But proud *Māgandiyā* felt insulted and
she thought to herself—"If this man has no need
of me, it is perfectly proper for him to say so, but
he declares me to be full of urine and dung. Very
well, by virtue of birth, lineage, social position,
wealth, and the charm of youth that I possess I shall
obtain a husband who is my equal, and then I
shall know what ought to be done to the monk
Gotama."

Enraged by the words of the Buddha, she con-
cieved a hatred towards Him. Later she was

---

1. The three daughters of Māra
2. *Buddhist Legends*, part i, p. 274.

given as a consort to the King of Udena. Taking
advantage of her position as one of the Royal
consorts, she bribed people and instigated them to
revile and drive the Buddha out of the city. When
the Buddha entered the city, they shouted at him,
saying: "You are a thief, a simpleton, a fool,
a camel, an ox, an ass, a denizen of hell, a beast.
You have no hope of salvation. A state of punishment is all that you can look forward to."

Venerable *Ānanda*, unable to hear this filthy
abuse, approached the Buddha and said—"Lord,
these citizens are reviling and abusing us. Let us
go elsewhere."

"Where shall we go, *Ānanda?*" asked the
Buddha.

"To some other city, Lord," said *Ānanda*.

"If men revile us there, where shall we go then?"
inquired the Buddha.

"To still another city, Lord," said *Ānanda*.

"*Ānanda*, one should not speak thus. Where
a difficulty arises, right there should it be settled.
Only under those circumstances is it permissible
to go elsewhere. But who are reviling you,
Ānanda?" questioned the Buddha.

"Lord, everyone is reviling us, slaves and all,"
replied *Ānanda*.

Admonishing Venerable *Ānanda* to practise patience, the Buddha said:

i. "As an elephant in the battle-field withstands the arrows shot from a bow, even so will I endure abuse. Verily, most people are undisciplined."

ii. "They lead the trained horses or elephants to an assembly. The King mounts the trained animal. The best among men are the disciplined who endure abuse."

iii. "Excellent are trained mules, so are thorough-bred horses of Sindh and noble tusked elephants; but the man who is disciplined surpasses them all."[1]

Again He addressed Venerable *Ānanda* and said—"Be not disturbed. These men will revile you only for seven days, and, on the eighth day they will become silent. A difficulty encountered by the Buddhas lasts no longer than seven days."[2]

10th Year at Pārileyyaka Forest.

While the Buddha was residing at Kosambi, a dispute arose between two parties of Bhikkhus— one versed in the Dhamma, the other in the Vinaya —with respect to the transgression of a minor rule of etiquette in the lavatory. Their respective supporters also were divided into two sections.

1. Dhammapada vv. 320, 321, 322.
2. See *Buddhist Legends,* vol. 1, p. 176.

Even the Buddha could not settle the differences of these quarrelsome monks. They were adamant and would not listen to His advice. The Buddha thought —"Under present conditions the jostling crowd in which I live makes my life one of discomfort. Moreover these monks pay no attention to what I say. Suppose I were to retire from the haunts of men and live a life of solitude." In pursuance of this thought, without even informing the Sangha, alone He retired to the Pārileyyaka Forest and spent the rainy season at the foot of a beautiful Sal-tree.

It was on this occasion, according to the story, that an elephant and a monkey ministered to His needs.[1]

11th Year at *Ekanālā*, brahmin village.

The following *Kasibhāradvāja Sutta*[2] was delivered here:

On one occasion the Buddha was residing at Ekanālā in Dakkhinagiri, the brahmin village in Magadha. At that time about five-hundred ploughs belonging to *Kasibhāradvāja* brahmin were harnessed for the sowing. Thereupon the Exalted One, in the forenoon, dressed Himself and taking bowl and robe went to the working place of the brahmin. At that time the distribution of food by the brahmin was taking place. The Buddha

1. Dhammapadaṭṭhakathā, Kosambaka Vatthu.
2. Sutta Nipāta, p. 12,

went to the place where food was being distributed and stood aside. The brahmin *Kasibhāradvāja* saw the Buddha waiting for alms. Seeing Him, he spoke thus—"I, O ascetic, plough and sow; and having ploughed and sown, I eat. You also, O ascetic, should plough and sow; and having ploughed and sown, you should eat."

"I, too, O brahmin, plough and sow; having ploughed and sown, I eat." said the Buddha.

"But we see not the Venerable *Gotama's* yoke, or plough, or ploughshare, or goad, or oxen, albeit the Venerable *Gotama* says—'I too plough and sow; and having ploughed and sown, I eat," remarked the brahmin.

Then the brahmin *Bhāradvāja* addressed the Exalted One thus:

"A farmer you claim to be, but we see none of your tillage. Being questioned about ploughing, please answer us so that we may know your ploughing."

The Buddha answered:

"Confidence (*saddhā*) is the seed, discipline (*tapo*) is the rain, wisdom (*paññā*) my yoke and plough, modesty (*hiri*) the pole of my plough, mind (*mano*) the rein, and mindfulness (*sati*) my ploughshare and goad.

"I am controlled in body, controlled in speech, temperate in food. With truthfulness I cut away weeds. Absorption in the Highest (*Arahantship*) is the release of the oxen.

"Perseverance (*viriya*) is my beast of burden that carries me towards the bond-free state (*Nibbāna*) Without turning it goes, and having gone it does not grieve.

"Thus is the tilling done: it bears the fruit of Deathlessness. Having done this tilling, one is freed from all sorrow."

Thereupon the brahmin *Kasibhāradvāja*, filling a large bronze bowl with milk-rice, offered it to the Exalted One, saying "May the Venerable *Gotama* eat the milk-rice! The Venerable *Gotama* is a farmer, since the Venerable *Gotama* tills a crop that bears the fruit of Deathlessness."

The Exalted One, however, refused to accept this saying:

"What is obtained by reciting verses is not fit to be eaten by me. This, O brahmin, is not the rule of seers. The Enlightened reject such food. While this principle lasts, this is the livelihood.

"Serve the unique, cankerless, great sage of holy calm with other kind of food and drink, for He is like a field to him that desires to sow good deeds."

12th Year at Verañjā.

A brahmin of Verañjā, hearing that the Buddha was residing at Verañjā near Naleru's Nimba tree with a large company of His disciples, approached Him and raised several questions with regard to His conduct. The brahmin was so pleased with His answers that he became a follower of the Buddha and invited Him and His disciples to spend the rainy season at Verañjā. The Buddha signified His assent as usual by His silence.

Unfortunately at this particular time there was a famine at Verañjā and the Buddha and His disciples were compelled to live on food intended for horses. A horse-dealer very kindly provided them with coarse food available, and the Buddha partook of such food with perfect equanimity.

One day, during this period, Venerable *Sāriputta*, arising from his solitary meditation, approached the Buddha and respectfully questioned Him thus: "Which Buddha's Dispensation endured long and which did not?"

The Buddha replied that the Dispensations of the Buddhas *Vipassi*, *Sikhī* and *Vessabhū* did not endure long, while the Dispensations of the Buddhas *Kakusandha*, *Konāgamana* and *Kassapa* endured long.[1]

The Buddha attributed this to the fact that some Buddhas did make no great effort in preach-

1.   Vinaya Piṭaka, Suttavibhanga (*Pārājikā*) pp. 1-11.
     Miss I. B. Horner, *Book of the Discipline*, Part 1, pp.1–23

ing the Dhamma in detail and promulgated no
rules and regulations for the discipline of the
disciples, while other Buddhas did so.

Thereupon Venerable *Sāriputta* respectfully implored the Buddha to promulgate the Fundamental Precepts (*Pātimokkha*) for the future discipline
of the Sangha so that the Holy Life may endure
long.

"Be patient, *Sāriputta,* be patient," said the
Buddha and added:

"The Tathāgata alone is aware of the time for
it. Until certain defiling conditions arise in the
Sangha the Tathāgata does not promulgate Means
of Discipline for the disciples and does not lay
down the Fundamental Precepts (*Pātimokkha*).
When such defiling conditions arise in the Sangha,
then only the Tathāgata promulgates Means of
Discipline and lays down the Fundamental Precepts for the disciples in order to eradicate such
defilements.

"When, *Sāriputta*, the Sangha attains long
standing (*rattaññumahattaṁ*), full development
(*vepullamahattaṁ*), great increase in gains (*lābhag-
gamahattaṁ*) and greatness in erudition (*bahus-
sutamahattaṁ*), defiling conditions arise in the
Sangha. Then does the Tathāgata promulgate
Means of Discipline and the Fundamental Precepts to prevent such defilements.

"*Sāriputta*, the Order of disciples is free from troubles, devoid of evil tendencies, free from stain, pure, and well established in virtue. The last of my five-hundred disciples is a Sotāpanna (*Stream-Winner*) not liable to fall, steadfast and destined for enlightenment."[1]

(The rainy season at Verañjā forms the subject of the Introduction to the *Pārājikā Book* of the Vinaya Piṭaka).

At the end of this rainy season the Buddha went on a preaching tour to Soreyya, Saṁkassa, Kannakujja, Payāga, and then, crossing the river, stayed some time in Benares and returned thence to Vesāli to reside at the Pinnacle Hall in Mahāvana.

13th Year was spent at Cāliya Rock.

14th Year at Jetavana Monastery, Sāvatthi.

The Venerable *Rāhula* received his Higher Ordination at this time on the completion of his twentieth year.

15th Year at Kapilavatthu.

The pathetic death of King *Suppabuddha*, who was angry with the Buddha for leaving his daughter, Princess *Yasodharā*, occurred in this year.

It may be mentioned that the Buddha spent only one rainy season in his birthplace.

---

1. The Buddha was referring to Venerable Ānanda.

16th Year at the city of Ālavī.

[1]The conversion of *Ālavaka* the demon, who feasted on human flesh, took place in this year.

Ālavaka, a ferocious demon, was enraged to see the Buddha in his mansion. He came up to Him and asked Him to depart. "Very well, friend," said the Buddha and went out. "Come in," said he. The Buddha came in. For the second and third time he made the same request and the Buddha obeyed. But when he commanded Him for the fourth time, the Buddha refused and asked him to do what he could.

"Well, I will ask you a question," said *Ālavaka*, "If you will not answer, I will scatter your thoughts, or rive your heart, or take you by your feet and fling you across the Ganges."

"Nay, friend," replied the Buddha, "I see not in this world inclusive of gods, brahmas, ascetics, and brahmins, amongst the multitude of gods and men, any who could scatter my thoughts, or rive my heart, or take me by my feet and fling me across the Ganges. However, friend, ask what you wish."

Ālavaka then asked the following questions

*"Herein, which is man's best possession?
Which well practised yields happiness?*

1. Sutta Nipāta, Ālavaka Sutta, p. 31, Chalmers, *Teachings of the Buddha,* p. 45.

Which indeed is the sweetest of tastes?
How lived, do they call the best life?"

To these questions the Buddha answered thus:

"Herein confidence is man's best possession.
Dhamma well practised yields happiness.
Truth indeed is the sweetest of tastes.
Life lived with understanding is best, they say."

Ālavaka next asked the Buddha:

"How does one cross the flood?
How does one cross the sea?
How does one overcome sorrow?
How is one purified?"

The Exalted One replied:

"By confidence one crosses the flood, by heedful-
ness the sea.
By effort one overcomes sorrow, by wisdom is
one purified."

Ālavaka then inquired:

"How is wisdom gained? How are riches found?
How is renown gained? How are friends bound?
Passing from this world to the next how does one
not grieve?"[1]

In answer the Buddha said:

"The heedful, intelligent person of confidence
gains wisdom by hearing the Dhamma of the Pure
Ones that leads to Nibbāna. He who does what is
proper, persevering and strenuous, gains wealth.

---

1. See *Kindred Sayings*, part 1, pp. 276-277.

By truth one attains to fame. Generosity binds friends. That faithful householder who possesses these four virtues—truthfulness, good morals, courage and liberality—grieves not after passing away."

"Well, ask many other ascetics and brahmins whether there is found anything greater than truthfulness, self-control, generosity, and patience."

Understanding well the meaning of the Buddha's words, *Ālavaka* said:

"How could I now ask diverse ascetics and brahmins? Today I know what is the secret of my future welfare.

"For my own good did the Buddha come to Ālavī. Today I know where gifts bestowed yield fruit in abundance. From village to village, from town to town will I wander honouring the Fully Enlightened One and the perfection of the sublime Dhamma."

17th Year was spent at Rajagaha.

18th Year was spent at Cāliya Rock.

19th and 20th years were spent at Rajagaha.

Buddha and Angulimāla

It was in the 20th year that the Buddha converted the notorious murderer *Angulimāla.*[1] Ahimsaka (*Innocent*) was his original name. His,

---

1. *Psalms of the Brethren,* pp. 318-325.
    See Angulimāla Sutta, No. 86, Majjhima Nikāya vol 2, p. 97.

father was chaplain to the King of *Kosala*. He received his education at Taxila, the famous educational centre in the olden days, and became the most illustrious and favourite pupil of his renowned teacher. Unfortunately his colleagues grew jealous of him, concocted a false story, and succeeded in poisoning the teacher's mind against him. The enraged teacher, without any investigation, contrived to put an end to his life by ordering him to fetch a thousand human right-hand fingers as teacher's honorarium. In obedience to the teacher, though with great reluctance, he repaired to the Jalini forest, in Kosala, and started killing people to collect fingers for the necessary offering. The fingers thus collected were hung on a tree, but as they were destroyed by crows and vultures he later wore a garland of those fingers to ascertain the exact number. Hence he was known by the name *Aṅgulimāla* (*Finger-wreathed*). When he had collected 999 fingers, so the books state, the Buddha appeared on the scene. Overjoyed at the sight, because he thought that he could complete the required number by killing the great ascetic, he stalked the Buddha drawing his sword. The Buddha by His psychic powers created obstacles on the way so that *Aṅgulimāla* would not be able to get near Him although He walked at His usual pace. *Aṅgulimāla* ran as fast as he could but he could not overtake the Buddha. Panting and sweating, he stopped and cried: "Stop, ascetic." The Buddha calmly said: "Though I walk, yet have I stopped. You too, *Añgulimāla* stop." The bandit thought—'These ascetics speak the truth, yet He says He has stopped, whereas it is I who have stopped. What does He mean?'

Standing, he questioned Him:

"Thou who art walking, friar, dost say: 'Lo I have stopped!'

And me thou tellest, who have stopped, I have not stopped!

I ask thee, friar, what is the meaning of thy words?

How sayest thou that thou hast stopped but I have not?"

The Buddha sweetly replied:

"Yea, I have stopped, *Añgulimāla*, evermore,

Towards all living things renouncing violence;

Thou holdest not thy hand against thy fellow-men,

Therefore 'tis I have stopped, but thou still goest on."[1]

Añgulimāla's good Kamma rushed up to the surface. He thought that the great ascetic was none other but the Buddha *Gotama* who out of compassion had come to help him.

Straightway he threw away his armour and sword and became a convert. Later, as requested by him he was admitted into the Noble Order by

1. *Psalms of the Brethren*, pp. 320, 321.

the Buddha with the mere utterance—'Come, O Bhikkhu!' (*Ehi Bhikkhu*).

News spread that *Angulimāla* had become a Bhikkhu. The King of *Kosala*, in particular, was greatly relieved to hear of his conversion because he was a veritable source of danger to his subjects.

But Venerable *Angulimāla* had no peace of mind, because even in his solitary meditation he used to recall memories of his past and the pathetic cries of his unfortunate victims. As a result of his evil Kamma, while seeking alms in the streets he would become a target for stray stones and sticks and he would return to the monastery 'with broken head and flowing blood, cut and crushed' to be reminded by the Buddha that he was merely reaping the effects of his own Kamma.

One day as he went on his round for alms he saw a woman in travail. Moved by compassion, he reported this pathetic woman's suffering to the Buddha. He then advised him to pronounce the following words of truth, which later came to be known as the *Angulimāla Paritta*.

"Sister, since my birth in the Arya clan (i.e. since his ordination) I know not that I consciously destroyed the life of any living being. By this truth may you be whole, and may your child be whole."

---

1. *Yato' ham bhagini ariyāya jātiyā jāto n'ābhijānāmi sañcicca pānna jivitā voropetā. Tena saccena sotthi te hotu, sotthi gabbhassā'ti.*

He studied this Paritta[1] and, going to the presence of the suffering sister, sat on a seat separated from her by a screen, and uttered these words. Instantly she was delivered of the child with ease. The efficacy of this Paritta persists to this day.

In due course Venerable *Aṅgulimāla* attained Arahantship.

Referring to his memorable conversion by the Buddha, he says:

"Some creatures are subdued by force,
Some by the hook, and some by whips,
But I by such a One was tamed,
Who needed neither staff nor sword."[2]

The Buddha spent the remaining twenty-five years of His life mostly in Sāvatthi at the Jetavana Monastery built by *Anāthapindika*, the millionaire, and partly at Pubbārāma, built by *Visākhā*, the chief benefactress.

---

1. Protective Discourse.
2. *Psalms of the Brethren*, p. 328.

CHAPTER 13

THE BUDDHA'S DAILY ROUTINE

"The Lord is awakened. He teaches the Dhamma for awakening."

MAJJHIMA NIKĀYA

The Buddha can be considered the most ener-getic and the most active of all religious teachers that ever lived on earth. The whole day He was occupied with His religious activities except when He was attending to His physical needs. He was methodical and systematic in the performance of His daily duties. His inner life was one of medita-tion and was concerned with the experiencing of Nibbānic Bliss, while His outer life was one of selfless service for the moral upliftment of the world. Himself enlightened, He endeavoured His best to enlighten others and liberate them from the ills of life.

His day was divided into five parts, namely, (i) The Forenoon Session, (ii) The Afternoon Session, (iii) The First Watch, (iv) The Middle Watch and (v) The Last Watch.

The Forenoon Session

Usually early in the morning He surveys the world with His Divine Eye to see whom he could help. If any person needs His spiritual assistance, uninvited He goes, often on foot, some times by air using His psychic powers, and converts that person to the right path. As a rule He goes in search of the vicious and the impure, but the pure and the virtuous come in search of Him. For instance, the Buddha went of His own accord to convert the robber and murderer *Aṅgulimāla* and the wicked demon *Ālavaka*, but pious young *Visākhā*, generous millionaire *Anāthapiṇḍika*, and intellectual *Sāriputta* and *Moggallāna* came up to Him for spiritual guidance.

While rendering such spiritual service to whomsoever it is necessary, if He is not invited to partake of alms by a lay supporter at some particular place, He, before whom Kings prostrated themselves, would go in quest of alms through alleys and streets, with bowl in hand, either alone or with His disciples. Standing silently at the door of each house, without uttering a word, He collects whatever food is offered and placed in the bowl and returns to the monastery. Even in His eightieth year when He was old and in indifferent health, He went on His rounds for alms in Vesāli.

Before midday He finishes His meals, Immediately after lunch He daily delivers a short discourse to the people, establishes them in the Three Refuges and the Five Precepts and if any person is spiritually advanced, he is shown the Path to Sainthood. At times He grants Ordina-

tion to them if they seek admission to the Order
and then retires to His chamber.

The Afternoon Session

After the noon meal He takes a seat in the
monastery and the Bhikkhus assemble to listen to
His exposition of the Dhamma. Some approach
Him to receive suitable objects of meditation
according to their temperaments; others pay
their due respects to Him and retire to their cells
to spend the afternoon.

After His discourse or exhortation to His
disciples, He Himself retires to His private Per-
fumed Chamber to rest. If He so desires, He lies
on His right side and sleeps for a while with
mindfulness. On rising, He attains to the Ecstasy
of Great Compassion (*Mahā Karuṇā Samāpatti*)
and surveys, with His Divine Eye, the world,
especially the Bhikkhus who retired to solitude
for meditation and other disciples in order to give
them any spiritual advice that is needed. If the
erring ones who need advice happen to be at a
distance, there He goes by psychic powers, admo-
nishes them and retires to His chamber.

Towards evening the lay followers flock to
Him to hear the Dhamma. Perceiving their innate
tendencies and their temperaments with the

Buddha-Eye,[1] He preaches to them for about one hour. Each member of the audience, though differently constituted, thinks that the Buddha's sermon is directed in particular to him. Such was the Buddha's method of expounding the Dhamma. As a rule the Buddha converts others by explaining His teachings with homely illustrations and parables, for He appeals more to the intellect than to emotion.

To the average man the Buddha at first speaks of generosity, discipline, and heavenly bliss. To the more advanced He speaks on the evils of material pleasures and on the blessings of renunciation. To the highly advanced He expounds the Four Noble Truths.

On rare occasions as in the case of *Aṅgulimāla* and *Khemā* did the Buddha resort to His psychic powers to effect a change of heart in His listeners.

The sublime teachings of the Buddha appealed to both the masses and the intelligentsia alike. A Buddhist poet sings:

"Giving joy to the wise, promoting the intelligence of the middling, and dispelling the darkness of the dull-witted, this speech is for all people."[2]

---

1. *Buddhacakkhu* constitutes the knowledge of the one's inclinations (āsaya) and the innate tendencies (*āsayānusaya ñāṇa*) and the knowledge of the dullness and keenness of faculties such as confidence, mindfulness, concentration, energy and wisdom (*indriyaparoparyattanañāṇa*)

2 *Satapañcasataka*, v. 78.

Both the rich and the poor, the high and the low, renounced their former faiths and embraced the new Message of Peace. The infant Sāsana,[1] which was inaugurated with a nucleus of five ascetics, soon developed into millions and peacefully spread throughout Central India.

The First Watch

This period of the night extends from 6 to 10 p.m. and was exclusively reserved for instruction to Bhikkhus. During this time the Bhikkhus were free to approach the Buddha and get their doubts cleared, question Him on the intricacies of the Dhamma, obtain suitable objects of meditation, and hear the doctrine.

The Middle Watch

During this period which extends from 10 p.m. to 2 a.m. Celestial Beings such as Devas and Brahmas, who are invisible to the physical eye, approach the Buddha to question Him on the Dhamma. An oft-recurring passage in the Suttas is; "Now when the night was far spent a certain Deva of surpassing splendour came to the Buddha, respectfully saluted Him and stood at a side." Several discourses and answers given to their queries appear in the Saṁyutta Nikāya.

---

1. The Dispensation of the Buddha.

The Last Watch

The small hours of the morning, extending from 2 to 6 a.m. which comprise the last watch, are divided into four parts.

The first part is spent in pacing up and down (*cankamana*). This serves as a mild physical exercise to Him. During the second part, that is from 3 to 4 a. m. He mindfully sleeps on His right side. During the third part, that is from 4 to 5 a.m., He attains the state of Arahantship and experiences Nibbānic bliss. For one full hour from 5 to 6 a.m. He attains the Ecstasy of Great Compassion (*Mahā Karuṇāsamāpatti*) and radiates thoughts of loving-kindness towards all beings and softens their hearts. At this early hour He surveys the whole world with His Buddha-Eye to see whether He could be of service to any. The virtuous and those that need His help appear vividly before Him though they may live at a remote distance. Out of compassion for them He goes of His own accord and renders necessary spiritual assistance.

The whole day He is fully occupied with His religious duties. Unlike any other living being He sleeps only for one hour at night. For two full hours in the morning and at dawn He pervades the whole world with thoughts of boundless love and brings happiness to millions. Leading a life of voluntary poverty, seeking His alms without inconveniencing any, wandering from place to place for eight months throughout the year preaching His sublime Dhamma, He tirelessly worked for the good and happiness of all till His eightieth year.

According to the Dharmapradipikā the last watch is divided into these four parts.

According to the commentaries the last watch consists of three parts. During the third part the Buddha attains the Ecstasy of Great Compassion.

CHAPTER 14

THE BUDDHA'S PARINIBBĀNA (DEATH)

"*The sun shines by day. The moon is radiant by night. Armoured shines the warrior King. Meditating the brāhmana shines. But all day and night the Buddha shines in glory.*"

DHAMMAPADA

The Buddha was an extraordinary being. Nevertheless He was mortal, subject to disease and decay as are all beings. He was conscious that He would pass away in His eightieth year. Modest as He was He decided to breathe His last not in renowned cities like Sāvatthi or Rājagaha, where His activities were centred, but in a distant and insignificant hamlet like Kusinara.

In His own words the Buddha was in His eightieth year like "a worn-out cart." Though old in age, yet, being strong in will, He preferred to traverse the long and tardy way on foot accompanied by His favourite disciple, Venerable *Ānanda*. It may be mentioned that Venerable *Sāriputta* and *Moggallāna*, His two chief disciples, predeceased Him. So did Venerable *Rāhula* and *Yasodharā*.

Rājagaha, the capital of Magadha, was the starting point of His last journey.

Before his impending departure from Rājagaha King *Ajātasattu*, the parricide, contemplating an unwarranted attack on the prosperous Vajjian Republic, sent his Prime Minister to the Buddha to know the Buddha's view about his wicked project.

Conditions of welfare

The Buddha declared that (i) as long as the Vajjians meet frequently and hold many meetings; (2) as long as they meet together in unity, rise in unity and perform their duties in unity; (3) as long as they enact nothing not enacted, abrogate nothing that has already been enacted, act in accordance with the already established ancient Vajjian principles; (4) as long as they support, respect, venerate and honour the Vajjian elders, and pay regard to their worthy speech; (5) as long as no women or girls of their families are detained by force or abduction; (6) as long as they support, respect, venerate, honour those objects of worship —internal and external—and do not neglect those righteous ceremonies held before; (7) as long as the rightful protection, defence and support for the Arahants shall be provided by the Vajjians so that Arahants who have not come may enter the realm and those who have entered the realm may live in peace—so long may the Vajjians be expected not to decline, but to prosper.

Hearing these seven conditions of welfare which the Buddha Himself taught the Vajjians, the Prime Minister, *Vassakāra*, took leave of the Buddha, fully convinced that the Vajjians could not be overcome by the King of Magadha in battle, without diplomacy or breaking up their alliance.

The Buddha thereupon availed Himself of this opportunity to teach seven similar conditions of welfare mainly for the benefit of His disciples. He summoned all the Bhikkhus in Rājagaha and said:

(1) "As long, O disciples, as the Bhikkhus assemble frequently and hold frequent meetings, (2) as long as the Bhikkhus meet together in unity, rise in unity, and perform the duties of the Sangha in unity; (3) as long as the Bhikkhus shall promulgate nothing that has not been promulgated, abrogate not what has been promulgated, and act in accordance with the already prescribed rules; (4) as long as the Bhikkhus support, respect, venerate and honour those long-ordained Theras of experience, the fathers and leaders of the Order, and respect their worthy speech; (5) as long as the Bhikkhus fall not under the influence of uprisen attachment that leads to repeated births; (6) as long as the Bhikkhus shall delight in forest retreats; (7) as long as the Bhikkhus develop mindfulness within themselves so that disciplined co-celibates who have not come yet may do so and those who are already present may live in peace—so long may the Bhikkhus be expected not to decline, but to prosper. As long as these seven conditions of welfare shall continue to exist amongst the Bhikkhus, as long as the Bhikkhus are well-instructed in these conditions—so long may they be expected not to decline, but to prosper.

With boundless compassion the Buddha enlightened the Bhikkhus on seven other conditions of welfare as follows:

"As long as the Bhikkhus shall not be fond of, or delight in, or engage in, business; as long as the Bhikkhus shall not be fond of, or delight in, or engage in, gossiping; as long as the Bhikkhus shall not be fond of, or delight in, sleeping; as long as the Bhikkhus shall not be fond of, or delight in, or indulge in, society; as long as the Bhikkhus shall neither have, nor fall under, the influence of base desires; as long as the Bhikkhus shall not have evil friends or associates and shall not be prone to evil—so long the Bhikkhus shall not stop at mere lesser, special acquisition without attaining Arahantship."

Furthermore, the Buddha added that as long as the Bhikkhus shall be devout, modest, conscientious, full of learning, persistently energetic, constantly mindful and full of wisdom—so long may the Bhikkhus be expected not to decline, but to prosper.

Sāriputta's Praise

Enlightening the Bhikkhus with several other discourses, the Buddha, accompanied by Venerable *Ānanda*, left Rājagaha and went to Ambalaṭṭhika and thence to Nālandā, where He stayed at the Pāvārika mango grove. On this occasion the Venerable *Sāriputta* approached the Buddha and extolled the wisdom of the Buddha, saying: "Lord, so pleased am I with the Exalted One that

methinks there never was, nor will there be, nor
is there now, any other ascetic or brahman who
is greater and wiser than the Buddha as regards
self enlightenment."

The Buddha, who did not approve of such an
encomium from a disciple of His, reminded Venerable *Sāriputta* that he had burst into such a song
of ecstasy without fully appreciating the merits of
the Buddhas of the past and of the future.

Venerable *Sāriputta* acknowledged that he had
no intimate knowledge of all the supremely Enlightened Ones, but maintained that he was acquainted with the Dhamma lineage, the process
through which all attain supreme Buddhahood,
that is by overcoming the five Hindrances—
namely, (i) sense-desires, (ii) ill-will, (iii) sloth and
torpor, (iv) restlessness and brooding, (v) indecision; by weakening the strong passions of the heart
through wisdom; by thoroughly establishing the
mind in the four kinds of Mindfulness; and by
rightly developing the seven factors of Enlightenment.

Pātaliputta

From Nālandā the Buddha proceeded to Pata-
ligama where *Sunīdha* and *Vassakāra*, the chief
ministers of Magadha, were building a fortress to
repel the powerful Vajjians. Here the Buddha
resided in an empty house and, perceiving with His
supernormal vision thousands of deities haunting
the different sites, predicted that Pataliputta would

become the chief city inasmuch as it is a residence for Ariyas, a trading centre and a place for the interchange of all kinds of wares, but would be subject to three dangers arising from fire, water and dissension.

Hearing of the Buddha's arrival at Pātaligama, the ministers invited the Buddha and His disciples for a meal at their house. After the meal was over the Buddha exhorted them in these verses:

"Wheresoe'er the prudent man shall take up his abode.

Let him support the brethren there, good men of self-control,

And give the merit of his gifts to the deities who haunt the spot.

Revered, they will revere him: honoured, they honour him again,

Are gracious to him as a mother to her own, her only son.

And the man who has the grace of the gods, good fortune he beholds."[1]

In honour of His visit to the city they named the gate by which He left 'Gotama-Gate''. and they desired to name the ferry by which He would cross "Gotama-Ferry", but the Buddha crossed the overflowing Ganges by His psychic powers

---

1. Prof. Rhys Davids—Dialogues of the Buddha—vol ii, p. 91.

while the people were busy making preparations
to cross.

Future states

From the banks of the Ganges He went to
Koṭigama and thence to the village of Nadika
and stayed at the Brick Hall. Thereupon the
Venerable *Ānanda* approached the Buddha and
respectfully questioned Him about the future
states of several persons who died in that village.
The Buddha patiently revealed the destinies of the
persons concerned and taught how to acquire
the Mirror of Truth so that an Arya disciple endowed therewith may predict of himself thus:
'Destroyed for me is birth in a woeful state, animal
realm, Peta realm, sorrowful, evil, and low states.
A Stream-Winner am I, not subject to fall, assured
of final Enlightenment.'

The Mirror of the Dhamma (Dhammādāsa)

"What, O *Ānanda*, is the Mirror of the
Dhamma?

"Herein a noble disciple reposes perfect confidence in the Buddha reflecting on His virtues
thus:

"Thus, indeed, is the Exalted One, a Worthy
One, a fully Enlightened One, Endowed with
wisdom and conduct, an Accomplished One,
Knower of the worlds, an Incomparable Chario-

teer for the training of individuals, the Teacher of gods and men, Omniscient, and Holy.[1]"

He reposes perfect confidence in the Dhamma reflecting on the characteristics of the Dhamma thus:

"Well expounded is the Dhamma by the Exalted One, to be self-realized, immediately effective, inviting investigation, leading onwards (to Nibbana), to be understood by the wise, each one for himself.[2]"

He reposes perfect confidence in the Sangha reflecting on the virtues of the Sangha thus:

"Of good conduct is the Order of the disciples of the Exalted One; of upright conduct is the Order of the disciples of the Exalted One; of wise conduct is the Order of the disciples of the Exalted One. These four pairs of persons constitute eight individuals. This Order of the disciples of the Exalted One is worthy of gifts, of hospitality, of offerings, of reverence, is an incomparable field of merit to the world.[3]"

---

1. *Iti'pi so bhagavā arahaṁ, sammā sambuddho, vijjāca-ranasampanno, sugato, lokavidhū anuttaro purisadamma-sārathi satthā devamanussānaṁ, buddho, bhagavā'ti.*
2. *Svākkhāto bhagavatā dhammo, sandiṭṭhiko, akāliko, ehi-passiko, opanayiko, paccattam veditabbo viññūhi'ti.*
3. *Supaṭipanno bhagavato sāvakasangho, ujupatipanno, bha-gavato sāvakasangho, ñāyapatipanno bhagavato sāva-kasangho, sāmicipatipanno bhagavato sāvakasango, yadidam cattāri purisayugāni aṭṭhapurisapuggalā, esa bhagavato sāvakasangho. āhuneyyo, pāhuneyyyo dak-khineyyo, añjalikaraṇiyo, anuttaraṁ, puññakkettaṁ lokassā'ti.*

He becomes endowed with virtuous conduct
pleasing to the Aryas, unbroken, intact, unspotted,
unblemished, free, praised by the wise, untarnished
by desires, conducive to concentration.

From Nadika the Buddha went to the flourishing
city of Vesali and stayed at the grove of *Ambapāli*,
the beautiful courtesan. Anticipating her visit,
the Buddha in order to safeguard His disciples,
advised them to be mindful and reflective and
taught them the way of mindfulness.

Ambapāli

Ambapāli, hearing of the Buddha's arrival at
her mango grove, approached the Buddha and
respectfully invited Him and His disciples for a
meal on the following day. The Buddha accepted
her invitation in preference to the invitation of
the Licchavi nobles which He received later. Although the Licchavi Nobles offered a large sum of
money to obtain from her the opportunity of providing this meal to the Buddha, she politely declined this offer. As invited, the Buddha had His
meal at *Ambapāli's* residence. After the meal
Ambapāli, the courtesan, who was a potential
Arahant, very generously offered her spacious
mango grove to the Buddha and His disciples.[1]

As it was the rainy season the Buddha advised
His disciples to spend their Retreat in or around

---

1. Later Ambapāli entered the Order and attained Arahantship.

Vesali, and He Himself decided to spend the
Retreat, which was His last and forty-fifth one, at
Beluva, a village near Vesali.

The Buddha's Illness

In this year He had to suffer from a severe
sickness, and "sharp pains came upon Him even
unto death". With His iron will, mindful and
reflective, the Buddha bore them without any
complaint.

The Buddha was now conscious that He would
soon pass away. But He thought that it would
not be proper to pass away without addressing
His attendant disciples and giving instructions to
the Order. So He decided to subdue His sickness
by His will and live by constantly experiencing the
bliss of Arahantship.[1]

Immediately after recovery, the Venerable
Ānanda approached the Buddha, and expressing
his pleasure on His recovery, remarked that he
took some little comfort from the thought that the
Buddha would not pass away without any instruction about the Order.

The Buddha made a memorable and significant
reply which clearly reveals the unique attitude of
the Buddha, Dhamma and the Sangha.

The Buddha's Exhortation

"What, O *Ānanda*, does the Order of disciples
expect of me? I have taught the Dhamma making

---

1. *Jīvitasaṁkhāram adhiṭṭhāya.*

no distinction between esoteric and exoteric doctrine.[1] In respect of the truths the Tathagata
has no closed fist of a teacher. It may occur to
anyone: "It is I who will lead the Order of Bhikkhus," or "The Order of Bhikkhus is dependent
upon me," or "It is he who should instruct any
matter concerning the Order."

"The Tathagata, *Ānanda*, thinks not that it is he
who should lead the Order of Bhikkhus, or that
the Order is dependent upon him. Why then
should He leave instructions in any matter concerning the Order?"

"I, too, *Ānanda*, am now decrepit, aged. old,
advanced in years, and have reached my end. I
am in my eightieth year. Just as a worn-out cart
is made to move with the aid of thongs, even so methinks the body of the Tathagata is moved with the

---

1. *Anantaraṁ abāhiraṁ karitvā*—These two terms refer
    to both individuals and teachings. "This much of my
    doctrine will I not teach others"—such a thought means
    limiting the Dhamma to an inner circle. "This much
    of my doctrine will I teach others"—such a thought
    means barring the Dhamma to others. "To this person
    I shall teach"—by such a thought a limitation is made
    to an inner circle. "To this person I shall not teach"—
    such a thought implies individual discrimination. The
    Buddha makes no such distinctions both with regard
    to His teaching or His disciples. The Buddha had
    nothing esoteric in His Teachings. Nor had He an inner
    circle or outer circle amongst His disciples.

aid of thongs.[1] Whenever, *Ānanda*, the Tathagata lives plunged in signless mental one-pointedness, by the cessation of certain feelings and unmindful of all objects, then only is the body of the Tathagata at ease.[2] ''

"Therefore, *Ānanda*, be ye islands[3] unto yourselves. Be ye a refuge to yourselves. Seek no external refuge. Live with the Dhamma as your island, the Dhamma as your refuge. Betake to no external refuge."[4]

"How, *Ānanda*, does a Bhikkhu live as an island unto himself, as a refuge unto himself, seeking no external refuge, with the Dhamma as an island, with the Dhamma as a refuge, seeking no external refuge? ''

"Herein, *Ānanda*, a Bhikkhu lives strenuous, reflective, watchful, abandoning covetousness in this world, constantly developing mindfulness with respect to body, feelings, consciousness, and Dhamma.[5] ''

---

1. *Vedhamissakena.*
2. Referring to the bliss of Arahantship (*phalasamāpatti*).
3. Havens.
4. *Attadīpā viharatha attasaranā anaññasaranā; dhammadīpā viharatha, dhammasaranā, anaññasaranā.*
5. These are the four kinds of Satipaṭṭhānas (Foundations of Mindfulness). Here the term *dhamma* is used in a different sense and it cannot adequately be rendered by one English word - as it refers to both mental and physical objects.
See Satipaṭṭhāna Sutta, Majjhima Nikāya No. 10.

"Whosoever shall live either now or after my death as an island unto oneself, as a refuge unto oneself, seeking no external refuge, with the Dhamma as an island, with the Dhamma as a refuge, seeking no external refuge, those Bhikkhus shall be foremost amongst those who are intent on discipline."

Here the Buddha lays special emphasis on the importance of individual striving for purification and deliverance from the ills of life. There is no efficacy in praying to others or in depending on others. One might question why Buddhists should seek refuge in the Buddha, Dhamma, and the Sangha when the Buddha had explicitly advised His followers not to seek refuge in others. In seeking refuge in the Triple Gem (Buddha, Dhamma and Sangha) Buddhists only regard the Buddha as an instructor who merely shows the Path of Deliverance, the Dhamma as the only way or means, the Sangha as the living examples of the way of life to be lived. By merely seeking refuge in them Buddhists do not consider that they would gain their deliverance.

Though old and feeble the Buddha not only availed Himself of every opportunity to instruct the Bhikkhus in various ways but also regularly went on His rounds for alms with bowl in hand when there were no private invitations. One day as usual He went in quest of alms in Vesali and after His meal went with Venerable *Ānanda* to the Capala Cetiya, and, speaking of the delightfulness of Vesali and other shrines in the city, addressed the Venerable *Ānanda* thus:

"Whosoever has cultivated, developed, mastered, made a basis of, experienced, practised, thoroughly acquired the four Means of Accomplishment (*Iddhipāda*)[1] could, if he so desires, live for an aeon (*kappa*)[2] or even a little more (*kappāvasesaṁ*). The Tathagata, O *Ānanda*, has cultivated, developed, mastered, made a basis of, experienced, practised, thoroughly acquired the four Means of Accomplishment. If He so desires, the Tathagata could remain for an aeon or even a little more."

The text adds that "even though a suggestion so evident and so clear was thus given by the Exalted One, the Venerable *Ānanda* was incapable of comprehending it so as to invite the Buddha to remain for an aeon for the good, benefit, and the happiness of the many, out of compassion for the world, for the good, benefit, and happiness of gods and men".

---

1. The four Iddhipādas are—Will (*Chanda*), Effort (*Viriya*), Thought (*Citta*), and Investigation or Wisdom (*Vimaṁsā*)
2. Here the term *kappa* means the normal life-term which was about 100 years. *Kappāvasesam* means an extra fraction of a *kappa*—i.e. about 120 or so.

The Sutta attributes the reason to the fact that the mind of Venerable *Ānanda* was, at the moment, dominated by Mara the Evil One.

The Buddha Announces His Death

The Buddha appeared on earth to teach the seekers of Truth things as they truly are and a unique path for the deliverance of all ills of life. During His long and successful ministry He fulfilled His noble mission to the satisfaction of both Himself and His followers. In His eightieth year He felt that His work was over. He had given all necessary instructions to His earnest followers— both the householders and the homeless ones—and they were not only firmly established in His Teachings but were also capable of expounding them to others. He therefore decided not to control the remainder of His life-span by His will-power and by experiencing the bliss of Arahantship. While residing at the Capala Cetiya the Buddha announced to Venerable *Ānanda* that He would pass away in three months' time.

Venerable *Ānanda* instantly recalled the saying of the Buddha and begged of Him to live for a *kappa* for the good and happiness of all.

"Enough *Ānanda*, beseech not the Tathagata. The time for making such a request is now past," was the Buddha's reply.

He then spoke on the fleeting nature of life and went with Venerable *Ānanda* to the Pinnacled

Hall at Mahavana and requested him to assemble all the Bhikkhus in the neighbourhood of Vesali.

To the assembled Bhikkhus the Buddha spoke as follows:

"Whatever truths have been expounded to you by me, study them well, practise, cultivate and develop them so that this Holy life may last long and be perpetuated out of compassion for the world, for the good and happiness of the many, for the good and happiness of gods and men".

"What are those truths? They are:

The Four Foundations of Mindfulness,
The Four Kinds of Right Endeavour
The Four Means of Accomplishment,
The Five Faculties,
The Five Powers,
The Seven Factors of Enlightenment, and
The Noble Eightfold Path[1]."

He then gave the following final exhortation and publicly announced the time of His death to the Sangha.

The Buddha's Last Words

"Behold, O Bhikkhus, now I speak to you. Transient are all conditioned things. Strive on

---

1. These are the 37 Constituents of Enlightenment (*Bodhi-pakkhiyadhammā*)

with diligence.[1] The passing away of the Tathagata will take place before long. At the end of
three months from now the Tathagata will pass
away."

"Ripe is my age. Short is my life. Leaving
you I shall depart. I have made myself my refuge.
O Bhikkhus, be diligent, mindful and virtuous.
With well-directed thoughts guard your mind. He
who lives heedfully in this Dispensation will escape life's wandering and put an end to suffering."[2]

Casting His last glance at Vesali, the Buddha
went with Venerable *Ānanda* to Bhandagama.
and addressing the Bhikkhus said:

*Morality, concentration, wisdom and Deliverance
supreme.*

*These things were realized by the renowned
Gotama.*

*Comprehending them, the Buddha taught the
doctrine to the disciples.*

*The Teacher with sight has put an end to sorrow
and has extinguished all passions.*

---

1. *Vayadhammā saṁkhārā, appamādena sampādetha.*
2. *Paripakko vayo mayhaṁ parittaṁ mama jīvitaṁ.*
   Pahāya vo gamissāmi kataṁ me sarana mattano
   Appamattā satīmanto susīlā hotha bhikkhavo
   Susamāhita samkappā sacittamanurakkhatha
   Yo imasmiṁ dhammavinaye appamatto vihessati
   Pahāya jātisamsāram dukkhasantaṁ karissati.

The Four Great References

Passing thence from village to village, the Buddha arrived at Bhoganagara and there taught the Four Great Citations or References (*Mahā-padesa*) by means of which the Word of the Buddha could be tested and clarified in the following discourse:

(1) A Bhikkhu may say thus—From the mouth of the Buddha Himself have I heard, have I received thus: 'This is the Doctrine, this is the Discipline, this is the teaching of the Master?' His words should neither be accepted nor rejected. Without either accepting or rejecting such words, study thoroughly every word and syllable and then put them beside the Discourses (*Sutta*) and compare them with the Disciplinary Rules (*Vinaya*). If, when so compared, they do not harmonise with the Discourses and do not agree with the Disciplinary Rules, then you may come to the conclusion. "Certainly this is not the word of the Exalted One, this has been wrongly grasped by the Bhikkhu."

Therefore you should reject it.

If, when compared and contrasted, they harmonise with the Discourses and agree with the Disciplinary Rules, you may come to the conclusion: "Certainly this is the word of the Exalted One, this has correctly been grasped by the Bhikkhu".

Let this be regarded as the First Great Reference.

(2) Again a Bhikkhu may say thus—'In such a monastery lives the Sangha together with leading Theras. From the mouth of that Sangha have

I heard, have I received thus: 'This is the Doctrine, this is the Discipline, this is the Master's Teaching.' His words should neither be accepted nor rejected. Without either accepting or rejecting such words, study thoroughly every word and syllable and then put them beside the Discourses (*Sutta*) and compare them with the Disciplinary Rules (*Vinaya*). If, when so compared, they do not harmonise with the Discourses and do not agree with the Disciplinary Rules, then you may come to the conclusion: "Certainly this is not the word of the Exalted One, this has been wrongly grasped by the Bhikkhu."

Therefore you should reject it.

If, when compared and contrasted, they harmonise with the Discourses and agree with the Disciplinary Rules, you may come to the conclusion: "Certainly this is the word of the Exalted One, this has correctly been grasped by the Bhikkhu."

Let this be regarded as the second Great Reference.

(3) Again a Bhikkhu may say thus—'In such a monastery dwell many Theras and Bhikkhus of great learning, versed in the teachings, proficient in the Doctrine, Vinaya. Discipline, and Matrices (*Mātikā*). From the mouth of those Theras have I heard, have I received thus: 'This is the Dhamma, this is the Vinaya, this is the Teaching of the Master. His words should neither be accepted nor rejected. Without either accepting or reject-

ing such words, study thoroughly every word and syllable and then put them beside the Discourses (*Sutta*) and compare them with the Disciplinary Rules (*Vinaya*). If, when so compared, they do not harmonise with the Discourses and do not agree with the Disciplinary Rules, then you may come to the conclusion: "Certainly this is not the word of the Exalted One, this has been wrongly grasped by the Bhikkhu."

Therefore you should reject it.

If, when compared and contrasted, they harmonise with the Suttas and agree with the Vinaya, then you may come to the conclusion: "Certainly this is the word of the Exalted One, this has been correctly grasped by the Bhikkhu."

Let this be regarded as the Third Great Reference.

(4) Again a Bhikkhu may say thus—'In such a monastery lives an elderly Bhikkhu of great learning, versed in the teachings, proficient in the Dhamma, Vinaya, and Matrices. From the mouth of that Thera have I heard, have I received thus: 'This is the Dhamma, this is the Vinaya, this is the Master's Teaching.' His words should neither be accepted nor rejected. Without either accepting or rejecting such words, study thoroughly every word and syllable and then put them beside the Discourses (*Sutta*) and compare them with the Disciplinary Rules (*Vinaya*). If, when so compared, they do not harmonise with the Dis-

courses and do not agree with the Disciplinary Rules, then you may come to the conclusion: "Certainly this is not the word of the Exalted One, this has been wrongly grasped by the Bhikkhu."

Therefore you should reject it.

If, when compared and contrasted, they harmonise with the Suttas and agree with the Vinaya, then you may come to the conclusion: "Certainly this is the Dhamma, this is the Vinaya, this is the Master's Teachings."

Let this be regarded as the Fourth Great Reference.

These, Bhikkhus, are the Four Great References.

The Buddha's Last Meal

Enlightening the disciples with such edifying discourses, the Buddha proceeded to Pava where the Buddha and His disciples were entertained by *Cunda* the smith. With great fervour *Cunda* prepared a special delicious dish called '*Sūkaramaddava*'.[1] As advised by the Buddha, *Cunda* served only the Buddha with the *Sūkaramaddava* and buried the remainder in the ground.

---

1. According to the commentary it is flesh of a boar neither too young nor too old, but not killed for His sake (*pavattamaṁsa*). Some say it is a kind of mushroom. It is also believed to be a special kind of delicious dish by that name, or a nutritious chemical food. See *Questions of Milinda*—Vol. 1, p. 244 and *Dialogues of the Buddha* part 2 p. 136 n. 1.

After the meal the Buddha suffered from an attack of dysentery and sharp pains came upon Him. Calmly He bore them without any complaint.

Though extremely weak and severely ill, the Buddha decided to walk to *Kusinārā*[1] His last resting place, a distance of about three *gāvutas*[2] from Pava. In the course of this last journey it is stated that the Buddha had to sit down in about twenty-five places owing to His weakness and illness.

On the way He sat at the foot of a tree and asked Venerable *Ānanda* to fetch some water as He was feeling thirsty. With difficulty Venerable *Ānanda* secured some pure water from a streamlet which, a few moments earlier, was flowing fouled and turbid, stirred up by the wheels of fivehundred carts.

At that time a man named *Pukkusa*, approached the Buddha, and expressed his admiration at the serenity of the Buddha, and, hearing a sermon about His imperturbability, offered Him a pair of robes of gold.

1. According to the commentary the Buddha chose Kusinārā to pass away for three reasons. First, to preach the *Mahāsudassana Sutta* in order to inspire people to be more virtuous; secondly to convert Subhadda, His last disciple, who could not have been converted by any other but Himself; thirdly to enable Dona, a brahmin, to distribute His relics peacefully amongst His followers.
2. A little more than six miles.

As directed by the Buddha, he robed the Buddha with one and Venerable *Ānanda* with the other.

When Venerable *Ānanda* placed the pair of robes on the Buddha, to his astonishment, he found the skin of the Buddha exceeding bright, and said —'How wonderful a thing is it, Lord and how marvellous, that the colour of the skin of the Exalted One should be so clear, so exceeding bright. For when I placed even this pair of robes of burnished gold and ready for wear on the body of the Exalted One, it seemed as if it had lost its splendour.'

Thereupon the Buddha explained that on two occasions the colour of the skin of the Tathagata becomes clear and exceeding bright—namely on the night on which the Tathagata attains Buddhahood and on the night the Tathagata passes away.

He then pronounced that at the third watch of the night on that day He would pass away in the Sala Grove of the Mallas between the twin Sala trees, in the vicinity of Kusinara.

Cunda's Meritorious Meal

He took His last bath in the river Kukuttha and resting a while spoke thus—"Now it may happen, *Ānanda*, that some one should stir up remorse in *Cunda* the smith, saying: 'This is evil to thee, *Cunda*, and loss to thee in that when the Tathagata had eaten His last meal from thy provisions, then He died.' Any such remorse in *Cunda* the smith should be checked by saying: 'This is good to thee, *Cunda*, and gain to thee, in that when the Tathagata had eaten His last meal from thy provision, then He died. From the very mouth of the Exalted One, *Cunda*, have I heard, from His very mouth have I received this saying: 'These two offerings of food are of equal fruit, and of equal profit, and of much greater fruit and of much greater profit than any other, and which are the two? The offering of food which when a Tathagata has eaten He attains to supreme and perfect insight, and the offering of food which when a Tathagata has eaten He passes away by that utter cessation in which nothing whatever remains behind—these two offerings of food are of equal fruit and of equal profit, and of much greater fruit, and of much greater profit than any other. There has been laid up by *Cunda* the smith a Kamma redounding to length of life, redounding to good birth, redounding to good fortune, redounding to good fame, redounding to the inheritance of heaven and of sovereign power.' In this way, *Ānanda*, should be checked any remorse in *Cunda* the smith."

Uttering these words of consolation out of compassion to the generous donor of His last meal, He went to the Sāla Grove of the Mallas and asked Venerable *Ānanda* to prepare a couch with the head to the north between the twin Sāla trees. The Buddha laid Himself down on His right side with one leg resting on the other, mindful and self-possessed.

How the Buddha is Honoured

Seeing the Sāla trees blooming with flowers out of season, and other outward demonstrations of piety, the Buddha exhorted His disciples thus:

"It is not thus, *Ānanda*, that the Tathagata is respected, reverenced, venerated, honoured, and revered. Whatever Bhikkhu or Bhikkhuni, Upāsaka or Upāsika lives in accordance with the Teaching, conducts himself dutifully, and acts righteously, it is he who respects, reverences, venerates, honours, and reveres the Tathagata with the highest homage. Therefore, *Ānanda*, should you train yourselves thus—"Let us live in accordance with the Teaching, dutifully conducting ourselves, and acting righteously."

At this moment the Venerable *Upavāna*, who was once attendant of the Buddha, was standing in front of the Buddha fanning Him. The Buddha asked Him to stand aside. ·

Venerable *Ānanda* wished to know why he was asked to stand aside as he was very serviceable to the Buddha.

The Buddha replied that Devas had assembled in large numbers to see the Tathagata and they were displeased because he was standing in their way concealing Him.

The Four Sacred Places

The Buddha then spoke of four places, made sacred by His association, which faithful followers should visit with reverence and awe. They are:

1. The birthplace of the Buddha[1],
2. The place where the Buddha attained Enlightenment[2],
3. The place where the Buddha established the Incomparable Wheel of Truth[3] (*Dhammacakka*), and
4. The place where the Buddha attained Parinibbāna[4].

"And they", added the Buddha, "who shall die with a believing heart, in the course of their pilgrimage, will be reborn, on the dissolution of their body, after death, in a heavenly state."

Conversion of Subhadda

At that time a wandering ascetic, named *Subhadda*[5], was living at Kusinara. He heard the

---

1. Lumbini on the Indian borders of Nepal.
2. Buddha Gayā, about 8 miles from the Gayā station.
3. Sāranāth.
4. Kusinārā—modern Kasiā —about 32 miles form Gorakhpur station.
5. This Subhadda should be distinguished from another Subhadda who entered the Order in his old age. It was the latter who remarked that the death of the Buddha was no occasion for sorrow as the Bhikkhus were free to do whatever they liked, without being bound by the injunctions of the Master. This remark of Subhadda prompted Venerable Kassapa to take immediate steps to hold a convocaion of the Dhamma and the Vinaya.

news that the Ascetic Gotama would attain Parinibbāna in the last watch of the night. And he
thought—I have heard grown-up and elderly
teachers, and their teachers, the wandering ascetics,
say that seldom and very seldom, indeed, do Exalted, Fully Enlightened Arahants arise in this world.
Tonight in the last watch the Ascetic *Gotama* will
attain Parinibbāna. A doubt has arisen in me,
and I have confidence in the Ascetic *Gotama*.
Capable, indeed, is the Ascetic *Gotama* to teach the
doctrine so that I may dispel my doubt.

Thereupon *Subhadda*, the wandering ascetic,
went to Upavattana Sāla grove of the Mallas
where the Venerable *Ānanda* was, and approaching him spoke as follows: "I have heard grown-
up and elderly teachers and their teachers, the
wandering ascetics, say that seldom, and very
seldom, indeed, do Exalted, Fully Enlightened
Arahants arise in this world. Tonight in the last
watch the Ascetic Gotama will attain Parinibbāna. A doubt has arisen in me, and I have confidence in the Ascetic *Gotama*. Capable, indeed,
is the Ascetic *Gotama* to teach the doctrine so
that I may dispel my doubts. Shall I, O *Ānanda*,
obtain a glimpse of the Ascetic *Gotama?*"

"Enough, friend *Subhadda*, do not worry the
Accomplished One. The Exalted One is wearied,"
said the Venerable *Ānanda*.

For the second and third time *Subhadda* repeated his request, and for the second and third
time Venerable *Ānanda* replied in the same manner.

The Buddha heard the conversation between the Venerable *Ānanda* and *Subhadda*, and addressing *Ānanda*, said:

'Nay, *Ānanda*, do not prevent *Subhadda*. Let *Subhadda*, O *Ānanda*, behold the Accomplished One. Whatsoever *Subhadda* will ask of me, all that will be with the desire for knowledge, and not to annoy me. And whatever I shall say in answer he will readily understand."

Thereupon the Venerable *Ānanda* introduced *Subhadda* to the Buddha.

Subhadda exchanged friendly greetings with the Buddha and sitting aside said: "There are these ascetics and priests, O *Gotama*, who are leaders of companies and congregations, who are heads of sects and are well-known, renowned religious teachers, esteemed as good men by the multitude, as, for instance, *Pūrana Kassapa*, *Makkhali Gosāla*, *Ajita Kesakambali*, *Pakudha Kaccāyana*, *Sañjaya Belaṭṭhiputta*, *Nigantha Nātaputta*[1]—have they all, as they themselves claim, thoroughly understood the Truth or not, or have some of them understood. and some not?."

"Let it be, O *Subhadda!* Trouble not yourself as to whether all or some have realized it or not. I shall teach the doctrine to you. Listen and bear it well in mind. I shall speak."

"So be it, Lord!" replied *Subhadda*.

---

1. They all flourished in the time of the Buddha.

The Buddha spoke as follows:

"In whatever Dispensation there exists not the Noble Eightfold Path, neither is the First Samaṇa, nor the Second, nor the Third, nor the Fourth to be found therein. In whatever Dispensation, O Subhadda, there exists the Noble Eightfold Path, there also are to be found the First Samaṇa, the Second Samaṇa. the Third Samaṇa, the Fourth Samaṇa. In this Dispensation, O *Subhadda*, there exists the Noble Eightfold Path.

"Here, indeed, are found the First Samaṇa[1], the Second Samaṇa[2], the Third Samaṇa,[3] and the Fourth Samaṇa. The other foreign schools are empty of Samaṇas.[4] If, O *Subhadda*, the disciples live rightly, the world would not be void of Arahants.[5]

"My age was twenty-nine when I went forth as a seeker after what is good. Now one and fifty years are gone since I was ordained. Outside this fold there is not a single ascetic who acts even partly in accordance with this realizable doctrine."

Thereupon *Subhadda* spoke to the Buddha as follows:

1. The first Samaṇa is the *Sotāpanna*, Stream-Winner.
2. The *Sakadāgāmi*, Once-Returner.
3. The *Anāgāmi*, Never-Returner.
4. The *Arahant*, The Worthy One, who is the Perfect Saint.
5. *Suññā parappavādā samaṇehi aññehi. Ime ca Subhadda bhikkhū sammā vihareyyuṁ asuñño loko arahantehi assā'ti.*

"Excellent, Lord, excellent! It is as if, O Lord, a man were to set upright that which was overturned, or were to reveal that which was hidden, or were to point the way to one who has gone astray, or were to hold a lamp amidst the darkness, so that whoever has eyes may see, even so has the doctrine been expounded in various ways by the Exalted One.

"And I, Lord, seek refuge in the Buddha, the Doctrine, and the Order. May I receive the Lesser and the Higher Ordination in the presence of the Exalted One"!

"Whoever, *Subhadda*," said the Buddha, "being already committed to the other doctrines desires the Lesser[1] and the Higher Ordination,[2] remains on

---

1. *Pabbajjā*—Renunciation. This refers to the ordination as a novice, which is done by donning the yellow robe after having shaved hair and beard and taking the Three Refuges and the Ten Precepts. The novice is called a Sāmanera. He has cut himself off from the world and its ways. Henceforth by him even his parents are addressed "lay-disciples."

2. *Upasampadā*—This refers to the Higher Ordination, which is bestowed only after the completion of the 20th year of life. He who receives it is a full member of the Order and is called a Bhikkhu.
    He is bound to observe the *Pātimokkha Precepts,* the commission of any of the major offences of which involves 'defeat' and expulsion from the Order. If willing, he could remain as a Sāmanera.
    See page 106, note 1.

probation for four months. At the end of four months, the disciples approving, he is ordained and raised to the status of a Bhikkhu. Nevertheless, on understanding, I make individual exception."

Then said *Subhadda:*

"If, Lord, those already committed to other doctrines, who desire the Lesser and the Higher Ordination in this Dispensation, remain on probation for four months, I too will remain on probation; and after the lapse of that period, the disciples approving, let me be received into the Order and raised to the status of a Bhikkhu."

Thereupon the Buddha addressed *Ānanda* and said:

"Then, *Ānanda,* you may ordain *Subhadda."*

"So, be it, Lord!" replied *Ānanda.*

And *Subhadda,* the wandering ascetic, spoke to the Venerable *Ānanda* as follows:

"It is a gain to you, O Venerable *Ānanda*! It is indeed a great gain to you, for you have been anointed by the anointment of discipleship in the presence of the Exalted One by Himself."

---

1. A probation is not demanded of the Buddhist aspirant to ordination.

Subhadda received in the presence of the Buddha the Lesser and the Higher Ordination.

And in no long time after his Higher Ordination, the Venerable *Subhadda*, living alone, remote from men, strenuous, energetic, and resolute, realized, in this life itself, by his own intuitive knowledge, the consummation of that incomparable Life of Holiness, and lived abiding in that state for the sake of which sons of noble families rightly leave the householder's life for the homeless life. He perceived that rebirth was ended, completed was the Holy Life, that after this life there was none other.

And the Venerable *Subhadda* became one of the Arahants. He was the last personal convert of the Buddha.

The Last Words to Ānanda

The Venerable *Ānanda* desired to know what they should do with the body of the Tathāgata.

The Buddha answered. Do not engage yourselves in honouring the remains of the Tathāgata. Be concerned about your own welfare. (i.e. Arahantship). Devote yourselves to your own welfare. Be heedful, be strenuous, and be intent on your own good. There are wise warriors, wise brahmins, wise householders who are firm believers in the Tathāgata. They will do honour to the remains of the Tathāgata.

At the conclusion of these interesting religious talks Venerable *Ānanda* went aside and stood weeping at the thought: "Alas! I am still a learner with work yet to do. But my Master will finally pass away—He who is my sympathiser".

The Buddha, noticing his absence, summoned him to His presence and exhorted him thus— "Enough, O *Ānanda*! Do not grieve, do not weep. Have I not already told you that we have to separate and divide and sever ourselves from everything that is dear and pleasant to us?

"O *Ānanda*, you have done much merit. Soon be freed from Defilements."

The Buddha then paid a tribute to Venerable *Ānanda*, commenting on his salient virtues.

After admonishing Venerable *Ānanda* in various ways, the Buddha ordered him to enter Kusinara and inform the Mallas of the impending death of the Tathāgata. Mallas were duly informed, and came weeping with their wives, young men, and maidens, to pay their last respects to the Tathāgata.

The Last Scene

Then the Blessed One addressed *Ānanda* and said:

"It may be, *Ānanda*, that you will say thus: Without the Teacher is the Sublime Teaching! There is no Teacher for us.' Nay, *Ānanda*, you should not think thus. Whatever Doctrine and Discipline have been taught and promulgated by me, *Ānanda*, they will be your Teacher when I am gone."[1]

"Let the Sangha, O *Ānanda*, if willing, abrogate the lesser and minor rules after my death."[2] remarked the Buddha.

Instead of using the imperative form the Buddha has used the subjunctive in this connection. Had it been His wish that the lesser rules should be abolished, He could have used the imperative. The Buddha foresaw that Venerable *Kassapa*, presiding over the First Council, would, with the consent of the Sangha, not abrogate any rule—hence His use of the subjunctive, states the commentator.

As the Buddha has not clearly stated what these minor rules were and as the Arahants could not come to any decision about them, they preferred not to alter any rule but to retain all intact.

Again the Buddha addressed the disciples and said: "If, O disciples, there be any doubt as to the Buddha, or the Doctrine, or the Order, or the Path, or the Method, question me, and repent not afterwards thinking,—we were face to face with the Teacher, yet we were not able to question the

1. *Yo ca kho mayā dhammo ca vinayo ca desito paññatto so 'vo mamaccayena satthā.*

2. *Ākamkhamāno, Ānanda, sangho, mamaccayena khuddā- nukhuddakāni sikkhāpadāni samūhantu!*

Exalted One in His presence." When He spoke thus the disciples were silent.

For the second and third time the Buddha addressed the disciples in the same way. And for the second and third time the disciples were silent.

Then the Buddha addressed the disciples and said: "Perhaps it may be out of respect for the Teacher that you do not question me. Let a friend, O disciples, intimate it to another."

Still the disciples were silent.

Thereupon the Venerable *Ānanda* spoke to the Buddha as follows:

"Wonderful, Lord! Marvellous, Lord! Thus am I pleased with the company of disciples. There is not a single disciple who entertains a doubt or perplexity with regard to the Buddha, the Doctrine, the Order, the Path and the Method."

"You speak out of faith, *Ānanda*, with regard to this matter. There is knowledge in the Tathāgata, that in this company of disciples there is not a single disciple who entertains a doubt or perplexity with regard to the Doctrine, the Order, the Path and the Method. Of these five hundred disciples, *Ānanda*, he who is the last is a Stream-Winner, not subject to fall but certain and destined for Enlightenment.'

---

1. The reference was to the Venerable Ānanda, who encouraged by those words, attained Arahantship later.

Lastly the Buddha addressed the disciples and gave His final exhortation.

"Behold, O disciples, I exhort you. **Subject to change are all component things. Strive on with diligence** (*Vayadhammā saṁkhārā, Appāmadena sampādetha*).

These were the last words of the Blessed One.

The Passing Away

The Buddha attained to the first Ecstasy (*Jhāna*). Emerging from it, He attained in order to the second, third, and fourth Ecstasies. Emerging from the fourth Ecstasy, He attained to "The Realm of the Infinity of Space" (*Akāsānañcāyatana*). Emerging from it He attained to "The Realm of the Infinity of Consciousness" (*Viññānañcāyatana*). Emerging from it, He attained to "The Realm of Nothingness" (*Ākiñcaññāyatana*). Emerging from it, He attained to "The Realm of Neither Perception nor Non-perception" (*N'eva saññā nāsaññāyatana*). Emerging from it, He attained to "The cessation of Perceptions and Sensations". (*Saññāvedayita-Nirodha*).

Venerable *Ānanda*, who had then not developed the Divine Eye, addressed Venerable *Anuruddha* and said: "O Venerable *Anuruddha*, the Exalted One has passed away."

"Nay, brother *Ānanda*, the Exalted One has not passed away but has attained to 'The Cessation of Perceptions and Sensations.

Then the Buddha, emerging from "The Cessation of Perceptions and Sensations", attained to "The Realm of Neither Perception nor Non-perception." Emerging from it, He attained to "The Realm of Nothingness." Emerging from it, He attained to "The Realm of the Infinity of Consciousness." Emerging from it, He attained to "The Realm of the Infinity of Space." Emerging from it, He attained to the fourth Ecstasy. Emerging from it, He attained to the third Ecstasy. Emerging from it, He attained to the second Ecstasy. Emerging from it, He attaind to the first Ecstasy. Emerging from it, He attained to the second Ecstasy. Emerging from it, He attained to the third Ecstasy. Emerging from it, He attained to the fourth Ecstasy. Emerging from it, and immediately after, the Buddha finally passed away.[1]

---

1. The death of the Buddha occurred in 543 B.C. on a Vesak fullmoon day.

CHAPTER 15

THE DHAMMA

HE TEACHINGS OF THE BUDDHA

What is Buddhism ?

"This doctrine is profound, hard to see, difficult to under-stand, calm, sublime, not within the sphere of logic, subtle, to be understood by the wise"

MAJJHIMA NIKĀYA

Tipitaka

The Buddha has passed away, but the sublime Teaching, which He expounded during His long and successful ministry and which He unreservedly bequeathed to humanity, still exists in its pristine purity.

Although the Master has left no written records of His Teachings, His disciples preserved them, by committing to memory and transmitting them orally from generation to generation.

Three months after the Death of the Buddha, in the eighth year of King *Ajātasattu's* reign, 500 pre-eminent Arahants concerned with preserving the purity of the Doctrine held a Convocation at Rajagaha to rehearse it. The Venerable *Ānanda* Thera, the Buddha's beloved attendant who had the special privilege and honour of hearing the discourses from the Buddha Himself, and the

Venerable *Upāli* Thera were chosen to answer questions about the Dhamma (*Doctrine*) and the Vinaya (*Discipline*) respectively.

This First Council compiled and arranged in its present form the Pali Tipiṭaka, which represents the entire body of the Buddha's Teaching.

Two other Councils[1] of Arahants were held 100 and 236 years later respectively, again to rehearse the Word of the Buddha because attempts were being made to pollute the pure Teaching.

About 83 B.C., during the reign of the pious Simhala King *Vaṭṭa Gāmani Abhaya*[2], a Council of Arahants was held, and the Tipiṭaka was, for the first time in the history of Buddhism, committed to writing at Aluvihara[3] in Ceylon.

Thanks to the indefatigable efforts of those noble and foresighted Arahants, there is no room either now or in the future for higher critics or progressive scholars to adulterate the pure Teaching.

---

1. See Mahāvamsa Translation pp. 14-50.

2. Ibid. pp. 19—50.

3. A hamlet in the interior of Ceylon, about 24 miles from Kandy. This sacred rock temple is still a place of pilgrimage to the Buddhists of Ceylon. *Buddhaghosuppatti,* a biography of the Great Commentator Buddhaghosa, states that the amount of books written on ola leaves when piled up would exceed the height of six elephants.

The voluminous Tipiṭaka, which contains the essence of the Buddha's Teaching, is estimated to be about eleven times the size of the Bible.

The word Tipiṭaka[1] means three Baskets.   They are the Basket of Discipline (*Vinaya Piṭaka*), the Basket of Discourses (*Sutta Piṭaka*) and the Basket of Ultimate Doctrine (*Abhidhamma Piṭaka*).

Vinaya Pitaka

The Vinaya piṭaka, which is regarded as the sheet anchor of the Holy Order, deals mainly with the rules and regulations of the Order of Bhikkhus (*monks*) and Bhikkhunis (*nuns*). For nearly twenty years after the Enlightenment of the Buddha, no definite rules were laid down for control and discipline of the Sangha (*Order*). Subsequently as occasion arose, the Buddha promulgated rules for the future discipline of the Sangha. Reasons for the promulgation of rules, their various implications, and specific Vinaya ceremonies of the Sangha are fully described in the Vinaya piṭaka. The history of the gradual development of Sāsana[2] from its very inception, a brief account of the life and ministry of the Buddha, and details of the three Councils are some other additional relevant contents of the Vinaya Piṭaka. Indirectly it reveals useful information about ancient history, Indian customs, ancient arts and sciences. One who reads the

---

1.   Saṁskrit—Tripitaka.
2.   Dispensation—*Sāsana* is the Pāli term applied to the whole Buddhist Church.

Vinaya piṭaka cannot but be impressed by the democratic constitution of the Sangha, their holding of possessions in common, the exceptionally high moral standard of the Bhikkhus, and the unsurpassed administrative abilities of the Buddha, who anticipated even the present Parliamentary system. Lord Zetland writes; "And it may come as a surprise to many to learn that in the Assemblies of the Buddhists in India two thousand years and more ago are to be found the rudiments of our own Parliamentary practice of the present day."[1]

The *Vinaya Piṭaka* consists of the following five books:

1. *Pārājika Pāli*	*Vibhanga*	(Major Offences)
2. *Pācittiya Pāli*		(Minor Offences)
3. *Mahāvagga Pāli*	*Khandaka*	(Greater Section)
4. *Cullavagga Pāli*		(Lesser Sectlon)
5. *Parivāra Pāli*		(Epitome of the Vinaya)

Sutta Piṭaka

The *Sutta Piṭaka* consists chiefly of instructive discourses delivered by the Buddha to both the Sangha and the laity on various occasions. A few discourses, expounded by disciples such as the Venerables *Sāriputta*, *Moggallāna*, and *Ānanda*, are incorporated and are accorded as much veneration as the Word of the Buddha Himself, since they

---

1. See *Legacy of India,* Edited by G. T. Garrat, pp, X, XI.

were approved by Him. Most of the sermons were intended mainly for the benefit of Bhikkhus, and they deal with the Holy Life and with the exposition of the Doctrine. There are several other discourses which deal with both the material and the moral progress of His lay-followers. The *Sigālovāda Sutta*[1], for instance, deals mainly with the duties of a layman. There are also a few interesting talks given to children.

This Piṭaka may be compared to a book of prescriptions, since the discourses were expounded on diverse occasions to suit the temperaments of various persons. There may be seemingly contradictory statements, but they should not be misconstrued as they were uttered by the Buddha to suit a particular purpose; for instance, to the self same question He would maintain silence, when the inquirer was merely foolishly inquisitive, or give a detailed reply when He knew the inquirer to be an earnest seeker after the Truth.

The *Sutta Piṭaka* consists of the following five Nikāyas (*Collections*):

1. *Dīgha Nikāya* (Collection of Long Discourses)
2. *Majjhima Nikāya* (Collection of Middle-length Discourses)

---

1. Commenting on this Sutta, Mrs. Rhys Davids says—
"Happy would have been the village or the clan on the banks of the Ganges where the people were full of the kindly spirit of fellow-feeling and the noble spirit of justice, which breathe through these naive and simple sayings."
See Dialogues of the Buddha part III. p. 168.

3. *Saṁyutta Nikāya* (Collection of Kindred Sayings)
4. *Anguttara Nikāya* (Collection of Gradual Sayings)
5. *Khuddaka Nikāya* (Smaller Collection)

This fifth is subdivided into fifteen books:

1. *Khuddaka Pāṭha* (Shorter Texts)
2. *Dhammapada* (The Way of Truth)
3. *Udāna* (Paeans of Joy)
4. *Itivuttaka* ("Thus said" Discourses)
5. *Sutta Nipāta* (Collected Discourses)
6. *Vimāna Vatthu* (Stories of Celestial Mansions)
7. *Peta Vatthu* (Stories of Petas)
8. *Theragāthā* (Psalms of the Brethren)
9. *Therīgāthā* (Psalms of the Sisters)
10. *Jātaka* (Birth Stories of the Bodhisatta)
11. *Niddesa* (Expositions)
12. *Paṭisambhidā* (Book on Analytical Knowledge)
13. *Apadāna* (Lives of Arahants)
14. *Buddhavaṁsa* (History of the Buddha)
15. *Cariyā Piṭaka* (Modes of Conduct)

Abhidhamma Pitaka

The Abhidhamma Piṭaka is the most important and most interesting of the three containing as it does the profound philosophy of the Buddha's teaching in contrast to the simpler discourses in the Sutta Piṭaka. Abhidhamma, the Higher Doctrine of the Buddha, expounds the quintessence of His profound teachings.[1]

---

1. See "*The Manual of Abhidhamma*" by the Author.

According to some scholars Abhidhamma is not a teaching of the Buddha, but is a later elaboration of scholastic monks. Tradition, however, attributes the nucleus of the Abhidhamma to the Buddha Himself. The *Mātikā** or Matrices of the Abhidhamma, such as *Kusalā Dhammā* (Wholesome States), *Akusalā Dhammā* (Unwholesome States), and *Abyākatā Dhammā* (Indeterminate States), etc., which have been elaborated in the six books (*Kathāvatthu*[1] being excluded), were expounded by the Buddha. To the Venerable *Sāriputta* is assigned the honour of having explained all these topics in detail.

Whoever the great author or authors may have been, it has to be admitted that the Abhidhamma must be the product of an intellectual genius comparable only to the Buddha. This is evident from the intricate and subtle *Paṭṭhāna Pakaraṇa* which describes in detail the various causal relations.

To the wise truth-seekers, Abhidhamma is an indispensable guide and an intellectual treat. Here is found food for thought to original thinkers and to earnest students who wish to develop wisdom and lead an ideal Buddhist life. Abhidhamma is not a subject of fleeting interest designed for the superficial reader.

---

* Note the reference to *Mātikā* in the Parinibbāna Sutta. See. p. 251.

1. *Points of Controversy,* the authorship of which is attributed to Venerable Moggaliputta Tissa who presided at the Third Council in the time of King Asoka.

Modern Psychology, limited as it is, comes within the scope of Abhidhamma inasmuch as it deals with mind, thoughts, thought-processes, and mental properties; but it does not admit of a psyche or a soul. It teaches a psychology without a psyche.

If one were to read the Abhidhamma as a modern text-book on psychology, one would be disappointed. No attempt has here been made to solve all the problems that confront a modern psychologist.

Consciousness (*Citta*) is defined. Thoughts are analysed and classified chiefly from an ethical standpoint. All mental properties (*Cetasika*) are enumerated. The composition of each type of consciousness is set forth in detail. How thoughts arise is minutely described. *Bhavanga* and *Javana* thought-moments, which are explained only in the Abhidhamma, and which have no parallel in modern psychology, are of special interest to research students in psychology. Irrelevant problems that interest students and scholars, but have no relation to one's Deliverance, are deliberately set aside.

Matter is summarily discussed, but it has not been described for physicists. Fundamental units of matter, material properties, source of matter, relationship of mind and matter are explained. Abhidhamma does not attempt to give a systematised knowledge of mind and matter. It investigates these two composite factors of the so-called being, to help the understanding of things as they truly are. A philosophy has been developed on those lines. Based on that philosophy, an ethical system has been evolved to realize the ultimate Goal, Nibbāna. As Mrs. Rhys Davids rightly says: "Abhidhamma deals with (i) what we find (a) within us (b) around us and of (ii) what we aspire to find."

While the Sutta Piṭaka contains the conventional teaching (vohāra desanā), the Abhidhamma Pitaka contains the ultimate teaching (paramattha desanā).

It is generally admitted by most exponents of the Dhamma that a knowledge of the Abhidhamma is essential to comprehend fully the Teachings of the Buddha, as it presents the key that opens the door of reality.

The *Abhidhamma Piṭaka* is composed of the following seven works:

1. *Dhammasangani*   (Classification of Dhamma)
2. *Vibhanga*   (Divisions)
3. *Dhātukathā*   (Discourse on Elements)
4. *Puggala Paññatti*   (The Book on Individuals)
5. *Kathāvatthu*   (Points of Controversy)
6. *Yamaka*   (The Book of Pairs)
7. *Paṭṭhāna*   (The Book of Causal Relations)

Is Buddhism a Philosophy?

The sublime Dhamma, enshrined in these sacred texts, deals with truths and facts that can be tested and verified by personal experience

and is not concerned with theories and speculations, which may be accepted as profound truths
today and thrown overboard tomorrow. The
Buddha did not expound revolutionary philosophical theories, nor did He attempt to create a new
material science. In plain terms He explained
both what is within and what is without, so far as it
concerns emancipation from the ills of life, and
revealed the unique Path of Deliverance.

Furthermore, the Buddha did not teach all that
He knew. On one occasion while the Buddha
was staying in a forest, He took a handful of leaves
and said: "O Bhikkhus, what I have taught you is
comparable to the leaves in my hand, and what
I have not taught you, to the leaves in the forest."[1]

He taught what He deemed was absolutely
essential for one's purification, and was characteristically silent on questions irrelevant to His noble
mission. Incidentally, He forestalled many a
modern scientist and philosopher.

Heraclitus (500 B.C.) believed that everything
flows (*pante rhei*) and that the universe is a constant becoming. He taught that nothing ever is;
everything is becoming. It was he who made the
famous statement that a person cannot step into
the same stream twice. *Pythagoras* (532 B.C.)

---

1. Saṁyutta Nikāya vol. 5, pp. 437-438, *Kindred Sayings,*
    part 5, p. 370.

taught, among other things, the theory of transmigration of souls. *Descartes* (1596-1650) declared the necessity of examining all phenomena at the bar of reasonable doubt. *Spinoza* (1632-1677). while admitting the existence of a permanent reality, asserted that all existence is transitory. In his opinion sorrow was to be conquered by finding an object of knowledge which is not transient, not ephemeral, but is immutable, permanent, everlasting. *Berkely* (1685-1776) thought that the so-called atom was a metaphysical fiction. *Hume* (1711-1776) analysed the mind and concluded that consciousness consists of fleeting mental states. In the view of *Hegel* (1770-1831) "the entire phenomenon is a becoming." *Schopenhauer* (1788-1860) in his "World as Will and Idea" has presented the truth of suffering and its cause in Western garb. *Henri Bergson* (1859-1941) advocated the doctrine of change, and emphasized the value of intuition. *William James* (1842-1910) referred to a stream of consciousness and denied the existence of a soul.

The Buddha expounded these truths of transiency (*anicca*), sorrow (*dukkha*), and soul-lessness (*anattā*) more than 2500 years ago.

The moral and philosophical teachings of the Buddha are to be studied, to be practised, and above all to be realized by one's own intuitive wisdom. As such the Dhamma is compared to a raft which enables one to cross the ocean of life.[1]

---

1. Majjhima Nikāya, No. 22.

Buddhism, therefore, cannot strictly be called a philosophy because it is not merely "the love of, inducing the search after, wisdom."[1] Nor is Buddhism "a hypothetical interpretation of the unknown (as in metaphysics), or of the inexactly known (as in ethics or political philosophy)."[2]

If by philosophy is meant "an inquiry not so much after certain particular facts as after the fundamental character of this world in which we find ourselves, and of the kind of life which such a world it behoves us to live,"[3] Buddhism may approximate to a philosophy, but it is very much more comprehensive.[4]

Philosophy deals mainly with knowledge and is not concerned with practice; whereas Buddhism lays special emphasis on practice and realization.

Is Buddhism a Religion?

Prof. Rhys Davids writes:

"What is meant by religion? The word, as is well-known is not found in languages not related to our own, and its derivation is uncertain. Cicero, in one passage, derived it from *re* and *lego*, and held that its real meaning was the repeti-

1. Webster's Dictionary.
2. William Durrant, *The History of Philosophy*, p. 2.
3. Webb, *History of Philosophy*, p. 2.
4. A philosophy in the sense of an epistomological system which furnishes a complete reply to the question of *the what*, of *the what is life?*—this is not." (Dr. Dahlke, *Buddhism*, p. 25.)

tion of prayers and incantations. Another interpretation
derives the word from *re* and *logo*, and makes its original
sense that of attachment, of a continual binding (that is,
no doubt to the gods). A third derivation connects the word
with *lex*, and explains it as a law-abiding, scrupulously conscientious frame of mind."[1]

Buddhism is not strictly a religion in the sense
in which that word is commonly understood, for
it is not "a system of faith and worship," owing
any allegiance to a supernatural God.

Buddhism does not demand blind faith from
its adherents. Hence mere belief is dethroned and
for it is substituted 'confidence based on knowledge.' It is possible for a Buddhist to entertain
occasional doubts until he attains the first stage
of Sainthood (*Sotāpatti*) when all doubts about the
Buddha, Dhamma, and the Sangha are completely
resolved. One becomes a genuine follower of
the Buddha only after attaining this stage.[2]

The confidence of a follower of the Buddha is
like that of a patient in respect of a noted physician, or of a student regarding his teacher.
Although a Buddhist seeks refuge in the Buddha as
his incomparable guide and teacher who indicates
the Path of Purity, he makes no servile surrender.

---

1. *Buddhism*, p. 1.
2. An ordinary adherent may be genuine enough as a follower, but he is not a sharer by realization of the
   Buddha-Dhamma.

A Buddhist does not think that he can gain purity
merely by seeking refuge in the Buddha or by
mere faith in Him.   It is not within the power even
of a Buddha to wash away the impurities of
others. Strictly speaking, one can neither purify
nor defile another. The Buddha, as Teacher, may
be instrumental, but we ourselves are responsible
for our purification.

In the Dhammapada the Buddha says:

> "*By oneself alone is evil done: by oneself is one defiled.*
> *By oneself alone is evil avoided: by oneself alone is one*
> *purified.*
> *Purity and impurity depend on oneself.*
> *No one can purify another,*" (v. 145).

A Buddhist is not a slave to a book or to any
individual.   Nor does he sacrifice his freedom of
thought by becoming a follower of the Buddha.
He is at full liberty to exercise his own freewill
and develop his knowledge even to the extent of
attaining Buddhahood himself, for all are potential
Buddhas.   Naturally Buddhists quote the Buddha
as their authority, but the Buddha Himself discarded all authority.

Immediate realization is the sole criterion of
truth in Buddhism.   Its keynote is rational understanding (*Sammā diṭṭhi*).   The Buddha advises
seekers of truth not to accept anything merely on
the authority of another but to exercise their own
reasoning and judge for themselves whether a
thing is right or wrong.

On one occasion the citizens of Kesaputta, known as *Kālāmas*, approached the Buddha and said that many ascetics and brahmins who came to preach to them used to exalt their own doctrines and denounce those of others, and that they were at a loss to understand which of those worthies were right.

[1]"Yes, O Kālāmas, it is right for you to doubt, it is right for you to waver. In a doubtful matter, wavering has arisen," remarked the Buddha and gave them the following advice which applies with equal force to modern rationalists as it did to those sceptic brahmins of yore.

"Come, O Kālāmas, Do not accept anything on mere hearsay (i.e., thinking that thus have we heard it from a long time). Do not accept anything by mere tradition (i.e., thinking that it has thus been handed down through many generations). Do not accept anything on account of rumours ('i.e., by believing what others say without any investigation). Do not accept anything just because it accords with your scriptures. Do not accept anything by mere supposition. Do not accept anything by mere inference. Do not accept anything by merely considering the appearances. Do not accept anything merely because it agrees with your preconceived notions. Do not accept anything merely because it seems acceptable

---

1. The bracketed explanatory parts of the foregoing translation are in accordance with the interpretations of the commentary and sub-commentary. The Pāli text of this important passage is as follows:

   "*Etha tumhe Kālāma. Mā anussavena, mā paramparāya, mā itikirāya, mā piṭasampadānena, mā takkahetu, mā nayahetu, mā ākāraparivitakkena, mā diṭṭhinijjhānak-khantiyā, mā bhabbarūpatāya, mā samaṇo no garū ti* (i.e., should be accepted). Do not accept anything thinking that the ascetic is respected by us (and therefore it is right to accept his word.)

"But when you know for yourselves—these things are immoral, these things are blameworthy, these things are censured by the wise, these things, when performed and undertaken, conduce to ruin and sorrow—then indeed do you reject them.

"When you know for yourselves—these things are moral, these things are blameless, these things are praised by the wise, these things,when performed and undertaken, conduce to well-being and happiness—then do you live and act accordingly."[1]

These wise sayings of the Buddha, uttered some 2500 years ago, still retain their original force and freshness even in this enlightened twentieth century.

With a homely illustration *Jnānasāra-samuccaya* repeats the same counsel in different words.

"Tāpāc chedāc ca nikasat svarṇam iva paṇḍitaih
Parīkshya blikshavo grāhyam madvaco na tu gauravāt"

"As the wise test gold by burning, cutting and rubbing it (on a piece of touchstone), so are you to accept my words after examining them and not merely out of regard for me."

The Buddha exhorted His disciple's to seek the truth, and not to heed mere persuasion even by superior authority.

Now, though it be admitted that there is no blind faith in Buddhism, one might question

---

1. Anguttara Nikāya vol. i, p. 189; *Kindred Sayings,* part i, pp. 171, 172.

whether there is no worshipping of Buddha images and such like idolatry amongst Buddhists.

Buddhists do not worship an image expecting worldly or spiritual favours, but pay their homage to what it represents. A Buddhist goes before an image and offers flowers and incense not to the image but to the Buddha. He does so as a mark of gratitude, reflecting on the virtues of the Buddha and pondering on the transiency of flowers. An understanding Buddhist designedly makes himself feel that he is in the noble presence of the Buddha, and thereby gains inspiration to emulate Him.

Referring to images, the great philospher Count Kaiserling writes: "I know nothing more grand in this world than the figure of the Buddha. It is the perfect embodiment of spirituality in the visible domain."[1]

Then again Buddhists do not worship the Bodhi-tree, but consider it a symbol of Enlightenment, and so, worthy of reverence.

Though such external forms of homage are prevalent amongst Buddhists, the Buddha is not worshipped as a God.

These external objects of homage are not absolutely necessary, but they are useful and they help one to concentrate one's attention. An intellectual could dispense with them as he could

---

1. *Travel Diary of a Philosopher.*

easily focus his attention on the Buddha, and thus visualize Him.

For our own good, and out of gratitude, we pay such homage, but what the Buddha expects from His disciples is not obeisance but the actual observance of His teaching.

Just before the Buddha passed away, many disciples came to pay their respects to Him. One Bhikkhu, however, remained in his cell absorbed in meditation. This matter was reported to the Buddha who summoned Him and, on enquiring the reason for his absence, was told: "Lord, I knew that Your Reverence would pass away three months hence, and I thought the best way of honouring the Teacher was by attaining Arahantship even before the decease of Your Reverence."

The Buddha extolled the praiseworthy conduct of that loyal and dutiful Bhikkhu, saying: "Excellent, excellent! He who loves me should emulate this Bhikkhu. He honours me best who practises my teaching best."[1]

On another occasion the Buddha remarked: "He who sees the Dhamma sees me."[2]

Furthermore, it must be mentioned that there are no petitionary or intercessory prayers in Buddhism. However much one may pray to the Buddha one cannot be saved. The Buddha does not

1. See *Buddhist Legends,* vol. 3. pp. 249, 250.
2. Saṁyutta Nikāya vol. 3. p. 129.

and cannot grant worldly favours to those who pray to Him. A Buddhist should not pray to be saved, but should rely on himself and strive with diligence to win his freedom and gain purity. Advising His disciples not to depend on others but to depend on oneself and to be self-reliant, the Buddha says:

Tumhehi kiccaṁ ātappaṁ akkhātāro tathāgatā[1]
"Striving should be done by yourselves. The Tathāgatas are teachers."

The Buddha not only speaks of the futility of prayers[2] but also disparages a slave mentality. Instead of prayers the Buddha emphasizes the importance of meditation that promotes self-discipline, self-control, self-purification and self-enlightenment. It serves as a tonic both to the mind and heart. Meditation is the essence of Buddhism.

In Buddhism there is not, as in most other religions, an Almighty God to be obeyed and feared. Buddhism denies the existence of a supernatural

---

1. Dhammapada v. 276.
2. Comp. "Prayer is an activity in which I frankly confess I am not an adept." Canon B. H. Streeter in *Modern Churchman*—Sept. 1924, p. 347.
   "I do not understand how men continue to pray unless they are convinced there is a listening ear."
   Rev. C. Beard, *Reformation,* p. 419.
   Sir Radhakrishnan states—"Prayers take the character of private communications, selfish bargaining with God. It seeks for objects of earthly ambitions and inflames the sense of self. Meditation on the other hand is self-change."

power, conceived as an Almighty Being or a cause-less force. There are no Divine revelations nor Divine messengers or prophets. A Buddhist is therefore not subservient to any higher super-natural power which controls his destinies and which arbitrarily rewards and punishes. Since Buddhists do not believe in revelations of a Divine Being, Buddhism does not claim the monopoly of truth and does not condemn any other religion. "Intolerance is the greatest enemy of religion". With His characteristic tolerance, the Buddha advised His disciples not to get angry, discontented, or displeased even when others spoke ill of Him, or of His Teaching, or of His Order. "If you do so," the Buddha said, "you will not only bring yourselves into danger of spiritual loss, but you will not be able to judge whether what they say is correct or not correct"—a most enlightened sentiment. Denouncing unfair criticism of other faiths, the Buddha states: "It is as a man who looks up and spits at heaven—the spittle does not soil the heaven, but it comes back and defiles his own person."[1]

Buddhism expounds no dogmas that one must blindly believe, no creeds that one must accept on good faith without reasoning, no superstitious rites and ceremonies to be observed for formal entry into the fold, no meaningless sacrifices and penances for one's purification.

---

1. See Sri Radhakrishnan, *Gautama the Buddha*.

Buddhism cannot, therefore, be strictly called a religion, because it is neither a system of faith and worship, nor "the outward act or form by which men indicate their recognition of the existence of a God or Gods having power over their own destiny to whom obedience, service, and honour are due."[1]

Karl Marx said: "Religion is the soul of soulless conditions, the heart of a heartless world, the opium of the people." Buddhism is not such a religion, for all Buddhist nations grew up in the cradle of Buddhism and their present cultural advancement is clearly due mainly to the benign-influence of the teachings of the Buddha.

However, if, by religion, is meant "a teaching which takes a view of life that is more than superficial, a teaching which looks into life and not merely at it, a teaching which furnishes men with a guide to conduct that is in accord with this in-look, a teaching which enables those who give it heed to face life with fortitude and death with serenity,"[2] or a system of deliverance from the ills of life, then certainly Buddhism is a religion of religions.[3]

---

1. Webster's Dictionary.
2. Ex-Bhikkhu Silācāra. See Ceylon Daily News—Vesak Number May 1939.
3. Dr. Dahlke, in arguing What Buddhism is, writes— "With this, sentence of condemnation is passed upon Buddhism as a religion. Religion, in the ordinary sense as that which points beyond this life to one essentially different, it cannot be."
   Buddhism and its Place in the Mental World, p. 27.

Is Buddhism an Ethical System?

Buddhism contains an excellent moral code, including one for the monks and another for the laity, but it is much more than an ordinary moral teaching.

Morality (*sīla*) is only the preliminary stage and is a means to an end, but not an end in itself. Though absolutely essential, it alone does not lead to one's Deliverance or perfect purity. It is only the first stage on the Path of Purity. Beyond morality is wisdom (*paññā*). The base of Buddhism is morality, and wisdom is its apex. As the pair of wings of a bird are these two complementary virtues. Wisdom is like unto man's eyes; morality is like unto his feet. One of the appellatives of the Buddha is *Vijjācaraṇasampanna*-endowed with wisdom and conduct.

Of the Four Noble Truths that form the foundation of Buddhism, the first three represent the philosophy of the Buddha's teaching; the fourth the ethics of Buddhism based on that philosophy.

Morality in Buddhism is not founded on any doubtful divine revelation, nor is it the ingenious invention of an exceptional mind, but it is a rational and practical code based on verifiable facts and individual experience. In the opinion of Prof. Max Muller the Buddhist moral code is one of the most perfect which the world has ever known.

Prof. Rhys Davids says: "Buddhist or no Buddhist I have examined every one of the great religious systems of the world; and in none of those have I found anything to surpass in beauty and comprehensiveness the Noble Eightfold Path of the Buddha. I am content to shape my life according to that path."

It is interesting to note that according to Buddhism there are deeds which are ethically good and bad, deeds which are neither good nor bad, and deeds which tend to the ceasing of all deeds. Good deeds are essential for one's emancipation, but when once the ultimate goal of the Holy Life is attained, one transcends both good and evil.

The Buddha says: "Righteous things (*dhamma*) you have to give up: how much more the unrighteous things (*adhamma*)."[1]

The deed which is associated with attachment (*lobha*), illwill (*dosa*) and delusion (*moha*) is evil. That deed which is associated with non-attachment (*alobha*), goodwill (*adosa*), and wisdom (*paññā*), is good.

The deeds of an Arahant, a Stainless One, possess no ethical value as he has gone beyond both good and evil. This does not mean that he is passive. He is active, but his activity is selfless and is directed to help others to tread the path he has trodden himself. His deeds, ordinarily accepted as good, lack creative power as regards

1. Majjhima Nikāya, Sutta No. 22.

himself. Unlike the actions of a worldling his actions do not react on himself as a Kammic effect.

His actions, in Pali, are called *kiriya* (functional). Purest gold cannot further be purified.

The mental states of the four types of supramundane Path consciousness, namely, *Sotāpatti* (Stream-Winner), *Sakadāgāmi* (Once-Returner), *Anāgāmi* (Non-Returner) and *Arahatta* (Worthy), though wholesome (*kusala*), do not tend to accumulate fresh Kamma, but, on the contrary, tend to the gradual cessation of the individual flux of becoming, and therewith to the gradual cessation of good and evil deeds. In these types of supramundane consciousness the wisdom factor (*paññā*), which tends to destroy the roots of Kamma, is predominant; while in the mundane types of consciousness volition (*cetanā*) which produces Kammic activities is predominant.

What is the criterion of morality according to Buddhism?

The answer is found in the admonition given by the Buddha to young Samaṇera *Rāhula*.

"If there is a deed, Rāhula, you wish to do, reflect thus: Is this deed conducive to my harm, or to others' harm, or to that of both? Then is this a bad deed entailing suffering. From such a deed you must resist.

"If there is a deed you wish to do, reflect thus: Is this deed not conducive to my harm, nor to others' harm, nor to that of both? Then is this a good deed entailing happiness. Such a deed you must do again and again."[1]

In assessing morality a Buddhist takes into consideration the interests both of himself and others—animals not excluded.

In the *Karanīya Metta Sutta* the Buddha exhorts: "As the mother protects her only child even at the risk of her own life; even so let one cultivate boundless thoughts of loving-kindness towards all beings."[2]

The Dhammapada states:

"All fear punishment, to all life is dear. Comparing others with oneself, let one neither hurt nor kill."[3]

To understand the exceptionally high standard of morality the Buddha expects from His ideal followers, one must carefully read the Dhammapada, Sigālovāda Sutta, Vyāgghapajja Sutta, Mangala Sutta, Metta Sutta, Parābhava Sutta, Vasala Sutta, Dhammika Sutta, etc.

As a moral teaching it excels all other ethical systems, but morality is only the beginning and not the end of Buddhism.

In one sense Buddhism is not a philosophy, in another sense it is the philosophy of philosophies.

1. Majjhima Nikāya, Rāhulovāda Sutta, No. 61.
   See pp. 130-133.
2. Sutta Nipāta
3. V. 129

In one sense Buddhism is not a religion, in another sense it is the religion of religions.

What Buddhism is

Buddhism is neither a metaphysical path nor a ritualistic path.

It is neither sceptical nor dogmatic.

It is neither eternalism nor nihilism.

It is neither self-mortification nor self-indulgence.

It is neither pessimism nor optimism but realism.

It is neither absolutely this-worldly nor other-worldly.

It is not extravert but introvert.

It is not theo-centric but homo-centric.

It is a unique Path of Enlightenment.

The original Pali term for Buddhism is *Dhamma*, which, literally, means that which upholds or sustains (him who acts in conformity with its principles and thus prevents him from falling into woeful states). There is no proper English equivalent that exactly conveys the meaning of the Pali term.

The Dhamma is that which really is. It is the Doctrine of Reality. It is a Means of Deliverance from suffering and Deliverance itself. Whether the Buddhas arise or not the Dhamma exists from all eternity. It is a Buddha that realizes this Dhamma, which ever lies hidden from the ignorant eyes of men, till He, an Enlightened One, comes and compassionately reveals it to the world.

"Whether the Tathāgatas appear or not, O Bhikkhus, it remains a fact, an established principle, a natural law that all conditioned things are transient (*anicca*), sorrowful (*dukkha*) and that everything is soulless (*anatta*). This fact the Tathāgata realizes, understands and when He has realized and understood it, announces, teaches, proclaims, establishes, discloses, analyses, and makes it clear, that all conditoned things are transient, sorrowful, and that everything is soulless."[1]

In the Majjhima Nikāya the Buddha says: "One thing only does the Buddha teach, namely, suffering and the cessation of suffering."[2]

This is the Doctrine of Reality.

Udāna states: "Just as, O Bhikkhus, the mighty ocean is of one flavour, the flavour of salt, even so, O Bhikkhus, this Dhamma is of one flavour, the flavour of Deliverance (*Vimutti*)."[3]

This is the Means of Deliverance.

This sublime Dhamma is not something apart from oneself. It is purely dependent on oneself and is to be realized by oneself. As such the Buddha exhorts:

1. Anguttara Nikāya Part I, p. 286.
2. Majjhima Nikāya Vol. I, p. 140 No. 22.
3. P. 67.

"*Attadīpā viharatha attapaṭisaraṇā*"[1]—Abide with oneself as an island, with oneself as a refuge.

"*Dhammadīpā viharatha, dhamma paṭisaraṇā, n'añña patisaraṇā*—Abide with the Dhamma as an island, with the Dhamma as a refuge.   Seek not for external refuge.[2]

---

1. Parinibbāna Sutta; see chapter 14.
2. Ibid.

CHAPTER 16

SOME SALIENT CHARACTERISTICS
OF BUDDHISM

―――――

"Well expounded is the Dhamma by the Exalted One, to be self-realized, with immediate fruit, inviting investigation, leading on to Nibbāna, to be comprehended by the wise, each for himself."

MAJJHIMA NIKĀYA

Foundations of Buddhism

The four Noble Truths, which the Buddha Himself discovered and revealed to the world, are the chief characteristics and the unshakable foundations of Buddhism.

They are suffering (the *raison d'etre* of Buddhism), its cause, i.e., craving, its end, i.e., Nibbana (the *summum bonum* of Buddhism), and the Middle Way.

The first three represent the philosophy of Buddhism, while the fourth represents the ethics of Buddhism, in accordance with that philosophy.

All these four Truths which comprise the Dhamma of the Buddha are dependent on this body itself. They are incontrovertible facts wholly associated with man and other beings.

Whether the Buddhas arise or not these Truths exist in the universe. It is the Buddhas that reveal them to the world.

Buddhism rests on the pivot of suffering. Although Buddhism emphasizes the existence of suffering yet it does not follow that Buddhism is a pessimistic religion. On the contrary it is neither totally pessimistic nor totally optimistic but realistic. One would be justified in calling the Buddha a pessimist if He had merely emphasized the truth of suffering without suggesting a means to end suffering and gain eternal happiness. The Buddha perceived the universality of sorrow and prescribed a remedy for this universal sickness of humanity. The highest conceivable happiness, according to the Buddha, is Nibbana, which is the total extinction of suffering.

The Author of the article on "Pessimism" in the *Encyclopaedia Britannica* writes:

"Pessimism denotes an attitude of hopelessness towards life, a vague general opinion that pain and evil predominate in human affairs. The original doctrine of the Buddha is in fact as optimistic as any optimism of the West. To call it 'pessimism' is merely to apply to it a characteristically Western Principle according to which happiness is impossible without personality. The true Buddhist looks forward with enthusiasm to absorption into eternal Bliss."

Happiness

The Buddha does not expect His followers to be constantly brooding on the ills of life and so make their lives unhappy.

Joy (*pīti*) has to be cultivated by every Buddhist as one of the essentials or prerequisites of Enlightenment. In the opinion of many unbiased writers,

Buddhists are reputed to be the happiest people in the whole world. They have no inferiority complex that they are wretched sinners.

The members of the Noble Order, who lead the Holy Life in the fullest possible manner, are perhaps the happiest persons. *"Aho sukhaṁ, aho sukhaṁ"*—Oh, happy indeed! Oh, happy indeed! "We shall be living in Joy"—are some of the oft-repeated favourite sayings of His followers.

One day a certain deity approached the Buddha and questioned Him thus:

"Who in the forest make their wonted haunt-—
The saintly livers of the holy life—
Who by one daily meal do break their fast:
Tell me how look they so serene of hue?"[1]

The Buddha replied;

"They make no lamentation o'er the past,
They yearn not after that which is not come,
By what now is do they maintain themselves;
Hence comes it that they look serene of hue."[1]

Happily the Bhikkhus live in the eternal present with no worries about either the past or the future.

Causal Law in Terms of Happiness

In the Saṁyutta Nikāya is found an interesting interpretation of the Dependent Origination (*Paṭicca Samuppāda*) in terms of happiness. The Buddha says:

---

1. *Kindred Sayings*, part 1, pp. 7, 8.

"Suffering leads to Confidence (*Saddhā*); Confidence to Rapture (*Pāmojja*); Rapture to Joy (*Pīti*); Joy to Tranquillity (*Passaddhi*); Tranquillity to Happiness (*Sukha*); Happiness to Concentration (*Samādhi*); Concentration to Knowledge and Vision of things as they truly are (*Yathābhūtañāṇadassana*); the Knowledge and Vision of things as they truly are to Repulsion (*Nibbidā*); Repulsion to Non-attachment (*Virāga*); Non-attachment to Deliverance (*Vimutti*); Deliverance to the Extinction of Passions (*Khaye-Nāṇa*); i. e., to Arahantship."[1]

This important passage clearly indicates how suffering can lead to happiness and ultimately to Sainthood.

Tolerance of Buddhism

No blind faith is necessary to understand these four Noble Truths. The first two Truths, which are mundane (*lokiya*), can be experienced by worldlings, themselves. The second two Truths, which are supramundane (*lokuttara*) can be experienced by attaining Saintship.

It is on the bed-rock of these facts, which could be verified by personal experience and tested by anybody, that the Buddha-Dhamma is built, and not on the fear of the unknown. Buddhism is therefore rational and intensely practical.

In the Dhamma there is nothing that is impractical or irrational. The Buddha practised what He taught; He taught what He practised. What He most emphasizes in His teaching is practice, for

---

1. Saṁyutta Nikāya, vol. ii, p. 32; *Kindred Sayings*, part ii, p. 27.

creeds alone cannot purify a person.
The Dhammapada states:

"Though much he recites the Scared Texts but acts not accordingly, that heedless man is like a cow-herd who counts others' kine; he has no share in the blessings of a recluse," (v. 19).

A rational and practical system cannot contain any mysterious or esoteric doctrine.   In the Pari-nibbāna Sutta the Buddha emphatically declares:

"I have taught the truth without making any distinction between esoteric and exoteric doctrine; for in respect of the truth Tathāgata has no such thing as the closed fist   of teacher who keeps something back."

Anantaraṁ and *abāhiraṁ* are the words used by the Buddha.   If the Buddha had thought—"This much of my doctrine I will not teach others," or "Only this much of my doctrine I will teach others," He would have fallen into the category of teachers who keep a closed fist.   If the Buddha had thought—"To these persons I will teach" or "To these persons I will not teach"—the Buddha would have created an inner circle and outer circle.   The Buddha makes no such distinction.[1]

With respect to secret doctrines the Buddha says in the Anguttara Nikāya.:[2]

"O disciples, there are three to whom secrecy belongs and not openness.   Who are they?   Secrecy belongs to women, not openness; secrecy belongs to priestly wisdom, not openness; secrecy belongs to false doctrine not openness.   The

1.   See p. 243.
2.   Part I, p. 261.

doctrines and rules proclaimed by the perfect Buddha shine before all the world and not in secret."

It is true that the Buddha had not expressed His view about some problems that perplex mankind. He was characteristically silent on these controversial subjects because they were irrelevant to His noble mission and unessential to one's Emancipation.

On a certain occasion a certain Bhikkhu, named Mālunkyaputta, approached the Buddha and impatiently demanded an immediate solution of some speculative problems on the threat of discarding the robe forthwith.

"Lord," he said, "these theories have not been elucidated, have been set aside, and rejected by the Exalted One— whether the world is eternal or not eternal; whether the world is finite or infinite; whether the life-principle (jīva) is the same as the body or whether the life-principle is one and the body is another; whether the Tathāgata, after death, is or is not; whether the Tathāgata, after death both is and is not; whether the Tathāgata, after death neither is nor is not."[1]

The Buddha advised him not to waste time and energy over such idle speculation which was detrimental to moral progress.

"It is as if a person were pierced by an arrow thickly smeared with poison and he should say to the surgeon who wants to extract it: I shall not allow the arrow to be extracted until I know the details of the person who wounded me, the nature of the arrow with which I was pierced, etc. That

1. Majjhima Nikāya, Cūla Mālunkya Sutta, No. 63.

perṣon would die before this would ever be known by him. In the same way that person would die before these questions had ever been elucidated."

The solving of these metaphysical questions did not lead to aversion, passionlessness, enlightenment, or Nibbana.

On another occasion when His disciples sought information about these points He silenced them by citing the parable of the elephant and blind men.[1]

An elephant was presented to some blind men to describe what it looked like. Those who touched the different parts of the elephant's body expressed their own peculiar ideas about the elephant. They argued amongst themselves and their arguments naturally ended in a quarrel.

Useless speculations that do not tend to Emancipation and that merely gratify curiosity, the Buddha dismisses with His characteristic silence.

Buddhism does not profess to provide an explanation to all ethical and philosophical problems that interest mankind. Neither does it deal with idle speculations and theorisings that do not tend to edification. Buddhism has a practical and specific purpose—the cessation of suffering—and with that goal in view all irrelevant side issues are completely set aside. Nevertheless, every encouragement is given to keen investigation into the real nature of life.

---

1. See Udāna, vi, p. 4; Woodward, *Some Sayings of the Buddha,* pp. 287, 288.

No coercions, persecutions, or fanaticisms play any part in Buddhism. To the unique credit of Buddhism it must be said that throughout its peaceful march of 2500 years no drop of blood has been shed in the name of the Buddha, no mighty monarch has wielded his powerful sword to propagate the Dhamma, and no conversion has been made either by force or by repulsive methods. Yet the Buddha was the first and the greatest missionary that lived on earth. Buddhism has spread, and is still spreading rapidly throughout the world, and is making peaceful penetration to all countries mainly owing to the intrinsic merit and unsurpassing beauty of its teachings and not at all with the aid of Imperialism, militarism or any other indirect proselytising agencies.

Aldous Huxley—writes.—"Alone of all the great world religions Buddhism made its way without persecution, censorship or inquisition. In all these respects its record is enormously superior to that of Christianity, which made its way among people wedded to materialism and which was able to justify the bloodthirsty tendencies of its adherents by an appeal to savage bronze-age literature of the Old Testament."

Lord Russell remarks: "Of the great religions of history, I prefer Buddhism, especially in its earliest forms; because it has had the smallest element of persecution."

In the name of the Buddha no sacred place was reddened with the blood of innocent women, no sincere thinkers were burnt alive, and there was no merciless roasting of heretics.

Buddhism which teaches nothing mysterious does not speak of miracles. The Buddha no doubt possessed supernormal powers as a result of His mental culture, but He did not perform miracles. *Yamaka Pāṭihāriya*,[1] for instance, erroneously rendered "Twin Miracle," is a psychic phenomenon which only a Buddha can perform. In this particular case, by His psychic powers, He makes fire and water issue from the pores of the body simultaneously.

Buddhism appeals more to the intellect than to the emotion. It is concerned more with the character of the devotees than with their numerical strength.

On one occasion Upāli the millionaire, a follower of Niganṭha Nātaputta, approached the Buddha and was so pleased with the Buddha's exposition of the Dhamma that he instantly expressed his desire to become a follower of the Buddha. But the Buddha advised him, saying—"Of a verity, O householder, make a thorough investigation. It is well for a distinguished man like you to make a thorough investigation."

Upāli, who was overwhelmed with joy at this unexpected utterance of the Buddha, said:

"Lord, if I had become a follower of another teacher, his followers would have taken me round the streets in procession proclaiming that such and such a millionaire had renounced his former religion and had embraced theirs. But, Lord, you advise me to investigate further. The more pleased

---

1. See p. 120.
1. See p. 120.

am I with this salutary advice of yours.   And he appreciatively
repeated—for the second time I seek refuge in the Buddha,
the Dhamma, and the Sangha."

Though he became a Buddhist by conviction,
the Buddha, quite in keeping with His boundless
compassion and perfect tolerance, advised him to
support his former religious teacher in accordance
with his practice.

Exhorting all seekers of truth not to be
influenced by external authorities or by mere per-
suasions, the Buddha even went to the extent of
requesting His disciples not to bow down submissively to superior authority.

Buddhism is saturated with this spirit of free
inquiry and complete tolerance.   It is the teaching
of the open mind and the sympathetic heart which,
lighting and warming the whole universe with its
twin rays of wisdom and compassion, sheds its
genial glow on every being struggling in the ocean
of birth and death.

So compassionate and tolerant was the Buddha
that He did not exercise His power to give commandments to His lay-followers.   Instead of using
the Imperative—Thou shalt or thou shalt not—
He says—It behoves you to do this, it behoves
you not to do this.

The ordinary precepts which Buddhists are
expected to observe are not commandments but
modes of discipline (*sikkhāpada*) which they take
of their own accord.

This tolerance and sympathy the Buddha extended to men, women, and all living beings.

Buddhism and Caste

It was the Buddha who, for the first time in the known history of mankind, attempted to abolish slavery and "invented the higher morality and the idea of the brotherhood of the entire human race and in striking terms condemned" the degrading caste-system which was firmly rooted. In Indian Society at that time. The Buddha declared:

> "*By birth is not one an outcast,*
> *By birth is not one a brahmin.*
> *By deeds is one an outcast,*
> *By deeds is one a brahmin.*"[1]

Vāseṭṭha Sutta[2] relates that two young brahmins had a discussion with regard to what constitutes a brahmin. One maintained that birth made a brahmin, while the other contended that conduct made a brahmin. As neither could convince the other both of them agreed to refer the matter to the Buddha.

So they approached the Buddha and presented their case before Him.

The Buddha at first reminded the questioners that although in the case of plants, insects, quadrupeds, serpents, fishes and birds there are

1. Sutta Nipāta—Vasala Sutta.
2. Ibid, p. 115.

many species and marks by which they could be distinguished, yet in the case of men there are no such species and marks. Then He explained how men differentiated themselves according to their various occupations. In conclusion the Buddha commented:

"*Birth makes no brahmin, nor non-brahmin makes;*
'Tis life and doing that mould the brahmin true.
Their lives mould farmers, tradesmen, merchants serfs;
Their lives mould robbers, soldiers, chaplains, kings."

Another interesting dialogue concerning this problem of caste appears in the Madhura Sutta.[1] The King of Madhura makes the following report to the Venerable *Kaccāna.*

"The brahmins say thus, *Kaccāna,* 'The brahmins are the most distinguished of the four divisions into which the people are classified; every other division is inferior. The brahmins alone are accounted pure, not those who are not brahmins. The brahmins are the legitimate sons of Brahma, born from his mouth, specially made by him, heirs of Brahma. What do you, Sir, say to this?"

The Venerable *Kaccāna* replied that it was an empty assertion and pointed out how a wealthy person could employ as his servant a member of any class or caste and how a vicious person could be born in a woeful state and a virtuous person in

---

1. Majjhima Nikāya, Vol. ii, pp.83-90.

a blissful state despite their particular castes, adding that a criminal, irrespective of his caste, would be punished for his crime. He emphasized the fact that all joining the Order receive equal honour and reverence without any discrimination.

According to Buddhism caste or colour does not preclude one from becoming an adherent of the Buddha or from entering the noble Order of the Sangha where all are treated as Ariyas. Fishermen, scavengers, courtesans, together with warriors and brahmins, were freely admitted into the Order and were also given positions of rank.

Upāli, the barber, was made, in preference to all others, chief disciple in matters pertaining to the Vinaya discipline. *Sunīta*, who was honoured by Kings and nobles as an Arahant, was a timid scavenger. The philosophic Sāti was the son of a fisherman. The courtesan *Ambapāli* joined the Order and attained Arahantship. *Rajjumālā*, who was converted by the Buddha as she was about to commit suicide, was a slave girl. So was *Punnā* whose invitation to spend a rainy season was accepted by the Buddha in preference to that of the millionaire *Anāthapindika*, her own master. *Subhā* was the daughter of a smith. *Cāpā* was the daughter of a deer-stalker. Such instances could be multiplied from the books to show that portals of Buddhism were wide open to all without any distinction.

The Buddha provided equal opportunities for all and raised, rather than lowered, the status of people.

In Buddhism one finds milk for the babe and meat for the strong, and it appeals equally to both the rich and the poor.

Buddhism and Women

It was also the Buddha who raised the status of women and brought them to a realization of their importance to society.

Before the advent of the Buddha women in India were not held in high esteem. One Indian writer, Hemacandra, looked down upon women as "the torch lighting the way to hell"—*Naraka-mārgadvārasya dīpikā.*

The Buddha did not humiliate women, but only regarded them as feeble by nature. He saw the innate good of both men and women and assigned to them their due places in His teaching. Sex is no barrier for purification or service.

Sometimes the Pali term used to connote women is *mātugāma* which means 'mother-folk' or 'society of mothers.' As a mother a woman holds an honourable place in Buddhism. The mother is regarded as a convenient ladder to ascend to heaven, and a wife is regarded as the 'best friend' (*paramā sakhā*) of the husband.

Although at first the Buddha refused to admit women into the Order on reasonable grounds, yet later He yielded to the entreaties of Venerable *Ānanda* and His foster-mother, *Mahā Pajāpati Gotamī*, and founded the Order of Bhikkhunis (*Nuns*). It was the Buddha who thus founded the first society for women with rules and regulations.

Just as Arahants *Sāriputta* and *Moggallāna* were made the two chief disciples in the Order of Bhikkhus, the oldest democratically constituted celibate Order, even so the Arahants *Khemā* and *Uppalavaṇṇā* were made the two chief female disciples in the Order of Bhikkhunis. Many other female disciples, too, were named by the Buddha Himself as amongst most distinguished and pious followers. Amongst the Vajjis, too, freedom to women was regarded as one of the causes that led to their prosperity. Before the advent of the Buddha women did not enjoy sufficient freedom and were deprived of an opportunity to exhibit their innate spiritual capabilities and their mental gifts. In ancient India, as is still seen today, the birth of a daughter to a family was considered an unwelcome and cumbersome addition.

On one occasion while the Buddha was conversing with King *Kosala*, a messenger came and informed the King that a daughter was born unto him. Hearing it, the King was naturally displeased. But the Buddha comforted and stimulated him, saying:

"A woman child, O Lord of men, may prove
Even a better offspring than a male."[1]

To women who were placed under various dis-
abilities before the appearance of the Buddha,
the establishment of the Order of Bhikkhunis was
certainly a blessing. In this Order queens, princes-
ses, daughters of noble families, widows, bereaved
mothers, helpless women, courtesans—all despite
their caste or rank met on a common footing,
enjoyed perfect consolation and peace, and breathed that free atmosphere which was denied to
those cloistered in cottages and palatial mansions.
Many, who otherwise would have fallen into
oblivion, distinguished themselves in various ways
and gained their emancipation by seeking refuge
in the Order.

Khemā, the first chief female disciple, was the
beautiful consort of King Bimbisāra. She was
at first reluctant to see the Buddha as she heard
that the Buddha used to refer to external beauty
in disparaging terms. One day she paid a casual
visit to the monastery merely to enjoy the scenery
of the place. Gradually she was attracted to the
hall where the Buddha was preaching. The
Buddha, who read her thoughts, created by His
psychic powers a handsome young lady, standing
aside fanning Him. *Khemā* was admiring her
beauty. The Buddha made this created image
change from youth to middle age and old age,

---

1. *Kindred Sayings,* part I, p. 111. See p. 202.

till it finally fell on the ground with broken teeth, grey hair, and wrinkled skin. Then only did she realize the vanity of external beauty and the fleeting nature of life. She thought:

"Has such a body come to be wrecked like that? Then so will my body also."

The Buddha read her mind and said:

"They who are slaves to lust drift down the stream,
Like to a spider gliding down the web
He of himself wrought. But the released,
Who all their bonds have snapt in twain,
With thoughts elsewhere intent, forsake the world,
And all delight in sense put far away."[1]

Khemā attained Arahantship and with the king's consent entered the Order. She was ranked foremost in Insight amongst the Bhikkhunis.

Paṭācārā, who lost her two children, husband, parents and brother, under very tragic circumstances, was attracted to the Buddha's presence by His will-power. Hearing the Buddha's soothing words, she attained the first stage of Sainthood and entered the Order. One day, as she was washing her feet she noticed how first the water trickled a little way and subsided, the second time it flowed a little further and subsided, and the third time it flowed still further and subsided. "Even so do mortals die," she pondered, "either in childhood, or in middle age, or when old." The

---

1. *Psalms of the Sisters*—p.. 82.

Buddha read her thoughts and, projecting His image before her, taught her the Dhamma. She attained Arahantship and later became a source of consolation to many a bereaved mother.

Dhammadinnā and *Bhaddā Kāpilāni* were two Bhikkhunis who were honoured exponents of the Dhamma.

In answer to Māra, the Evil One, it was Bhik-khunī *Somā*[1] who remarked:

"What should the woman-nature count in her who, with mind well-set and knowledge advancing, has right to the Dhamma? To one who entertains doubt with the question: 'Am I a woman in these matters, or am I a man, or what then am I?'—the Evil One is fit to talk."

Amongst the laity too there were many women who were distinguished for their piety, generosity, devotion, learning and loving-kindness.

Visākhā, the chief benefactress of the Order, stands foremost amongst them all.[2]

Suppiyā was a very devout lady who, being unable to procure some flesh from the market, cut a piece of flesh from her thigh to prepare a soup for a sick Bhikkhu.

Nakulamātā was a faithful wife who, by reciting her virtues, rescued her husband from the jaws of death.

1. See *Kindred Sayings*, Part i. p. 162.
2. See pp. 175-188.

Sāmāvati was a pious and lovable queen who, without any illwill, radiated loving-kindness towards her rival even when she was burnt to death through her machination.

Queen *Mallikā* on many occasions counselled her husband, King *Pasenadi*.

A maid-servant, *Khujjuttarā*, secured many converts by teaching the Dhamma.

Punabbasumātā was so intent on hearing the Dhamma that she hushed her crying child thus:

"*O silence, little Uttarā! Be still,*
Punabbasu, that I may hear the Norm
Taught by the Master, by the Wisest Man.
Dear unto us is our own child, and dear
Our husband; dearer still than these to me
Is't of this Doctrine to explore the Path."[1]

A contemplative mother, when questioned why she did not weep at the loss of her only child, said:

"*Uncalled he hither came, unbidden soon to go;*
E'en as he came, he went.   What cause is here for
woe?"[2]

Sumanā and *Subhaddā* were two sisters of exemplary character who had implicit faith in the Buddha.

---

1. *Kindred Sayings*, 5 Part I, p. 270.
2. Jātaka Translation v.p. 110, No. 354.

These few instances will suffice to illustrate
the great part played by women in the time of the
Buddha.

Buddhism and Harmlessness

The boundless kindness of the Buddha was
directed not only to all human beings but also to
the dumb animals as well. It was the Buddha who
banned the sacrifice of animals and admonished
His followers to extend their loving-kindness
(*Mettā*) to all living beings—even to the tiniest
creature that crawls at one's feet. No man, He
taught, has the right to destroy the life of another
as life is precious to all.

A Bhikkhu is expected to exercise this loving-
kindness to such an extent that he is forbidden by
the Vinaya rules even to dig or cause to dig the
ground. He cannot even drink water without it
being filtered.

Asoka, the greatest Buddhist King, wrote on
rock and monolith, saying: "The living must not
be nourished with the living. Even chaff with
insects must not be burnt."

A genuine Buddhist must practise this Metta
towards every living being and identify himself
with all, making no distinctions whatever. It is
this Buddhist Metta, one of the most salient characteristics of Buddhism, that attempts to break
all the barriers of caste, colour and creed which separate one man from another. If followers of
different faiths cannot meet on a common platform

like brothers and sisters just because they belong to different religions, then surely the religious teachers have failed in their noble missions.

In that noble Toleration Edict, which is based on the Culla Vyūha and Maha Vyūha Suttas, King *Asoka* says: "Concourse alone is best, that is, all should hearken willingly to the doctrines professed by others."

In its teaching Buddhism has no features to confine it to any particular nation or any particular country. It is universal in its appeal.

To the Buddhist there is no far or near, no enemy or foreigner, no renegade or untouchable, since universal love, realized through understanding, has established the brotherhood of all living beings. A real Buddhist is a citizen of the world.

Some salient characteristics of Buddhism are, therefore, its rationality, practicability, efficacy, non-aggressiveness, harmlessness, tolerance, and universality.

Buddhism is the noblest of all unifying and uplifting influences that has operated for more than 2500 years.

*   *   *

Nations have come and gone. Empires built on might and force have flourished and perished. But the Dhamma Empire of the Buddha, founded on love and reason, still flourishes and will continue to flourish as long as its followers adhere to its noble principles.

CHAPTER 17

THE FOUR NOBLE TRUTHS

_____

"*Light arose in me in things not heard before.*"

DHAMMACAKKA SUTTA

Truth (*Sacca*) is that which is. Its Saṁskrit equivalent is *Satya* which means an incontrovertible fact.

According to Buddhism there are four such Truths[1] pertaining to this so-called being.

In the Rohitassa Sutta the Buddha states:

"In this very one-fathom long body along with its perceptions and thoughts, do I proclaim the world, the origin of the world, the cessation of the world, and the path leading to the cessation of the world."[2]

In this particular context the term "world" (*loka*) implies suffering.

This interesting passage refers to the four Noble Truths which the Buddha Himself discovered by His own intuitive knowledge. Whether the Buddhas arise or not these Truths exist, and it is a Buddha that reveals them to the deluded world. They do not and cannot change with time because they are eternal Truths. The Buddha was not

_____

1. See Chapter 6.
2. Saṁyutta Nikāya, i. p. 62. See *Kindred Sayings*, part I. p. 86.

indebted to anyone for His realization of them. He Himself said: "They were unheard before."[1]

These Truths are in Pali termed *ariyasaccāni*. They are so called because they were discovered by the Greatest Ariya, the Buddha, who was far removed from passion.

The first Truth deals with *dukkha*, which for need of a better English equivalent, is rendered by suffering or sorrow. As a feeling *dukkha* means that which is difficult to be endured (*du* = difficult, *kha* = to endure). As an abstract truth *dukkha* is used in the sense of 'contemptible' (*du*) and 'emptiness' (*kha*). The world rests on suffering— hence it is contemptible. The world is devoid of any reality—hence it is empty or void. *Dukkha*, therefore, means contemptible void.

Average men are only surface-seers. An Ariya sees things as they truly are. To an Ariya all life is suffering and he finds no real happiness in this world which deceives mankind with illusory plea- sures. Material happiness is merely the gratifica- tion of some desire. "No sooner is the desired thing gained than it begins to be scorned." Ins- atiate are all desires.

---

1. Hence there is no justification for the statement that Buddhism is a natural outgrowth of Hinduism, although it has to be admitted that there exist some fundmental doctrines common to both and that is because those doctrines are in accordance with eternal truth or Dhamma.

All are subject to birth (*jāti*), and consequently to decay (*jarā*), disease (*vyādhi*), and finally to death (*maraṇa*). No one is exempt from these four inevitable causes of suffering.

Impeded wish is also suffering. We do not wish to be associated with things or persons we detest, nor do we wish to be separated from things or persons we love. Our cherished desires are not, however, always gratified. What we least expect or what we least desire is often thrust on us. At times such unexpected unpleasant circumstances become so intolerable and painful that weak ignorant folk are compelled to commit suicide as if such an act would solve the problem.

Real happiness is found within, and is not to be defined in terms of wealth, power, honours or conquests. If such worldly possessions are forcibly or unjustly obtained, or are misdirected, or even viewed with attachment, they will be a source of pain and sorrow for the possessors.

Ordinarily the enjoyment of sensual pleasures is the highest and only happiness to an average person. There is no doubt a momentary happiness in the anticipation, gratification, and recollection of such fleeting material pleasures, but they are illusory and temporary. According to the Buddha non-attachment (*virāgatā*) or the transcending of material pleasures is a greater bliss.

In brief, this composite body itself is a cause of suffering.

This First Truth of suffering which depends
on this so-called being and various aspects of life,
is to be carefully analysed and examined. This
examination leads to a proper understanding of
oneself as one really is.

The cause of this suffering is craving or attachment (*taṇhā*) which is the Second Noble Truth.

The Dhammapada states:

"From craving springs grief, from craving springs fear,
For him who is wholly free from craving, there is no
grief, much less fear." (V. 216)

This craving is a powerful mental force latent
in all, and is the chief cause of most of the ills of
life. It is this craving, gross or subtle, that leads
to repeated births in Saṁsāra and makes one cling
to all forms of life.

The grossest forms of craving are attenuated
on attaining *Sakadāgāmi*, the second stage of
Sainthood, and are eradicated on attaining *Anāgāmi*, the third stage of Sainthood. The subtle
forms of craving are eradicated on attaining
Arahantship.

Both suffering and craving can only be eradicated by following the Middle Way, enunciated by
the Buddha Himself, and attaining the supreme
Bliss of Nibbāna.

The Third Noble Truth is the complete cessation of suffering which is Nibbāna, the ultimate

Goal of Buddhists. It is achieved by the total eradication of all forms of craving.

This Nibbāna is to be comprehended by the mental eye by renouncing all internal attachment to the external world.[1]

This Truth has to be realized by developing the Noble Eightfold Path which is the Fourth Noble Truth. This unique path is the only straight route that leads to Nibbāna. It avoids the extreme of self-mortification that weakens one's intellect and the extreme of self-indulgence that retards one's moral progress.

It consists of the following eight factors.:

1) Right Understanding (*Sammā Diṭṭhi*),
2) Right Thoughts (*Sammā Saṁkappa*),
3) Right Speech (*Sammā Vācā*),
4) Right Action (*Sammā Kammanta*),
5) Right Livelihood (*Sammā Ājīva*),
6) Right Effort (*Sammā Vāyāma*),
7) Right Mindfulness (*Sammā Sati*), and
8) Right Concentration (*Sammā Samādhi*),

1. Right Understanding is explained as the knowledge of the four Noble Truths. In other words, it is the understanding of oneself as one really is, because, as the Rohitassa Sutta states, these truths are concerned with the 'one-fathom long body of man.'

The key-note of Buddhism is this right understanding.

---

1. See chapters 33, 34.

2.   Clear vision or right understanding leads to
clear thinking.   The second factor of the noble
Eightfold Path is, therefore, *Sammā Saṁkappa*.
The English renderings—'Right Resolutions', Right
Aspirations'—do not convey the actual meaning
of the Pali term. Right Ideas or Right Mindfulness
comes closer to the meaning. 'Right Thoughts'
may be suggested as the nearest English equivalent.

By *Saṁkappa* is meant the '*Vitakka*' mental
state, which, for want of a better rendering, may
be called 'initial application.' This important
mental state eliminates wrong ideas or notions
and helps the other moral adjuncts to be diverted
to Nibbāna.

It is one's thoughts that either defile or purify
a person. One's thoughts mould one's nature
and controls one's destiny. Evil thoughts tend
to debase one just as good thoughts tend to elevate
one. Sometimes a single thought can either destroy or save a world.

Sammā Saṁkappa serves the double purpose
of eliminating evil thoughts and developing pure
thoughts.

Right Thoughts, in this particular connection,
are threefold.

They consist of:

i.   *Nekkhamma*—Renunciation of worldly pleasures or selflessness which is opposed to attachment, selfishness, and self-possessiveness.

ii. *Avyāpāda*—Loving-kindness, goodwill, or benevolence, which is opposed to hatred, ill-will, or aversion, and

iii. *Avihiṁsā*—Harmlessness or compassion, which is opposed to cruelty and callousness.

These evil and good forces are latent in all. As long as we are worldlings these evil forces rise to the surface at unexpected moments in disconcerting strength. When once they are totally eradicated on attaining Arahantship, one's stream of consciousness gets perfectly purified.

Attachment and hatred, coupled with ignorance, are the chief causes of all evil prevalent in this deluded world. "The enemy of the whole world is lust, through which all evils come to living beings. This lust when obstructed by some cause is transformed into wrath."

One is either attached to desirable external objects or is repulsed with aversion in the case of undesirable objects. Through attachment one clings to material pleasures and tries to gratify one's desire by some means or other. Through aversion one recoils from undesirable objects and even goes to the extent of destroying them as their very presence is a source of irritation. With the giving up of egoism by one's own intuitive insight, both attachment and hatred automatically disappear.

The Dhammapada states:

"There is no fire like lust, no grip like hate,
There is no net like delusion, no river like craving." (V. 251)

I. As one ascends the spiritual ladder one renounces by degrees both gross and subtle attachment to material pleasures like grown-up children giving up their petty toys. Being children, they cannot be expected to possess an adult's understanding, and they cannot be convinced of the worthlessness of their temporary pleasures. With maturity they begin to understand things as they truly are and they voluntarily give up their toys. As the spiritual pilgrim proceeds on the upward path by his constant meditation and reflection, he perceives the futility of pursuing base material pleasures and the resultant happiness in forsaking them. He cultivates non-attachment to the fullest degree. "Happy is non-attachment in this world, so is the transcending of all sensual pleasures," is one of the early utterances of the Buddha.

ii. The other most rebellious passion is anger, aversion, illwill, or hatred, all of which are implied by the Pali term *vyāpāda*. It consumes the person in whom it springs and consumes others as well. The Pali term *avyāpāda*, literally, non-enmity, corresponds to that most beautiful virtue *Mettā* (Saṁskrit *Maitrī*) which means loving-kindness or goodwill towards all without any distinction. He whose mind is full of loving-kindness can harbour no hatred towards any. Like a mother who makes no difference between herself and her only child and protects it even at the risk of her own life, even so does the spiritual pilgrim who follows this middle path radiate his thoughts of loving-kindness identifying himself with all. Buddhist Mettā embraces all living beings, animals not excluded.

iii. *Avihiṁsā* or *Karuṇā*—Harmlessness or compassion is the third and the last member of *saṁkappa*.

Karuṇā is that sweet virtue which makes the tender hearts of the noble quiver at the sufferings of others. Like Buddhist Mettā, Buddhist Karuṇā too is limitless. It is not restricted only to co-religionists or co-nationals or to human beings alone. Limited compassion is not true *karuṇā*.

A compassionate one is as soft as a flower. He cannot bear the sufferings of others. He might at times even go to the extent of sacrificing his own life to alleviate the sufferings of others. In every Jātaka story it is evident that the Bodhisatta endeavoured his best to help the distressed and the forlorn and to promote their happiness in every possible way.

Karuṇā has the characteristics of a loving mother whose thoughts, words, and deeds always tend to relieve the distress of her sick child. It has the property of not being able to tolerate the sufferings of others. Its manifestation is perfect non-violence and harmlessness—that is, a compassionate person appears to be absolutely non-violent and harmless. The sight of the helpless states of the distressed is the proximate cause for the practice of *Karuṇā*. The consummation of *karuṇā* is the eradication of all forms of cruelty.   The direct enemy of *karunā* is cruelty and the indirect enemy is homely grief.

Buddhist mettā appeals to both the rich and the poor, for Buddhism teaches its followers to elevate the lowly, help the poor, the needy, and the forlorn, tend the sick, comfort the bereaved, pity the wicked, and enlighten the ignorant.

Compassion forms a fundamental principle of both Buddhist laymen and Bhikkhus.

Speaking of Buddhist harmlessness, Aldous Huxley writes:

"Indian pacifism finds its complete expression in the teaching of the Buddha.   Buddhism teaches *ahimsā* or harmlessness towards all beings.   It forbids even laymen to have anything to do with the manufacture and sale of arms, with the making of poison and intoxicants, with soldiering or the slaughtering of animals."

The Buddha advises His disciples thus:

"Wherefore, O Bhikkhus, however men may speak concerning you, whether in season or out of season, whether appropriately or inappropriately, whether courteously or rudely, whether wisely or foolishly, whether kindly or maliciously, thus, O Bhikkhus, must you train yourselves— Unsullied shall our minds remain, neither shall evil words escape our lips.   Kind and compassionate ever shall we abide with hearts harbouring no ill-will.   And we shall enfold those very persons with streams of loving thoughts unfailing, and forth from them proceeding we shall radiate the whole wide world with constant thoughts of loving-kindness, ample, expanding, measureless, free from enmity, free from ill-will. Thus must you train yourselves."

---

1. See chapter 42.

He whose mind is free from selfish desires, hatred and cruelty, and is saturated with the spirit of selflessness, loving-kindness and harmlessness, lives in perfect peace. He is indeed a blessing to himself and others.

3. Right Thoughts lead to Right Speech, the third factor. It deals with refraining from falsehood, slandering, harsh words, and frivolous talk.

He who tries to eradicate selfish desires cannot indulge in uttering falsehood or in slandering for any selfish end or purpose. He is truthful and trustworthy and ever seeks the good and beautiful in others instead of deceiving, defaming, denouncing or disuniting his own fellow beings. A harmless mind that generates loving-kindness cannot give vent to harsh speech which first debases the speaker and then hurts another. What he utters is not only true, sweet and pleasant but also useful, fruitful and beneficial.

4. Right Speech follows Right Action which deals with abstinence from killing, stealing and sexual misconduct.

These three evil deeds are caused by craving and anger, coupled with ignorance. With the gradual elimination of these causes from the mind of the spiritual pilgrim, blameworthy tendencies arising therefrom will find no expression. Under no pretence would he kill or steal. Being pure in mind, he would lead a pure life.

5. Purifying thoughts, words and deeds at the outset, the spiritual pilgrim tries to purify his livelihood by refraining from the five kinds of trade which are forbidden to a lay-disciple. They are trading in arms (*satthavaṇijjā*), human beings (*sattavaṇijjā*), flesh (*maṁsavaṇijjā*), i.e. breeding animals for slaughter, intoxicating drinks (*majjavaṇijjā*), and poison (*visavaṇijjā*).

Hypocritical conduct is cited as wrong livelihood for monks.

Strictly speaking, from an Abhidhamma standpoint, by right speech, right action and right-livelihood are meant three abstinences (*virati*) but not the three opposite virtues.

6. Right Effort is fourfold—namely:

i. The endeavour to discard evil that has already arisen,

ii. The endeavour to prevent the arising of unarisen evil,

iii. The endeavour to develop unarisen good, and,

iv. The endeavour to promote the good which has already arisen.

Right Effort plays a very important part in the Noble Eightfold Path. It is by one's own effort that one's deliverance is obtained and not by merely seeking refuge in others or by offering prayers.

In man are found a rubbish-heap of evil and a

store-house of virtue. By effort one removes this
rubbish-heap and cultivates these latent virtues.

7.   Right Effort is closely associated with Right
Mindfulness.   It is the constant mindfulness with
regard to body (*kāyānupassanā*), feelings (*vedanānupassanā*), thoughts (*cittānupassanā*), and mind
objects (*dhammānupassanā*).

Mindfulness on these four objects tend to
eradicate the misconceptions with regard to desirability (*subha*), so-called happiness (*sukha*), permanence (*nicca*), and an immortal soul (*atta*) respectively.

8.   Right Effort and Right Mindfulness lead to
Right Concentration. It is the one-pointedness of
the mind.

A concentrated mind acts as a powerful aid
to see things as they truly are by means of penetrative insight.

Of these eight factors of the Noble Eightfold
Path the first two are grouped in wisdom (*paññā*),
the second three in morality (*sīla*) and the last
three in concentration (*samādhi*).

$$
Sīla \quad = \begin{cases} \text{Right Speech} \\ \text{Right Action} \\ \text{Right Livelihood} \end{cases}
$$

$$
Samādhi \quad = \begin{cases} \text{Right Effort} \\ \text{Right Mindfulness} \\ \text{Right Concentration} \end{cases}
$$

$$Pa\dot{n}\dot{n}\bar{a} \quad = \quad \left\{ \begin{array}{l} \text{Right Understanding} \\ \text{Right Thoughts} \end{array} \right.$$

According to the order of development *sīla*, *samādhi*, and *paññā* are the three stages of the Path.

Strictly speaking, from an ultimate standpoint, these factors that comprise the Noble Eightfold Path signify eight mental properties (*cetasika*) collectively found in the four classes of supramundane consciousness (*lokuttara citta*) whose object is Nibbāna.

They are:—*paññindriya* (faculty of wisdom), *vitakka* (initial application), *virati* (three abstinences,) *viriya* (energy), *sati* (mindfulness) and *ekaggatā* (one-pointedness) respectively.

All these factors denote the mental attitude of the aspirant who is striving to gain his Deliverance.

CHAPTER 18

KAMMA

"All living beings have Kamma as their own."

MAJJHIMA NIKĀYA

Kamma[1] is the law of moral causation. Rebirth is its corollary. Both Kamma and Rebirth are interrelated, fundamental doctrines in Buddhism.

These two doctrines were prevalent in India before the advent of the Buddha. Nevertheless, it was the Buddha who explained and formulated them in the completeness in which we have them today.

What is the cause of the inequality that exists amongst mankind?

How do we account for the unevenness in this ill-balanced world?

Why should one be brought up in the lap of luxury, endowed with excellent mental, moral, and physical qualities, and another in absolute poverty, in abject misery? Why should one be born a millionaire and another a pauper? Why should one be a mental prodigy and another an idiot? Why should one be born with saintly characteristics and another with criminal tendencies? Why should some be linguists, artists, mathematicians, and musicians from the very cradle? Why should others be congenitally blind, deaf, and deformed? Why should some be blessed and others cursed from their birth?

---

1. Saṁskrit Karma.

Either there is a definite cause for this inequality or there is not, If there is not, the inequality is purely accidental.

No sensible person would think of attributing this inequality to blind chance or pure accident.

In this world nothing happens to any person that he does not for some reason or other deserve. Usually the actual reason or reasons cannot be comprehended by men of ordinary intellect. The definite invisible cause or causes of the visible effect may not necessarily be confined to the present life, but could be traced to a proximate or remote past birth. With the aid of telesthesia and retrocognitive knowledge, may it not be possible for a highly developed seer to perceive events which are ordinarily imperceptible to the physical eye? Buddhists affirm such a possibility.

The majority of mankind attribute this inequality to a single cause such as the will of a Creator. The Buddha explicitly denies the existence of a Creator as an Almighty Being or as a causeless cosmic force.[1]

Now, how do modern scientists account for the inequality of mankind?

Confining themselves purely to sense-data, they attribute this inequality to chemico-physical causes, heredity, and environment.

Julian Huxley, a distinguished biologist, writes:

---

1. See chapter 23.

"Some genes control colour, others height or weight, others fertility or length of life,others vigour and the reverse, others shape or proportions. Possibly all, certainly the vast majority, of hereditary characteristics are gene-controlled. For mental characters, especially the more complex and subtle ones, the proof is more difficult, but there is every evidence that they are inheritable, and no evidence that their inheritance is due to a different mechanism from that for bodily characters. That which is inherited in our personality and bodily peculiarities depends somehow upon the interaction of this assorted battery of genes with which we are equipped at fertilization." [1]

One must admit that all such chemico-physical phenomena, revealed by scientists, are partly instrumental,—but could they be solely responsible for the subtle distinctions that exist amongst individuals? Yet, why should identical twins who are physically alike, inheriting like genes, enjoying the same privileges of upbringing, be temperamentally, intellectually and morally totally different?

Heredity alone cannot account for these vast differences. Strictly speaking, it accounts more plausibly for some of the similarities than for most of the differences.

The infinitesimally minute chemico-physical germ, which is supposed to be about 30 millionth part of an inch across, inherited from parents, explains only a portion of man, his physical foundation. With regard to the more complex and subtle mental, intellectual, and moral differences

1. *The Stream of Life*, p. 15.

we need more enlightenment. The theory of
heredity cannot satisfactorily account for the birth
of a criminal in a long line of honourable ancestors,
for the birth of a Saint in a family of evil repute,
for the arising of infant prodigies, men of genius
and great spiritual teachers.

Dealing with this question of heredity, Dr. Th.
Pascal writes in his interesting book on '*Reincarnation*':

"To return to the role played by the germ in the question
of heredity we repeat that the physical germ, of itself alone,
explains only a portion of man; it throws light on the physical
side of heredity, but leaves in as great darkness as ever the
problem of moral and intellectual faculty. If it represented
the whole man, one would expect to find in any individual
the qualities manifested in his progenitors and parents—
never any other; these qualities could not exceed the amount
possessed by the parents, whereas we find criminals from
birth in the most respectable families, and saints born to
parents who are the very scum of society. You may come
across identical twins, i.e., beings born from the same germ,
under the same conditions of time and environment, one of
whom is an angel and the other a demon, though their physical
forms closely resemble each other. Child prodigies are sufficiently numerous to trouble frequently the thinker with the
problem of heredity. In the lineage of these prodigies has
there been found a single ancestor capable of explaining
these faculties, as astonishing as they are premature? If, to
the absence of a cause in their progenitors is added the fact
that genius is not hereditary, that Mozarts, Beethovens and
Dantes have left no children stamped from birth as prodigies
or genius, we shall be forced to the conclusion that, within
the limits it has taken up, materialism is unable to explain
heredity. Nor is heredity always realized; many a physical

characteristic is not reproduced; in families tainted with dangerous physiological defects, many children escape the evil, and the diseased tendencies of the tissues remain latent in them, although they often affect their descendants. On the other hand extremely divergent mental types are often met with in the same family,[1] and many a virtuous parent is torn with grief on seeing the vicious tendencies of the child. So we find that heredity and environment either fail to fulfill their promise or else give what was not theirs to give."

According to Buddhism this inequality is due not only to heredity, environment, "nature and nurture",[2] but also to the operation of the law of Kamma or, in other words, to the result of our own inherited past actions and our present doings. We ourselves are responsible for our own happiness and misery. We create our own heaven. We create our own hell. We are the architects of our own fate.

The Cause of Inequality

Perplexed by the seemingly inexplicable, apparent disparity that exists amongst humanity, a young truth-seeker named *Subha* approached the Buddha and questioned him regarding it.

---

1. Of Shakespeare, Col. Ingersol writes:
    "Neither of his parents could read or write. He grew up in a small and ignorant village."

2. "Human inequality springs from two sources, nature and nurture."
    J.B.S. Haldane, *The Inequality of Mankind."* p. 23.

"What is the reason, what is the cause, O Lord, that we find amongst mankind the short-lived (*appāyukā*) and the long-lived (*dīghāyukā*), the diseased (*bavhābādhā*) and the healthy (*appābādhā*), the ugly (*dubbaṇṇā*) and the beautiful (*vaṇṇavantā*), the powerless (*appesakkā*) and the powerful (*mahesakkā*), the poor (*appabhogā*) and the rich (*mahābhogā*), the low-born (*nīcakulīnā*) and the high-born (*uccakulīnā*), the ignorant (*duppaññā*) and the wise (*paññavantā*)?

The Buddha's reply was:

"All living beings have actions (*Kamma*) as their own, their inheritance, their congenital cause, their kinsman, their refuge. It is Kamma that differentiates beings into low and high states."[1]

He then explained the causes of such differences in accordance with the law of cause and effect.

If a person destroys life, is a hunter, besmears his hand with blood, is engaged in killing and wounding, and is not merciful towards living beings, he, as a result of his killing, when born amongst mankind, will be short-lived.

---

1.   *Kammassakā mānava sattā, Kammadāyādā, Kammayoni, Kammabandhu, Kammapaṭisaraṇā, Kammaṁ satte vibhajati yadidaṁ hinappaṇitatāyā'ti.*

     Majjhima Nikāya, Cullakammavibhanga Sutta, No. 135, Cf. Venerable Nāgasena's reply to the identical question put by King Milinda.
     See Warren, *Buddhism in Translation*—p. 214.

If a person avoids killing, leaves aside cudgel and weapon, and is merciful and compassionate towards all living beings, he, as a result of his non-killing when born amongst mankind, will be long-lived.

If a person is in the habit of harming others with fist or clod, with cudgel or sword, he, as a result of his harmfulness, when born amongst mankind, will suffer from various diseases.

If a person is not in the habit of harming others, he, as a result of his harmlessness, when born amongst mankind, will enjoy good health.

If a person is wrathful and turbulent, is irritated by a trival word, gives vent to anger, ill-will and resentment, he, as a result of his irritability, when born amongst mankind, will become ugly.

If a person is not wrathful and turbulent, is not irritated even by a torrent of abuse, does not give vent to anger, ill-will and resentment, he, as a result of his amiability, when born amongst mankind, will become beautiful.

If a person is jealous, envies the gains of others, marks of respect and honour shown to others, stores jealousy in his heart, he, as a result of his jealousy, when born amongst mankind, will be powerless.

If a person is not jealous, does not envy the gains of others, marks of respect and honour shown to others, stores not jealousy in his heart, he, as a result of his absence of jealousy, when born amongst mankind, will be powerful.

If a person does not give anything for charity, he, as a result of his greediness, when born amongst mankind, will be poor.

If a person is bent on charitable giving, he, as a result of his generosity, when born amongst mankind, will be rich.

If a person is stubborn, haughty, honours not those who are worthy of honour, he, as a result of his arrogance and irreverance, when born amongst mankind, will be of low-birth.

If a person is not stubborn, not haughty, honours those who are worthy of honour, he, as a result of his humility and deference, when born amongst mankind, will be of high-birth.

If a person does not approach the learned and the virtuous and inquire what is good and what is evil, what is right and what is wrong, what should be practised and what should not be practised, what should be done and what should not be done, what conduces to one's welfare and what to one's ruin, he, as a result of his non-inquiring spirit, when born amongst mankind, will be ignorant.

If a person does approach the learned and the virtuous and makes inquiries in the foregoing manner, he, as a result of his inquiring spirit, when born amongst mankind, will be intelligent.[1]

Certainly we are born with hereditary characteristics. At the same time we possess certain innate abilities that science cannot adequately account for. To our parents we are indebted for the gross sperm and ovum that form the nucleus of this so-called being. There they remain dormant until this potential germinal compound is

---

1. With respect to this similarity of action and reaction the following note by Dr. Grimm will perhaps be of interest to the readers: "It is not difficult in all these cases also to show the law of affinity as the regulator of the grasping of a new germ that occurs at death. Whosoever devoid of compassion, can kill men or, animals, carries deep within himself the inclination to shorten life. He finds satisfaction or even pleasure in the short-livedness of other creatures. Short-lived germs have therefore some affinity which makes itself known after his death in the grasping of another germ which then takes place to his own detriment. Even so, germs bearing within themselves the power of developing into a deformed body, have an affinity for one who finds pleasure in ill-treating and disfiguring others.

vitalized by the Kammic energy needed for the production of the foetus. Kamma is therefore the indispensable conceptive cause of this being.

The accumulated Kammic tendencies inherited, in the course of previous lives, at times play a far greater role than the hereditary parental cells and genes in the formation of both physical and mental characteristics.

The Buddha, for instance, inherited, like every other person, the reproductive cells and genes from his parents. But physically, morally, and intellectually there was none comparable to Him in His long line of honourable ancestors. In the Buddha's own words, He belonged not to the Royal lineage, but to that of the Ariyan Buddhas. He was certainly a superman, an extraordinary creation of His own Kamma.

"An angry person begets within himself an affinity for ugly bodies and their respective germs, since it is the characteristic mark of anger to disfigure the face. "Whoever is jealous, niggardly, haughty, carries within himself the tendency to grudge everything to others and to despise them. Accordingly germs that are destined to develop in poor, outward circumstances, possess affinity for him.

"It is, of course, only a consequence of the above, that a change of sex may also ensue.

"Thus it is related in the *Dīgha Nikāya* No. 21 that Gopikā, a daughter of the Sakya house, was reborn after her death as Gopaka Devaputta, because the female mind has become repulsive to her, and she had formed a male mind within herself."

The Doctrine of the Buddha. p. 191.

According to the Lakkhana Sutta[1] the Buddha inherited exceptional physical features such as the thirty-two major marks, as the result of his past meritorious deeds. The ethical reason for acquiring each physical feature is clearly explained in the discourse.

It is obvious from this unique case that Kammic tendencies could not only influence our physical organism, but also nullify the potentiality of the parental cells and genes—hence the significance of the Buddha's enigmatic statement: "We are the heirs of our own actions."

Dealing with this problem of variation the Atthasālinī states :

"Depending on this difference in Kamma appears the difference in the birth of beings, high and low, base and exalted, happy and miserable. Depending on the difference in Kamma appears the difference in the individual features of beings as beautiful and ugly, high-born and low-born, well-built and deformed, Depending on the difference in Kamma appears the difference in worldly conditions of beings as gain and loss, fame and disgrace, blame and praise, happiness and misery"

"*By Kamma the world moves, by Kamma men*
Live; and by Kamma are all beings bound
As by its pin the rolling chariot wheel.
By Kamma one attains glory and praise.
By Kamma bondage, ruin, tyranny,
Knowing that Kamma bears fruit manifold,
Why say ye, 'In the world no Kamma is.'"[2]

---

1. Dīgha Nikāya, iii, 142, No. 30.
2. P. 65; *The Expositor,* i. 87.

Thus, from a Buddhist standpoint, our present mental, moral, intellectual, and temperamental differences are preponderantly due to our own actions and tendencies, both past and present.

Everything is not due to Kamma

Although Buddhism attributes this variation to the law of Kamma, as the chief cause amongst a variety, it does not however assert that everything is due to Kamma. The law of Kamma, important as it is, is only one of the twenty-four causal conditions (*paccaya*), described in Buddhist Philosophy.[1]

Refuting the erroneous view that "Whatsoever weal or woe or neutral feeling is experienced, is all due to some previous action (*pubbekatahetu*)," the Buddha states:

"So, then, owing to previous action, men will become murderers, thieves, unchaste, liars, slanderers, babblers, covetous, malicious, and perverse in view. Thus for those who fall back on the former deeds as the essential reason, there is neither the desire to do, nor effort to do, nor necessity to do this deed or abstain from that deed."[2]

This important text contradicts the belief that all physical circumstances and mental attitudes spring solely from past Kamma. If the present life is totally conditioned or wholly controlled by our past actions, then Kamma is certainly

1. See Compendium of Philosophy, p. 191, Manual of Abhidhamma by Nārada Thera.
2. Anguttara Nikāya—i, 173; *Gradual Sayings*, i. 157.

tantamount to fatalism or pre-determination or pre-destination. One will not be free to mould one's present and future. If this were true, freewill would be an absurdity. Life would be purely mechanical, not much different from a machine. Whether we are created by an Almighty God who controls our destinies and fore-ordains our future, or are produced by an irresistible past Kamma that completely determines our fate and controls our life's course, independent of any free action on our part, is essentially the same. The only difference then lies in the two words God and Kamma. One could easily be substituted for the other, because the ultimate operation of both forces would be identical.

Such a fatalistic doctrine is not the Buddhist law of Kamma.

The Five Niyāmas

According to Buddhism there are five orders or processes (*Niyāmas*)[1] which operate in the physical and mental realms.

They are:—

1. *Utu Niyāma*, physical inorganic order; e.g., seasonal phenomena of winds and rains, the unerring order of seasons, characteristic seasonal changes and events, causes of winds and rains, nature of heat, etc. belong to this group.

---

1. See *Abhidhammāvatāra*, p. 54; Mrs. Rhys Davids, *Buddhism*, p. 119.

2. *Bīja Niyāma*, order of germs and seeds (physical organic order); e.g., rice produced from rice seed, sugary taste from sugar-cane or honey, and peculiar characteristics of certain fruits. The scientific theory of cells and genes and the physical similarity of twins may be ascribed to this order.

3. *Kamma Niyāma*, order of act and result; e.g., desirable and undesirable acts produce corresponding good and bad results.

As surely as water seeks its own level, so does Kamma, given opportunity, produce its inevitable result,—not in the form of a reward or punishment but as an innate sequence. This sequence of deed and effect is as natural and necessary as the way of the sun and the moon, and is the retributive principle of Kamma.

Inherent in Kamma is also the continuitive principle.

Manifold experiences, personal characteristics, accumulated knowledge, and so forth are all indelibly recorded in the palimpsest-like mind. All these experiences and characters transmigrate from life to life. Through lapse of time they may be forgotten as in the case of our experiences of our childhood. Infant prodigies and wonderful children, who speak in different languages without receiving any instruction, are note-worthy examples of the continuitive principle of Kamma.

4. *Dhamma Niyāma*, order of the norm; e.g., the natural phenomena occurring at the birth of a Bodhisatta in his last birth. Gravitation and other similar laws of nature, the reason for being good, etc. may be included in this group.

5. *Citta Niyāma*, order of mind or psychic law; e.g., processes of consciousness, constituents of consciousness, power of mind, including telepathy, telesthesia, retro-cognition, premonition, clair-voyance, clair-audience, thought-reading, and such other psychic phenomena, which are inexplicable to modern science.

Every mental or physical phenomenon could be explained by these all-embracing five orders or processes which are laws in themselves. Kamma as such is only one of these five orders. Like all other natural laws, they demand no lawgiver.

Of these five, the physical inorganic order, the physical organic order and the order of the norm are more or less of the mechanical type though they can be controlled to some extent by human ingenuity and the power of mind. For example, fire normally burns, and extreme cold freezes, but man has walked unscathed over fire and meditated naked on Himalayan snows; horti-culturists have worked marvels with flowers and fruits; and Yogis have performed levitation. Psychic law is equally mechanical, but Buddhist training aims at control of mind, which is possible by right understanding and skilful volition. Kamma law operates quite automatically and, when the Kamma is powerful, man cannot interfere with its inexorable result though he may desire to do so; but here also right understanding and skilful volition can accomplish much and mould the future. Good Kamma, persisted in, can thwart the reaping of bad.

Kamma is certainly an intricate law whose working is fully comprehended only by a Buddha. The Buddhist aims at the final destruction of all Kamma.

Kamma-Vipāka (fruit of action) is one of the four unthinkables (*acinteyya*), states the Buddha in the Anguttara Nikaya.[1]

1. See *Gradual Sayings,* part 2, p. 90.

CHAPTER 19

WHAT IS KAMMA?

"Volition is Kamma."

ANGUTTARA NIKĀYA

Kamma

The Pali term *Kamma*, literally, means action or doing. Any kind of intentional action whether mental, verbal, or physical is regarded as Kamma. It covers all that is included in the phrase: "Thought, word and deed". Generally speaking, all good and bad actions constitute Kamma. In its ultimate sense Kamma means all moral and immoral volition (*kusala akusala cetanā*). Involuntary, unintentional or unconscious actions, though technically deeds, do not constitute Kamma, because volition, the most important factor in determining Kamma, is absent.[1]

The Buddha says:—"I declare, O Bhikkhus, that volition (*cetanā*) is Kamma, Having willed one acts by body, speech and thought.

Every volitional action of persons, except those of Buddhas and Arahants, is called Kamma. An exception is made in their case because they are delivered from both good and evil. They have eradicated both ignorance and craving, the roots of Kamma. "Destroyed are their (germinal) seeds

---

1. Anguttara Nikāya iii. p. 415, *The Expositor,* part I 117; Atthasālini, p. 88.

(*khīṇa-bījā*), selfish desires no longer grow," states the Ratana Sutta. This does not mean that the Buddhas and Arahants are passive. They are tirelessly active in working for the real well-being and happiness of all. Their deeds, ordinarily accepted as good or moral, lack creative power as regards themselves. Understanding things as they truly are, they have finally shattered their cosmic fetters—the chain of cause and effect.

Some religions attribute this unevenness to Kamma, but they differ from Buddhism when they state that even unintentional actions should be regarded as Kamma.

According to them, "the unintentional murderer of his mother is a hideous criminal. The man who kills or who harasses in any way a living being without intent, is none the less guilty, just as a man who touches fire is burnt."[1]

"This astounding theory undoubtedly leads to palpable absurdities.

"The embryo and the mother would both be guilty of making each other suffer. Further the analogy of the fire is logically fallacious. For instance, a man would not be guilty if he got another person to commit the murder, for one is not burnt if one gets another to put his hand into the fire. Moreover unintentional actions would be

---

1. See Poussin. *The Way to Nirvāna*, p. 68.

much worse than intentional wrong actions, for, according to the comparison, a man who touches fire without knowing that it would burn is likely to be more deeply burnt than the man who knows.

In the working of Kamma its most important feature is mind. All our words and deeds are coloured by the mind or consciousness we experience at such particular moments. "When the mind is unguarded, bodily action is unguarded; speech also is unguarded; thought also is unguarded. When the mind is guarded, bodily action is guarded; speech also is guarded; and thought also is guarded."[1]

"By mind the world is led, by mind is drawn: And all men own the sovereignty of mind."

"If one speaks or acts with a wicked mind, pain follows one as the wheel, the hoof of the draught-ox."[2]

"If one speaks or acts with a pure mind, happiness follows one as the shadow that never departs."[3]

Immaterial mind conditions all Kammic activities.

Kamma does not necessarily mean past actions. It embraces both past and present deeds. Hence, in one sense, we are the result of what we were, we will be the result of what we are. In another

---

1. Atthasālini p. 68. *The Expositor,* part I, p. 91.
2. Dhammapada, V. 1.
3. *Ibid,* V. 2.

sense, it should be added, we are not totally the result of what we were, we will not absolutely be the result of what we are. The present is no doubt the offspring of the past and is the parent of the future, but the present is not always a true index of either the past or the future—so complex is the working of Kamma. For instance, a criminal today may be a saint tomorrow, a good person yesterday may be a vicious one today.

It is this doctrine of Kamma that the mother teaches her child when she says: "Be good and you will be happy and we will love you. But if you are bad, you will be unhappy and we will not love you."

Like attracts like. Good begets good. Evil begets evil. This is the law of Kamma.

In short Kamma is the law of cause and effect in the ethical realm, or as some Westerners prefer to say, "action influence."

Kamma and Vipāka

Kamma is action, and *Vipāka*, fruit or result, is its reaction. Just as every object is accompanied by a shadow, even so every volitional activity is inevitably accompanied by its due effect. Like potential seed is Kamma. Fruit, arising from the tree, is the Vipāka, effect or result. As Kamma may be good or bad, so may Vipāka, fruit, be good or bad. As Kamma is mental, so Vipāka too is mental; it is experienced as happiness or bliss, unhappiness or misery according to the nature of the Kamma seed. *Ānisaṁsa* are the concomitant advantageous material conditons, such as prosperity health and longevity.

When *Vipāka's* concomitant material conditions are disadvantageous, they are known as *ādinava* (evil consequences), and appear as poverty, ugliness, disease, short life span and the like.

By Kamma are meant the Moral and Immoral types of mundane consciousness (*kusala akusala lokiya citta*), and by Vipāka, the resultant types of mundane consciousness (*lokiya vipākacitta*).

According to Abhidhamma,[1] Kamma constitutes the twelve types of immoral consciousness, eight types of moral consciousness pertaining to the Sentient Realm (*kāmāvacara*), five types of moral consciousness pertaining to the Realms of Forms (*rūpāvacara*), and four types of moral consciousness pertaining to the Formless Realms (*arūpāvacara*).

The eight types of supramundane (*lokuttara*) consciousness are not regarded as *Kamma*, because they tend to eradicate the roots of *Kamma*. In them the predominant factor is wisdom (*paññā*) while in the mundane it is volition. (*cetanā*).

---

1. See Compendium of Philosophy, — Abhidhammattha Sangaha, Chapter 1; Manual of Abhidhamma ch. 1.

The nine types of moral consciousness pertaining to the Realms of Form and the Formless Realms are the five *Rūpāvacara* and four *Arūpāvacara Jhānas* (*Ecstasies*) which are purely mental.

Words and deeds are caused by the first twenty types of mundane consciousness. Verbal actions are done by the mind by means of speech. Bodily actions are done by the mind through the instrument of the body. Purely mental actions have no other instrument than the mind.

These twenty-nine[1] types of consciousness are called Kamma because they have the power to produce their due effects quite automatically, independent of any external agency.

Those types of consciousness which one experiences as inevitable consequences of one's moral and immoral thoughts are called resultant consciousness pertaining to the Sentient Realm. The five types of resultant consciousness pertaining to the Realms of Form and the four types of resultant consciousness pertaining to the Formless Realms are called *Vipāka* or fruition of Kamma.

As we sow, so we reap somewhere and sometime, in this life or in a future birth. What we reap today is what we have sown either in the present or in the past.

The Saṁyutta Nikāya[2] states:

---

1. $20+5+4=29$
2. Vol. 1, p. 227; *Kindred Sayings*, part 1, p. 293.

"According to the seed that's sown,
So is the fruit ye reap therefrom
Doer of good (will gather) good.
Doer of evil, evil (reaps).
Sown is the seed, and planted well.
Thou shalt enjoy the fruit thereof."

Kamma is a law in itself which operates in its own field without the intervention of any external, independent ruling agency.

Inherent in Kamma is the potentiality of producing its due effect. The cause produces the effect, the effect explains the cause. The seed produces the fruit, the fruit explains the seed, such is their relationship. Even so are Kamma and its effect.

"The effect already blooms in the cause."

Happiness and misery, which are the common lot of humanity, are the inevitable effects of causes. From a Buddhist standpoint they are not rewards and punishments, assigned by a supernatural, omniscient ruling power to a soul that has done good or evil. Theists who attempt to explain everything by this one temporal life and an eternal future life, ignoring a past, may believe in a post-mortem justice, and may regard present happiness and misery as blessings and curses conferred on his creation by an omniscient and omnipotent Divine Ruler, who sits in heaven above controlling the destinies of the human race. Buddhism that emphatically denies an arbitrarily created immortal soul, believes in natural law and justice which cannot be suspended by either an Almighty God, or an All-compassionate Buddha. According to this natural law, acts bring their own rewards and punishments to the individual doer whether human justice finds him or not.

Some there are, who cavil thus: So you Buddhists too administer the opium of Kammic doctrine to the poor, saying:

"You are born poor in this life on acount of your past evil Kamma. He is born rich on account of his past good Kamma. So be satisfied with your humble lot, but do good to be rich in your next life.

"You are being oppressed now because of your past evil Kamma. That is your destiny. Be humble and bear your sufferings patiently. Do good now. You can be certain of a better and happier life after death."

The Buddhist doctrine of Kamma does not expound such fatalistic views. Nor does it vindicate a post-mortem justice. The All-merciful Buddha, who had no ulterior selfish motives, did not teach this law of Kamma to protect the rich and comfort the poor by promising illusory happiness in an after-life.

According to the Buddhist doctrine of Kamma, one is not always compelled by an iron necessity, for Kamma is neither fate nor predestination imposed upon us by some mysterious unknown power to which we must helplessly submit ourselves. It is one's own doing reacting on oneself, and so one has the power to divert the course of Kamma to some extent. How far one diverts it, depends on oneself.

The Cause of Kamma

Ignorance (*avijjā*) or not knowing things as they truly are, is the chief cause of Kamma. Dependent on ignorance arise Kammic activities (*avijjā paccayā saṁkhārā*), states the Buddha in the *Paṭicca Samuppāda* (Dependent Origination).

Associated with ignorance is its ally craving (*taṇhā*), the other root of Kamma. Evil actions are conditioned by these two causes. All good deeds of a worldling (*puthujjana*), though associated with the three wholesome roots of generosity (*alobha*), goodwill (*adosa*) and knowledge (*amoha*), are nevertheless regarded as Kamma because the two roots of ignorance and craving are dormant in him. The moral types of supramundane Path consciousness (*maggacitta*) are not regarded as Kamma because they tend to eradicate the two root causes.

The Doer of Kamma

Who is the doer of Kamma? Who reaps the fruit of Kamma? "Is it a sort of accretion about a soul?"

In answering these subtle questions, Venerable Buddhaghosa writes in the *Visuddhi Magga*:

"*No Doer is there who does the deed,*
Nor is there one who feels the fruit,
Constituent parts alone roll on,
This indeed is right discernment."[1]

---

1.   Vol. ii, p. 602. See Warren, *Buddhism in Translations*, p. 248
     The Path of Purity, iii, p 728.
     Kammassa   kārako   natthi — vipākassa   ca   vedako
     Suddhadhammā   pavattanti — evetaṁ   samma   dassanaṁ

According to Buddhism there are two realities—apparent and ultimate. Apparent reality is ordinary conventional truth (*sammuti sacca*). Ultimate reality is abstract truth (*paramattha sacca*).

For instance, the table we see is apparent reality. In an ultimate sense the so-called table consists of forces and qualities.

For ordinary purposes a scientist would use the term water, but in the laboratory he would say H_2O.

In the same way for conventional purposes such terms as man, woman, being, self and so forth are used. The so-called fleeting forms consist of psycho-physical phenomena which are constantly changing, not remaining for two consecutive moments the same.

Buddhists therefore do not believe in an unchanging entity, in an actor apart from action, in a perceiver apart from perception, in a conscious subject behind consciousness.

Who then is the doer of Kamma? Who experiences the effect?

Volition or will (*cetanā*) is itself the doer. Feeling (*vedanā*) is itself the reaper of the fruits of action. Apart from these pure mental states (*suddhadhammā*) there is none to sow and none to reap.

Just as, says the Venerable Buddhaghosa, in the case of those elements of matter that go under the name of tree, as soon as at any point the fruit springs up, it is then said the tree bears fruit or 'thus the tree has fructified,' so also in the case of 'aggregates' (*khandhas*) which go under the name of Deva or man, when a fruition of happiness or misery springs up at any point, then it is said 'that Deva or man is happy or miserable.'

In this respect Buddhists agree with Prof. William James when, unlike Descartes, he asserts:

"Thoughts themselves are the thinkers."[1]

Where is Kamma ?

"Stored within the psyche," writes a certain psycho-analyst, "but usually inaccessible and to be reached only by some, is the whole record, without exception, of every experience the individual has passed through, every influence felt, every impression received. The subconscious mind is not only an indelible record of individual experiences but also retains the impress of primeval impulses and tendencies, which so far from being outgrown as we fondly deem them in civilized man, are subconsciously active and apt to break out in disconcerting strength at unexpected moments."

A Buddhist would make the same assertion with a vital modification. Not stored within any postulatory 'psyche', for there is no proof of any such receptacle or store-house in this ever-changing complex machinery of man, but dependent on the individual psycho-physical continuity or flux is every experience the so-called being has passed

---

1. Psychology, p. 216.

through, every influence felt, every impression received, every characteristic—divine, human, or brutal—developed. In short the entire Kammic force is dependent on the dynamic mental flux (*citta santati*) ever ready to manifest itself in multifarious phenomena as occasion arises.

"Where, Venerable Sir, is Kamma?" King Milinda questioned the Venerable Nāgasena.

"O Mahārāja," replied the Venerable Nāgasena, "Kamma is not said to be stored somewhere in this fleeting consciousness or in any other part of the body. But dependent on mind and matter it rests manifesting itself at the opportune moment, just as mangoes are not said to be stored somewhere in the mango tree, but dependent on the mango tree they lie, springing up in due season." [1]

Neither wind nor fire is stored in any particular place, nor is Kamma stored anywhere within or without the body.

Kamma is an individual force, and is transmitted from one existence to another. It plays the chief part in the moulding of character and explains the marvellous phenomena of genius, infant prodigies, and so forth. The clear understanding of this doctrine is essential for the welfare of the world.

---

1. See Visuddhi Magga, ch XVII.

CHAPTER 20

THE WORKING OF KAMMA

"By Kamma is this world led."

ATTHASĀLINI

The working of Kamma is an intricate law which only a Buddha can fully comprehend. To obtain a clear understanding of this difficult subject it is necessary to acquaint oneself with thought-processes (*cittavīthi*) according to Abhidhamma.

Mind or consciousness, the essence of the so-called being, plays the most important part in the complex machinery of man. It is mind that either defiles or purifies one. Mind in fact is both the bitterest enemy and the greatest friend of oneself.

When a person is fast asleep and is in a dreamless state, he experiences a kind of consciousness which is more or less passive than active. It is similar to the consciousness one experiences at the moment of conception and at the moment of death. (*cuti*). The Buddhist philosophical term for this type of consciousness is *Bhavanga* which means factor of life, or indispensable cause or condition of existence. Arising and perishing every moment, it flows on like a stream not remaining the same for two consecutive moments.

We do experience this type of consciousness not only in a dreamless state but also in our waking state. In the course of our life we experience Bhavanga thought-moments more than any other type of consciousness. Hence *Bhavanga* becomes an indispensable condition of life.

Some scholars identify *Bhavanga* with subconsciousness. According to the *Dictionary of Philosophy* sub-consciousness is "a compartment of the mind alleged by certain psychologists and philosophers to exist below the threshold of consciousness."

In the opinion of Western philosophers subconsciousness and consciousness co-exist. But, according to Buddhist philosophy, no two types of consciousness co-exist.[1]

Nor is Bhavanga a sub-plane. It does not correspond to F. W. Myer's subliminal consciousness either. There does not seem to be any place for *Bhavanga* in Western philosophy. Perhaps we may be using these philosophical terms with different meanings.

---

1. According to Buddhist philosophy there is no moment when we do not ordinarily experience a particular kind of consciousness, hanging on to some object—whether physical or mental. The time limit of such a consciousness is termed one thought-moment. Each thought-moment is followed by another. The rapidity of the succession of such thought-moments is hardly conceivable by the ken of human knowledge. It pleases the commentators to say that during the time occupied by a flash of lightning billions and billions of thought-moments may arise.

Bhavanga is so called because it is an essential condition for continued existence. Life-continuum has been suggested as the closest English equivalent for *Bhavanga*.

This *Bhavanga* consciousness, which one always experiences as long as it is uninterrupted by external stimuli, vibrates for a thought-moment and passes away when a physical or mental object enters the mind. Suppose, for instance, the object presented is a physical form. Now, when the *Bhavanga* stream of consciousness is arrested, sensedoor consciousness (*pañcadvārāvajjana*), whose function is to turn the consciousness towards the object, arises and passes away. Immediately after this there arises visual consciousness (*cakkhuviññāṇa*) which sees the object, but yet knows no more about it. This sense operation is followed by a moment of the reception of the object so seen (*sampaṭicchana*). Next arises the investigating thought-moment (*santīraṇa*) which momentarily examines the object so seen. This is followed by the determining thought-moment (*votthapana*) when discrimination is exercised and freewill may play its part. On this depends the subsequent psychologically important stage *Javana*. It is at this stage that an action is judged, whether it be moral or immoral. Kamma is performed at this stage.

If viewed rightly (*yonisomanasikāra*), it becomes moral; if wrongly (*ayonisomanasikāra*), immoral. Irrespective of the desirability or the undesirability of the object presented to the mind, it is possible for one to make the Javana process moral or immoral. If, for instance, one meets an enemy, anger will arise automatically. A wise person might, on the contrary, with self-control, radiate a thought of love towards him. This is the reason why the Buddha states:

"By self is evil done,
By self is one defiled,
By self is no evil done,
By self is one purified.
Both defilement and purity depend on oneself.
No one is purified by another."[1]

It is an admitted fact that environment, circumstances, habitual tendencies and the like condition our thoughts. On such occasions freewill is subordinated. There exists however the possibility for us to overcome those external forces and produce moral and immoral thoughts exercising our own freewill.

An extraneous element may be a causative factor, but we ourselves are directly responsible for the actions that finally follow.

It is extremely difficult to suggest a suitable rendering for *Javana.*

Apperception is suggested by some. Impulse is suggested as an alternative rendering, which seems to be less satisfactory than apperception. Here the Pali term is retained.

---

1. Dhammapada, v. 165.

Javana, literally, means running. It is so called because, in the course of a thought-process, it runs consequently for seven thought-moments, or, at times of death, for five thought-moments with an identical object. The mental states occurring in all these thought-moments are similar, but the potential force differs.

This entire thought-process which takes place in an infinitesimal part of time ends with the registering consciousness (*tadālambana*) lasting for two thought-moments. Thus one thought-process is completed at the expiration of seventeen thought moments.

Books cite the simile of the mango tree to illustrate this thought-process.

A man, fast asleep, is lying at the foot of a mango tree with his head covered. A wind stirs the branches and a fruit falls beside the head of the sleeping man. He removes his head covering, and turns towards the object. He sees it and then picks it up. He examines it, and ascertains that it is a ripe mango fruit. He eats it, and swallowing the remnants with saliva, once more resigns himself to sleep.

The dreamless sleep corresponds to the unperturbed current of Bhavanga. The striking of the wind against the tree corresponds to past Bhavanga

---

1. See diagram i. p. 365.

Diagram i.

1. The thought-process runs as follows:—

```
1          2          3
* *       * *       * * *
Atita Bhavanga    Bhavanga Calana    Bhavanga Upaccheda
Past Bhavanga     Vibrating Bhavanga Arrest Bhavanga

4          5          6
* * *     * *       * *
Āvajjana          Pañca Viññāna      Sampaticchana
Sense-door        Sense-consciousness Receiving consciousness
consciousness

7          9    10   11   12   13   14   15
* *       * * * * * * * * * * * * * * * * * * * * *
Santīrana                JAVANA
Investigating consciousness

8          16   17
* * *     * *  * *
Votthapana        Tadālambana
Determining       Registering consciousness
consciousness
```

and the swaying of the branches to vibrating Bhavanga. The falling of the fruit represents the arrest Bhavanga. Turning towards the object corresponds to sense-door adverting consciousness; sight of the object, to perception; picking up, to receiving consciousness; examination, to investigating consciousness; ascertaining that it is a ripe mango fruit, to determining consciousness. The actual eating resembles the Javana process, and the swallowing of the morsels corresponds to retention. His resigning to sleep resembles the subsidence of the mind into Bhavanga again. Of the seven thought-moments, as stated above, the effect of the first thought-moment, the weakest in potentiality, one may reap in this life itself. This is called 'Immediately Effective' (*diṭṭhadhammavedaniya*) Kamma. If it does not operate in this life, it becomes ineffective (*ahosi*).

The next weakest is the seventh thought-moment. Its effect one may reap in the subsequent birth. Hence it is termed 'Subsequently Effective' (*upapajjavedaniya*) Kamma, which, too, automatically becomes ineffective if it does not operate in the second birth.

The effect of the intermediate thought-moments may take place at any time in the course of one's wanderings in Samsara until the final Emancipation. This type of Kamma is termed 'Indefinitely Effective' (*aparāpariyavedaniya*).

There is thus a *classification of Kamma with reference to its time of operation:-*

1. *Diṭṭhadhammavedaniya* (Immediately Effec- *Kamma* tive Kamma)
2. *Upapajjavedaniya* (Subsequently Effec- *Kamma* tive Kamma)
3. *Aparāpariyavedaniya* (Indefinitely Effec- *Kamma* tive Kamma) and
4. *Ahosi Kamma* (Ineffective Kamma)

Illustrations:

The result of a good Kamma reaped in this life:

A husband and his wife possessed only one upper garment to wear when they went out-of-doors. One day the husband heard the Dhamma from the Buddha and was so pleased with the Doctrine that he wished to offer his only upper garment, but his innate greed would not permit him to do so. He combatted with his mind and, ultimately overcoming his greed, offered the garment to the Buddha and exclaimed— "I have won, I have won." The king was delighted to hear his story and in appreciation of his generosity presented him thirty-two robes. The devout husband kept one for himself and another for his wife and offered the rest to the Buddha.[1]

The result of a bad Kamma reaped in this life:

A hunter who went hunting to the forest, followed by his dogs, met by the wayside a Bhikkhu who was proceeding on his alms round. As the hunter could not procure any game he thought it was due to the unfortunate meeting of the Bhikkhu. While returning home he met the same Bhikkhu and was deeply enraged at this second encounter. In spite of the entreaties of the innocent Bhikkhu the hunter set

---

1.   Buddhist Legends (Dhammapadaṭṭhakathā), pt. 2, p. 262.

the dogs on him. Finding no escape therefrom, the Bhikkhu climbed a tree. The wicked hunter ran up to the tree, and pierced the soles of the Bhikkhu's feet with the point of an arrow. The pain was so excruciating that the robe, the Bhikkhu was wearing, fell upon the hunter completely covering him. The dogs, thinking that the Bhikkhu had fallen from the tree, devoured their own master.[1]

Subsequently Effective Kamma:

A millionaire's servant returned home in the evening after his laborious work in the field, to see that all were observing the Eight Precepts as it was the full moon day. Learning that he also could observe them even for half a day, he took the precepts and fasted at night. Unfortunately he died on the following morning and as a result of his good action was born as a Deva.[2]

Ajātasattu, son of King Bimbisāra, was born, immediately after his death, in a state of misery as the result of killing his father.

Indefinitely Effective Kamma:

No person is exempt from this class of Kamma. Even the Buddhas and Arahants may reap the effects of their past Kamma.

The Arahant *Moggallāna* in the remote past, instigated by his wicked wife, attempted to kill his mother and father.[3] As a result of this he suffered long in a woeful state, and in his last birth was clubbed to death by bandits.

To the Buddha was imputed the murder of a female devotee of the naked ascetics.

1. Buddhist Legends p. 282.
2. Ibid., pt. i. p. 278.
3. According to some books he actually killed them.

This was the result of his having insulted a Pacceka Buddha in one of His previous births.

The Buddha's foot was slightly injured when Devadatta made a futile attempt to kill Him. This was due to His killing a step-brother of his in a previous birth with the object of appropriating his property.

*   *   *

There is another *classification of Kamma according to function (kicca):*

1. *Janaka Kamma* (Reproductive Kamma),
2. *Upatthambaka Kamma* (Supportive Kamma),
3. *Upapīḍaka Kamma* (Counteractive Kamma),
4. *Upaghātaka Kamma* (Destructive Kamma).

Every subsequent birth, according to Buddhism, is conditioned by the good or bad Kamma which predominated at the moment of death. This kind of Kamma is technically known as Reproductive (*janaka*) Kamma.

The death of a person is merely "the temporary end of a temporary phenomenon." Though the present form perishes another form which is neither absolutely the same nor totally different takes its place according to the thought that was powerful at the death moment since the Kammic force which hitherto actuated it is not annihilated with the dissolution of the body. It is this last thought-process which is termed 'Reproductive Kamma' that determines the state of a person in his subsequent birth.

As a rule the last thought-process depends on the general conduct of a person. In some exceptional cases, perhaps due to favourable or unfavourable circumstances, at the moment of death a good person may experience a bad thought and a bad person a good one. The future birth will be determined by this last thought-process, irrespective of the general conduct. This does not mean that the effects of the past actions are obliterated. They will produce their inevitable results at the appropriate moment. Such reverse changes of birth account for the birth of vicious children to virtuous parents and of virtuous children to vicious parents.

Now, to assist and maintain or to weaken and obstruct the fruition of this Reproductive Kamma another past Kamma may intervene. Such actions are termed 'Supportive' (*upattham bhaka*) Kamma and 'Counteractive' (*upapīḍaka*) Kamma respectively

According to the law of Kamma the potential energy of the Reproductive Kamma can be totally annulled by a more powerful opposing past Kamma, which, seeking an opportunity, may quite unexpectedly operate, just as a counteractive force can obstruct the path of a flying arrow and bring it down to the ground. Such an action is termed 'Destructive' (*upaghātaka*) Kamma which is more powerful than the above two in that it not only obstructs but also destroys the whole force.

As an instance of the operation of all the four, the case of Venerable Devadatta who attempted to kill the Buddha and who caused a schism in the Sangha may be cited.

His Reproductive good Kamma destined him to a birth in a royal family. His continued comfort and prosperity were due to the action of the Supportive Kamma. The Counteractive Kamma came into operation when he was subjected to such humiliation as a result of his being excommunicated from the Sangha. Finally the Destructive Kamma brought his life to a miserable end.

The following *classification is according to the priority of effect (vipākadānavasena):*

1. *Garuka Kamma,*
2. *Āsanna Kamma,*
3. *Āciṇṇa Kamma,* and
4. *Kaṭattā Kamma.*

The first is *Garuka Kamma* which means a weighty or serious action. It is so called because it produces its effects for certain in this life or in the next. On the moral side the weighty actions are the *Jhānas* or Ecstasies, while on the immoral side they are the subsequently-effective heinous crimes (*Ānantariya Kamma*)—namely, matricide, parricide, the murder of an Arahant, the wounding of the Buddha, and the creation of a schism in the Sangha.

If, for instance, any person were to develop the Jhānas and later to commit one of these heinous crimes, his good Kamma would be obliterated by the powerful evil Kamma. His subsequent birth will be conditioned by the evil Kamma in spite of his having gained the Jhanas earlier. For example, Venerable Devadatta lost his psychic powers and was born in a woeful state because he wounded the Buddha and caused a schism in the Sangha.

King *Ajātasattu*, as the Buddha remarked, would have attained the first stage of Sainthood if he had not committed parricide. In this case the powerful evil Kamma obstructed his spiritual attainment.

When there is no Weighty Kamma to condition the future birth a Death-proximate (*āsanna*) Kamma might operate. This is the action one does, or recollects, immediately before the dying-moment. Owing to its significance in determining the future birth, the custom of reminding the dying person of his good deeds and making him do good on his death-bed still prevails in Buddhist countries.

Sometimes a bad person may die happily and receive a good birth if fortunately he remembers or does a good act at the last moment. This does not mean that although he enjoys a good birth he will be exempt from the effects of the evil deeds he has accumulated during his life-time.

At times a good person, on the other hand, may die unhappily by suddenly remembering an evil act or by conceiving a bad thought, perchance compelled by unfavourable circumstances.

Habitual (*ācinṇa*) Kamma is the next in priority of effect. It is the Kamma that one constantly performs and recollects and towards which one has a great liking.

Habits whether good or bad become second nature. They more or less tend to mould the character of a person. At leisure moments we often engage ourselves in our habitual thoughts and deeds. In the same way at the death-moment, unless influenced by other circumstances, we, as a rule, recall to mind our habitual thoughts and deeds.

The last in this category is Cumulative (*kaṭattā*)[1] Kamma which embraces all that cannot be included in the foregoing three. This is as it were the reserve fund of a particular being.

The last classification is according to the plane in which the effects take place. They are:—

1. Evil actions (*akusala*) which may ripen in the Sense-Sphere (*kāmaloka*).

2. Good actions (*kusala*) which may ripen in the Sense-Sphere.

3. Good actions which may ripen in the Realms of Form (*rūpaloka*), and

4. Good actions which may ripen in the Formless Realms (*arūpaloka*).

---

1. Literally, 'because done'.

Evil actions which may ripen in the Sense-Sphere:

There are ten evil actions caused by deed, word, and mind which produce evil Kamma. Of them three are committed by deed—namely, killing (*pāṇātipāta*), stealing (*adinnādāna*), and sexual misconduct (*kāmesu micchācāra*).

Four are committed by word—namely, lying (*musāvāda*), slandering (*pisunavācā*), harsh speech (*pharusavāca*), and frivolous talk (*samphappalāpa*).

Three are committed by mind—namely, covetousness (*abhijjhā*), ill-will (*vyāpāda*), and false-view (*micchādiṭṭhi*)

Killing means the intentional destruction of any living being. The Pali term *pāṇa* strictly means the psycho-physical life pertaining to one's particular existence. The wanton destruction of this life force, without allowing it to run its due course, is *pāṇātipāta*. *Pāṇa* means that which breathes. Hence all animate beings, including animals, are regarded as *pāṇa*, but not plants[1] as they possess no mind. Bhikkhus, however, are forbidden to destroy even plant life. This rule, it may be mentioned, does not apply to lay-followers.

The following five conditions are necessary to complete the evil of killing—i. a living being.

---

1. "In plants there is no transmission of stimuli by nerves. Nerves are unknown to them as nerve—centres."
Dr. Karl V. Frisch—*You and Life*. p. 125.

ii.   knowledge that it is a living being, iii.   intention of killing.   iv.   effort to kill, and v.   consequent death.

The gravity of the evil depends on the goodness and the magnitude of the being concerned.
The killing of a virtuous person or a big animal is
regarded as more heinous than the killing of a
vicious person or a small animal because a greater
effort is needed to commit the evil and the loss
involved is considerably great.

The evil effects of killing are:—brevity of life,
ill-health, constant grief due to the separation
from the loved, and constant fear.

Five conditions are necessary for the completion
of the evil of stealing:—namely, i.   another's
property, ii. knowledge that it is so, iii. intention
of stealing, iv. effort to steal, and v. actual removal.

The inevitable consequences of stealing are:—
poverty, misery, disappointment, and dependent
livelihood.

Four conditions are necessary to complete the
evil of sexual misconduct—namely, i. the thought
to enjoy, ii. consequent effort, iii. means to gratify,
and iv. gratification.

The inevitable consequences of sexual misconduct are:—having many enemies, union with undesirable wives and husbands, and birth as a
woman or an eunuch.

Four conditions are necessary to complete the evil of lying— namely, i. an untruth, ii. deceiving intention, iii. utterance, and iv. actual deception.

The inevitable consequences of lying are:—being subject to abusive speech and vilification, untrustworthiness, and stinking mouth.

Four conditions are necessary to complete the evil of slandering—namely, i. persons that are to be divided, ii. the intention to separate them or the desire to endear oneself to another, iii. corresponding effort, and iv. the communication.

The inevitable consequence of slandering is the dissolution of friendship without any sufficient cause.

Three conditions are necessary to complete the evil of harsh speech—namely, i. a person to be abused, ii. angry thought, and iii. the actual abuse.

The inevitable consequences of harsh speech are:—being detested by others though absolutely harmless, and having a harsh voice.

Two conditions are necessary to complete the evil of frivolous talk—namely: i. the inclination towards frivolous talk, and ii. its narration.

The inevitable consequences of frivolous talk are:—defective bodily organs, and incredible speech.

Two conditions are necessary to complete the evil of covetousness—namely, i. another's possession, and ii. adverting to it, thinking—would this be mine!'

The inevitable consequence of covetousness is non-fulfilment of one's wishes.

Two conditions are necessary to complete the evil of illwill—namely, i. another person, and ii the thought of doing harm.

The inevitable consequences of illwill are:—ugliness, manifold diseases, and detestable nature.

False view is seeing things wrongly. False beliefs such as the denial of the efficacy of deeds are also included in this evil.

Two conditions are necessary to complete this evil—namely, i. perverted manner in which the object is viewed, and ii. the understanding of it according to that misconception.

The inevitable consequences of false view are:—base desires, lack of wisdom, dull wit, chronic diseases, and blameworthy ideas.

According to Buddhism there are ten kinds of false views—namely,[1] i. There is no such virtue as 'generosity' (dinnaṁ), This means that there

---

1. The Pāli text runs as follows:—
   "*N'atthi dinnaṁ, n'atthi iṭṭhaṁ, n'atthi hutaṁ, n'atthi sukaṭadukkaṭānaṁ kammānaṁ phalaṁ vipāko, n'atthi ayaṁ loko, n'atthi paraloko, n'atthi mātā, n'atthi pitā, n'atthi sattā apapātikā, n,atthi loke samaṇa-brāhamaṇā sammaggatā sammāpatipannā ye imañ ca lokaṁ parañ ca lokaṁ sayaṁ abhiññā sacchikatvā pavedenti.* See Dhammasangani—p. 233. The Expositor—pt. ii. 493, and Buddhist Psychology—p. 355.

is no good effect in giving alms. 2. There is no such virtue as 'liberal alms giving (*iṭṭhaṁ*)' or 3. 'Offering gifts to guests (*hutaṁ*),' Here, too, the implied meaning is that there is no effect in such charitable actions. 4. There is neither fruit nor result of good or evil deeds. 5. There is no such belief as 'this world' or 6. 'A world beyond' i.e., those born here do not accept a past existence, and those living here do not accept a future life. 7. There is no mother or 8. Father, i.e., there is no effect in anything done to them. 9. There are no beings that die and are being reborn (*opapātika*) 10. There are no righteous and well-disciplined recluses and brahmins who, having realized by their own super-intellect this world and world beyond, make known the same. (The reference here is to the Buddhas and Arahants).

Good Kamma which may ripen in the Sense-Sphere:

2. There are ten kinds of such meritorious actions (*kusalakamma*)—namely, (1) Generosity (*dāna*), (2) Morality (*sīla*), (3) Meditation (*bhāvanā*) (4) Reverence (*apacāyana*), (5) Service (*veyyāvacca*). (6) Transference of merit (*pattidāna*), (7) Rejoicing in others' good actions (*anumodanā*), (8) Hearing the doctrine (*dhamma savana*), (9) Expounding the doctrine (*dhammadesanā*) and (10) Straightening one's own views (*diṭṭhijjukamma*).

Sometimes these ten moral actions are regarded as twelve by introducing sub-divisions to (7) and (10).

Praising of others' Good Actions (*pasaṁsā*) is added to Rejoicing in others' merit (*anumodanā*). Taking the Three Refuges (*saraṇa*) and Mindfulness (*anussati*) are substituted for Straightening of one's views.

'Generosity' yields wealth. 'Morality' gives birth in noble families and in states of happiness. 'Meditation' gives birth in Realms of Form and Formless Realms, and helps to gain Higher Knowledge and Emancipation. 'Transference of merit' acts as a cause to give in abundance in future births. 'Rejoicing in others' merit' is productive of joy wherever one is born. Both 'expounding and hearing the Dhamma' are conducive to wisdom. 'Reverence' is the cause of noble parentage. 'Service' produces large retinue. 'Praising others good works' results in getting praise to oneself. 'Seeking the Three Refuges' results in the destruction of passions. 'Mindfulness' is conducive to diverse forms of happiness.

Kusala Kamma which may ripen in the Realms of Form:

These are the following five[1] kinds of (*Rūpa-Jhānas*) or Ecstasies which are purely mental:—

i.   The first *Jhāna* moral consciousness which consists of initial application (*vitakka*), sustained

---

1.   According to the Abhidhammatha Sangaha there are five Rūpa Jhānas, but the *Visuddhi Magga* mentions four Jhānas. There is no great difference between the two interpretations. In the former the Jhānas are divided into five according to the five constituents. In the latter the second Jhāna consists of the final three constituents without the first two.

application (*vicāra*), pleasurable interest (*pīti*), happiness (*sukha*), and one-pointedness (*ekaggatā*),

ii. The second *Jhāna* moral consciousness which consists of sustained application, pleasurable interest, happiness, and one-pointedness,

iii. The third *Jhāna* moral consciousness which consists of pleasurable interest, happiness and one-pointedness,

iv. The fourth *Jhāna* moral consciousness which consists of happiness and one-pointedness, and

v. The fifth *Jhāna* moral consciousness which consists of equanimity (*upekkhā*) and one pointedness.

These *Jhānas* have their corresponding effects in the Realms of Form.

Kusala Kamma which may ripen in the Formless Realms:

These are the four *Arūpa Jhānas* which have their corresponding effects in the Formless Realms-namely,

1. Moral consciousness dwelling in the 'Infinity of Space' (*Ākāsānañcāyatana*),
2. Moral consciousness dwelling on the 'Infinity of Consciousness' (*Viññāṇañcāyatana*),
3. Moral consciousness dwelling on 'Nothing ness' (*Ākiñcaññāyatana*), and
4. Moral consciousness wherein 'Perception neither is nor is not' (*N'eva saññān'āsaññāyatana*)[1].

---

1. For details see *A Manual of Abhidhamma* by Nārada Thera.

CHAPTER 21

NATURE OF KAMMA

"As you sow the seed so shall you reap the fruit."

SAMYUTTA NIKĀYA

Is one bound to reap all that one has sown in just proportion?

Not necessarily! In the Anguttara Nikāya the Buddha states:

"If any one says that a man must reap according to his deeds, in that case there is no religious life nor is an opportunity afforded for the entire extinction of sorrow. But if any one says that what a man reaps *accords* with his deeds, in that case there is a religious life and an opportunity is afforded for the entire extinction of sorrow."[1]

In Buddhism therefore there is every possibility to mould one's Kamma.

Although it is stated in the *Dhammapada*[2] that "not in the sky, nor in mid-ocean nor entering a mountain cave is found that place on earth, where abiding one may escape from (the consequence of) an evil deed," yet one is not bound to pay all the arrears of past Kamma. If such were the case, emancipation would be an impossibility. Eternal suffering would be the unfortunate result.

---

1. Anguttara Nikāya, part i. 249. See Warren, *Buddhism in Translations*, p. 218.
2. V. 127.

One is neither the master nor the servant of this Kamma. Even the most vicious person can by his own effort become the most virtuous person. We are always becoming something and that something depends on our own actions. We may at any moment change for the better or for the worse. Even the most wicked person should not be discouraged or despised on account of his evil nature. He should be pitied, for those who censure him may also have been in that same position at a certain stage. As they have changed for the better he may also change, perhaps sooner than they. Who knows what good Kamma he has in store for him? Who knows his potential goodness?

Angulimāla, a highway robber and the murderer of more than a thousand of his brethren became an Arahant and erased, so to speak, all his past misdeeds.

Ālavaka, the fierce demon who feasted on the flesh of human beings, gave up his carnivorous habits and attained the first stage of Sainthood.

Ambapāli, a courtesan, purified her character and attained Arahantship.

Asoka, who was stigmatised *Caṇḍa* (wicked), owing to his ruthlessness in expanding his Empire, became *Dharmāsoka*, or Asoka the Righteous, and changed his career to such an extent that today— "Amidst the tens of thousands of names of monarchs that crowd the columns of history, their majesties and graciousnesses, serenities and royal highnesses and the like the name of *Asoka* shines, and shines almost alone, a star."[1]

These are few striking examples which serve to show how a complete reformation of character can be effected by sheer determination.

It may so happen that in some cases a lesser evil may produce its due effect, while the effect of a greater evil may be minimised.

The Buddha says:

"Here, O Bhikkhus, a certain person is not disciplined in body, in morality, in mind, in wisdom, has little good and less virtue, and lives painfully in consequence of trifling misdeeds. Even a trivial act committed by such a person will lead him to a state of misery.

"Here, O Bhikkhus, a certain person is disciplined in body, in morality, in mind, in wisdom, does much good, is high-souled and lives with boundless compassion towards all.

"A similar evil committed by such a person ripens in this life itself and not even a small effect manifests itself (after death), not to say of a great one.[2]

"It is as if a man were to put a lump of salt into a small cup of water. What do you think, O Bhikkhus? Would now the small amount of water in this cup become saltish and undrinkable?

"Yes, Lord.

"And why?

---

1. H. G. Wells—*Outline of History.*
2. The reference here is to an Arahant who is not subject to any future sorrow.

"Because, Lord, there was very little water in the cup, and so it became saltish and undrinkable by this lump of salt.

"Suppose a man were to put a lump of salt into the river Ganges. What think you, O Bhikkhus? Would now the river Ganges become saltish and undrinkable by the lump of salt?

"Nay, indeed, Lord.

"And why not?

"Because, Lord, the mass of water in the river Ganges is great, and so it would not become saltish and undrinkable.

"In exactly the same way we may have the case of a person who does some slight evil deed which brings him to a state of misery, or, again, we may have the case of another person who does the same trival misdeed, yet he expiates it in his present life. Not even a small effect manifests itself (after death), not to say of a great one.

"We may have the case of a person who is cast into prison for the theft of a half-penny, penny, or for a hundred pence or, again, we may have the case of a person who is not cast into prison for a half-penny, for a penny, for a hundred pence.

"Who is cast into prison for a half-penny, for a penny, or for a hundred pence?

"Whenever any one is poor, needy and indigent, he is cast into prison for a half-penny, for a penny, or for a hundred pence.

"Who is not cast into prison for a half-penny, or for a pennny, or for a hundred pence?

"Whenever any one is rich, wealthy, and affluent, he is not cast into prison for a half-penny, for a penny, for a hundred pence.

"In exactly the same way we may have the case of a person who does some slight evil deed which brings him to a state of misery, or again we may have the case of another person who does the same trivial misdeed, and expiates it in the present life. Not even a small effect manifests itself (after death), not to say of a great one."[1]

Cause of Adverse Results

Good begets good, but any subsequent regrets on the part of the doer in respect of the good done, deprive him of the due desirable results.

The following case may be cited in illustration:

On one occasion King Pasenadi of Kosala approached the Buddha and said:

"Lord, here in Sāvatthi a millionaire householder has died. He has left no son behind him, and now I come here, after having conveyed his property to the palace. Lord, a hundred lakhs in gold, to say nothing of the silver. But this millionaire householder used to eat broken scraps of food and sour gruel. And how did he clothe himself? For dress he wore a robe of coarse hemp, and as to his coach, he drove in a broken-down cart rigged up with a leaf-awning."

Thereupon the Buddha said:

"Even so, O King, even so. In a former life, O King, this millionaire householder gave alms of food to a Pacceka Buddha called Tagarasikhi. Later, he repented of having given the food, saying within himself: 'It would be better if my servants and workmen ate the food I gave for alms.' And besides this he deprived his brother's only son of his life for the sake of his property. And because this millionaire householder gave alms of food to the Pacceka Buddha

---

1. Anguttara Nikāya pt. i. p. 249—See Warren, *Buddhism in Translation*, p. 227.

Tagarasikhi, in requital for this deed, he was reborn seven times in heavenly blissful states. And by the residual result of that same action, he became seven times a millionaire in this very Sāvatthi.

"And because this millionaire householder repented of having given alms, saying to himself: It would be better if my servants and workmen ate the food. Therefore as a requital for this deed, he had no appreciation of good food, no appreciation of fine dresses, no appreciation of an elegant vehicle, no appreciation of the enjoyments of the five senses.

"And because this millionaire householder slew the only son of his brother for the sake of his property, as requital for this deed, he had to suffer many years, many hundreds of years, many thousands of years, many hundreds of thousand of years of pain in states of misery. And by the residual of that same action, he is without a son for the seventh time, and in consequence of this, had to leave his property to the royal treasury."[1]

This millionaire obtained his vast fortune as a result of the good act done in a past birth, but since he repented of his good deed, he could not fully enjoy the benefit of the riches which Kamma provided him.

Beneficent and Maleficent Forces

In the working of Kamma it should be understood that there are beneficent and maleficent forces to counteract and support this self-operating

---

1. Saṁyutta Nikāya, pt. i, p. 91.
   See Warren, *Buddhism in Translations*, p. 296, and Grimm, *The Doctrine of the Buddha*, p. 248.

law.   Birth (*gati*), time or conditions (*kāla*), personality or appearance (*upadhi*) and effort (*payoga*) are such aids and hindrances to the fruition of Kamma.

If, for instance, a person is born in a noble family or in a state of happiness, his fortunate birth will sometimes hinder the fruition of his evil Kamma.

If, on the other hand, he is born in a state of misery or in an unfortunate family, his unfavourable birth will provide an easy opportunity for his evil Kamma to operate.

This is technically known as *Gati Sampatti* (favourable birth) and *Gati Vipatti* (unfavourable birth).

An unintelligent person, who, by some good Kamma, is born in a royal family, will, on account of his noble parentage, be honoured by the people. If the same person were to have a less fortunate birth, he would not be similarly treated.

King Duṭṭhagamani of Ceylon, for instance, acquired evil Kamma by waging war with the Tamils, and good Kamma by his various religious and social deeds.   Owing to his good Reproductive Kamma he was born in a heavenly blissful state. Tradition says that he will have his last birth in the time of the future Buddha Metteyya.   His evil Kamma cannot, therefore, successfully operate owing to his favourable birth.

To cite another example, King Ajātasattu, who committed parricide, became distinguished for his piety and devotion later owing to his association with the Buddha. He now suffers in a woeful state as a result of His heinous crime. His unfavourable birth would not therefore permit him to enjoy the benefits of his good deeds.

Beauty (*Upadhi Sampatti*), and ugliness (*Upadhi Vipatti*) are two other factors that hinder and favour the working of Kamma.

If, by some good Kamma, a person obtains a happy birth but unfortunately is deformed, he will not be able fully to enjoy the beneficial results of his good Kamma. Even a legitimate heir to the throne may not perhaps be raised to that exalted position if he happens to be physically deformed.

Beauty, on the other hand, will be an asset to the possessor. A good-looking son of a poor parent may attract the attention of others and may be able to distinguish himself through their influence.

Favourable time or occasion and unfavourable time or occasion (*Kalā Sampatti* and *Kalā Vipatti*) are two other factors that effect the working of Kamma; the one aids, and the other impedes the working of Kamma.

In the case of a famine all without exception will be compelled to suffer the same fate. Here the unfavourable conditions open up possibilities for evil Kamma to operate. The favourable conditions, on the other hand, will prevent the operation of evil Kamma.

Of these beneficent and maleficent forces the most important is effort (*Payoga*).   In the working of Kamma effort or lack of effort plays a great part. By present effort one can create fresh Kamma, new surroundings, new environment, and even a new world.   Though placed in the most favourable circumstances and provided with all facilities, if one makes no strenuous effort, one not only misses golden opportunities but may also ruin oneself.   Personal effort is essential for both worldly and spiritual progress.

If a person makes no effort to cure himself of a disease or to save himself from his difficulties, or to strive with diligence for his progress, his evil Kamma will find a suitable opportunity to produce its due effects.   If, on the contrary, he endeavours on his part to surmount his difficulties, to better his circumstances, to make the best use of the rare opportunities, to strive strenuously for his real progress, his good Kamma will come to his succour.

When ship-wrecked in deep sea, the Bodhisatta Mahā Janaka made a great effort to save himself, while the others prayed to the gods and left their fate in their hands. The result was that the Bodhisatta escaped while the others were drowned.

These two important factors are technically known as *Payoga Sampatti* and *Payoga Vipatti*.

Though we are neither absolutely the servants nor the masters of our Kamma, it is evident from these counteractive and supportive factors that the fruition of Kamma is influenced to some extent by external circumstances, surroundings, personality, individual striving, and the like.

It is this doctrine of Kamma that give consolation, hope, reliance, and moral courage to a Buddhist.

When the unexpected happens, difficulties, failures, and misfortunes confront him, the Buddhist realizes that he is reaping what he has sown, and is wiping off a past debt. Instead of resigning himself, leaving everything to Kamma, he makes a strenuous effort to pull out the weeds and sow useful seeds in their place, for the future is in his hands.

He who believes in Kamma, does not condemn even the most corrupt, for they have their chance to reform themselves at any moment. Though bound to suffer in woeful states, they have the hope of attaining eternal peace. By their deeds they create their own hells, and by their own deeds they can also create their own heavens.

A Buddhist who is fully convinced of the law of Kamma does not pray to another to be saved but confidently relies on himself for his emancipation. Instead of making any self-surrender, or propitiating any supernatural agency, he would rely on his own will-power and work incessantly for the weal and happiness of all.

This belief in Kamma, "validates his effort and kindles his enthusiasm," because it teaches individual responsibility.

To an ordinary Buddhist Kamma serves as a deterrent, while to an intellectual it serves as an incentive to do good.

This law of Kamma explains the problem of suffering, the mystery of the so-called fate and predestination of some religions, and above all the inequality of mankind.

*   *   *

We are the architects of our own fate. We are our own creators. We are our own destroyers. We build our own heavens. We build our own hells.

What we think, speak and do, become our own. It is these thoughts, words, and deeds that assume the name of Kamma and pass from life to life exalting and degrading us in the course of our wanderings in Saṁsara.

Says the Buddha:—

"Man's merits and the sins he here hath wrought:
That is the thing he owns, that takes he hence.
That dogs his steps, like shadows in pursuit.
Hence let him make good store for life elsewhere.
Sure platform in some other future world,
Rewards of virtue on good beings wait."

Kindred Sayings, i. p. 98.

CHAPTER 22

WHAT IS THE ORIGIN OF LIFE?

"Inconceivable is the beginning, O disciples, of this faring on. The earliest point is not revealed of the running on, the faring on, of beings, cloaked in ignorance, tied by craving,"

SAṀYUTTA NIKĀYA

Rebirth, which Buddhists do not regard as a mere theory but as a fact verifiable by evidence, forms a fundamental tenet of Buddhism, though its goal Nibbāna is attainable in this life itself. The Bodhisatta Ideal and the correlative doctrine of freedom to attain utter perfection are based on this doctrine of rebirth.

Documents record that this belief in rebirth, viewed as transmigration or reincarnation, was accepted by philosophers like *Pythagoras* and *Plato*, poets like *Shelly*, *Tennyson* and *Wordsworth*, and many ordinary people in the East as well as in the West.

The Buddhist doctrine of rebirth should be differentiated from the theory of transmigration and reincarnation of other systems, because Buddhism denies the existence of a transmigrating permanent soul, created by God, or emanating from a *Paramātma* (Divine Essence).

It is Kamma that conditions rebirth. Past Kamma conditions the present birth; and present Kamma, in combination with past Kamma, conditions the future. The present is the offspring of the past, and becomes, in turn, the parent of the future.

The actuality of the present needs no proof as it is self-evident. That of the past is based on memory and report, and that of the future on forethought and inference.

If we postulate a past, a present and a future life, then we are at once faced with the problem—"What is the ultimate origin of life?"

One school, in attempting to solve the problem, postulates a first cause, whether as a cosmic force or as an Almighty Being. Another school denies a first cause for, in common experience, the cause ever becomes the effect and the effect becomes the cause. In a circle of cause and effect a first cause[1] is inconceivable. According to the former, life has had a beginning, according to the latter, it is beginningless. In the opinion of some the conception of a first cause is as ridiculous as a round triangle.

One might argue that life must have had a beginning in the infinite past and that beginning or the First Cause is the Creator.

In that case there is no reason why the same demand may not be made of this postulated Creator.

With respect to this alleged First Cause men have held widely different views. In interpreting this First Cause, Paramātma, Brahma, Isvara,

---

1. "There is no reason to suppose that the world had a beginning at all. The idea that things must have a beginning is due to the poverty of our imagination." Bertrand Russell, *Why I am not a Christian.*

Jehovah, God, the Almighty, Allah, Supreme
Being, Father in Heaven, Creator, Order of Heaven,
Prime Mover, Uncaused Cause, Divine Essence,
Chance, Pakati, Padhāna are some significant
terms employed by certain religious teachers and
philosophers.

Hinduism traces the origin of life to a mystical
Paramātma from which emanate all *Ātmas* or
souls that transmigrate from existence to existence
until they are finally reabsorbed in Paramātma.
One might question whether there is any possibility for these reabsorbed *Ātmas* for a further transmigration.

Christianity, admitting the possibility of an
ultimate origin, attributes everything to the fiat of
an Almighty God.

"Whoever," as Sohopenhaeur says, "regards himself as
having come out of nothing must also think that he will
again become nothing, for that an eternity has passed before
he was, and then a second eternity had begun, through which
he will never cease to be, is a monstrous thought.

"Moreover, if birth is the absolute beginning, then death
must be the absolute end; and the assumption that man is
made out of nothing, leads necessarily to the assumption
that death is his absolute end."[1]

"According to the Theological principles," argues Spencer
Lewis, "man is created arbitrarily and without his desire,
and at the moment of creation is either blessed or unfortunate, noble or depraved, from the first step in the process
of his physical creation to the moment of his last breath,
regardless of his individual desires, hopes, ambitions, struggles
or devoted prayers. Such is theological fatalism.

1. See *The world as Will and Idea.*

"The doctrine that all men are sinners and have the essential sin of Adam is a challenge to justice, mercy, love and omnipotent fairness."

Huxley says—"If we are to assume that anybody has designedly set this wonderful universe going, it is perfectly clear to me that he is no more entirely benevolent and just, in any intelligible sense of the words, than that he is malevolent and unjust."

According to Einstein: "If this being (*God*) is omnipotent, then every occurrence, including every human action, every human thought, and every human feeling and aspiration is also his work; how is it possible to think of holding men responsible for their deeds and thoughts before such an Almighty Being?

"In giving out punishments and rewards, He would to a certain extent be passing judgment on himself. How can this be combined with the goodness and righteousness ascribed to him?"

According to Charles Bradlaugh—"The existence of evil is a terrible stumbling block to the Theist. Pain, misery, crime, poverty confront the advocate of eternal goodness, and challenge with unanswerable potency his declaration of Deity as all-good, all-wise, and all-powerful."

Commenting on human suffering and God, Prof. J. B. S. Haldane writes:—"Either suffering is needed to perfect human character, or God is not Almighty. The former theory is disproved by the fact that some people who have suffered very little but have been fortunate in their ancestry and education have very fine characters. The objection to the second is that it is only in connection with the universe as a whole that there is any intellectual gap to be filled by the postulation of a deity. And a creator could presumably create whatever he or it wanted."[1]

---

1. See his essay on "A Plea for Atheism," *Humanity's Gain from Unbelief.*

In "Despair," a poem of his old age, Lord Tennyson thus boldly attacks God, who, as recorded in Isaiah, says—"I make peace and create evil."[1]

"What! I should call on that infinite Love that has served us so well?

Infinite cruelty, rather, that made everlasting hell. Made us, foreknew us, foredoomed us, and does what he will with his own.

Better our dead brute mother who never has heard us groan."

Dogmatic writers of old authoritatively declared that God created man after his own image. Some modern thinkers state, on the contrary, that man created God after his own image.[2] With the growth of civilization man's conception of God grows more and more refined. There is at present a tendency to substitute this personal God by an impersonal God.

Voltaire states that God is the noblest creation of man.

---

1. Isaiah, XXV, 7.

2. "A strict demonstration of the existence of God is utterly impossible. Almost all the proofs that have been offered assume in the very premises the conclusion to be proved." Rev. W. Kirkus in *Orthodoxy Scripture and Reason,* p. 34.

   "We have got to recognize that evil falls within a universe for which God is responsible. We cannot absolve God for permitting the existence of sin and pain."

   —Canon. C. E. Raven, *The Grounds of Christian Assumption.*

It is however impossible to conceive of such an omnipotent, omnipresent being, an epitome of everything that is good—either in or outside the universe.

Modern science endeavours to tackle the problem with its limited systematized knowledge. According to the scientific standpoint, we are the direct products of the sperm and ovum cells provided by our parents. But science does not give a satisfactory explanation with regard to the development of the mind, which is infinitely more important than the machinery of man's material body. Scientists, while asserting "*Omne vivum ex vivo*" "all life from life" maintain that mind and life evolved from the lifeless.

Now from the scientific standpoint we are absolutely parent-born. Thus our lives are necessarily preceded by those of our parents and so on. In this way life is preceded by life until one goes back to the first protoplasm or colloid. As regards the origin of this first protoplasm or colloid, however, scientists plead ignorance.

What is the attitude of Buddhism with regard to the origin of life?

At the outset it should be stated that the Buddha does not attempt to solve all the ethical and philosophical problems that perplex mankind. Nor does He deal with speculations and theories that tend neither to edification nor to enlightenment. Nor does He demand blind faith from His adherents anent a First Cause. He is chiefly con-

cerned with one practical and specific problem—
that of suffering and its destruction, all side issues
are completely ignored.

On one occasion a Bhikkhu named *Mālunkyaputta*, not content to lead the Holy Life, and
achieve his Emancipation by degrees, approached
the Buddha and impatiently demanded an immediate solution of some speculative problems with
the threat of discarding the robes if no satisfactory answer was given.

"Lord," he said, "these theories have not been elucidated, have been set aside and rejected by the Blessed One—
whether the world is eternal or not eternal; whether the
world is finite or infinite. If the Blessed One will elucidate
these questions to me, then I will lead the Holy Life under
Him. If he will not, then I will abandon the precepts and
return to the lay life.

"If the Blessed One knows that the world is eternal, let
the Blessed One elucidate to me that the world is eternal;
if the Blessed One knows that the world is not eternal, let
the Blessed One elucidate that the world is not eternal—
in that case, certainly, for one who does not know and lacks
the insight, the only upright thing is to say: I do not know,
I have not the insight."

Calmly the Buddha questioned the erring Bhikkhu whether his adoption of the Holy Life was
in any way conditional upon the solution of
such problems.

"Nay, Lord," the Bhikkhu replied.

The Buddha then admonished him not to
waste time and energy over idle speculations
detrimental to his moral progress, and said:

"Whoever, Mālunkyaputta, should say, 'I will not lead the Holy Life under the Blessed One until the Blessed One elucidates these questions to me'—that person would die before these questions had ever been elucidated by the Accomplished One.

"It is as if a person were pierced by an arrow thickly smeared with poison, and his friends and relatives were to procure a surgeon, and then he were to say. 'I will not have this arrow taken out until I know the details of the person by whom I was wounded, nature of the arrow with which I was pierced, etc.' That person would die before this would ever be known by him.

"In exactly the same way whoever should say, 'I will not lead the Holy Life under the Blessed One until He elucidated to me whether the world is eternal or not eternal, whether the world is finite or infinite. . .' That person would die before these questions had ever been elucidated by the Accomplished One.

"If it be the belief that the world is eternal, will there be the observance of the Holy Life? In such a case—No! If it be the belief that the world is not eternal, will there be the observance of the Holy Life? In that case also— No! But, whether the belief be that the world is eternal or that it is not eternal, there is birth, there is old age, there is death, the extinction of which in this life itself I make known.

"Mālunkyaputta, I have not revealed whether the world is eternal or not eternal, whether the world is finite or infinite. Why have I not revealed these? Because these are not profitable, do not concern the bases of holiness, are not conducive to aversion, to passionlessness, to cessation, to tranquility, to intuitive wisdom, to enlightenment or to Nibbāna. Therefore I have not revealed these."[1]

---

1.   Majjhima Nikāya, Cūla Mālunkya Sutta No. 63.

According to Buddhism, we are born from the matrix of action (*Kammayoni*). Parents merely provide us with a material layer. Therefore being precedes being. At the moment of conception, it is Kamma that conditions the initial consciousness that vitalizes the foetus. It is this invisible Kammic energy, generated from the past birth, that produces mental phenomena and the phenomena of life in an already extant physical phenomena, to complete the trio that constitutes man.

Dealing with the conception of beings, the Buddha states:

"Where three are found in combination, there a germ of life is planted. If mother and father come together, but it is not the mother's fertile period, and the 'being-to-be born' (*gandhabba*) is not present, then no germ of life is planted. If mother and father come together, and it is the mother's fertile period, but the 'being-to-be-born' is not present then again no germ of life is planted. If mother and father come together and it is the mother's fertile period, and the 'being-to-be-born' is present, then by the conjunction of these three, a germ of life is there planted."[1]

Here *Gandhabba* (= *gantabba*) does not mean "a class of devas said to preside over the process of conception"[2] but refers to a suitable being ready to be born in that particular womb. This term is used only in this particular connection, and must not be mistaken for a permanent soul.

---

1. Ibid., Mahātanhāsaṁkhaya Sutta, No. 38, Although wick and oil may be present, yet an external fire should be introduced to produce a flame.

2. See F. L. Woodward, *Some Sayings of the Buddha.*, p. 40.

For a being to be born here, somewhere a being must die. The birth of a being, which strictly means the arising of the Aggregates (*khandhānaṁ pātubhāvo*), or psycho-physical phenomena in this present life, corresponds to the death of a being in a past life; just as, in conventional terms, the rising of the sun in one place means the setting of the sun in another place. This enigmatic statement may be better understood by imagining life as a wave and not as a straight line. Birth and death are only two phases of the same process. Birth precedes death, and death, on the other hand, precedes birth. This constant succession of birth and death connection with each individual life-flux constitutes what is technically known as *Saṁsāra*—recurrent wandering.

What is the ultimate origin of life?

The Buddha positively declares: "Without, cognizable beginning is this *Saṁsāra*. The earliest point of beings who, obstructed by ignorance and fettered by craving, wander and fare on, is not to be perceived."

---

1. *Anamataggo' yaṁ bhikkhave saṁsāro, pubbākoṭi na paññāyati avijjānīvaraṇānaṁ sattānam taṇhāsaṁyojanānaṁ sandhāvataṁ.*

   "Incalculable is the beginning, brethren, of this faring on. The earliest point is not revealed of the running on, the faring, of beings cloaked in ignorance, tied to craving." F. L. Woodward—*Kindred Sayings*, part iii, p. 118.

   "Inconceivable is the beginning of this Samsāra, not

This life-stream flows *ad infinitum*, as long as it is fed with the muddy waters of ignorance and craving. When these two are completely cut off, then only does the life-stream cease to flow; rebirth ends, as in the case of Buddhas and Arahants. A first beginning of this life-stream cannot be determined, as a stage cannot be perceived when this life force was not fraught with ignorance and craving.

It should be understood that the Buddha has here referred merely to the beginning of the life-stream of living beings. It is left to scientists to speculate on the origin and the evolution of the universe.

---

to be discovered a first beginning of beings, who, obstructed by ignorance and ensnared by craving, are hurrying and hastening through this round of rebirths." *Nyānatiloka Thera.*

Saṁsāra, literally, means recurrent wandering.

Atthasālinī defines Saṁsāra thus:—

Khandhānaṁ paṭipāṭi dhātu-āyatanāna ca
Abbhocchinnaṁ vattamānā saṁsāro' ti pavuccati.

Saṁsāra is the unbroken succession of aggregates, elements, and the sense-bases.

CHAPTER 23

THE BUDDHA ON THE SO-CALLED CREATOR-GOD

"I count your Brahma one th'unjust among,
Who made a world in which to shelter wrong."

JĀTAKA

The Pāli equivalent for the Creator-God in other religions is either *Issara* (Saṁskrit—*Īsvara*) or Brahma. In the Tipitaka there is absolutely no reference whatever to the existence of a God. On several occasions the Buddha denied the existence of a permanent soul (*Attā*). As to the denial of a Creator-God, there are only a few references. Buddha never admitted the existence of a Creator whether in the form of a force or a being.

Despite the fact that the Buddha placed no supernatural God over man some scholars assert that the Buddha was characteristically silent on this important controversial question. The following quotations will clearly indicate the viewpoint of the Buddha towards the concept of a Creator-God.

In the Anguttara Nikāya the Buddha speaks of three divergent views that prevailed in His time. One of these was: "Whatever happiness or pain or neutral feeling this person experiences all that is due to the creation of a Supreme Deity (*Issaranimmānahetu.*)"[1]

---

1. Añguttara Nikāya i, p. 174. Gradual Sayings, i, p. 158.

According to this view we are what we were willed to be by a Creator. Our destinies rest entirely in his hands. Our fate is pre-ordained by him. The supposed freewill granted to his creation is obviously false.

Criticising this fatalistic view, the Buddha says: "So, then, owing to the creation of a Supreme Deity men will become murderers, thieves, unchaste, liars, slanderers, abusive, babblers, covetous, malicious and perverse in view. Thus for those who fall back on the creation of a God as the essential reason, there is neither desire nor effort nor necessity to do this deed or abstain from that deed."[1]

In the Devadaha Sutta[2] the Buddha, referring to the self-mortification of naked ascetics, remarks: "If, O Bhikkhus, beings experience pain and happiness as the result of God's creation (*Issaranimmānahetu*), then certainly these naked ascetics must have been created by a wicked God (*pāpakena issarena*), since they suffer such terrible pain."

Kevaḍḍha Sutta narrates a humorous conversation that occurred between an inquisitive Bhikkhu and the supposed Creator.

---

1. Majjhima Nikāya ii, p. 222. Sutta No. 101.
2. Dīgha Nikāya i, p. 221, Sutta No. 11.

A Bhikkhu, desiring to know the end of the elements, approached Mahā Brahma and questioned him thus:

"Where, my friend, do the four great elements—earth, water, fire and air—cease, leaving no trace behind?" To this The Great Brahma replied: "I, brother, am Brahma, Great Brahma, the Supreme Being, the Unsurpassed, the Chief, the Victor, the Ruler, the Father of all beings who have been or are to be."

For the second time the Bhikkhu repeated his question, and the Great Brahma gave the same dogmatic reply:

When the Bhikkhu questioned him for the third time, the Great Brahma took the Bhikkhu by the arm, led him aside, and made a frank utterance:

"O Brother, these gods of my suite believe as follows: 'Brahma sees all things, knows all things, has penetrated all things.' Therefore, was it that I did not answer you in their presence. I do not know, O brother, where these four great elements—earth, water, fire and air—cease, leaving no trace behind. Therefore it was an evil and a crime, O brother, that you left the Blessed One, and went elsewhere in quest of an answer to this question. Turn back, O brother, and having drawn near to the Blessed One, ask Him this question, and as the Blessed One shall explain to you so believe."

Tracing the origin of Mahā Brahma, the so-called Creator-God, the Buddha comments in the Pāṭika Sutta.[1]

---

1. Dīgha Nikāya (No. 24) iii, p. 29. *Dialogues of the Buddha.* iii, pp. 26, 27.

"On this, O disciples, that being who was first born (in a new world evolution) thinks thus: "I am Brahma, the Great Brahma, the Vanquisher, the All-Seer, the Disposer, the Lord, the Maker, the Creator, the Chief, the Assigner, the Master of Myself, the Father of all that are and are to be. By me are these beings created. And why is that so? A while ago I thought: Would that other beings too might come to this state of being! Such was the aspiration of my mind, and lo! these beings did come.

"And those beings themselves who arose after him, they too think thus: "This Worthy must be Brahma, the Great Brahma, the Vanquisher, the All-Seer, the Disposer, the Lord, the Maker, the Creator, the Chief, the Assigner, the Master of Myself, the Father of all that are and are to be.

"On this, O disciples, that being who arose first becomes longer lived, handsomer, and more powerful, but those who appeared after him become shorter lived, less comely. less powerful. And it might well be, O disciples, that some other being, on deceasing from that state, would come to this state (on earth) and so come, he might go forth from the household life into the homeless state. And having thus gone forth, by reason of ardour, effort, devotion, earnestness, perfect intellection, he reaches up to such rapt concentration, that with rapt mind he calls to mind his former dwelling place, but remembers not what went before. He says thus: 'That Worshipful Brahma, the Vanquisher, the All-Seer, the Disposer, the Lord, the Maker, the Creator, the Chief, the Assigner, the Master of Myself, the Father of all that are and aɪe to be, he by whom we were created, he is permanent, constant, eternal, unchanging, and he will remain so for ever and ever. But we who were created by that Brahma, we have come hither all impermanent, transient, unstable, short-lived, destined to pass away.'

"Thus was appointed the beginning of all things, which ye, sirs, declare as your traditional doctrine, to wit, that it has been wrought by an over-lord, by Brahma.""

In the Bhūridatta Jātaka[1] (No. 543) the Bodhisatta questions the supposed Divine justice of the
Creator as follows:

"He who has eyes can see the sickening sight,
Why does not Brahma set his creatures right?

If his wide power no limits can restrain,
Why is his hand so rarely spread to bless?

Why are his creatures all condemned to pain?
Why does he not to all give happiness?

Why do fraud, lies, and ignorance prevail?
Why triumphs falsehood—truth and justice fail?

I count you Brahma one th'unjust among,
Who made a world in which to shelter wrong."

Refuting the theory that everything is the creation of a Supreme Being, the Bodhisattā states
in the *Mahābodhi Jātaka* (No. 528):

"If there exists some Lord all powerful to fulfil
In every creature bliss or woe, and action good or
ill;
That Lord is stained with sin. Man does but
work his will."

---

1. Jātaka Translation, vol. vi, p. 110.
2. Ibid, vol. p. 122.

CHAPTER 24

REASONS TO BELIEVE IN REBIRTH

"I recalled my varied lot in former existences"

MAJJHIMA NIKĀYA

How are we to believe in rebirth?

The Buddha is our greatest authority on rebirth. On the very night of His Enlightenment, during the first watch, the Buddha developed retro-cognitive knowledge which enabled Him to read His past lives.

"I recalled," He declares, "my varied lot in former existences as follows: first one life, then two lives, then three, four, five, ten, twenty up to fifty lives, then a hundred, a thousand, a hundred thousand and so forth."[1]

During the second watch the Buddha, with clairvoyant vision, perceived beings disappearing from one state of existence and reappearing in another. He beheld the "base and the noble, the beautiful and the ugly, the happy and the miserable, passing according to their deeds."[1]

These are the very first utterances of the Buddha regarding the question of rebirth. The textual references conclusively prove that the Buddha did not borrow this stern truth of rebirth from

---

1. Majjhima Nikāya, Mahāsaccaka Sutta, No. 36, i. 248.

any pre-existing source, but spoke from personal knowledge—a knowledge which was supernormal, developed by Himself, and which could be developed by others as well.

In His first paean of joy (*udāna*), the Buddha says:

"Through many a birth (*anekajāti*), wandered I, seeking the builder of this house. Sorrowful indeed is birth again and again (*dukkhājātipunappunam*)."[1]

In the *Dhammacakka Sutta*,[2] His very first discourse, the Buddha, commenting on the second Noble truth, states: "This very craving is that which leads to rebirth" (*y'āyam tanhā ponobhavikā*). The Buddha concludes this discourse with the words: "This is my last birth. Now there is no more rebirth (*ayam antimā jāti natthi dāni punabbhavo*)."

The *Majjhima Nikāya* relates that when the Buddha, out of compassion for beings, surveyed the world with His Buddha-vision before He decided to teach the Dhamma, He perceived beings who, with fear, view evil and a world beyond (*paralokavajjabhayadassāvino*).[3]

In several discourses the Buddha clearly states that beings, having done evil, are, after death (*parammaranā*), born in woeful states, and beings having done good, are born in blissful states,

---

1. Dhammapada, v. 153.
2. Mahā Vagga, p. 10, Samyutta Nikāya v. 428. See ch. 6.
3. Majjhima Nikāya i, 169.

Besides the very interesting *Jātaka* stories, which deal with His previous lives and which are of ethical importance, the *Majjhima Nikāya* and the *Anguttara Nikāya* make incidental references to some of the past lives of the Buddha.

In the *Ghaṭīkāra Sutta*,[1] the Buddha relates to the Venerable *Ānanda* that He was born as *Jotipāla*, in the time of the Buddha *Kassapa*, His immediate predecessor. The *Anāthapiṇḍikovāda Sutta*[2] describes a nocturnal visit of *Anāthapiṇḍika* to the Buddha, immediately after his rebirth as a Deva. In the *Anguttara Nikāya*,[3] the Buddha alludes to a past birth as *Pacetana* the wheelright. In the *Samyutta Nikāya*, the Buddha cites the names of some Buddhas who preceded Him.

An unusual direct reference to departed ones appears in the *Parinibbāna Sutta*.[4] The Venerable *Ānanda* desired to know from the Buddha the future state of several persons who had died in a particular village. The Buddha patiently described their destinies.

Such instances could easily be multiplied from the Tipitaka to show that the Buddha did expound the doctrine of rebirth as a verifiable truth.[5]

---

1. Majjhima Nikāya ii, 45 (No. 81).
2. Ibid., iii. 258 (No. 143).
3. Part i, 111.
4. Dīgha Nikāya ii, 91 (No. 16).
5. Cp. Mr. J. G. Jennings, *The Vedantic Buddhism of the Buddha.*

Following the Buddha's instructions, His disciples also developed this retro-cognitive knowledge and were able to read a limited, though vast, number of their past lives. The Buddha's power in this direction was limitless.

Certain Indian Rishis, too, prior to the advent of the Buddha, were distinguished for such supernormal powers as clairaudience, clairvoyance, telepathy, telesthesia, and so forth.

Although science takes no cognizance of these supernormal faculties, yet, according to Buddhism, men with highly developed mental concentration cultivate these psychic powers and read their past just as one would recall a past incident of one's present life. With their aid, independent of the five senses, direct communication of thought and direct perception of other worlds are made possible.

Some extraordinary persons, especially in their childhood, spontaneously develop, according to the laws of association, the memory of their past births and remember fragments of their previous lives.[1] (*Pythagoras*) is said to have distinctly remembered a shield in a Grecian temple as having been carried by him in a previous incarnation at the siege of Troy."[2] Somehow or other these wonderful children lose that memory later, as is the case with many infant prodigies.

1. The case of Shanti Devi of India is a striking example. See *The Bosat,* vol. xiii, No. 2. p. 27.
2. William W. Atkinson and E. D. Walter, *Reincarnation and the Law of Kamma.*

Experiences of some dependable modern psychists, ghostly phenomena, spirit communication, strange alternate and multiple personalities[1] also shed some light upon this problem of rebirth.

In hypnotic states some can relate experiences of their past lives, while a few others, like *Edgar Cayce* of America, were able not only to read the past lives of others but also to heal diseases.[2]

The phenomenon of secondary personalities has to be explained either as remnants of past personal experiences or as "possession by an invisible spirit." The former explanation appears more reasonable, but the latter cannot totally be rejected.

---

1. *Psalms of the Brethren* (*Theragāthā*) gives an interesting account of a Brahmin named Vangīsa, "who won favour as a teacher by tapping on skulls with his finger nails and discovering thereby where their former occupants were reborn."
    Certain persons at times exhibit different personalities in the course of their particular lives. Prof. James cites some remarkable cases in his *Principles of Psychology*. See F. W. H. Myers, *Human Personality and its survival of bodily Death*. The Visuddhi Magga mentions an interesting incident of a deva entering into the body of a layman. See *The Path of Purity,* part i, p. 48.
    The writer himself has met persons who were employed as mediums by invisible beings to convey their thoughts and some others who were actually possessed by evil spirits. When in this hypnotic state they speak and do things of which normally they are totally innocent and which they cannot afterwards recall.

2. See *Many Mansions* and *The World Within* by Gina Cerminara.

How often do we meet persons whom we have never before met, but who, we instinctively feel, are familiar to us? How often do we visit places and instinctively feel impressed that we are perfectly acquainted with those surroundings?[1]

The Dhammapada commentary relates the story of a husband and wife who, seeing the Buddha, fell at His feet and saluted Him, saying—"Dear son, is it not the duty of sons to care for their mother and father when they have grown old. Why is it that for so long a time you have not shown yourself to us? This is the first time we have seen you?"

---

1. "It was such experiences that led Sir Walter Scott to a sense of metempsychosis. His biographer Lockhart quotes in his *Life of Scott* the following entry in Scott's diary for February 17th, 1828.

"I cannot, I am sure, tell if it is worth marking down, that yesterday at dinner time, I was strangely haunted by what I would call the sense of pre-existences, viz., a confused idea that nothing that passed was said for the first time, that the same topics had been discussed and the persons had stated the same opinions on them. The sensation was so strong as to resemble what is called a mirage in the desert and calenture on board ship.

"Bulwer Lytton describes these mysterious experiences as that strange kind of inner and spiritual memory which often recalls to us places and persons we have never seen before, and which Platonists would resolve to be the unquenched and struggling consciousness of a former life." H. M. Kitchener, *The Theory of Reincarnation,* p. 7.

The writer also has met some persons who remember fragments of their past births and also a distinguished doctor in Europe who hypnotises people and makes them describe some of their past lives.

The Buddha attributed this sudden outburst of parental love to the fact that they had been His parents several times during His past lives and remarked:

"*Through previous association or present advantage*

That old love springs up again like the lotus in the water."[1]

There arise in this world highly developed personalities, and Perfect Ones like the Buddhas. Could they evolve suddenly? Could they be the products of a single existence?

How are we to account for personalities like *Confucius*, *Pānini*, *Buddhaghosa*, *Homer* and *Plato*, men of genius like *Kālidāsa*, *Shakespeare*, infant prodigies like *Ramanujan*, *Pascal*, *Mozart*, *Beethoven* and so forth?

Could they be abnormal if they had not led noble lives and acquired similar experiences in the past? Is it by mere chance that they are born of those particular parents and placed under those favourable circumstances?

Infant prodigies, too, seem to be a problem for scientists. Some medical men are of opinion that prodigies are the outcome of abnormal glands, especially the pituitary, the pineal and the adrenal gland. The extraordinary hypertrophy of glands of particular individuals may also be due to a past Kammic cause. But how, by mere hypertrophy of glands, one *Christian Heineken* could talk

1. See *Buddhist Legends*, vol. 3, p. 108.

within a few hours of his birth, repeat passages
from the Bible at the age of one year, answer any
question on Geography at the age of two, speak
French and Latin at the age of three, and be a
student of philosophy at the age of four; how
John Stuart Mill could read Greek at the age of
three; how *Macaulay* could write a world history
at the age of six; how *William James Sidis,* wonder
child of the United States, could read and write at
the age of two, speak French, Russian, English
German with some Latin and Greek at the age of
eight; how *Charles Bennet* of Manchester could
speak in several languages at the age of three; are
wonderful events incomprehensible to nonscient
ists.[1] Nor does science explain why glands should
hypertrophy in just a few and not in all.   The real
problem remains unsolved.

Heredity alone cannot account for prodigies
"else their ancestry would disclose it, their poste
rity, in even greater degree than themselves, would
demonstrate it "

The theory of heredity should be supplemented
by the doctrine of Kamma and rebirth for an
adequate explanation of these puzzling problems

Is it reasonable to believe that the present span
of life is the only existence between two eternities
of happiness and misery?   The few years we spend
here, at most but five score years, must certainly
be an inadequate preparation for eternity.

---

1.   Ceylon Observer, November 21, 1948.

If one believes in the present and a future, it is logical to believe in a past.

If there be reason to believe that we have existed in the past, then surely there are no reasons to disbelieve that we shall continue to exist after our present life has apparently ceased.[1]

It is indeed a strong argument in favour of past and future lives that "in this world virtuous persons are very often unfortunate and vicious persons prosperous."[2]

We are born into the state created by ourselves. If, in spite of our goodness, we are compelled to lead an unfortunate life, it is due to our past evil Kamma. If, in spite of our wickedness, we are prosperous, it is also due to our past good Kamma. The present good and bad deeds will, however, produce their due effects at the earliest possible opportunity.

A Western writer says:

"Whether we believe in a past existence or not, it forms the only reasonable hypothesis which bridges certain gaps in human knowledge concerning facts of everyday life. Our reason tells us that this idea of past birth and Kamma alone can explain, for example, the degrees of differences that exist between twins; how men like Shakespeare with a very limited experience are able to portray, with marvellous exactitude, the most diverse types of human character, scenes, and so forth, of which they could have no

1. "We have come to look upon the present as the child of the past and as the parent of the future." T. H. Huxley.
2. Addison.

actual knowledge, why the work of the genius invariably transcends his experience, the existence of infant precocity, and the vast diversity in mind and morals, in brain and physique, in conditions, circumstances and environments, observable throughout the world."

What do Kamma and Rebirth explain?

1. They account for the problem of suffering for which we ourselves are responsible.

2. They explain the inequality of mankind.

3. They account for the arising of geniuses and infant prodigies.

4. They explain why identical twins who are physically alike, enjoying equal privileges, exhibit totally different characteristics, mentally, morally, temperamentally and intellectually.

5. They account for the dissimilarities amongst children of the same family, though heredity may account for the similarities.

6. They account for the extraordinary innate abilities of some men.

7. They account for the moral and intellectual differences between parents and children.

8. They explain how infants spontaneously develop such passions as greed, anger and jealousy.

9. They account for instinctive likes and dislikes at first sight.

10. They explain how in us are found "a rubbish heap of evil and a treasure-house of good."

11. They account for the unexpected outburst

of passion in a highly civilised person, and for the sudden transformation of a criminal into a saint.

12.   They explain how profligates are born to saintly parents, and saintly children to profligates.

13.   They explain how, in one sense, we are the result of what we were, we will be the result of what we are; and, in another sense, we are not absolutely what we were, and we will not be absolutely what we are.

14.   They explain the causes of untimely deaths and unexpected changes in fortune.

15.   Above all they account for the arising of omniscient, perfect spiritual teachers, like the Buddhas, who possess incomparable physical, mental and intellectual characteristics.

CHAPTER 25

THE WHEEL OF LIFE

PATICCA-SAMUPPĀDA

"No God no Brahma can be found,
No matter of this wheel of life,
Just bare phenomena roll
Dependent on conditions all!"

VISUDDHI MAGGA

The process of rebirth has been fully explained by the Buddha in the *Paṭicca-Samuppāda*.

Paṭicca means 'because of' or 'dependent upon' *samuppāda* 'arising' or 'origination,' Although the literal meaning of the term is 'arising because of' or 'dependent arising or origination,' it is applied to the whole causal formula which consists of twelve interdependent causes and effects, technically called *paccaya* and *paccayuppanna*.

The method of the *Paṭicca-Samuppāda* should be understood as follows:

Because of A arises B. Because of B arises C. When there is no A, there is no B. When there is no B, there is no C. In other words—'this being so, that is; this not being so, that is not.' (*imasmim sati, idam hoti; imasmim asati, idam na hoti*.)

Paṭicca-Samuppāda is a discourse on the process of birth and death, and not a philosophical theory of the evolution of the world. It deals

with the cause of rebirth and suffering with a
view to helping men to get rid of the ills of life.
It makes no attempt to solve the riddle of an
absolute origin of life.

It merely explains the 'simple happening of a
state, dependent on its antecedent state.'[1]

Ignorance (*avijjā*) of the truth of suffering, its
cause, its end, and the way to its end, is the chief
cause that sets the wheel of life in motion. In
other words, it is the not-knowingness of things
as they truly are, or of oneself as one really is. It
clouds all right understanding.

"Ignorance is the deep delusion wherein we
here so long are circling round,"[2] says the Buddha.

When ignorance is destroyed and turned into
knowingness, all causality is shattered as in the
case of the Buddhas and Arahants.

In the *Itivuttaka*[3] the Buddha states—"Those
who have destroyed delusion and broken through
the dense darkness, will wander no more: causality exists no more for them."

Ignorance of the past, future, both past and
future and "The Dependent Origination" is also
regarded as Avijjā.

---

1. *Tabbhāvabhāvībhāvākāramatta* - Abhidhammattha San-
     gaha.
     See Manual of Abhidhamma by Nārada Thera, p. 360.
2. Sutta Nipāta v. 730.
3. P. 14.

Dependent on ignorance arise conditioning activities (*saṁkhārā*).

Saṁkhārā is a multisignificant term which should be understood according to the context. Here the term signifies immoral (*akusala*), moral (*kusala*) and unshakable (*āneñja*) volitions (*cetanā*) which constitute Kamma that produces rebirth. The first embraces all volitions in the twelve types of immoral consciousness; the second, all volitions in the eight types of Beautiful (*sobhana*) moral consciousness and the five types of moral *rūpajhāna* consciousness; the third, all volitions in the four types of moral *arūpajhāna* consciousness.

Saṁkhārā, as one of the five aggregates, implies fifty of the fifty-two mental states, excluding feeling and perception.

There is no proper English equivalent which gives the exact connotation of this Pali term.

The volitions of the four supramundane Path consciousness (*lokuttara maggacitta*) are not regarded as *saṁkhārā* because they tend to eradicate ignorance. Wisdom (*paññā*) is predominant in supramundane types of consciousness while volition (*cetanā*) is predominant in the mundane types of consciousness.

All moral and immoral thoughts, words and deeds are included in *saṁkhārā*. Actions, whether good or bad, which are directly rooted in, or indirectly tainted with ignorance, and which must necessarily produce their due effects, tend to prolong wandering in *Saṁsāra*. Nevertheless, good deeds, freed from greed, hate and delusion, are necessary to get rid of the ills of life. Accordingly the Buddha compares His Dhamma to a raft whereby one crosses the ocean of life. The activities of Buddhas and Arahants, however, are not treated as *saṁkhārā* as they have eradicated ignorance.

Ignorance is predominant in immoral activities. while it is latent in moral activities. Hence both moral and immoral activities are regarded as caused by ignorance.

Dependent on past conditioning activities arises relinking or rebirth-consciousness (*patisandhi-viññāna*) in a subsequent birth. It is so called because it links the past with the present, and is the initial consciousness one experiences at the moment of conception.

Viññāṇa strictly denotes the nineteen types of rebirth-consciousness (*paṭisandhi-viññāna*) described in the Abhidhamma. All the thirty-two types of resultant consciousness (*vipāka citta*) experienced during lifetime, are also implied by the term.

The foetus in the mother's womb is formed by the combination of this relinking-consciousness with the sperm and ovum cells of the parents. In this consciousness, are latent all the past impressions, characteristics and tendencies of that particular individual life-flux.

This rebirth-consciousness is regarded as pure[1] as it is either devoid of immoral roots of lust, hatred, and delusion[2] or accompanied by moral roots.[3]

Simultaneous with the arising of the relinking-consciousness there occur mind and matter (*nāma-rūpa*) or, as some scholars prefer to say, "corporeal organism."

The second and third factors (*samkhārā* and *viññāna*) pertain to the past and present lives of an individual. The third and fourth factors (*viññāna* and *nāma-rūpa*). on the contrary, are contemporaneous.

This compound *nāma-rūpa* should be understood as *nāma* (mind) alone, *rūpa* (matter) alone, and *nāmarūpa* (mind and matter) together. In the case of Formless Planes (*arūpa*) there arises only mind: in the case of Mindless (*asañña*) Planes, only matter; in the case of Sentient Realm (*kāma*) and Realms of Form (*rūpa*), both mind and matter.

Nāma here means the three aggregates—feeling (*vedanā*), perception (*sañña*) and mental states (*samkhārā*)—that arise simultaneous with the re-linking-consciousness. *Rūpa* means the three

---

1. "Radiant is this consciousness." (*pabhassaram idam cittam*) says the Buddha in the Anguttara Nikāya vol. 1, p. 10. According to the commentator the Buddha was thus referring to the rebirth-consciousness.
2. In the case of 'Rootless Resultants' (*Ahetuka-vipāka*).
3 In the case of 'Resultants with Roots' (*Sahetukavipāka*).

decads—*kāya* (body), *bhāva* (sex), and *vatthu* (seat of consciousness)—that also arise simultaneous with the relinking-consciousness, conditioned by past Kamma.

The body-decad is composed of the four elements—namely, 1. the element of extension (*paṭhavi*), 2. the element of cohesion (*āpo*), 3. the element of heat (*tejo*), 4. the element of motion (*vāyo*); its four derivatives (*upādā rūpa*)—namely, 5. colour (*vaṇṇa*), 6. odour (*gandha*), 7. taste (*rasa*), 8. nutritive essence (*ojā*), 9. vitality (*jīvitindriya*) and 10. body (*kāya*).

Sex-decad and base decad also consist of the first nine and sex (*bhāva*) and seat of consciousness (*vatthu*) respectively.

From this it is evident that sex is determined by past Kamma at the very conception of the being.

Here *kāya* means the sensitive part of the body (*pasāda*).

Sex is not developed at the moment of conception but the potentiality is latent. Neither the heart nor the brain, the supposed seat of consciousness, has been evolved at the moment of conception, but the potentiality of the seat is latent.

In this connection it should be remarked that the Buddha did not definitely assign a specific seat for consciousness as He has done with the other senses. It was the cardiac theory (the view that the heart is the seat of consciousness) that prevailed in His time, and this was evidently supported by the *Upanishads*. The Buddha could have accepted the popular theory, but He did not commit Himself. In the *Paṭṭhāna*, the Book of Relations, the Buddha refers to the seat of consciousness, in such indirect terms as "*yaṁ rūpaṁ nissāya*—depending on that material thing", without positively asserting whether that *rūpa* was either the heart (*hadaya*) or the brain. But, according to the view of commentators like Venerable Buddhaghosa and Anuruddha, the seat of consciousness is definitely the heart. It should be understood that the Buddha neither accepted nor rejected the popular cardiac theory.

During the embryonic period the six sense-bases (*salāyatana*) gradually evolve from these psycho-physical phenomena in which are latent infinite potentialities. The insignificant infinitesimally small speck now develops into a complex six senses-machine.

Human machine is very simple in its beginning but very complex in its end. Ordinary machines, on the other hand, are complex in the beginning but very simple in the end. The force of a finger is sufficient to operate even a most gigantic machine.

The six-senses-human machine now operates almost mechanically without any agent like a soul to act as the operator. All the six senses—eye, ear, nose, tongue, body and mind—have their respective objects and functions. The six sense-objects such as forms, sounds, odours, sapids, tangibles and mental objects collide with their respective sense-organs giving rise to six types of consciousness. The conjunction of the sense-bases, sense-objects and the resultant consciousness is contact (*phassa*) which is purely subjective and impersonal.

The Buddha states:

"Because of eye and forms, visual consciousness arises; contact is the conjunction of the three. Because of ear and sounds, arises auditory consciousness; because of nose and odours, arises olfactory consciousness; because of tongue and sapids, arises gustatory consciousness; because of body and tangibles. arises tactile consciousness; because of mind and mental objects, arises mind-consciousness. The conjuction of these three is contact."[1]

It should not be understood that mere collision is contact (*na sangatimatto eva phasso*).

Dependent on contact feelings (*vedanā*) arise.

Strictly speaking, it is feeling that experiences an object when it comes in contact with the senses. It is this feeling that experiences the desirable or undesirable fruits of an action done in this or in a previous birth. Besides this mental state there is no soul or any other agent to experience the result of the action.

Feeling or. as some prefer to say, sensation, is a mental state common to all types of con-

---

1. Saṁyutta Nikāya, part ii, p. 70; *Kindred Sayings,* part ii, p. 50.

sciousness. Chiefly there are three kinds of feelings
—namely pleasurable (*somanassa*), unpleasurable
(*domanassa*), and neutral (*adukkhamasukha*). With
physical pain (*dukkha*) and physical happiness
(*sukha*) there are altogether five kinds of feelings.
The neutral feeling is also termed *upekkhā* which
may be indifference or equanimity.

According to *Abhidhamma* there is only one
type of consciousness accompanied by pain.
Similarly there is only one accompanied by happiness. Two are connected with an unpleasurable feeling. Of the 89 types of consciousness,
in the remaining 85 are found either a pleasurable
or a neutral feeling.

It should be understood here that *Nibbānic*
bliss is not associated with any kind of feeling.
Nibbānic bliss is certainly the highest happiness
(*Nibbānaṁ paramaṁ sukhaṁ*), but it is the happiness of relief from suffering. It is not the enjoyment of any pleasurable object.

Dependent on feeling arises craving (*taṇhā*)
which, like ignorance, is the other most important
factor in the "Dependent Origination." Attachment, thirst, clinging are some renderings for this
Pāli term.

Craving is threefold—namely, craving for sensual pleasures (*kāmataṇhā*), craving for sensual
pleasures associated with the view of eternalism,
(*bhavataṇhā*) i.e., enjoying pleasures thinking that
they are imperishable, and craving for sensual

pleasures with the view of nihilism (*vibhavataṇhā*) i.e., enjoying pleasures thinking that everything perishes after death. The last is the materialistic standpoint.

Bhavataṇhā and *vibhavataṇhā* are also inter- preted as attachment to Realms of Form (*rūpa- bhava*) and Formless Realms (*arūpabhava*) res- pectively. Usually these two terms are rendered by craving for existence and non-existence.

There are six kinds of craving corresponding to the six sense objects such as form, sound and so on. They become twelve when they are treated as internal and external. They are reckoned as 36 when viewed as past, present and future, When multiplied by the foregoing three kinds of craving, they amount to 108.

It is natural for a worldling to develop a cra- ving for the pleasures of sense. To overcome sense-desires is extremely difficult. The most powerful factors in the wheel of life are ignorance and craving, the two main causes of the Dependent Origination. Ignorance is shown as the past cause that conditions the present; and craving, the present cause that conditions the future.

Dependent on craving is grasping (*upādāna*) which is intense craving. *Taṇhā* is like groping in the dark to steal an object. *Upādāna* corresponds to the actual stealing of the object. Grasping is caused by both attachment and error. It gives rise to the false notions, of "I" and "mine."

Grasping is fourfold-namely, Sensuality, False Views, Adherence to rites and ceremonies, and the Theory of a soul.

The last two are also regarded as false views.

Dependent on grasping arises *bhava* which, literally, means becoming. It is explained as both moral and immoral actions which constitute Kamma (*Kammabhava*)—active process of becoming—and the different planes of existence (*upapatti-bhava*)—passive process of becoming. The subtle difference between *samkhārā* and *kammabhava* is that the former pertains to the past and the latter to the present life. By both are meant Kammic activities. It is only the *Kammabhava* that conditions the future birth.

Dependent on becoming arises birth (*jāti*) in a subsequent life.

Birth strictly speaking, is the arising of the psycho-physical phenomena (*khandhānam pātu-bhāvo*).

Old age and death (*jarāmarana*), are the inevitable results of birth.

If, on account of a cause, an effect arises, then, if the cause ceases, the effect also must cease.

The reverse order of the *Paticca-Samuppāda* will make the matter clear.

Old age and death are only possible in and with a psycho-physical organism, that is to say, a six-senses-machine. Such an organism must be born, therefore it presupposes birth. But birth is the inevitable result of past Kamma or action, which is conditioned by grasping due to craving. Such craving appears when feeling arises. Feeling is the outcome of contact between senses and objects.

Therefore it presupposes organs of sense which cannot exist without mind and body. Mind originates with a rebirth-consciousness, conditioned by activities, due to ignorance of things as they truly are.

The whole formula may be summed up thus:

Dependent on Ignorance arise Conditioning Activities.

Dependent on Conditioning Activities arises Relinking-Consciousness.

Dependent on Relinking-Consciousness arise Mind and Matter.

Dependent on Mind and Matter arise the six Spheres of Sense.

Dependent on the Six Spheres of Sense arises Contact

Dependent on Contact arises Feeling.

Dependent on Feeling arises Craving.

Dependent on Craving arises Grasping.

Dependent on Grasping arise Actions (*Kamma bhava*).

Dependent on Actions arises Birth.

Dependent on Birth arise Decay, Death, Sorrow, Lamentation Pain, Grief, and Despair.

Thus does the entire aggregate of suffering arise.

THE WHEEL OF LIFE

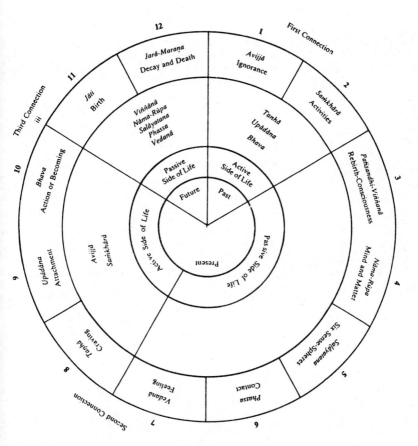

Diagram 4

The complete cessation of Ignorance leads to the cessation of Conditioning Activities.

The cessation of Conditioning Activities leads to the cessation of Relinking-Consciousness.

The cessation of Relinking-Consciousness leads to the cessation of Mind and Matter.

The cessation of Mind and Matter leads to the cessation of the six Spheres of Sense.

The cessation of the six Spheres of Sense leads to the cessation of Contact.

The cessation of Contact leads to the cessation of Feeling.

The cessation of Feeling leads to the cessation of Craving.

The cessation of Craving leads to the cessation of Grasping.

The cessation of Grasping leads to the cessation of Actions.

The cessation of Actions leads to the cessation of Birth.

The cessation of Birth leads to the cessation of Decay, Death, Sorrow, Lamentation, Pain, Grief, and Despair.

Thus does the cessation of this entire aggregate of suffering result.

The first two of these twelve factors pertain to the past, the middle eight to the present, and the last two to the future.

Of them Moral and Immoral Activities (*samkhārā*) and Actions (*bhava*) are regarded as Kamma.

Ignorance (*avijjā*), Craving (*taṇhā*), and Grasping (*upādāna*) are regarded as Passions or Defilements (*kilesa*); Relinking—Consciousness (*paṭisandhi-viññāṇa*), Mind and Matter (*nāma-rūpa*), Spheres of Sense (*salāyatana*), Contact (*phassa*), Feeling (*vedanā*), Birth (*jāti*), Decay and Death (*jarā-maraṇa*) are regarded as Effects (*vipāka*).

Thus Ignorance, Activities, Craving, Grasping and Kamma, the five causes of the past, condition the present five effects (*phala*)-namely, Relinking-Consciousness, Mind and Matter, Spheres of Sense, Contact, and Feeling. In the same way Craving, Grasping, Kamma, Ignorance, and Activities of the present condition the above five effects of the future.

This process of cause and effect continues *ad infinitum*. A beginning of this process cannot be determined as it is impossible to conceive of a time when this life-flux was not encompassed by ignorance. But when this ignorance is replaced by wisdom and the life-flux realizes the *Nibbāna Dhātu*, then only does the rebirth process terminate.

"'Tis Ignorance entails the dreary round —now here, now there—of countless births and deaths."

"But, no hereafter waits for him who knows!"[1]

---

1. Chambers. *Buddha's Teachings*, vv. 729, 730.

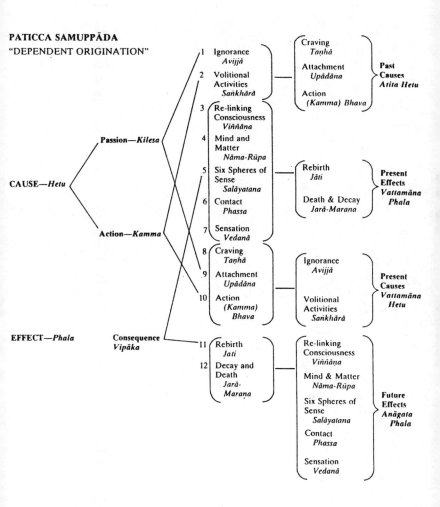

PATICCA SAMUPPĀDA
"DEPENDENT ORIGINATION"

1 Ignorance
  Avijjā
2 Volitional
  Activities
  Sankhārā
3 Re-linking
  Consciousness
  Viññāna
4 Mind and
  Matter
  Nāma-Rūpa
5 Six Spheres of
  Sense
  Salāyatana
6 Contact
  Phassa
7 Sensation
  Vedanā
8 Craving
  Tanhā
9 Attachment
  Upādāna
10 Action
   (Kamma)
   Bhava
11 Rebirth
   Jati
12 Decay and
   Death
   Jarā-Marana

Passion—*Kilesa*

Action—*Kamma*

CAUSE—*Hetu*

EFFECT—*Phala*

Consequence
Vipāka

Craving
Tanhā
Attachment
Upādāna
Action
(Kamma) *Bhava*

Past
Causes
Atita Hetu

Rebirth
Jāti

Death & Decay
Jarā-Marana

Present
Effects
*Vattamāna
Phala*

Ignorance
Avijjā

Volitional
Activities
Sankhārā

Present
Causes
*Vattamāna
Hetu*

Re-linking
Consciousness
Viññāna

Mind & Matter
Nāma-Rūpa

Six Spheres of
Sense
Salāyatana

Contact
Phassa

Sensation
Vedanā

Future
Effects
*Anāgata
Phala*

CHAPTER 26

MODES OF BIRTH AND DEATH

"Again, again the slow wits seek rebirth,
Again, again comes birth and dying comes,
Again, again men bear us to the grave."

SAMYUTTA NIKĀYA

The Paṭicca-Samuppāda describes the process of rebirth in subtle technical terms and assigns death to one of the following four causes:

1. Exhaustion of the Reproductive Kammic energy (*kammakkhaya*).

The Buddhist belief is that, as a rule, the thought, volition, or desire, which is extremely strong during lifetime, becomes predominant at the time of death and conditions the subsequent birth. In this last thought-process is present a special potentiality. When the potential energy of this Reproductive (*janaka*) Kamma is exhausted, the organic activities of the material form in which is embodied the life-force, cease even before the end of the life-span in that particular place. This often happens in the case of beings who are born in states of misery (*apāya*) but it can happen in other planes too.

2. The expiration of the life-term (*āyukkhaya*), which varies in different planes.

Natural deaths, due to old age, may be classed under this category.

There are different planes of existence with varying age-limits. Irrespective of the Kammic force that has yet to run, one must, however, succumb to death when the maximum age-limit is reached. If the Reproductive Kammic force is extremely powerful, the Kammic energy. rematerialises itself in the same plane or, as in the case of Devas, in some higher realm.

3. The simultaneous exhaustion of the Reproductive Kammic energy and the expiration of the life-term (*ubhayakkhaya*).

4. The opposing action of a stronger Kamma unexpectedly obstructing the flow of the Reproductive Kamma before the life-term expires (*upacchedaka-kamma*).

Sudden untimely deaths of persons and the deaths of children are due to this cause.

A more powerful opposing force can check the path of a flying arrow and bring it down to the ground. So a very powerful Kammic force of the past is capable of nullifying the potential energy of the last thought-process, and may thus destroy the psychic life of the being. The death of Venerable Devadatta, for instance, was due to a Destructive Kamma which he committed during his lifetime.

The first three are collectively called "timely deaths" (*kāla-maraṇa*), and the fourth is known as "untimely death" (*akālamaraṇa*).

An oil lamp, for instance, may get extinguished owing to any of the following four causes-namely, the exhaustion of the wick, the exhaustion of oil, simultaneous exhaustion of both wick and oil, or some extraneous cause like a gust of wind,

So may death be due to any of the foregoing four causes.

Explaining thus the causes of death, Buddhism states that there are four modes of birth-namely, 1. egg-born beings (*aṇḍaja*), 2. womb-born beings (*jalābuja*), 3. moisture-born beings (*saṁsedaja*), and 4. beings having spontaneous births (*opapātika*).

This broad classification embraces all living beings.

Birds and oviparous snakes belong to the first division.

The womb-born creatures comprise all human beings, some devas inhabiting the earth, and some animals that take conception in a mother's womb.

Embryos, using moisture as nidus for their growth, like certain lowly forms of animal life, belong to the third class.

Beings having a spontaneous birth are generally invisible to the physical eye. Conditioned by their past Kamma, they appear spontaneously, without passing through an embryonic stage. Petas and Devas normally, and Brahmas belong to this class.

CHAPTER 27

PLANES OF EXISTENCE

"Not to be reached by going is world's end."

ANGUTTARA NIKĀYA

According to Buddhism the earth, an almost insignificant speck in the universe, is not the only habitable world, and humans are not the only living beings. Indefinite are world systems and so are living beings. Nor is "the impregnated ovum the only route to rebirth." By traversing one cannot reach the end of the world[1], says the Buddha.

Births may take place in different spheres of existence. There are altogether thirty-one places in which beings manifest themselves according to their moral or immoral Kamma.

There are four states of unhappiness (*Apāya*)[2] which are viewed both as mental states and as places.

They are:

1. *Niraya* (*ni+aya*; devoid of happiness)— woeful states where beings atone for their evil Kamma. They are not eternal hells where beings are subject to endless suffering. Upon the exhaustion of the evil Kamma there is a possibility for

---

1. See *Kindred Sayings*, part 1, pp. 85, 86.
2. *Apa + aya* = devoid of happiness.

beings born in such states to be reborn in blissful states as the result of their past good actions.

2. *Tiracchāna-yoni* (*tiro* = across; *acchāna* = going), the animal kingdom. Buddhist belief is that beings are born as animals on account of evil Kamma. There is, however, the possibility for animals to be born as human beings as a result of the good Kamma accumulated in the past. Strictly speaking, it should be more correct to state that Kamma which manifested itself in the form of a human being may manifest itself in the form of an animal or *vice versa*, just as an electric current can be manifested in the forms of light, heat and motion successively—one not necessarily being evolved from the other.

It may be remarked that at times certain animals particularly dogs and cats, live a more comfortable life than even some human beings due to their past good Kamma.

It is one's Kamma that determines the nature of one's material form which varies according to the skilfulness or unskilfulness of one's actions.

3. *Peta-yoni* (*pa*+*ita*) lit., departed beings, or those absolutely devoid of happiness. They are not disembodied spirits of ghosts. They possess deformed physical forms of varying magnitude, generally invisible to the naked eye. They have no planes of their own, but live in forests, dirty surroundings, etc. There is a

special book, called *Petavatthu*, which exclusively deals with the stories of these unfortunate beings. Saṁyutta Nikāya also relates some interesting accounts of these Petas.

Describing the pathetic state of a Peta, the Venerable *Moggallāna* says:—

"Just now as I was descending Vultures' Peak Hill, I saw a skeleton going through the air, and vultures, crows, and falcons kept flying after it, pecking at its ribs, pulling it apart while it uttered cries of pain. To me, friend, came this thought :—O but this is wonderful ! O but this is marvellous that a person will come to have such a shape, that the individuality acquired will come to have such a shape."

"This being," the Buddha remarked, "was a cattle-butcher in his previous birth, and as the result of his past Kamma he was born in such a state."[1]

According to the *Questions of Milinda* there are four kinds of Petas—namely, the *Vantāsikas* who feed on vomit, the *Khuppipāsino* who hunger and thirst, the *Nijjhāmataṇhikā*, who are consumed by thirst, and the *Paradattūpajīvino* who live on the gifts of others.

As stated in the Tirokuḍḍa Sutta[2] these last mentioned Petas share the merit performed by their living relatives in their names, and could thereby pass on to better states of happiness.

---

1. See *Kindred Sayings*, part ii, p. 170.
2. Khuddaka Pāṭha.

4. *Asura-yoni*—the place of the Asura-demons. Asura, literally, means those who do not shine or those who do not sport. They are also another class of unhappy beings similar to the Petas. They should be distinguished from the Asuras who are opposed to the Devas.

*　　　*　　　*

Next to' these four unhappy states (*Duggati*) are the seven happy states (*Sugati*). They are:—

1. *Manussa*[1]—The Realm of human beings.

The human realm is a mixture of both pain and happiness. Bodhisattas prefer the human realm as it is the best field to serve the world and perfect the requisites of Buddhahood. Buddhas are always born as human beings.

2. *Cātummahārājika* — the lowest of the heavenly realms where the Guardian Deities of the four quarters of the firmament reside with their followers.

3. *Tāvatṁisa*—lit., thirty-three—the Celestial Realm of the thirty-three Devas[2] where

---

1. Literally, those who have an uplifted or developed mind (*mano ussannaṁ etasaṁ*). The Saṁskrit equivalent of *manussa* is *manushya* which means the sons of Manu. They are ‚so called because they became civilized after Manu the seer.

2. A Chinese Buddhist book states that on each of the four sides of this Plane are eight heavens (32) and a central one where King Sakka dwells. *Guide to Buddhahood.*

Deva Sakka is the King.　The origin of the name is attributed to a story which states that thirty-three selfless volunteers led by Magha (another name for Sakka), having performed charitable deeds, were born in this heavenly realm.　It was in this heaven that the Buddha taught the Abhidhamma to the Devas for three months.

4.　*Yāma*—'The Realm of the Yāma Devas.' That which destroys pain is Yāma.

5.　*Tusita*—lit., happy dwellers, is 'The Realm of Delight.'

The Bodhisattas who have perfected the requisites of Buddhahood reside in this Plane until the opportune moment comes for them to appear in the human realm to attain Buddhahood.　The Bodhisatta Metteyya, the future Buddha, is at present residing in this realm awaiting the right opportunity to be born as a human being and become a Buddha.

The Bodhisatta's mother, after death, was born in this realm as a Deva (god).　From here he repaired to Tāvatiṁsa Heaven to listen to the Abhidhamma taught by the Buddha.

6.　*Nimmānaratī*—'The Realm of the Devas who delight in the created mansions.'

7.　*Paranimmitavasavattī*—"The Realm of the Devas who make others' creation serve their own ends.'

The last six are the realms of the Devas whose physical forms are more subtle and refined than those of human beings and are imperceptible to the naked eye. These celestial beings too are subject to death as all mortals are. In some respects, such as their constitution, habitat, and food they excel humans, but do not as a rule transcend them in wisdom. They have spontaneous births, appearing like youths and maidens of fifteen or sixteen years of age.

These six Celestial Planes are temporary blissful abodes where beings are supposed to live enjoying fleeting pleasures of sense.

The four unhappy states (*Duggati*) and the seven happy states (*Sugati*) are collectively termed *Kāmaloka*—Sentient Sphere.

*   *   *

Superior to these Sensuous Planes are the Brahma Realms or Rūpaloka (Realms of Form) where beings delight in jhānic bliss, achieved by renouncing sense-desires.

Rūpaloka consists of sixteen realms according to the jhānas or Ecstasies cultivated. They are as follows:—

(a) The Plane of the First Jhāna;

1. *Brahma Pārisajja* — The Realm of the Brahma's Retinue.

2. *Brahma Purohita* — The Realm of the Brahma's Ministers.

3. *Māha Brahma*—The Realm of the Great Brahmas.

The highest of the first three is Mahā Brahma. It is so called because the dwellers in this Realm excel others in happiness, beauty, and age-limit owing to the intrinsic merit of their mental development.

(b) The Plane of the Second Jhāna;

4. *Parittābhā*—The Realm of Minor Lustre,

5. *Appamāṇābhā*—The Realm of Infinite Lustre,

6. *Ābhassarā*—The Realm of the Radiant Brahmas.

(c) The Plane of the Third Jhāna;

7. *Parittasubhā*-The Realm of the Brahmas of Minor Aura.

8. *Appamāṇasubhā*—The Realm of the Brahmas of Infinite Aura,

9. *Subhakiṇhā*—The Realm of the Brahmas of Steady Aura,

(d) The Plane of the Fourth Jhāna;

10. *Vehapphala*—The Realm of the Brahmas of Great Reward.

11. *Asaññasatta*—The Realm of Mindless Beings,

12. *Suddhāvāsa*—The Pure Abodes which are further subdivided into five, viz:

i. *Aviha*—The Durable Realm,

ii. *Atappa*—The Serene Realm,

iii. *Sudassa*—The Beautiful Realm,

iv. *Sudassi*—The Clear-Sighted Realm.
v. *Akaniṭṭha*—The Highest Realm.

Only those who have cultivated the Jhānas or Ecstasies are born on these higher planes. Those who have developed the First Jhāna are born in the first Plane; those who have developed the Second and Third Jhānas are born in the second Plane; those who have developed the Fourth and Fifth Jhānas are born in the third and fourth Planes respectively.

The first grade of each plane is assigned to those who have developed the Jhānas to an ordinary degree, the second to those who have developed the Jhānas to a greater extent, and the third to those who have gained a complete mastery over the Jhānas.

In the eleventh plane, called the *Asaññasatta*, beings are born without a consciousness.

Here only a material flux exists. Mind is temporarily suspended while the force of the Jhāna lasts. Normally both mind and matter are inseparable. By the power of meditation it is possible, at times, to separate matter from mind as in this particular case. When an Arahant attains the Nirodha Samāpatti, too, his consciousness ceases to exist temporarily. Such a state is almost inconceivable to us. But there may be inconceivable things which are actual facts.

The Suddhāvāsas or Pure Abodes are the exclusive Planes of Anāgāmis or Never-Returners. Ordinary beings are not born in these states. Those who attain Anāgāmi in other planes are reborn in these Pure Abodes. Later, they attain Arahantship and live in those planes until their life-term ends.

*   *   *

There are four other planes called *Arūpaloka* which are totally devoid of matter or bodies. Buddhists maintain that there are realms where mind alone exists without matter. "Just as it is possible for an iron bar to be suspended in the air because it has been flung there, and it remains as long as it retains any unexpended momentum, even so the Formless being appears through being flung into that state by powerful mind-force, there it remains till that momentum is expended. This is a temporary separation of mind and matter, which normally co-exist."[1]

It should be mentioned that there is no sex distinction in the Rūpaloka and the Arūpaloka.

The Arūpaloka is divided into four planes according to the four Arūpa Jhānas.

They are:—

1. *Ākāsānañcāyatana*—The Sphere of the Conception of Infinite Space.

2. *Viññānañcāyatana*—The Sphere of the Conception of Infinite Consciousness.

---

1. Kassapa Thera.

3. *Ākiñcaññāyatana*—The Sphere of the Conception of Nothingness,

4. *N'eva Saññā Nāsaññayatana*—The Sphere of Neither Perception nor Non-Perception.[1]

*   *   *   *

It should be remarked that the Buddha did not attempt to expound any cosmological theory.

The essence of the Buddha's teaching is not affected by the existence or non-existence of these planes.   No one is bound to believe anything if it does not appeal to his reason.   Nor is it proper to reject anything because it cannot be conceived by one's limited knowledge.

---

1. For details and the life-term of various planes see *A Manual* of *Abhidhamma* by Nārada Thera, pp. 234-246.

CHAPTER 28

HOW REBIRTH TAKES PLACE

"The pile of bones of (all the bodies of) one man
Who has alone one aeon lived
Would make a mountain's height—
So said the mighty seer."

ITIVUTTAKA

To the dying man at this critical stage, according to Abhidhamma philosophy, is presented a *Kamma, Kamma Nimitta*, or *Gati Nimitta*.

By Kamma is here meant some good or bad act done during his lifetime or immediately before his dying moment. It is a good or bad thought. If the dying person had committed one of the five heinous crimes (*Garuka Kamma*) such as parricide etc. or developed the Jhānas (*Ecstasies*), he would experience such a Kamma before his death. These are so powerful that they totally eclipse all other actions and appear very vividly before the mind's eye. If he had done no such weighty action, he may take for his object of the dying thought-process a Kamma done immediately before death (*Āsanna Kamma*); which may be called a 'Death-Proximate Kamma.'

In the absence of a 'Death-Proximate Kamma' a habitual good or bad act (*Ācinna Kamma*) is presented, such as the healing of the sick in the case of a good physician, or the teaching of the Dhamma in the case of a pious Bhikkhu, or stealing in the case of a thief. Failing all these, some casual trivial good or bad act (*Katattā Kamma*) becomes the object of the dying thought-process.

THE PLANES OF EXISTENCE

The Age Limit

ARŪPALOKA (4) Formless Realms	N'eva Saññā N'āsaññayatana			48,000	M.K.
	Ākiñcaññāyatana			60,000	,,
	Viññānañcāyatana			40,000	,,
	Akāsānañcāyatana			20,000	,,
RŪPALOKA (16) Realms of Form	Catuttha Jhāna Bhūmi	**SUDDHĀVĀSA** Pure Abodes	Akaniṭṭha	16,000	,,
			Sudassi	8,000	,,
			Sudassa	4,000	,,
	Fourth Jhāna Realm		Atappa	2,000	,,
			Aviha	1,000	,,
			Asaññasatta	500	,,
			Vehapphala	500	,,
	Tatiya Jhāna Bhūmi Third Jhāna Realm		Subhakinha	64	,,
			Appamānasubha	32	,,
			Parittasubha	16	,,
	Dutiya Jhāna Bhūmi Second Jhāna Realm		Ābhassara	8	,,
			Appamāṇābha	4	,,
			Parittābha	2	,,
	Pathama Jhāna Bhūmi First Jhāna Realm		Mahā Brahma	1	A.K.
			Brahma Purohita	1/2	,,
			Brahma Pārisajja	1/3	,,
KĀMALOKA (11) Sentient Existence	**SUGATI (7)** Happy States — **DEVALOKA (6)** Celestial Realms		Paranimmitavasavatti	16,000	C.Y.
			Nimmānarati	8,000	,,
			Tusita	4,000	,,
			Yāma	2,000	,,
			Tāvatimsa	1,000	,,
			Cātummahārājika	500	,,
	Manussa—Human Realm			**No Limit**	
	DUGGATI (4) Evil States	Asurayoni			,,
		Petayoni			,,
		Tiracchāna yoni			,,
		Niraya			,,

M.K. = Māhā Kappa
A.K. = Asaṅkheyya Kappa
C.Y. = Celestial Years

Diagram iv.

Kamma Nimitta or 'symbol,' means a mental reproduction of any sight, sound, smell, taste, touch or idea which was predominant at the time of some important activity, good or bad, such as a vision of knives or dying animals in the case of a butcher, of patients in the case of a physician, and of the object of worship in the case of a devotee, etc.......

By *Gati Nimitta*, or 'symbol of destiny' is meant some symbol of the place of future birth. This frequently presents itself to dying persons and stamps its gladness or gloom upon their features. When these indications of the future birth occur, if they are bad, they can at times be remedied. This is done by influencing the thoughts of the dying man. Such premonitory visions[1] of destiny may be fire, forests, mountainous regions, a mother's womb, celestial mansions, and the like.

Taking for the object a Kamma, or a Kamma symbol, or a symbol of destiny, a thought-process runs its course even if the death be an instantaneous one.

For the sake of convenience let us imagine that the dying person is to be reborn in the human kingdom and that the object is some good Kamma.

His *Bhavanga* consciousness is interrupted, vibrates for a thought-moment and passes away; after which the mind-door consciousness (*mano-*

---

1. For details with regard to these "premonitory visions of the place of rebirth" see Dr. W. T. Evans-Wents, *The Tibetan Book of the Dead*, p. 183.

dvāravajjana) arises and passes away. Then comes the psychologically important stage—Javana process—which here runs only for five thought-moments by reason of its weakness, instead of the normal seven. It lacks all reproductive power; its main function being the mere regulation of the new existence (*abhinavakaraṇa*). The object here being desirable, the consciousne::s he experiences is a moral one. The Tadālambana-consciousness which has for its function a registering or identifying for two moments of the object so perceived, may or may not follow. After this occurs the death-consciousness (*cuticitta*), the last thought-moment to be experienced in this present life.

There is a misconception amongst some that the subsequent birth is conditioned by this last death-consciousness (*cuticitta*) which in itself has no special function to perform. What actually conditions rebirth is that which is experienced during the Javana process.

With the cessation of the decease-consciousness death actually occurs. Then no material qualities born of mind and food (*cittaja* and *āhāraja*) are produced. Only a series of material qualities born of heat (*utuja*) goes on till the corpse is reduced to dust.[1]

---

1. According to Buddhism material qualities are produced in four ways.
   i.   *Kamma* i.e. past moral and immoral actions;
   ii. *Utu*, i.e. physical change or the *Tejo* (heat) element which includes both heat and cold;
   iii. *Citta*, i.e. mind and mental properties,
   iv. *Āhāra* i.e., nutriment that exists in food.

Simultaneous with the arising of the rebirth-consciousness there spring up the 'body-decad,' 'sex-decad,' and 'base-decad' (*Kāya-bhāva-vatthu-dasaka*).[1]

According to Buddhism, therefore, sex is determined at the moment of conception and is conditioned by Kamma not by any fortuitous combination of sperm and ovum-cells.[2]

The passing away of the consciousness of the past birth is the occasion for the arising of the new consciousness in the subsequent birth. However, nothing unchangeable or permanent is transmitted from the past to the present.

Just as the wheel rests on the ground only at one point, so, strictly speaking, we live only for one thought-moment. We are always in the present, and that present is ever slipping into the irrevocable past. Each momentary consciousness of this ever-changing life-process, on passing away, transmits its whole energy, all the indelibly recorded impressions on it, to its successor. Every fresh consciousness, therefore, consists of the potentialities of its predecessors together with something more. At death, the consciousness perishes, as in truth it perishes every moment, only to give birth to another in a rebirth. This renewed conscious-

---

1. See p. 424.
2. Compare "The sex of the individual is determined at conception by the chromosome make-up of the gametes. Through this, the embryo is endowed with a potentiality of developing towards one sex" Frank Alexander, *Psychosomatic Medicine* p. 219.

ness inherits all past experiences. As all impressions are indelibly recorded in the ever-changing palimpsest-like mind, and all potentialities are transmitted from life to life, irrespective of temporary disintegration, thus there may be reminiscence of past births or past incidents. Whereas if memory depended solely on brain cells, such reminiscence would be impossible.

"This new being which is the present manifestation of the stream of Kamma-energy is not the same as, and has no identity with, the previous one in its line—the aggregates that make up its composition being different from, having no identity with, those that make up the being of its predecessor. And yet it is not an entirely different being since it has the same stream of Kamma-energy, though modified perchance just by having shown itself in that manifestation, which is now making its presence known in the sense-perceptible world as the new being"[1]

Death, according to Buddhism, is the cessation of the psycho-physical life of any one individual existence. It is the passing away of vitality (*āyu*), i.e., psychic and physical life (*jīvitindriya*), heat (*usma*) and consciousness (*viññāṇa*).

Death is not the complete annihilation of a being, for though a particular life-span ends, the force which hitherto actuated it is not destroyed.

Just as an electric light is the outward visible manifestation of invisible electric energy, so we are the outward manifestations of invisible Kammic

---

1.   Bhikkhu Sīlācāra.

energy.   The bulb may break, and the light may be
extinguished, but the current remains and the light
may be reproduced in another bulb. In the same
way, the Kammic force remains undisturbed by
the disintegration of the physical body, and the
passing away of the present consciousness leads to
the arising of a fresh one in another birth. But
nothing unchangeable or permanent "*passes*" from
the present to the future.

In the foregoing case, the thought experienced
before death being a moral one, the resultant rebirth-consciousness takes for its material an
appropriate sperm and ovum cell of human parents.   The rebirth-consciousness (*paṭisandhi viññāṇa*) then lapses into the Bhavanga state.*

The continuity of the flux, at death, is unbroken
in point of time, and there is no breach in the
stream of consciousness.

Rebirth takes place immediately, irrespective
of the place of birth, just as an electro-magnetic
wave, projected into space, is immediately reproduced in a receiving radio set. Rebirth of the
mental flux is also instantaneous and leaves no
room whatever for any intermediate state[1] (*antara-
bhava*). Pure Buddhism does not support the

---

* See *A Manual of Abhidhamma* by Nārada Thera, p. 273.
1. According to Tibetan works, writes Dr. Evans-Wents,
   there is an intermediate state where beings remain for
   one, two, three, five, six or seven weeks, until the forty-
   ninth day. This view is contrary to the teachings of
   Buddhism.
   The Tibetan Book of the Dead, pp. XLII-XLIII, 58, 160-165

belief that a spirit of the deceased person takes lodgement in some temporary state until it finds a suitable place for its "reincarnation."

This question of instantaneous rebirth is well expressed in the Milinda Pañha:

The King Milinda questions:

"Venerable Nāgasena, if somebody dies here and is reborn in the world of Brahma, and another dies here and is reborn in Kashmir, which of them would arrive first?

"They would arrive at the same time, O King.

"In which town were you born, O King?

"In a village called Kalasi, Venerable Sir.

"How far is Kalasi from here, O King?

"About two hundred miles, Venerable Sir.

"And how far is Kashmir from here, O King?

"About twelve miles, Venerable Sir.

"Now think of the village of Kalasi, O King.

"I have done so, Venerable Sir.

"And now think of Kashmir, O King.

"It is done, Venerable Sir.

"Which of these two, O King, did you think the more slowly and which the more quickly?

"Both equally quickly, Venerable Sir.

"Just so, O King, he who dies here and is reborn in the world of Brahma, is not reborn later than he who dies here and is reborn in Kashmir."

'Give me one more simile, Venerable Sir."

"What do you think, O King? Suppose two birds were

flying in the air and they should settle at the same time, one upon a high and the other upon a low tree, which bird's shade would first fall upon the earth, and which bird's later?"

"Both shadows would appear at the same time, not one of them earlier and the other later."[1]

＊　　　　＊　　　　＊

The question might arise: Are the sperm and ovum cells always ready, waiting to take up the rebirth-thought?

According to Buddhism, living beings are infinite in number, and so are world systems. Nor is the impregnated ovum the only route to rebirth. Earth, an almost insignificant speck in the universe, is not the only habitable plane, and humans are not the only living beings.[2] As such it is not impossible to believe that there will always be an appropriate place to receive the last thought vibrations. A point is always ready to receive the falling stone.

---

1. Milinda's Questions, part 1, pp. 127-128.
2. "There are about 1,000,000 planetary systems in the Milky Way in which life may exist."
   See Fred Hoyle, *The Nature of the Universe*, pp. 87-89.

CHAPTER 29

WHAT IS IT THAT IS REBORN?
(No-Soul)

"Neither the same nor yet another.'

VISUDDHI MAGGA

Apart from mind and matter, which constitute this so-called being, Buddhism does not assert the existence of an immortal soul, or an eternal ego, which man has obtained in a mysterious way from an equally mysterious source.

A soul which is eternal must necessarily remain always the same without any change whatever. If the soul which is supposed to be the essence of man is eternal, there could be neither a rise nor a fall. Nor could one explain why "different souls are so variously constituted at the outset."

To justify the existence of endless felicity in an eternal heaven and unending torment in an eternal hell, it is absolutely necessary to postulate an immortal soul.

"It should be said," writes Bertrand Russell, "that the old distinction between soul and body has evaporated, quite as much because 'matter' has lost its solidity as because mind has lost its spirituality. Psychology is just beginning to be scientific. In the present state of psychology belief in immortality can at any rate claim no support from science."[1]

According to the learned author of the *Riddle of the Universe*:[2]

"This theological proof that a personal creator has breathed an immortal soul (generally regarded as a portion of the Divine Soul) into man is a pure myth. The cosmological proof that the 'moral order of the world' demands the eternal duration of the human soul is a baseless dogma. The teleological proof that the 'higher destiny' of man involves the perfecting of his defective, earthly soul beyond the grave —rests on a false anthropism. The moral proof—that the defects and the unsatisfied desires of earthly existence must be fulfilled by 'compensative justice' on the other side of eternity—is nothing more than a pious wish. The ethnological proof—that the belief in immortality, like the belief in God, is an innate truth, common to all humanity—is an error in fact. The ontological proof—that the soul, being a simple, immaterial, and indivisible entity cannot be involved in the corruption of death—is based on an entirely erroneous view of the psychic phenomena; it is a spiritualistic fallacy. All these and similar 'proofs of athanatism' are in a parlous condition; they are definitely annulled by the scientific criticism of the last few decades."

If nothing in the form of a spirit or soul passes from this life to the other, what is it that is reborn?

In this question it is taken for granted that there is some thing to be reborn.

---

1. *Religion and Science*, p. 132.
2. P. 166.

A few centuries ago it was argued-"*Cogito, ergo sum* (I think, therefore I am). True, but first it has to be proved that there is an "I" to think.

We say that the sun rises in the East and sets in the West, although we know that actually it is not so. We have to admit that one cannot strike an identical place twice although to all appearance one has done so.

Everything changes so soon. For no two moments are we identically the same.

Buddhists agree with Bertrand Russell when he says:

"There is obviously some reason in which I am the same person as I was yesterday, and, to take an even more obvious example, if I simultaneously see a man and hear him speaking, there is some sense in which the I that sees is the same as the I that hears."[1]

Until recently scientists believed in an indivisible and indestructible atom. "For sufficient reasons physicists have reduced this atom to a series of events; for equally good reasons psychologists find that mind has not the identity of a single continuing thing but is a series of occurrences bound together by certain intimate relations. The question of immortality, therefore, has become the question whether these intimate relations exist between occurrences connected with a living body and other occurrences which take place after that body is dead."[2]

As C.E.M. Joad says in *The Meaning of Life*:

1. *Religion and Science,* p. 132.
2. Ibid, p. 166.

"Matter has since disintegrated under our very eyes. It is no longer solid; it is no longer enduring; it is no longer determined by compulsive laws; and more important than all it is no longer known."

The so-called atoms, it seems, are both "divisible and destructible." The electrons and protons that compose atoms "can meet and annihilate one another, while their persistence, such as it is, is rather that of a wave lacking fixed boundaries, and in process of continual change both as regards shape and position, than that of a thing."

Bishop *Berkley*, who showed that this so-called atom was a metaphysical fiction, held that there existed a spiritual substance called a soul.

Hume in his search after a soul declares:

"There are some philosophers who imagine we are every moment intimately conscious of what we call our self: that we feel its existence and its continuance in existence and are certain, beyond the evidence of a demonstration, both of its perfect identity and simplicity. For my part, when I enter most intimately into what I call myself, I always stumble on some particular perception or other—of heat or cold, light or shade, love or hatred, pain or pleasure. I never can catch myself at any time without a perception. and never can observe anything but the perception..."[1]

Bergson says:

"All consciousness is time existence; and a conscious state is not a state that endures without changing. It is a

---

1. William James, *Principles of Psychology,* p. 351.

change without ceasing; when change ceases, it ceases; it is itself nothing but change."

Watson, a distinguished psychologist, states:

"No one has ever touched a soul, or has seen one in a test tube, or has in any way come into relationship with it as he has with the other objects of his daily experience. Nevertheless to doubt its existence is to become a heretic, and once might possibly even had led to the loss of one's head. Even today a man holding a public position dare not question it."[1]

Dealing with this question of soul, Prof. James writes:

"This soul-theory is a complete superfluity, so far as according for the actually verified facts of conscious experience goes. So far no one can be compelled to subscribe to it for definite scientific reasons.

"This me is an empirical aggregate of things objectively known. The I which knows them cannot itself be an aggregate, neither for psychological purpose need it be considered to be an unchanging metaphysical entity like the soul, or a principal like the pure Ego viewed as out of time. It is a thought, at each moment different from that of the last moment, but appropriative of the latter, together with all that the latter calls its own. All the experimental facts find their place in this description, unencumbered with any hypothesis save that of the existence of passing thoughts or states of mind."[2]

He concludes his interesting chapter on the soul with the words:

---

1. Watson, *Behaviourism*, p. 4.
2. *Principles of Psychology*, p. 215.

"And in this book the provisional solution which we have reached must be the final word":

"*The thoughts themselves are the thinkers.*"

And this is an echo of the very words of the Buddha from 2500 years ago in the valley of the Ganges.

Buddhism, teaching a psychology without a psyche, resolves the living being into mind and matter (*nāma-rūpa*) which are in a state of constant flux.

In the ancient days the Indian sages too believed in an indivisible atom which they called *Paramāṇu.* According to the ancient belief 36 *Paramāṇus* constitute one *Aṇu;* 36 *Aṇus,* one *Tajjāri;* 36 *Tajjāris,* one *Rathareṇu.* The minute particles of dust seen dancing in the sunbeam are called *Rathareṇus.* One *Paramāṇu* is, therefore, 1/46,656th part of a *Rathareṇu.* With His supernormal vision the Buddha analysed the *Paramāṇu* and declared that the *Paramāṇu* consists of interrelated forces known as *Paramatthas* or essentials of matter.

These *Paramatthas* are *Paṭhavi, Āpo, Tejo,* and *Vāyo.*

Paṭhavi. means the element of extension, the substratum of matter. Without it objects cannot occupy space. The qualities of hardness and softness which are relative are two conditions of this same element.

Āpo is the element of cohesion. Unlike *paṭhavi* it is intangible. It is this element which makes the scattered atoms of matter cohere and gives us the idea of body. When solid bodies are melted, this element becomes more prominent in the resulting fluid. This element is found even in minute particles when solid bodies are reduced to powder. The element of extension and cohesion are so closely interrelated that when cohesion ceases extension disappears.

Tejo is the element of heat. Cold is also a form of *tejo*. Both heat and cold are included in *tejo* because they possess the power of maturing bodies or, in other words, it is the vitalising energy. Preservation and decay are due to this element. Unlike the other three essentials of matter this element, also called *utu*, has the power to regenerate by itself.

Vāyo is the element of motion. Movements are caused by this element. Motion is regarded as the force or the generator of heat.

"Motion and heat in the material realm correspond respectively to consciousness and Kamma in the mental."

These four are the fundamental units of matter and are invariably combined with the four derivatives-namely, colour (*vaṇṇa*), odour (*gandha*) taste (*rasa*), and nutritive essence (*ojā*).

The four elements and the derivatives are inseparable and interrelated, but one element may preponderate over another, as for instance, the element of extension preponderates in earth; cohesion, in water; heat, in fire; and motion, in air.

Thus, matter consists of forces and qualities which are in a state of constant flux. According to Buddhism matter endures only for 17 thought-moments.[1]

Mind, the more important part in the complex machinery of man, consists of fifty-two mental states. Feeling or sensation (*vedanā*) is one, perception (*saññā*) is another. The remaining fifty are collectively called volitional activities (*saṁkhāra*), a rendering which does not exactly convey the meaning of the Pāli term. Of them volition or *cetanā* is the most important factor. All these psychic states arise in a consciousness (*Viññāṇa*).

According to Buddhist philosophy there is no moment when one does not experience a particular kind of consciousness, hanging on to some object—whether physical or mental. The time limit of such a consciousness is termed one thought-moment. Each thought-moment is followed by another. Thus the succession of mental states contains a time element. The rapidity of the succession of such thought-moments is hardly conceivable.

1. It pleases the commentators to say that the time duration of one thought-moment is even less than the one-millionth part of the time occupied by a flash of lightning.

Each unit of consciousness consists of three instants (*khaṇa*). They are arising or genesis (*uppāda*), static or development (*ṭhiti*) and cessation or dissolution (*bhaṅga*).

Immediately after the cessation stage of a thought-moment there occurs the genesis stage of the subsequent thought-moment. Each momentary consciousness of this ever-changing life process, on passing away, transmits its whole energy, all the indelibly recorded impressions, to its successor. Every fresh consciousness consists of the potentialities of its predecessors together with something more. There is therefore a continuous flow of consciousness like a stream without any interruption. The subsequent thought-moment is neither absolutely the same as its predecessor— since its composition is not identical—nor entirely different—being the same stream of life. There is no identical being, but there is an identity in process.

It must not be understood that consciousness is in bits joined together like a train or a chain. On the contrary, "it constantly flows on like a river receiving from the tributary streams of sense constant accretions to its flood, and ever dispensing to the world around it the thought-stuff it has gathered by the way."[1] It has birth for its source and death for its mouth.

Here occurs a juxtaposition of fleeting states of consciousness but not a superposition of such states, as some appear to believe. No state once

----
1. See *Compendium of Philosophy-Introduction*, p. 12.

gone ever recurs—none absolutely identical with what goes before. These states constantly change, not remaining the same for two consecutive moments. Worldlings, enmeshed in the web of illusion, mistake this apparent continuity to be something eternal and go to the extent of introducing an unchanging soul (the supposed doer and observer of all actions) into this ever-changing consciousness.

The four kinds of psychic phenomena, combined with the physical phenomena, form the five aggregates (*pañcakkhanda*), the complex-compound termed a living being.

Ones individuality is the combination of these five aggregates.

We see a vast expanse of water in the sea, but the water of the ocean consists of countless drops. An infinite number of particles of sand constitute the sea-beach, but it appears as one long sheet. Waves arise and dash against the shore, but, strictly speaking, no single wave comes from the deep blue sea to lose its identity on the shore. In the cinematograph we see a moving scene, but to represent that motion a series of momentary pictures must appear on the screen.

One cannot say that the perfume of a flower depends on the petal or on the pistil or on the colour, for the perfume is in the flower.

In the same way one's individuality is the combination of all the five aggregates.

The whole process of these psycho—physical phenomena which are constantly becoming and passing away, is at times called, in conventional terms, the self or *attā* by the Buddha; but it is a process, and not an identity that is thus termed.

Buddhism does not totally deny the existence of a personality in an empirical sense. It denies, in an ultimate sense (*paramattha saccena*), an identical being or a permanent entity, but it does not deny a continuity in process. The Buddhist philosophical term for an individual is *santati*, that is, a flux or continuity. This uninterrupted flux or continuity of psycho-physical phenomena, conditioned by Kamma, having no perceptible source in the beginningless past nor any end to its continuation in the future, except by the Noble Eightfold Path, is the Buddhist substitute for the permanent ego or eternal soul in other religious systems.

         *   *   *

How is rebirth possible without a soul to be reborn?

Birth, according to Buddhism, is the arising of the *khandas*, the aggregates or groups (*khandhānam pātubhāvo*).

Just as the arising of a physical state is conditioned by a preceding state as its cause, so the appearance of these psycho-physical phenomena is conditioned by causes anterior to its birth. The present process of becoming is the result of the craving for becoming in the previous birth, and the present instinctive craving conditions life in a future birth.

As the process of one life-span is possible without a permanent entity passing from one thought-moment to another, so a series of life-processes is possible without anything to transmigrate from one existence to another.

The Buddhist doctrine of rebirth should be differentiated from the theory of reincarnation which implies the transmigration of a soul and its invariable material rebirth.

In the *Milinda Pañha* and *Visuddhi Magga* the Venerable Nāgasena and Buddhaghosa have employed several similes to illustrate the truth that nothing transmigrates from one life to another.

The simile of the flame is very striking. Life is compared to a flame. Rebirth is the transmitting of this flame from one group to another. The flame of life is continuous although there is an apparent break at so-called death.

King Milinda questions;

"Venerable Nāgasena does rebirth take place without anything transmigrating.

'Yes, O King, rebirth takes place without anything transmigrating?

"Give me an illustration, Venerable Sir.

"Suppose, O King, a man were to light a light from light pray, would the one light have passed over to the other light?"

"Nay, indeed, Venerable Sir,

"In exactly the same way, O King, does rebirth take place without anything transmigrating.

"Give me another illustration.

"Do you remember, O King, having learnt, when you were a boy, some verse or other from your teacher of poetry?

"Yes, Venerable Sir.

"Pray, O King, did the verse pass over to you from your teacher?

"Nay, indeed, Venerable Sir.

"In exactly the same way, O King, does rebirth take place without anything transmigrating."

          *   *   *

Again King Milinda questions:

"Venerable Nāgasena, what is it that is born into the next existence?

"O King, it is mind and body that is born into the next existence?

"It is this same mind and body that is born into the next existence.

"O King, it is not this same mind and body that is born into the next existence, but with this mind and body, O King, one does a deed—it may be good, or it may be evil—and by reason of this deed another mind and body is born into the next existence.

"Venerable Sir, if it is not this mind and body that is born into the next existence, is one not freed from one's evil deeds?

"If one were not born into another existence, one would be freed from one's evil deeds: but, O King, inasmuch as one is born into another existence, therefore is one not freed from one's evil deeds.

"Give me an illustration.

"O King, it is as if a man were to take away another man's mangoes, and the owner of the mangoes were to seize him, and show him to the king and say—'Sire, this man hath taken away my mangoes'; and the other were to say, 'Sire, I did not take away his mangoes. The mangoes which this man planted were different from those which I took away. I am not liable to punishment.' Pray, O King, would the man be liable to punishment?

"Assuredly, Venerable, Sir, he would be liable to punishment.

"For what reason?

"Because, in spite of what he might say, he would be liable to punishment for the reason that the last mangoes were derived from the first mangoes.

"In exactly, the same way, O King, with this mind and body one does a deed—it may be good, or it may be bad —and by reason of this deed another mind and body is born into the next existence. Therefore is one not freed from one's evil deeds."[1]

The Venerable *Buddhaghosa* elucidates this intricate point by citing the similes of echo, light, impression of a seal, and reflection in a mirror.

A modern writer illustrates this process by a series of billiard balls in close contact.

"If, for instance, another ball is rolled against the last stationary ball, the moving ball will stop dead, and the foremost stationary ball will move on. The first moving ball does not pass over, it remains behind, it dies; but it is undeniably the movement of that ball, its momentum, its Kamma, and not any newly created movement, which is reborn in the foremost ball."[2]

---

1. See Warren—*Buddhism in Translations,* pp. 234, 235.
2. Dr. Ananda Coomarasvami—*Buddha and the Gospel of Buddhism,* p. 106.

In like manner—to use conventional terms-
the body dies and its Kammic force is reborn in
another without anything transmigrating from
this life to the other.   The last thought-moment
of this life perishes conditioning another thought-
moment in a subsequent life.   The new being is
neither absolutely the same-since it has changed-
nor totally different-being the same stream of
Kamma energy.   There is merely a continuity of
a particular life-flux; just that and nothing more.

CHAPTER 30

MORAL RESPONSIBILITY

"By self is one defiled,
By self is one purified."

DHAMMAPADA

Is it the doer of the act or another who reaps its results in the succeeding birth? [1]

To say that he who sows is absolutely the same as he who reaps is one extreme, and to say that he who sows is totally different from he who reaps is the other extreme. Avoiding these two extremes, the Buddha teaches the doctrine of the middle way in terms of cause and effect. "Neither the same nor another" (*na ca so na ca añño*), writes the Venerable Buddhaghosa in the Visuddhi Magga. The evolution of the butterfly may be cited in illustration.

Its initial stage was an egg. Then it turned into a caterpillar. Later it developed into a chrysalis, and eventually into a butterfly. This process occurs in the course of one lifetime. The butterfly is neither the same as, nor totally different from, the caterpillar. Here also there is a flux of life, or a continuity.

Venerable Nāgasena explains this point by citing the illustration of a lamp that burns through-

---

1. See *The Questions of Milinda,* part I. p. 111 and Dr. Dahlke, *Buddhism and Science,* p. 64.

out the night. The flame of the first watch is
not identical with that of the last watch, yet
throughout the night the light burns in dependence upon one and the same lamp. As with the
flame so there is a continuity of life—each succeeding stage depending upon the preceding one.

*If there be no soul, can there be any moral res-
ponsibility?*

Yes, because there is a continuity or identity
in process, which is substituted for an identical
personality.

A child, for instance, becomes a man. The
latter is neither absolutely the same as the former-
since the cells have undergone a complete change-
nor totally different—being the identical stream
of life. Nevertheless, the individual, as man,
is responsible for whatever he has done in his
childhood. Whether the flux dies here and is
reborn elsewhere, or continues to exist in the
same life, the essential factor is this continuity.
Suppose a person was 'A' in his last birth, and
is 'B' in this. With the death of 'A' the physical
vehicle, the outward manifestation of Kammic
energy is relinquished and, with the birth of 'B'
a fresh physical vehicle arises. Despite the ap-,
parent material changes, the invisible stream of
consciousness (*cittasantati*) continues to flow,
uninterrupted by death, carrying along with it

---

1. See "*Anatta and Moral Responsibility*" by Mr. A. D.
Jayasundara, Mahabodhi Journal, vol. 41, p. 93.

all the impressions received from the tributary streams of sense. Conventionally speaking, must not 'B' be responsible for the actions of 'A' who was his predecessor?

Some may object that in this case there is no memory owing to the intervening death.

But is identity or memory absolutely essential in assessing moral responsibility?

Strictly speaking, neither is essential.

If, for instance, a person were to commit a crime and suddenly, losing his memory, were to forget the incident, would he not be responsible for his act?

His forgetfulness would not exempt him from responsibility for the commission of that crime. To this, some may ask: "What is the use of punishing him, for he is not aware that he is being punished for that crime? Is there any justice here?"

Of course, there is not, if we are arbitrarily governed by a God who rewards and punishes us.

Buddhists believe in a just and rational law of Kamma that operates automatically and speak in terms of cause and effect instead of rewards and punishments.

In the words of Bhikkhu Silācāra: "If a person does something in sleep, gets out of bed and walks over the edge of a verandah, he will fall into the road below and in all likelihood break an arm or leg. But this will happen not at all as a punishment for sleep-walking, but merely as its result. And the fact that he did not remember going out on the verandah would not make the slightest difference to the result of his fall from it, in the shape of broken bones. So the follower of the Buddha takes measures to see that he does not walk over verandahs or other dangerous places, asleep or awake, so as to avoid hurting himself or anyone who might be below and on whom he might fall."

The fact that a person does not remember his past is no hindrance to the intelligent understanding of the working of Kammic law. It is the knowledge of the inevitability of the sequence of Kamma in the course of one's life in Saṁsāra that helps to mould the character of a Buddhist.

CHAPTER 31

KAMMIC DESCENT AND KAMMIC ASCENT

"Kamma differentiates beings into high and low states."
                                                      MAJJHIMA NIKĀYA

Is Kammic descent possible? In other words, can a man be born as an animal?

The Buddhist answer may not be acceptable to all, for Buddhism does recognize this possibility.

Material forms, through which the life-continuum expresses itself, are merely temporary visible manifestations of the Kammic energy. The present physical body is not directly evolved from the past physical form, but is the successor of this past form—being linked with it through the same stream of Kammic energy.

Just as an electric current can be manifested in the forms of light, heat and motion successively-one not necessarily being evolved from the other-so this Kammic energy may manifest itself in the form of a Deva, man, animal, or other being,—one form having no physical connection with the other. It is one's Kamma that determines the nature of one's material form, which varies according to the skilfulness or unskilfulness of one's past actions, and this again depends entirely on the evolution of one's understanding of reality.

Instead of saying that man becomes an animal, or *vice versa*, it would be more correct to say that the Kammic force which manifested itself in the form of man may manifest itself in the form of an animal.

In the course of our wanderings in Saṁsāra-to speak in conventional terms—we gather various experiences, receive manifold impressions, acquire diverse characteristics. Our very thought, word, or deed is indelibly recorded in the palimpsest-like mind. The different natures we thus acquire in the course of such successive births whether as men, Devas, animals or Petas, lie dormant within us, and as long as we are worldlings these undestroyed natures may, at unexpected moments, rise to the surface "in disconcerting strength" and reveal our latent Kammic tendencies.

It is quite natural for us to remark after witnessing an unexpected outburst of passion in a highly cultured person: "How could he have done such a thing? Who would have thought that he would commit such an act!"

There is nothing strange in this misdemeanour of his. It is just a revelation of a hidden part of his intricate self. This is the reason why men normally of lofty motives are sometimes tempted to do things which one would least expect of them.

Devadatta, for example, a noble prince by birth, a leading member of the Holy Order, was possessed of supernormal powers. Overcome by jealousy, latent in him, he made several attempts to kill his own master the Buddha.

Such is the intricate nature of man. One's immediate past is not always a true index to one's immediate future. Every moment we create fresh Kamma. In one sense we are truly what we were, and we will be what we are. In another sense we are not absolutely what we were, and we will not be what we are. Who was yesterday a criminal may today become a saint, who today is holy may tomorrow turn out to be a wretched sinner.

We can safely and rightly be judged by this eternal present. Today we sow the seeds of the future. At this very moment we may act the part of a brute and create our own hell, or, on the other hand, act the part of a superman and create our own heaven. Each present thought-moment conditions the next thought-moment. The subsequent birth also, according to Buddhist philosophy, is determined by the last thought-process we experience in this life. Just as through the course of one's life each thought perishes, giving up all its potentialities to its successor, even so the last thought-process of this life ends, transmitting all its acquired characteristics and natures to the succeeding moment-namely, the first thought-moment (*paṭisandhi viññāṇa*) in the subsequent birth.

Now, if the dying person cherishes a base desire or idea, or experiences a thought, or does an act which befits an animal, his evil Kamma will condition him to birth in animal form. The Kammic force which manifested itself in the form of a man will manifest itself in the form of

an animal. This does not imply that thereby all
his past good Kammic tendencies are lost. They
too lie dormant seeking an opportunity to rise
to the surface. It is such a good Kamma that
will later effect birth as a human being.

The last thought-process does not, as a rule,
depend on the sum-total of our actions in our
lifetime. Generally speaking, a good person gets a
good birth, and a bad person, a bad one. Under
exceptional circumstances, however, the unexpected may happen.

Queen *Mallik*ā,[1] for example, led a good life,
but as the result of experiencing an evil thought
at her dying moment, she was born in a state of
woe. As her good Kamma was powerful the
expiation lasted only for a few days.

"Is this justifiable?" one might ask.

If a holy person, due to some provocation,
were to commit a murder, he would be charged
as a murderer. His past good actions would no
doubt stand to his credit and have their due effect,
but the brutal act could not be obliterated by his
past good. Perhaps his past good record would
tend to mitigate the sentence, but never could it
acquit him altogether of his heinous crime. This
unexpected event would compel him to live in an

---

1.   Wife of King Kosala who lived in the time of the Buddha.

uncongenial atmosphere amongst similar criminals. Is this fair? Imagine how one single immoral act may degrade a noble man!

On one occasion two ascetics *Punna* and *Seniya* who were practising ox-asceticism and dog-asceticism came to the Buddha and questioned Him as to their future destiny:

The Buddha replied:

"In this world a certain person cultivates thoroughly and constantly the practices, habits, mentality, and manners of a dog. He, having cultivated the canine practices, habits, mentality, and manners thoroughly and constantly, upon the breaking up of the body, after death, will be reborn, amongst dogs. Certainly if he holds such a belief as this—'By virtue of this practice, austerity or noble life, I shall become a god or a deity of some kind'—that is a false belief of his. For one who holds a false belief I declare that there is one of two future states—the state of torment or the animal kingdom. Thus, failing a state of torment, successful canine asceticism only delivers one to companionship with dogs."[1]

In the same way the Buddha declared that he who observes ox-asceticism will, after death, be born amongst oxen.

So there is the possibility for a Kammic descent in one bound in the so-called evolutionary scale of beings.

But the contrary, a Kammic ascent, is also possible.

---

1. Majjhima Nikāya, Sutta No. 57.

When, for instance, an animal is about to die, it may experience a moral consciousness that will ripen into a human birth. This last thought-process does not depend wholly on any action or thought of the animal, for generally speaking, its mind is dull and it is incapable of doing any moral action. This depends on some past good deed done during a former round of its existence which has long been prevented from producing its inevitable results. In its last moment the animal therefore may conceive ideas or images which will cause a human birth.

Poussin, a French writer, illustrates this fact by the law of heredity: "A man may be like his grandfather but not like his father. The germs of disease have been introduced into the organism of an ancestor, for some generations they remain dormant. But suddenly they manifest themselves in actual diseases."

So intricate is the nature of this doctrine of Kamma and Rebirth!

                *   *   *

Whence we came, whither we go, and when we go, we know not. The fact that we must go we know for certain.

Our cherished possessions, our kith and kin follow us not—nay, not even our bodies which we call our own. From elements they came, to elements they return. Empty fame and vain glory vanish in thin air.

Alone we wander in this tempest-tossed sea of Saṁsāra wafted hither and thither by our own Kamma, appearing here as an animal or man and there perchance as a god or Brahma.

We meet and part and yet we may meet again incognito. For seldom do we find a being who, in the course of our wandering, had not at one time been a mother, a father, a sister, a son, a daughter.

"If a man," says the Buddha, "were to prune out the grasses, sticks, boughs, and twigs in this India and collecting them together, should make a pile laying them in a four inch stack, saying for each: "This is my mother, this is my mother's mother,'—the grasses, sticks, boughs, twigs in this India would be used up, ended but not the mothers of that man's mother.

So closely bound are we during our journeyings in Saṁsāra.

The countless lives we have led and the innumerable sufferings we were subject to in the infinite past are such that the Buddha remarks:

"The bones of a single person wandering in Samsāra would be a cairn, a pile, a heap as Mount Vepulla, were there a collector of these bones and were the collections not destroyed.

"Long time have you suffered the death of father and mother, of sons, daughters, brothers and sisters, and while you were thus suffering, you have verily shed tears upon this long way, more than there is water in the four oceans.

"Long time did your blood flow by the loss of your heads when you were born as oxen, buffaloes, rams, goats, etc.

"Long time have you been caught as dacoits or highway-men or adulterers, and through your being beheaded, verily more blood has flowed upon this long way than there is water in the four oceans.

"And thus have you for long time undergone sufferings, undergone torment, undergone misfortune, and filled the graveyards full, verily long enough to be dissatisfied with every form of existence, long enough to turn away and free yourself from them all."[1]

---

1. See *The Book of The Gradual Sayings* I pp. 31-34.

CHAPTER 32

A NOTE ON THE DOCTRINE
OF KAMMA AND REBIRTH IN THE WEST

The Doctrine of Kamma and rebirth is the key-stone of the philosophy of Plato. Beings are for ever travelling through "a cycle of necessity"; the evil they do in one semicircle of their pilgrimage is expiated in the other. In the Republic, we find Kamma personified as "Lachesis, the daughter of necessity," at whose hands disembodied beings choose their incarnations. Orpheus chooses the body of a swan. Thersites that of an ape, Agamemmon that of an eagle. "In like manner, some of the animals passed into men, and into one another, the unjust passing into the wild, and the just into the tame."

In the period preceding the Persian Wars, the contact of the West with the East caused a revolt against the simple eschatology of Homer, and the search began for a deeper explanation of life. This quest, it is interesting to note, was begun by the Ionian Greeks of Asia Minor, who were influenced by India.

Pythagoras,[1] who was born about 580 B.C. on

---

1. Pythagoras remembered having fought, as Euphorbus in the Trojan War. Empedocles had been in past births a boy, a girl, a bird and a scaly fish in the ocean. (Frag. 117, Diels.)

the Island of Samos, travelled widely and, according to his biographer, studied the teaching of the Indians. It was he who taught the West the Doctrine of Kamma and Rebirth.

"It is not too much," says Garbe in his *Greek Thinkers*,[1] "to assume that the curious Greek, who was a contemporary of the Buddha, would have acquired a more or less exact knowledge of the East, in that age of intellectual fermentation, through the medium of Persia."

REBIRTH AS VIEWED BY OTHERS

Bhagavad Gītā:—
"As a man, casting off worn-out garments, taketh the new ones, so the dweller in the body, casting off worn-out bodies, entereth into others that are new."
"For certain is death for the born, and certain is birth for the dead."

Herodotus:—
"The Egyptians propounded the theory that the human soul is imperishable, and that where the body of anyone dies it enters into some other creature that may be ready to receive it."

Pythagoras:
"All have souls, all is soul, wandering in the organic world and obeying eternal will or law."

Plato:—
"Soul is older than body. Souls are continually born over again into this life."

Ovid on Pythagoras: translated by Dryden—

---

1. i. 127.

"Death so called, is but old matter dressed
In some new form: and in varied vest
From tenement to tenement though tossed,
The soul is still the same, the figure only lost.
And as the softened wax new seals receives,
This face assumes, and that impression leaves,
Now called by one, now by another name,
The form is only changed, the wax is still the
*   same,*

Then, to be born is to begin to be
Some other thing we were not formerly.
That forms are changed I grant;
That nothing can continue in the figure it began"

Schopenhauer:—

"We find the doctrine of Metempsychosis, springing from the earliest and noblest ages of the human race, always spread abroad in the earth as the belief of the great majority of mankind, nay really as the teaching of all religions, with the exception of the Jews and the two which have proceeded from it in the most subtle form however, and coming nearest to the truth as has already been mentioned in Buddhism. Accordingly while Christians console themselves with the thought of meeting in another world in which one regains one's complete personality and knows oneself at once, in these other religions the meeting again is already going on— only incognito. In the succession of births those who now stand in close connection or contact with us will also be born along with us at our next birth, and will have the same or analogous relations and sentiments towards us as now, whether these are of a friendly or hostile description.

"Taught already in the Vedas, as in all sacred books of India, metempsychosis is well known to be the kernel of Brahmanism and Buddhism. It accordingly prevails at the present day in the whole of the non-Mohammedan Asia, thus among more than half of the whole human race, as the firmest conviction and with an incredibly strong practical influence. It was also the belief of the Egyptians from whom it was received with enthusiasm by Orpheus, Pythagoras and Plato: the Pythagoreans, however, specially retain it. That it was also taught in the mysteries of the Greeks undeniably follows the ninth book of Plato's Laws."

"The Edda also especially in the 'Volusna' teaches metempsychosis; not less was it the foundation of the Druids".

"According to all this, the belief in metempsychosis presents itself as the natural conviction of man, whenever he reflects at all in an unprejudiced manner......"

THE WORLD AS WILL AND IDEA

Hume:—

"Metempsychosis is the only system of immortality that philosophy can hearken to."

Disraeli:—

"There is no system so simple, and so little repugnant to our understanding as that of metempsychosis. The pains and pleasures of this life are by this system considered as the recompense or the punishment of our actions in another state."

Dante:—

"And then son, who through thy mortal weight shall again return below."

Emerson:—

"We must infer our destiny from the preparation we are driven by instinct to have innumerable experiences which are of no visible value, and which we may receive through many lives before we shall assimilate or exhaust them."

Lessing:—

"Why should I not come back as often as I am capable of acquiring fresh knowledge, fresh experience? Do I bring away so much from one that there is nothing to repay the trouble of coming back?"

Huxley:—

"Like the doctrine of evolution itself, that of transmigration has its roots in the realm of reality.

"Everyday experience familiarises us with the facts which are grouped under the name of heredity. Everyone of us bears upon him obvious marks of his parentage perhaps of remoter relationships. More particularly the sum of tendencies to act in a certain way, which we call character, is often to be traced through a long series of progenitors and collaterals. So we may justly say that this character, this moral and intellectual essence of a man does veritably pass over from one fleshly tabernacle to another, and does really transmigrate from generation to generation. In the new-born infant the character of the stock lies latent, and the ego is little more than a bundle of potentialities, but, very early these become actualities: from childhood to age they manifest themselves in dullness or brightness, weakness or strength, viciousness or uprightness; and with each feature modified by confluence with another character, if by nothing else, the character passes on to its incarnation in new bodies.

"The Indian philosophers called character, as thus defined, 'Karma'. It is this Karma which passed from life
to life and linked them in the chain of transmigrations;
and they held that it is modified in each life, not merely by
confluence of parentage but by its own acts."

Tennyson:—

> *"Or if through lower lives I came*
> *Tho' all experience past became,*
> *Consolidate in mind and frame,*
> *I might forget my weaker lot;*
> *For is not our first year forgot*
> *The haunts of memory echo not."*

Wordsworth :—

> *"Our birth is but a sleep and a forgetting*
> *The soul that rises with us, our life's star*
> *Hath had elsewhere its setting,*
> *And cometh from after :*
> *Not in entire forgetfulness,*
> *And not in utter nakedness."*

Shelley :—

"If there be no reasons to suppose that we have existed
before that period at which existence apparently commences,
then there are no grounds for supposing that we shall continue to exist after our existence has apparently ceased."

Professor Francis Bowen of Harvard University in urging Christians to accept rebirth writes :

"Our life on earth is rightly held to be a discipline and
a preparation for a higher and eternal life hereafter, but
if limited to the duration of a single mortal body, it is so

brief as to seem hardly sufficient for so grand a purpose. Three score years and ten must surely be an inadequate preparation for eternity. But what assurance have we that the probation of the soul is confined within such narrow limits? Why may it not be continued or repeated through a long series of successive generations, the same personality animating one after another an indefinite number of tenements of flesh and carrying forward into each the training it has received, the character it has formed, the temper and dispositions it has indulged, in the steps of existence immediately preceding. It need not remember its past history even whilst bearing the fruits and the consequence of that history deeply ingrained into its present nature. How many long passages of any one life are now completely lost to memory, though they may have contributed largely to build up the heart and the intellect which distinguish one man from another? Our responsibility surely is not lessened by such forgetfulness. We still seem accountable for the misuse of time, though we have forgotten how or on what we have wasted it. We are even now reaping the bitter fruits, through enfeebled health and vitiated desires and capacities, of many forgotten acts of self-indulgence, wilfulness and sin—forgotten just because they were so numerous.

"If every birth were an act of absolute creation, the introduction to life of an entirely new creature, we might reasonably ask why different souls are so variously constituted at the outset? If metempsychosis is included in the scheme of the divine government of the world, this difficulty disappears altogether. Considered from this point of view, every one is born into the state which he had fairly earned by his own previous history. The doctrine of inherited sin and its consequence is a hard lesson to be learned. But no one can complain of the dispositions and endowments which he has inherited so to speak from himself, that is from his former self in a previous state of existence. What we call death is only the introduction of another life on earth, and if this be not a higher and better life than the one just ended, it is our own fault."

PRE-EXISTENCE

"*I laid me down upon the shore*
And dreamed a little space;
I heard the great waves break and roar;
The sun was on my face.

"*My idle hands and fingers brown*
Played with the pebbles grey;
The waves came up, the waves went down;
Most thundering and gay.

"*The pebbles they were smooth and round*
And warm upon my hands;
Like little people I had found
Sitting among the sands.

"*The grains of sand so shining small.*
Soft through my fingers ran;
The sun shown down upon it all.
And so my dream began;

How all of this had been before,
How ages far away.
I lay on some forgotten shore
As here I lie today.

"*The waves came up shinning up the sands,*
As here today they shine;
And in my pre-Pelasgian hands
The sand was warm and fine.

" *I have forgotten whence I came*
Or what my home might be,
Or by what strange and savage name
I called that thundering sea.

" *I only know the sun shone down*
As still it shines today.
And in my fingers long and brown
The little pebbles lay."[1]

1. Frances Cornford-
   An Anthology of Modern Verse,
   Chosen by A. Methuen, London.
   Methuen and Co., and reproduced in
   "The Buddhist Annual of Ceylon." 1927.

CHAPTER 33

NIBBĀNA

"Nibbāna is bliss supreme."
DHAMMAPADA

Nibbāna is the *summum bonum* of Buddhism.

However clearly and descriptively one may write on this profound subject, however glowing may be the terms in which one attempts to describe its utter serenity, comprehension of Nibbana is impossible by mere perusal of books. Nibbāna is not something to be set down in print, nor is it a subject to be grasped by intellect alone; it is a supramundane state (*Lokuttara Dhamma*) to be realized only by intuitive wisdom.

A purely intellectual comprehension of Nibbāna is impossible because it is not a matter to be arrived at by logical reasoning (*atakkāvacara*). The words of the Buddha are perfectly logical, but Nibbāna, the ultimate Goal of Buddhism, is beyond the scope of logic. Nevertheless, by reflecting on the positive and negative aspects of life, the logical conclusion emerges that in contradistinction to a conditioned phenomenal existence, there must exist a sorrowless, deathless, non-conditioned State.

The Jātaka Commentary relates that the Bodhisatta himself in his birth as the ascetic Sumedha contemplated thus:

"Even as, although Misery is,
Yet Happiness is also found,
So, though indeed Existence is,
Non-existence should be sought.

"Even as, although there may be Heat,
Yet grateful Cold is also found,
So, though the threefold Fire exists,
Likewise Nirvāna should be sought.

"Even as, although there Evil is,
That which is Good is also found,
So, though 'tis true that birth exists.
That which is not birth should be sought."[1]

Definition

The Pāli word *Nibbāna* (Saṁskrit—Nirvāna) is composed of *'Ni* and *'Vāna'*. *Ni* is a negative particle. *Vāna* means weaving or craving. This craving serves as a cord to connect one life with another.

"It is called Nibbāna in that it is a departure (*Ni*) from that craving which is called *Vāna*, lusting."[2]

As long as one is bound up by craving or attachment one accumulates fresh Kammic activities which must materialise in one form or other in the eternal cycle of birth and death. When all forms of craving are eradicated, reproductive

---

1. Warren, *Buddhism in Translations,* p. 6.
2. Abhidhammattha Sangaha. See Compendium of Philosophy, p. 168.

Kammic forces cease to operate, and one attains Nibbāna, escaping the cycle of birth and death. The Buddhist conception of Deliverance is escape from the ever-recurring cycle of life and death and not merely an escape from sin and hell.

Nibbāna is also explained as the extinction of the fire of lust (*lobha*), hatred (*dosa*), and delusion (*moha*).

"The whole world is in flames," says the Buddha. "By what fire is it kindled? By the fire of lust, hatred and delusion; by the fire of birth, old age, death, sorrow, lamentation, pain, grief and despair is it kindled."

Nibbāna, in one sense, may be interpreted as the extinction of these flames. One must not thereby infer that Nibbāna is nothing but the extinction of these flames.[1] The *means* should be differentiated from the *end*. Here the extinction of the flames is the means of attaining Nibbāna.

Is Nibbāna nothingness :

To say that Nibbāna is nothingness simply because one cannot perceive it with the five senses, is as illogical as to conclude that light does not exist simply because the blind do not see it. In a well-known fable the fish, who was acquainted only with water, arguing with the turtle, triumphantly concluded that there existed no land, because he received "No" to all his queries.

---

1. *Khayamattam' eva na nibbānam ti vattabbam*—Abhidhamāvatāra.

"Once upon a time there was a fish. And just because it was a fish, it had lived all its life in the water and knew nothing whatever about anything else but water. And one day as it swam about in the pond where all its days had been spent, it happened to meet a turtle of its acquaintance who had just come back from a little excursion on the land."

"Good day, Mr. Turtle!" said the fish. "I have not seen you for a long time. Where have you been?"

"Oh", said the turtle, "I have just been for a trip on dry land."

"On dry land!" exclaimed the fish. "What do you mean by on dry land? There is no dry land. I had never seen such a thing. Dry land is nothing."

"Well," said the turtle good-naturedly. "If you want to think so, of course you may; there is no one who can hinder you. But that's where I've been, all the same."

"Oh, come," said the fish. "Try to talk sense. Just tell me now what is this land of yours like? Is it all wet?"

"No, it is not wet," said the turtle.

"Is it nice and fresh and cool?" asked the fish.

"No, it is not nice and fresh and cool," the turtle replied.

"Is it clear so that light can come through it?"

"No, it is not clear. Light cannot come through it."

"Is it soft and yielding, so that I could move my fins about in it and push my nose through it?"

"No, it is not soft and yielding, You could not swim in it."

"Does it move or flow in streams?"

"No, it neither moves nor flows in streams?"

"Does it ever rise up into waves then, with white foams in them?" asked the fish, impatient at this string of Noes.

"No!" replied the turtle, truthfully, "It never rises up into waves that I have seen."

"There now," exclaimed the fish triumphantly. "Didn't
I tell you that this land of yours was just nothing? I have
just asked, and you have answered me that it is neither
wet nor cool, not clear nor soft and that it does not flow
in streams nor rise up into waves, And if it isn't a single one
of these things what else is it but nothing? Don't tell me."

"Well, well", said the turtle, "If you are determined to
think that dry land is nothing, I suppose you must just go
on thinking so. But any one who knows what is water
and what is land would say you were just a silly fish, for
you think that anything you have never known is nothing
just because you have never known it."

"And with that the turtle turned away and, leaving the
fish behind in its little pond of water, set out on another
excursion over the dry land that was nothing."[1]

It is evident from this significant story that
neither can the turtle, who is acquainted with both
land and sea, explain to the fish the real nature of
land, nor can the fish grasp what is land since it
is acquainted only with water. In the same way
Arahants who are acquainted with both the mundane and the supramundane cannot explain to a
worldling what exactly the supramundane is in
mundane terms, nor can a worldling understand
the supramundane merely by mundane knowledge.

If Nibbāna is nothingness, then it necessarily
must coincide with space (Ākāsa). Both space
and Nibbāna are eternal and unchanging. The
former

1. Quoted from Bhikkhu Silācāra's booklet, *The Four
Noble Truths.*

is eternal because it is nothing in itself. The latter is spaceless and timeless. With regard to the difference between space and Nibbāna, it may briefly be said that space *is not*, but Nibbāna *is*.

The Buddha, speaking of the different planes of existence, makes special reference to a 'Realm of Nothingness' (*Ākiñcaññāyatana*).

The fact that Nibbāna is realized as one of the mental objects (*vatthudhamma*), decidedly proves that it is not a state of nothingness. If it were so, the Buddha would not have described its state in such terms as "Infinite" (*Ananta*), "Non-condi-tioned" (*Asaṁkhata*), "Incomparable" (*Anūpa-meya*), "Supreme" (*Anuttara*), "Highest" (*Para*), "Beyond" (*Pāra*), "Highest Refuge" (*Parāyana*), "Safety" (*Tāṇa*), "Security" (*Khema*), "Happi-ness" (*Siva*), "Unique" (*Kevala*), "Abodeless, (*Anālaya*), "Imperishable" (*Akkhara*), "Absolute Purity" (*Visuddha*), "Supramundane" (*Lokuttara*), "Immortality" (*Amata*), "Emancipation" (*Mutti*), "Peace" (*Santi*), etc.

In the Udāna and Itivuttaka the Buddha refers to Nibbāna as follows:—

"There is, O Bhikkhus, an unborn (*ajāta*), unoriginated (*abhūta*), unmade (*akata*) and non-conditioned state (*asaṁ-khata*). If, O Bhikkhus, there were not this unborn, un-originated, unmade and non-conditioned, an escape for the born, originated, made, and conditioned, would not be, possible here. As there is an unborn, unoriginated, unmade, and non-conditioned state, an escape for the born, originated made, conditioned is possible."[1]

The Itivuttaka states:

"*The born, become, produced, compounded, made,*
And thus not lasting, but of birth and death
An aggregate, a nest of sickness, brittle,
A thing by food supported, come to be,—
'Twere no fit thing to take delight in such.
Th'escape therefrom, the real, beyond the sphere
Of reason, lasting, unborn, unproduced,
The sorrowless, the stainless path that ends
The things of woe, the peace from worries,
*   —bliss.*"[2]

The Nibbāna of Buddhists is, therefore, neither a state of nothingness nor a mere cessation. What it is not, one can definitely say. What precisely it

---

1. According to the commentary these four terms are used as synonyms.

    Ajāta means that it has not sprung up on account of causes or conditions (*hetupaccaya*). *Abhūta* (lit., not become) means that it has not arisen. As it has not sprung up from a cause and has not come into being, it is not made (*akata*) by any means. Becoming and arising are the characteristics of conditioned things such as mind and matter, but Nibbāna, being not subject to those conditions, is non-conditioned (*asaṁkhata*). See Woodward, *Verses of Uplift*, p. 98. *As it was said,* p. 142.

2. Woodward, *As it was said,* p. 142.

is, one cannot adequately express in conventional terms as it is unique. It is for self-realization (*paccattaṁ veditabbo*).

Sopādisesa and Anupādisesa Nibbāna Dhātu.

References are frequently made in the books to Nibbāna as Sopādisesa[1] and Anupādisesa Nibbāna Dhātu.

These in fact are not two kinds of Nibbāna, but the one single Nibbāna receiving its name according to experience of it before and after death.

Nibbāna is attainable in this present life itself if the seeker fits himself for it. Buddhism nowhere states that its ultimate goal can be reached only in a life beyond. Here lies the difference between the Buddhist conception of Nibbāna and the non-Buddhist conception of an eternal heaven which is attainable only after death.

When Nibbāna is realized in the body, it is called *Sopādisesa Nibbāna Dhātu*. When an Arahant attains Pari-Nibbāna after the dissolution of the body, without any remainder of any physical existence, it is called *Anupadisesa Nibbāna Dhātu*.

In the Itivuttaka the Buddha says:

"There are, O Bhikkhus, two elements of Nibbāna·
"What two? "The element of Nibbāna with the basis (*upādi*) still remaining and that without basis.

---

1. *Sa* = with, *upādi* = aggregates—mind and body, *sesa*, remaining. The aggregates are called *Upādi* because they are firmly grasped by craving and ignorance.

"Herein, O Bhikkhus, a Bhikkhu is an Arahant, one who has destroyed the Defilements, who has lived the life, done what was to be done, laid aside the burden, who has attained his goal, who has destroyed the fetters of existence, who, rightly understanding, is delivered. His five sense-organs still remain, and as he is not devoid of them he undergoes the pleasant and the unpleasant experiences. That destruction of his attachment, hatred and delusion is called 'the Element of Nibbāna with the basis still remaining.'

"What O Bhikkus, is 'the Element of Nibbāna without the basis'?

"Herein, O Bhikkhus, a Bhikkhu is an Arahant...is delivered. In this very life all his sensations will have no delight for him, they will be cooled. This is called 'the Element of Nibbāna without a basis.'[1]

> "*These two Nibbāna-states are shown by Him*
> *Who seeth, who is such and unattached.*
> *One state is that in this same life possessed*
> *With base remaining, tho' becoming's stream*
> *Be cut off. While the state without a base*
> *Belongeth to the future, wherein all*
> *Becomings utterly do come to cease.*
> *They who, by knowing this state uncompounded*
> *Have heart's release, by cutting off the stream,*
> *They who have reached the core of dhamma, glad*
> *To end, such have abandoned all becomings.*"[2]

---

1. Since he will not be reborn.
2. P. 38, Woodward, *As it Was Said*, p. 144.

CHAPTER 34

CHARACTERISTICS OF NIBBĀNA

What is Nibbāna, friend ? The destruction of lust, the destruction of hatred, the destruction of delusion—that, friend, is called Nibbāna."

SAMYUTTA NIKĀYA

In contradistinction to Saṁsāra, the phenomenal existence, Nibbāna is eternal (*dhuva*), desirable (*subha*), and happy (*sukha*).

According to Buddhism all things, mundane and supramundane, are classified into two divisions, namely, those conditioned by causes (*saṁkhata*) and those not conditioned by any cause (*asaṁkhata*).

"These three are the features of all conditioned things (*saṁkhatalakkhaṇāni*):—arising (*uppāda*), cessation (*vaya*), and change of state (*ṭhitassa aññathattaṁ*),"[1]

Arising or becoming is an essential characteristic of everything that is conditioned by a cause or causes. That which arises or becomes is subject to change and dissolution. Every conditioned thing is constantly becoming and is perpetually changing. The universal law of change applies to everything in the cosmos—both mental and physical—ranging from the minutest germ or

---

1. See *Gradual Sayings*, i, p. 135.

tiniest particle to the highest being or the most massive object. Mind, though imperceptible, changes faster even than matter.

Nibbāna, a supramundane state, realized by Buddhas and Arahants, is declared to be not conditioned by any cause. Hence it is not subject to any becoming, change and dissolution. It is birthless (*ajāta*), decayless (*ajara*), and deathless (*amara*). Strictly speaking, Nibbāna is neither a cause nor an effect. Hence it is unique (*kevala*).

Everything that has sprung from a cause must inevitably pass away, and as such is undesirable (*asubha*).

Life is man's dearest possession, but when he is confronted with insuperable difficulties and unbearable burdens, then that very life becomes an intolerable burden. Sometimes he tries to seek relief by putting an end to his life as if suicide would solve all his individual problems.

Bodies are adorned and adored. But those charming, adorable and enticing forms, when disfigured by time and disease, become extremely repulsive.

Men desire to live peacefully and happily with their near ones, surrounded by amusements and pleasures, but, if by some misfortune, the wicked world runs counter to their ambitions and desires, the inevitable sorrow is then almost indescribably sharp.

The following beautiful parable aptly illustrates the fleeting nature of life and its alluring pleasures.

A man was forcing his way through a thick forest beset with thorns and stones. Suddenly to his great consternation, an elephant appeared and gave chase. He took to his heels through fear, and, seeing a well, he ran to hide in it. But to his horror he saw a viper at the bottom of the well. However, lacking other means of escape, he jumped into the well, and clung to a thorny creeper that was growing in it. Looking up, he saw two mice—a white one and a black one—gnawing at the creeper. Over his face there was a beehive from which occasional drops of honey trickled.

This man, foolishly unmindful of this precarious position, was greedily tasting the honey. A kind person volunteered to show him a path of escape. But the greedy man begged to be excused till he had enjoyed himself.

The thorny path is saṁsāra, the ocean of life. Man's life is not a bed of roses. It is beset with difficulties and obstacles to overcome, with opposition and unjust criticism, with attacks and insults to be borne. Such is the thorny path of life.

The elephant here resembles death; the viper, old age; the creeper, birth; the two mice, night and day. The drops of honey correspond to the fleeting sensual pleasures. The man represents the so-called being. The kind person represents the Buddha.

The temporary material happiness is merely the gratification of some desire. When the desired thing is gained, another desire arises. Insatiate are all desires.

Sorrow is essential to life, and cannot be evaded.

Nibbāna, being non-conditioned, is eternal, (*dhuva*), desirable (*subha*), and happy (*sukha*).

The happiness of Nibbāna should be differentiated from ordinary worldly happiness. Nibbānic bliss grows neither stale nor monotonous. It is a form of happiness that never wearies, never fluctuates. It arises by allaying passions (*vupasama*) unlike that temporary worldly happiness which results from the gratification of some desire (*vedayita*).

In the Bahuvedaniya Sutta[1] the Buddha enumerates ten grades of happiness beginning with the gross material pleasures which result from the pleasant stimulation of the senses. As one ascends higher and higher in the moral plane the type of happiness becomes ever more exalted, sublime and

---

1. Majjhima Nikāya, No. 57.

subtle, so much so that the world scarcely re-
cognizes it as happiness. In the first *Jhāna* one
experiences a transcendental happiness (*sukha*),
absolutely independent of the five senses. This
happiness is realized by inhibiting the desire for
the pleasures of the senses. highly prized by the
materialist. In the fourth *Jhāna* however, even
this type of happiness is discarded as coarse and
uprofitable, and equanimity (*upekkhā*) is termed
happiness.

The Buddha says[1]:

"Fivefold, Ānanda, are sensual bonds, What are the
five? Forms cognizable by the eye—desirable. lovely,
charming, infatuating, accompanied by thirst, and arousing
the dust of the passions; sounds cognizable by the ear; odours
cognizable by the nose; flavours cognizable by the tongue;
contacts cognizable by the body—desirable, lovely charming,
infatuating, accompanied by thirst, and arousing the dust
of passions. These, Ānanda, are the five sensual bonds. Whatever happiness or pleasure arises from these sensual bonds, is
known as sensual happiness.

"Whoso should declare: 'This is the highest happiness
and pleasure which beings may experience-' I do not grant
him that, and why? Because there is other happiness more
exalted and sublime.

"And what is that other happiness more exalted and
sublime? Here a Bhikkhu lives, completely separated from
sense-desires, remote from immoral states, with initial and
sustained application born of seclusion, in joy and happiness
abiding in the First Ecstasy (*Paṭhama Jhāna*). This is happiness more exalted and sublime.

---

1. Majjhima Nikāya, No. 57 *The Blessing*, No. 4, pp. 129–
132.

"But should anyone declare:— 'This is the highest happiness and pleasure which beings may experience'— I do not grant him that, and why? Because there is another happiness yet more exalted and sublime.

"Here a Bhikkhu, stilling initial and sustained application, having tranquillity within, mind one-pointed, initial and sustained application having ceased, as a result of concentration lives in joy and happiness, abiding in the Second Ecstasy (*Dutiya Jhāna*). This is the other happiness more exalted and sublime.

"Yet should anyone declare that this is the highest happiness and pleasure experienced by beings—I do not grant it. There is happiness more exalted.

"Here a Bhikkhu, eliminating joy, abides serene, mindful, and completely conscious, experiencing in the body that of which the Ariyas say:— 'Endowed with equanimity and mindfulness he abides in bliss.' Thus he lives abiding in the Third Ecstasy (*Tatiya Jhāna*). This is the other happiness and pleasure more exalted and sublime.

"Still should anyone declare that this is the highest happiness—I do not grant it. There is happiness more exalted.

"Here a Bhikkhu, abandoning pleasure and pain, leaving behind former joy and grief—painless, pleasureless, perfect in equanimity and mindfulness—lives abiding in the Fourth Ecstasy (*Catuttha Jhāna*). This is the other happiness more exalted and sublime.

"However, were this declared to be the highest happiness—I do not grant it. There is happiness more sublime.

"Here a Bhikkhu, passing entirely beyond the perception of form, with the disappearance of sense reaction, freed from attention to perceptions of diversity, thinks:

'Infinity is Space'—and lives abiding in the Realm of infinite Space (*Ākāsānañcāyatana*). This other happiness is more exalted and sublime.

"Nevertheless, if this were declared the highest happiness— I do not grant it. There is happiness more sublime.

"Here a Bhikkhu, transcending entirely the Realm of Infinite Space, thinks: 'Infinite is Consciousness,' and lives abiding in the Realm of Infinite Consciousness (*Viññāṇañcāyatana*). This other happiness is more exalted and sublime.

"And yet should this be declared the highest happiness— I do not grant. There is higher happiness.

"Here a Bhikkhu, transcending the Realm of Infinite Consciousness, thinks: 'There is nothing whatsoever' and lives abiding in the Realm of Nothingness (*Ākiñcaññāyatana*). This other happiness is more exalted and sublime than that.

"And still were this declared the highest happiness—I do not grant it. There is happiness more exalted.

"Here a Bhikkhu, passing entirely beyond the Realm of Nothingness, lives abiding in the Realm of Neither Perception nor Non-Perception (*N'eva saññā n'āsaññāyatana*). This other happiness is more exalted and sublime.

"Yet whoso should declare: 'This is the highest bliss and pleasure which beings may experience'—I do not grant him that, and why? Because yet another happiness is more exalted and sublime.

"And what is this other happiness more exalted and sublime? Here a Bhikkhu, utterly transcending the Realm of Neither Perception nor Non-Perception, lives, having attained to the Cessation of perception and sensation (*Saññāvedayita—Nirodha*). This, Ānanda, is the other happiness more exalted and sublime.

Of all the ten grades of happiness this is the highest and the most sublime. This transcendental state is Nirodha Samāpatti, that is, experiencing Nibbāna in this life itself.

As the Buddha Himself has anticipated, one may ask: "How can that state be called highest happiness when there is no consciousness to experience it."

The Buddha replies: "Nay, disciples, the Tathāgata does not recognize bliss merely because of a pleasurable sensation, but, disciples, wherever bliss is attained there and there only does the Accomplished One recognize bliss."[1]

"I proclaim," says the Buddha, "that everything experienced by the senses is sorrow." But why? Because one in sorrow craves to be happy, and the so-called happy crave to be happier still. So insatiate is worldly happiness.

In conventional terms the Buddha declares: "*Nibbānaṁ paramaṁ sukhaṁ* Nibbāna is the highest bliss," It is bliss supreme because it is not a kind of happiness experienced by the senses. It is a blissful state of positive relief from the ills of life.

The very fact of the cessation of suffering is ordinarily termed happiness, though this is not an appropriate word to depict its real nature.

---

1. Majjhima Nikāya, No. 57.

Where is Nibbāna?

In the Milinda Pañha the Venerable *Nāgasena* answers this question thus:

"There is no spot looking East, South, West, or North, above, below or beyond, where Nibbāna is situate, and yet *Nibbāna is,* and he who orders his life aright, grounded in virtue and with rational attention, may realize it whether he lives in Greece, China, Alexandria, or in Kosala.

"Just as fire is not stored up in any particular place but arises when the necessary conditions exist, so Nibbāna is said not to exist in a particular place, but it is attained when the necessary conditions are fulfilled."

In the *Rohitassa Sutta* the Buddha states: "In this very one-fathom-long body, along with its perceptions and thoughts, do I proclaim the world, the origin of the world, the cessation of the world and the path leading to the cessation of the world."[1]

Here world means suffering. The cessation of the world, therefore, means the cessation of suffering which is Nibbāna.

One's Nibbāna is dependent upon this one-fathom body. It is not something that is created nor is it something to be created.[2]

---

1. *Imasmiṁ byāmamatte y'eve kalebare sasaññīmhi samanake lokaṅ ca paññāpemi, lokasamudayaṅ ca, lokanirodhaṅ ca, lokanirodhagāminiṁ paṭipadaṅ ca, paññāpemi.* Saṁyutta Nikāya, i, p. 62.

2. *Pattabbam eva h' etaṁ maggena, na uppādetabbaṁ.* Verily this (Nibbāna) is to be attained (or realized) by means of the four Paths of Sainthood, and is not to be *produced—Visuddhi Magga.*

Nibbāna is there where the four elements of cohesion (*āpo*), extension (*paṭhavi*), heat (*tejo*), and motion (*vāyo*) find no *footing*.

Referring to where Nibbāna is, Saṁyutta Nikāya states:[1]

"*Where the four elements that cleave, and stretch, And burn, and move no further footing find.*"

In the *Udāna*[2] the Buddha says:

"Just as, O Bhikkhus, notwithstanding those rivers that reach the great ocean and the torrents of rain that fall from the sky, neither a deficit nor a surplus is perceptible in the great ocean, even so despite the many Bhikkhus that enter the remainderless *Pari-Nibbāna* there is neither a deficit nor a surplus in the element of Nibbāna."

Nibbāna is, therefore, not a kind of heaven where a transcendental ego resides, but a Dhamma (an attainment) which is within the reach of us all.

An eternal heaven, which provides all forms of pleasures desired by man and where one enjoys happiness to one's heart's content, is practically inconceivable. It is absolutely impossible to think that such a place could exist permanently anywhere.

Granting that there is no place where Nibbāna is stored up, King *Milinda* questions Venerable *Nāgasena* whether there is any basis whereon a

1. Kindred Sayings, pt. i, p. 23.
   Yattha āpo ca paṭhavi tejo vāyo na gadhati.
2. See Woodward, *Verses of Uplift,* pp. 66-67.

man stand and, ordering his life aright, realize
Nibbāna.

"Yes, O King, there is such a basis.

"Which, then, Venerable Nāgasena, is that basis?

"Virtue, O King, is that basis. For, if grounded in virtue, and careful in attention, whether in the land of the
Scythians or the Greeks, whether in China or in Tartary,
whether in Alexandria or in Nikumba, whether in Benares
or in Kosala, whether in Kashmir or in Gandhara, whether
on a mountain top or in the highest heavens,—wherever
he may be, the man who orders his life aright will attain
Nibbāna."[1]

What Attains Nibbāna?

This question must necessarily be set aside as
irrelevant, for Buddhism denies the existence of
a permanent entity or an immortal soul.[2]

The so-called being of which we often hear as
the "vestment of the soul" is a mere bundle of
conditioned factors.

The Arahant Bhikkhuni *Vajirā* says:

*"And just as when the parts are rightly set,
The word chariot ariseth (in our minds).
So doth our usage covenant to say
A being when the aggregates are there."*[3]

---

1. *Questions of King Milinda,* pp. 202-204.
2. See Chapter 29.
3. *Kindred Sayings,* part 1, p. 170.

According to Buddhism the so-called being consists of mind and matter (*nāma-rūpa*) which constantly change with lightning rapidity. Apart from these two composite factors there exists no permanent soul or an unchanging entity. The so-called "I" is also an illusion.

Instead of an eternal soul or an illusory "I" Buddhism posits a dynamic life-flux (*santati*) which flows *ad infinitum* as long as it is fed with ignorance and craving. When these two root causes are eradicated by any individual on attaining Arahantship, they cease to flow with his final death.

In conventional terms one says that the Arahant has attained *Parinibbāna* or passed away into Nibbāna.

"As right now, and here" there is neither a permanent ego nor an identical being it is needless to state that there can be no "I" or a soul (*attā*) in Nibbāna.

The Visuddhi Magga states:—

"Misery only doth exist, none miserable;
Nor doer is there, nought save the deed is found;
Nibbāna is, but not the man who seeks it;
The path exists, but not the traveller on it."[1]

The chief difference between the Buddhist concepion of Nibbāna and the Hindu conception

---

1. *Dukkham' eva hi na koci dukkhito*
Kārako no kiriyā,' va vijjati
Atthi nibbuti na nibbuto pumā
Maggam atthi gamako na vijjati.

of Nirvāna or Mukti lies in the fact that Buddhists view their goal without an eternal soul and creator, while Hindus do believe in an eternal soul and a creator.

This is the reason why Buddhism can neither be called Eternalism nor Nihilism.

In Nibbāna nothing is 'eternalised' nor is anything 'annihilated.'

As Sir Edwin Arnold says:—
"*If any teach Nirvāna is to cease,*
Say unto such they lie.
If any teach Nirvāna is to live,
Say unto such they err."

* * *

It must be admitted that this question of Nibbāna is the most difficult in the Teaching of the Buddha. However much we may speculate we shall never be in a position to comprehend its real nature. The best way to understand Nibbāna is to try to realize it with our own intuitive knowledge.

Although Nibbāna cannot be perceived by the five senses and lies in obscurity in so far as the average man is concerned, the only straight path that leads to Nibbāna has been explained by the Buddha with all the necessary details and is laid open to all. The goal is now clouded. but the method of achievement is perfectly clear and when that achievement is realized, the Goal is as clear as "the moon freed from clouds."

CHAPTER 35

THE WAY TO NIBBĀNA

(I)

_____

*"This Middle Path leads to tranquillity, realization,
enlightenment and nibbāna."*

DHAMMACAKKA SUTTA

The way to Nibbāna is the Middle Path (*Maj-jhimā Paṭipadā*) which avoids the extreme of self-mortification that weakens the intellect and the extreme of self-indulgence that retards moral progress.

This Middle Path consists of the following eight factors: Right Understanding, Right Thoughts, Right Speech, Right Action, Right Livelihood, Right Effort, Right Mindfulness, and Right Concentration.

The first two are classified as Wisdom (*paññā*), the second three as Morality (*sīla*), and the last three as Concentration (*samādhi*).

According to the order of development Morality, Concentration, and Wisdom are the three stages on the Grand Highway that leads to Nibbāna.

These three stages are embodied in the beautiful ancient verse:

*Sabba pāpassa akaraṇaṁ—kusalassa upasampadā
Sacittapariyodapanaṁ—etaṁ Buddhāna sāsanaṁ*

To cease from all evil
To cultivate good
To purify one's mind—
This is the advice of all the Buddhas.

*   *   *

We reap what we sow. Evil results in pain, and good in happiness. Our pain and happiness are the direct results of our own good and evil.

A person with a right understanding realizes this just law of action and reaction and, of his own accord, refrains from evil and does good to the best of his ability. He does so for his own good and for the good of others. He considers it his duty to live as a blessing to himself and to all others.

Knowing that life is precious to all and that none has any right whatever to destroy the life of another, he extends compassion and loving-kindness towards every living being, even to the tiniest creature that crawls at his feet, and refrains from killing or causing injury to any living being.

There is no rule that one is to be preyed upon by another. However, the strong do mercilessly kill the weak and feast on their flesh. This is animal instinct. Such actions by animals are excusable because they know not what they do, but when those who are gifted with reason and understanding perpetrate such crimes, there is no excuse. Whether to satisfy one's palate or as pastime, it is not justifiable to kill or to cause

another living being to be killed. If the killing
of animals is wrong, how much more heinous
is it to kill human beings—individually or collectively, employing brutal or so-called civilized
methods—for the sake of peace, religion, or any
other seemingly good purpose?

Honesty, trustworthiness, and uprightness also
are the characteristics of a person with right understanding. Such a person tries to abstain from all
forms of stealing "whether in its dissembled or
obvious forms." Abstaining from sexual misconduct, which debases the exalted nature of man,
he tries to be pure and chaste. He avoids false
speech, harsh language, slander and frivolous talk
and speaks only what is true, sweet, kind and
helpful. As certain drinks and drugs promote
heedlessness and mental distraction, he avoids
intoxicating liquor and cultivates heedfulness and
clarity of vision.

These elementary principles of regulated behaviour are essential to one who treads the Path to
Nibbāna, chiefly because they tend to control
both deeds and words. Violation of them intro-
duces obstacles that hinder his moral progress on
the Path. Observance of them means smooth and
steady progress along the Path.

Having progressed a step further in his gradual
advance, the aspirant now tries to control his
senses.

To control craving for food and to promote
buoyancy of mind and body, abstemiousness or

fasting at least once a month is advisable. Plain
and simple living is preferable to a luxurious life
which makes one a slave to passions. A life of
celibacy is recommended, as one's valuable energy
thus conserved could then be utilised wholly for
the intellectual and moral welfare of oneself and
others. In such a life one is detached from additional worldly bonds that impede moral progress.
Almost all spiritual teachers, it would appear,
have nourished their bodies sparingly and have led
a life of strict celibacy, simplicity, voluntary poverty, and self-control.

While he progress slowly and steadily, with
regulated word and deed and sense-restraint, the
Kammic force of the striving aspirant compels him
to renounce worldly pleasures and adopt the
ascetic life. To him then comes the idea that:

> "*A den of strife is household life,*
> *And filled with toil and need,*
> *But free and high as the open sky*
> *Is the life the homeless lead.*"[1]

Thus realizing the vanity of sensual pleasures,
he voluntarily foresakes all earthly possessions,
and donning the ascetic garb tries to lead the
Holy Life in all its purity.

It is not, however, the external appearance
that makes a man holy but internal purification
and an exemplary life. Transformation should

---

1. Sutta Nipāta, Pabbajjā Sutta, v. 406.

come from within, not from without.   It is not absolutely necessary to retire to solitude and lead the life of an ascetic to realize   Nibbāna. The life of a Bhikkhu no doubt expedites and facilitates spiritual progress, but even as a layman Sainthood may be attained.

He who attains Arahantship as a layman in the face of all temptations is certainly more praiseworthy than a Bhikkhu who attains Arahantship living amidst surroundings that are not distracting.

Concerning a minister who attained Arahantship while seated on an elephant decked in his best apparel, the Buddha remarked:

"Even though a man be richly adorned, if he
walks in peace,

If he be quiet, subdued, certain and pure,
And if he refrains from injuring any living being,
That man is a Brahmin, that man is a hermit,
that man is a monk."[1]

There have been several such instances of laymen who realized Nibbāna without renouncing the world.   The most devout and generous lay-follower *Anāthapindika* was a Sotāpanna,[2] the Sakya *Mahānāma* was a Sakadāgāmi,[3] the potter *Ghatīkāra* was an Anāgāmi[4] and King *Suddhodana* died as an Arahant.[5]

---

1. Dhammapada, v. 142.
2. "Stream—Winner"—The first stage of Sainthood.
3. "Once—Returner"—The second stage of Sainthood.
4. "Never—Returner"—The third stage of Sainthood.
5. "The Worthy One"—The final stage of Sainthood.

A Bhikkhu is expected to observe the four kinds of Higher Morality—namely,

*Pātimokkha Sila-*The Fundamental Moral Code,[1]

Indriyasaṁvara Sīla—Morality pertaining to sense-restraint,

Ājīvapārisuddhi Sīla—Morality pertaining to purity of livelihood,

*Paccayasannissita Sīla*M—orality pertaining to the use of the necessaries of life.

These four kinds of morality are collectively called *Sīla-Visuddhi* (Purity of Virtue), the first of the seven stages of Purity on the way to Nibbāna.

When a person enters the Order and receives his Higher Ordination (*Upasampadā*), he is called a Bhikkhu. There is no English equivalent that exactly conveys the meaning of this Pāli term Bhikkhu. "Mendicant Monk" may be suggested as the nearest translation, not in the sense of one who begs but in the sense of one who lives on alms.

There are no vows for a Bhikkhu. Of his own accord he becomes a Bhikkhu in order to lead the Holy Life as long as he likes. He is at liberty to leave the Order at any time.

A Bhikkhu is bound to observe 220 rules,[2] apart from several other minor ones. The four

---

1. Various rules which a Bhikkhu is expected to observe.
2. Excluding the seven modes of settling disputes (*adhikaraṇasmatha dhamma*).

major rules which deal with perfect celibacy, stealing, murder, and false claims to higher spiritual powers, must strictly be observed. If he violates any one of them, he becomes defeated (*pārājikā*) and automatically ceases to be a Bhikkhu. If he wishes, he can re-enter the Order and remain as a *Sāmaṇera* (novice). In the case of other rules, which he violates, he has to make amends according to the gravity of the offence.

Among the salient characteristics of a Bhikkhu are purity, perfect celibacy, voluntary poverty, humility, simplicity, selfless service, self-control, patience, compassion and harmlessness.

The life of a Bhikkhu or, in other words, renunciation of worldly pleasures and ambitions, is only an effective means to attain Nibbāna, but is not an end in itself.

CHAPTER 36
THE WAY TO NIBBĀNA
(II)

MEDITATION

"One way to acquire gain, another that leads to Nibbāna."
                                          DHAMMAPADA

Concentration (*Samādhi*)

Securing a firm footing on the ground of morality, the aspirant then embarks upon the higher practice of Samādhi, the control and culture of the mind, the second stage of the Path of Purity.

Samādhi is one-pointedness of the mind. It is concentration of the mind on one object to the entire exclusion of all else.

According to Buddhism there are forty subjects of meditation (*kammaṭṭhāna*) which differ according to the temperaments of individuals.

They are:

(*a*) The ten Kasiṇas[1] (devices)—namely, i.

---

1. *Kasiṇa* here means whole, all, complete. It is so called because the projected light issuing from the conceptualized image of the Kasiṇa object could be extended everywhere without limitation.

In the case of earth Kasiṇa one makes a circle of about one span and four fingers in diameter and, covering it with dawn-coloured clay, smoothes it well. If there be not enough clay of the dawn colour, he may introduce some other kind of clay beneath. This concentrative circle is known as Kasiṇa-Maṇḍala.

The remaining Kasiṇas should be similarly understood. Details are given in the *Visuddhi Magga*. It may be mentioned that light and space Kasiṇas are not found in the Text. When they are excluded there are thirty-eight subjects.

earth Kasiṇa, ii. water Kasiṇa, iii. fire Kasiṇa, iv. air Kasiṇa, v. blue Kasiṇa, vi. yellow Kasiṇa, vii. red Kasiṇa, viii. white Kasiṇa, ix. light Kasiṇa and x. space Kasiṇa.

(b) The ten Impurities (*asubha*)[1]—namely, ten corpses which are respectively:— . i. bloated (*uddhumātaka*), ii. discoloured (*vinīlaka*), iii. festering (*vipubbaka*), iv. dissected (*vicchiddaka*), v. gnawed-to-pieces (*vikkhāyitaka*), vi. scattered-in-pieces (*vikkhittaka*), vii. mutilated and scattered-in-pieces (*hata-vikkhittaka*), viii. bloody (*lohitaka*), ix. worm-infested (*pulapaka*), and x. skeleton (*aṭṭhika*).

(c) The ten Reflections (*anussati*)[2]—namely, eight Reflections on:— i. The Buddha (*Buddhānussati*), ii. The Doctrine (*Dhammānussati*), iii. The Sangha (*Sanghānussati*), iv. Virtue (*sīlānussati*), v. Liberality (*cāgānussati*), vi. Devas (*devatānussati*), vii. Peace (*upasamānussati*), viii. Death (*maraṇānussati*), respectively, together with ix. Mindfulness regarding the body (*kāyagatāsati*)

1. These ten kinds of corpses were found in ancient cemeteries and charnel places where dead bodies were not buried or cremated and where flesh-eating beasts and birds frequent. In modern days it is impossible to obtain such corpses as subjects for meditation.

2. *Anussati*—lit., means constant mindfulness.

and x. Mindfulness regarding respiration (*ānāpānasati*).

(*d*) The four Illimitables or the four Modes of Sublime Conduct (*Brahmavihāra*)- namely, Loving-kindness (*mettā*), Compassion (*karunā*), Appreciative Joy (*muditā*), and Equanimity (*upekkhā*).

(*e*) The One Perception—i.e., the Perception of the loathsomeness of material food (*āhāre paṭikkūlasaññā*).[1]

(*f*) The One Analysis—i.e., The Analysis of the four Elements (*catudhātuvavatthāna*).[2]

(*g*) The four Arūpa Jhānas—namely,

The Realm of the Infinity of Space (*Ākāsānañcāyatana*), The Realm of the Infinity of Consciousness (*Viññāṇañcāyatana*), The Realm of Nothingness (*Ākiñcaññāyatana*), and the Realm of Neither Perception nor Non-Perception (*N'eva saññā n'āsaññāyatana*).

Suitability of Subjects for different Temperaments

According to the Texts the ten Impurities and the Mindfulness regarding the Body such as the

---

1. *Āhāre paṭikkūlasaññā*—i.e., the feeling of loathsomeness of food in its search, eating, etc.

2. *Catudhātuvavatthānaṁ*—i.e., the investigation of the four primary elements of extension (*paṭhavi*), cohesion (*āpo*), heat (*tejo*), and motion (*vāyo*), with regard to their special characteristics.

thirty-two parts are suitable for those of a lustful temperament because they tend to create a disgust for the body which fascinates the senses.

The four Illimitables and the four coloured Kasiṇas are suitable for those of a hateful temperament.

The Reflections on the Buddha and so forth are suitable for those of a devout temperament. The Reflections on Death and Peace, Perception on the loathsomeness of material food, and Analysis of the four Elements are suitable for those of an intellectual temperament.   The remaining objects, chiefly Reflection on the Buddha, Meditation on Loving-Kindness, Mindfulness regarding the Body and Reflection on Death are suitable for all, irrespective of temperament.

There are six kinds of Temperaments (*carita*). They are:—

   i.   Lustful Temperament (*rāgacarita*),
   ii.   Hateful Temperament (*dosacarita*),
   iii. Ignorant Temperament (*mohacarita*),
   iv.   Devout Temperament (*saddhācarita*),
   v.   Intellectual Temperament (*buddhicarita*), and
   vi.   Discursive Temperament (*vitakkacarita*).

Carita signifies the intrinsic nature of a person which is revealed when one is in normal state without being preoccupied with anything.   The temperaments of people differ owing to the diversity of their actions or Kamma.   Habitual actions tend to form particular temperaments.

Rāga or lust is predominant in some while *dosa* or anger, hatred, illwill in others. Most people belong to these·two categories. There are a few others who lack intelligence and are more or less ignorant (*mohacarita*). Akin to ignorant are those whose minds oscillate unable to focus their attention deliberately on one thing (*vitakkacarita*). By nature some are exceptionally devout (*saddhācarita,*) while others are exceptionally intelligent (*buddhicarita*).

Combining these six with one another, we get 63 types. With the inclusion of speculative temperament (*diṭṭhicarita*) there are 64 types.

The subjects of meditation are variously adapted to these different temperaments and types of people.

Before practising Samādhi, the qualified aspirant should give a careful consideration to the subject of meditation. In ancient days it was customary for pupils to seek the guidance of a competent teacher to choose a suitable subject according to their temperaments. But, today if no competent teacher is available, the aspirant must exercise his own judgement and choose one he thinks most suited to his character.

When the subject has been chosen, he should withdraw to a quiet place where there are the fewest distractions. The forest, a cave, or any lonely place is most desirable, for there one is least liable to interruption during the practice.

It should be understood that solitude is within us all.   If our minds are not settled,   even a quiet forest would not be a congenial place.   But if our minds are settled, even the heart of a busy town may be congenial.   The atmosphere in which we live acts as an indirect aid to tranquillize our minds.

Next to be decided by the aspirant is the most convenient time when he himself and his surroundings are in the best possible condition for the practice.

Early in the morning when the mind is fresh and active, or before bedtime, if one is not over-tired, is generally the most appropriate time for meditation.   But whatever the time selected, it is advisable daily to keep to that particular hour, for our minds then become conditioned to the practice.

The meditating posture, too, serves as a power-ful aid to concentration.

Easterners generally sit cross-legged, with the body erect.   They sit placing the right foot on the left thigh and the left foot on the right thigh.   This is the full position.   If this posture is difficult, as it certainly is to many, the half position may be adopted, that is, simply placing the right foot on the left thigh or the left foot on the right thigh.

When this triangular position is assumed, the whole body is well balanced.

The right hand should be placed on the left hand, the neck straightened so that the nose is in a perpendicular line with the navel. The tongue should rest on the upper palate. The belt should be loosened, and clothes neatly adjusted. Some prefer closed eyes so as to shut out all unnecessary light and external sights.

Although there are certain advantages in closing the eyes, it is not always recommended as it tends to drowsiness. Then the mind gets out of control and wanders aimlessly, vagrant thoughts arise, the body loses its erectness, quite unconsciously the mouth opens itself, saliva drivels, and the head nods.

The Buddhas usually sit with half closed eyes looking through the tip of the nose not more than a distance of four feet away.

Those who find the cross-legged posture too difficult may sit comfortably in a chair or any other support, sufficiently high to rest the feet on the ground.

It is of no great importance what posture one adopts provided it is easy and relaxed.

The aspirant who is striving to gain one-pointedness of the mind should endeavour to control any unwholesome thoughts at their very inception.

As mentioned in the Sutta Nipāta[1] he may be attacked by the ten armies of the Evil One. They are: i. sensual desires, (*kāma*), ii. discouragement (*arati*), iii. hunger and thirst (*khuppipāsā*), iv.

---

1. Padhāna Sutta. See p. 28.

attachment (*taṇhā*), v. sloth and torpor (*thīna-middha*), vi. fear (*bhaya*), vii. doubt (*vicikicchā*), viii. detraction and stubbornness (*makkha, thambha*), ix. gain, praise, honour and ill-gotten fame (*lābha, siloka, sakkāra, micchāyasa*), and x. self-praise and contempt for others (*attukkaṁsana paravambhana*).

On such occasions the following practical suggestions given by the Buddha will be beneficial to all.

1. Harbouring a good thought opposite to the encroaching one, e.g., loving-kindness in case of hatred.

2. Reflecting upon possible evil consequences, e.g., anger sometimes results in murder.

3. Simple neglect or becoming wholly inattentive to them.

4. Tracing the cause which led to the arising of the unwholesome thoughts and thus forgetting them in the retrospective process.

5. Direct physical force.

Just as a strong man overpowers a weak person, so one should overcome evil thoughts by bodily strength. "With teeth clenched and tongue pressed to the palate," advises the Buddha, "the monk by main force must constrain and coerce his mind; and thus with clenched teeth and taut tongue, constraining and coercing his mind, those evil and unsalutary thoughts will disappear and go to decay; and with their disappearing, the mind will become settled, subdued, unified, and concentrated."[1]

Having attended to all these necessary preliminaries, the qualified aspirant retires to a solitary place, and summoning up confidence as to the certainty of achieving his goal, he makes a persistent effort to develop concentration.

A physical object like a Kasiṇa circle only aids concentration. But a virtue like loving-kindness has the specific advantage of building up that particular virtue in the character of the person.

While meditating one may intelligently repeat the words of any special formula, since they serve as an aid to evoke the ideas they represent.

However intent the aspirant may be on the object of his meditation he will not be exempt from the initial difficulties that inevitably confront a beginner. "The mind wanders, alien thoughts dance before him, impatience overcomes him owing to the slowness of progress, and his efforts slacken in consequence." The determined aspirant only welcomes these obstacles, the difficulties he cuts through and looks straight to his goal, never for a moment turning away his eyes from it.

Suppose, for instance, an aspirant takes an earth-kasiṇa for his object (*kammaṭṭhāna*).

The surface of a circle of about one foot in diameter is covered with clay and smoothed well.

1.   Majjhima Nikāya, Vitakka Saṅthāna Sutta, No. 20.

This concentrative circle is known as the preliminary object (*parikamma nimitta*). He sets it down some four feet away and concentrates on it, saying—pathavi, pathavi (earth, earth), until he becomes so wholly absorbed in it that all adventitious thoughts get automatically excluded from the mind. When he does this for some time —perhaps weeks or months or years—he would be able to visualize the object with closed eyes. On this visualized image (*uggaha nimitta*), which is a mental replica of the object, he concentrates until it develops into a conceptualized image (*patibhāga nimitta*).

According to the Visuddhi Magga the difference between the first visualized image and the second conceptualized image is that "in the former a fault of the kasina object appears while the latter is like the disc of a mirror taken out of a bag, or a well-burnished conch-shell, or the round moon issuing from the clouds."

The conceptualized image neither possesses colour nor form. It is just a mode of appearance and is born of perception.

As he continually concentrates on this abstract concept he is said to be in possession of "proximate concentration' (*upacāra samādhi*) and the innate five Hindrances to spiritual progress (*nīvarana*)—namely, sensual desires (*kāmacchanda*), hatred (*vyāpāda*), sloth and torpor (*thīnamiddha*); restlessness and worry (*uddhaccakukkucca*), and indecision (*vicikicchā*), are temporarily inhibited by means of one-pointedness (*ekaggatā*), zest (*pīti*), initial application, (*vitakka*), happiness (*sukha*), and sustained application (*vicāra*) respectively.

Eventually he gains 'ecstatic concentration' (*appanā samādhi*) and becomes absorbed in Jhana, enjoying the calmness and serenity of a onepointed mind.

This one-pointedness of the mind, achieved by inhibiting the Hindrances, is termed 'Purity of Mind' (*cittavisuddhī*), the second stage on the Path of Purity.

For the water-kasiṇa one may take a vessel full of colourless water, preferably rain water, and concentrate on it, saying- āpo, āpo, (water, water) until he gains one-pointedness of the mind.

To develop the fire-kasiṇa one may kindle a fire before him and concentrate on it through a hole, a span and four fingers wide, in a rush-mat, a piece of leather, or a piece of cloth.

One who develops the air-kasiṇa concentrates on the wind that enters through window-space or a hole in the wall, saying-vāyo, vāyo (air, air).

To develop the colour kasiṇas one may make a disc (maṇḍala) of the prescribed size and colour it blue, yellow, red, or white and concentrate on it repeating the name of the colour as in the case of the earth-kasina.

He may even concentrate on blue, yellow, red and white flowers.

Light-kasiṇa may be developed by concentrating on the moon or an unflickering lamplight or on a circle of light made on the ground or the wall by sunlight or moonlight entering through a wall-crevice or holes, saying-*āloka, āloka* (light, light).

Space-kasiṇa could be developed by concentrating on a hole; a span and four fingers wide, in either a well-covered pavilion or a piece of leather or a mat, saying-*okāsa, okāsa* (space, space).

Asubha:—

The ten kinds of corpses were found in ancient Indian cemeteries where dead bodies were not buried or cremated and where flesh-eating animals frequent. In modern days finding them is out of question.

Anussati:—

Buddhānussati— is the reflection on the virtues of the Buddha as follows:—

"Such indeed is that Exalted One—Worthy, Fully Enlightened, Endowed with Wisdom and Conduct, Well-farer, Knower of the Worlds, an Incomparable Charioteer for the training of individuals, Teacher of gods and men, Omniscient, and Holy."

Dhammānussati—is the reflection on the characteristics of the Doctrine as follows:—

"Well-expounded is the doctrine by the Blessed One, to be realized by oneself, of immediate fruit, inviting investigation,[1] leading to Nibbāna, to be understood by the wise, each one for himself."

Sanghānussati—is the reflection on the virtues of the pure members of the Holy Celibate Order as follows:—

"Of good conduct is the Order of the disciples of the Blessed one; of upright conduct is the Order of the disciples of the Blessed One; of wise conduct is the Order of the disciples of the Blessed One; of dutiful conduct is the Order of the disciples of the Blessed One. These four pairs of persons constitute eight individuals. This Order of the disciples of the Blessed One is worthy of offerings, is worthy of hospitality, is worthy of gifts, is worthy of reverential salutation, is an incomparable field of merit to the world."

Sīlānussati—is the reflection on the perfection of one's own virtuous conduct.

Cāgānussati—is the reflection on one's own charitable nature.

Devatānussati—"Deities are born in such exalted states on account of their faith and other virtues. I too possess them." Thus when one reflects again and again on one's own faith and

---

1. *Ehi-passiko:* inviting to come and see.

other virtues, placing deities as witnesses, it is called Devatanussati.

Upasamānussati—is the reflection on the attributes of Nibbana such as the cessation of suffering and the like.

Maranānussati—is the reflection on the termination of psycho-physical life.

Contemplation on death enables one to comprehend the fleeting nature of life. When one understands that death is certain and life is uncertain, one endeavours to make the best use of one's life by working for self-development and for the development of others instead of wholly indulging in sensual pleasures. Constant meditation on death does not make one pessimistic and lethargic, but, on the contrary, it makes one more active and energetic. Besides, one can face death with serenity.

While contemplating death one may think that life is like a flame, or that all so-called beings are the outward temporary manifestations of the invisible Kammic energy just as an electric light is the outward manifestation of the invisible electric energy. Using various similies as one likes, one may meditate on the uncertainty of life and on the certainty of death.

Kāyagatāsati—is the reflection on the 32 impure parts of the body such as hair, hair of the body, nails, teeth, skin, flesh, sinews, bones, marrow, kidneys, heart, liver, diaphragm, spleen, lungs, bowels, mesentery, stomach, faeces, brain, bile, phlegm, pus, blood, sweat, lymph, tears, grease, saliva, nasal mucus, articular fluid, and urine."

This meditation on the loathsomeness of the body leads to dispassion. Many Bhikkhus in the time of the Buddha attained Arahantship by meditating on these impurities. If one is not conversant with all the thirty-two parts, one may meditate on one part such as bones, flesh, or skin.

Inside this body is found a skeleton. It is filled with flesh which is covered with a skin. Beauty is nothing but skin deep. When one reflects on the impure parts of the body in this manner, passionate attachment to this body gradually disappears.

This meditation may not appeal to those who are not sensual. They may meditate on the innate creative possibilities of this complex machinery of man.

Ānāpānasati—is mindfulness on respiration. *Āna* means inhalation and *apāna*, exhalation.

In some books these two terms are explained in the reverse order.

Concentration on the breathing process leads to one-pointedness of the mind and ultimately to Insight which leads to Arahantship.

This is one of the best subjects of meditation which appeals equally to all. The Buddha also practised this *ānāpānasati* before His Enlightenment.

A detailed exposition of this meditation is found in the *Satipaṭṭhāna Sutta* and in the *Visuddhi Magga*.

A few practical hints are given here for the benefit of the average reader.

Adopting a convenient posture, breathe out and close the mouth. Then breathe through the nostrils naturally and not forcefully. Inhale first and mentally count one. Exhale and count two, concentrating on the breathing process. In this manner one may count upto ten constantly focussing one's attention on respiration. It is possible for the mind to wander before one counts upto ten. But one need not be discouraged. Let one try till one succeeds. Gradually one may increase the number of series—say five series of ten. Later one may concentrate on respiration without counting. Some prefer counting as it aids concentration, while some others prefer not to count. What is essential is concentration and not counting which is secondary. When one does this concentration, one feels light in body and mind and very peaceful too. One might perhaps feel as if one were floating in the air. When this concentration is practised for a certain period, a day will come when one will realize that this so-called body is supported by mere breath and that body perishes when breathing ceases. One instantly realizes impermanence. Where there is change there cannot be a permanent entity or an immortal soul. Insight could then be developed to gain Arahantship.

It is now clear that the object of this concentration on respiration is not merely to gain one pointedness but also to cultivate Insight in order to obtain deliverance.

This simple method may be pursued by all without any harm.

For more details readers are referred to the Visuddhi Magga.

Ānāpāna Sati according to the Satipaṭṭhāna Sutta—"Mindfully he inhales, mindfully he exhales.

1. "When making a long inhalation, he knows: 'I make a long inhalation'; when making a long exhalation, he knows: 'I make a long exhalation.'

2. "When making a short inhalation he knows: "I make a short inhalation'; when making a short exhalation, he knows: 'I make a short exhalation.'

3. "Clearly perceiving the entire breathing process (i.e., the beginning, middle and end), 'I will inhale' thus he trains himself; clearly perceiving the entire breathing process, 'I will exhale': thus he trains himself.

4. "Calming the respirations, 'I will inhale': thus he trains himself; calming the respirations, 'I will exhale': thus he trains himself."

Brahmavihāra

Here *Brahma* means sublime or noble as in Brahmacariya (sublime life); *vihāra* means mode or state of conduct, or state of living. They are also termed *appamaññā* (limitless, boundless), because these thoughts are radiated towards all beings without limit or obstruction.

Mettā (Saṁskrit-Maitrī) loving-kindness, benevolence, goodwill-is defined as that which softens one's heart. It is not carnal love or personal affection. The direct enemy of *Mettā* is hatred, illwill or aversion (*kodha*), its indirect enemy is personal affection (*pema*). Mettā embraces all beings without exception. The culmination of Mettā is the identification of oneself with all beings (*sabbattatā*). It is the wish for the good and happiness of all. Benevolent attitude is its chief characteristic. It discards illwill.

Karuṇā (compassion) is defined as that which makes the hearts of the good quiver when others are subject to suffering, or that which dissipates the sufferings of others. Its chief characteristic is the wish to remove the sufferings of others. Its direct enemy is wickedness (*hiṁsā* and its indirect enemy is passionate grief (*domanassa*). Compassion embraces sorrow-stricken beings and it eliminates cruelty.

Muditā is not mere sympathy but sympathetic or appreciative joy. Its direct enemy is jealousy (*issā*) and its indirect enemy is exhilaration (*pahāsa*). Its chief characteristic is happy acquiescence in others' prosperity and success (*anumo-danā*). Mudita embraces all prosperous beings. It eliminates dislike (*arati*) and is the congratulatory attitude of a person.

Upekkhā— lit., means to view impartially, that is, with neither attachment nor aversion. It is not hedonic indifference but perfect equanimity or well-balanced mind. It is the balanced state of mind amidst all vicissitudes of life, such as praise and blame, pain and happiness, gain and loss, repute and disrepute. Its direct enemy is attachment (*rāga*) and its indirect enemy is callousness. Upekkhā discards clinging and aversion. Impartial attitude is its chief characteristic.

Here *upekkhā* does not mean mere neutral feeling, but implies a sterling virtue. Equanimity, mental equilibrium are its closest equivalents. *Upekkhā* embraces the good and the bad, the loved and the unloved, the pleasant and the unpleasant.

Visuddhimagga describes in detail the method to cultivate the Brahmavihāras in order to develop the Jhānas.

When once the aspirant succeeds in cultivating the Jhānas. he can, without difficulty, develop the five supernormal powers (*abhiññā*)-namely, Divine Eye (*dibbacakkhu*), Divine Ear (*dibbasota*), Reminiscence of past births (*pubbe nivāsānussati-ñāṇa*), Thought-reading (*paracittavijānana*), and various psychic powers (*iddhividha*).

Samādhi and these supernormal powers. it may be mentioned, are not essential for the attainment of Arahantship, though they would undoubtedly be an asset to the possessor. There are, for instance, dry-visioned Arahants (*sukkhavipassaka*) who, without the aid of the jhānas, attain Arahantship straightway by merely cultivating Insight. Many men and women attained Arahantship in the time of the Buddha Himself without developing the jhānas.

It is only one who has gained the fifth *Jhāna* that could develop the five kinds of *Abhiññā*.

Dibbacakkhu is the Celestial or Divine Eye, also called clairvoyance, which enables one to see heavenly or earthly things, far or near, that are imperceptible to the physical eye.

Cutūpapātañāṇa, knowledge with regard to the dying and reappearing of beings, is identical with this Celestial Eye. *Anāgataṁsañāṇa*, knowledge with regard to the future and *Yathākammūpagata-ñāṇa*, knowledge with regard to the faring of beings according to their own good and bad actions, are two other kinds of knowledge belonging to the same category.

Dibbasota is the Celestial Ear, also called clair-audience, which enables one to hear subtle or coarse sounds far or near.

Pubbenivāsānussatiñāṇā is the power to remember the past lives of oneself and others. With regard to this knowledge the Buddha's power is limitless, while in the case of others it is limited.

Paracittavijānana is the power to discern the thoughts of others.

Iddhividha is the power to fly through the air, walk on water, dive into the earth, create new forms etc.

CHAPTER 37
NĪVARANA OR HINDRANCES

"There are these five corruptions of the heart, tainted by which the heart is neither soft, nor pliable, nor gleaming, nor easily broken up, nor perfectly composed for the destruction of the corruptions."

SAṀYUTTA NIKĀYA

Nīvaraṇa (Nī + var, to hinder, to obstruct) is that which hinders one's progress or that which obstructs the path to Emancipation and heavenly states. It is also explained as that which "muffles, enwraps, or trammels thought."

There are five kinds of *Nīvaraṇas* or Hindrances. They are: (i) Sensual desires (*Kāmacchanda*), (ii) Illwill (*Vyāpāda*), (iii) Sloth and Torpor (*Thīna-Middha*), (iv) Restlessness and Worry (*Uddhacca-Kukkucca*), and (v) Doubts (*Vicikicchā*).

1. *Kāmacchanda* means sensual desires or attachment to pleasurable sense-objects such as form, sound, odour, taste, and contact. This is regarded · as one of the Fetters, too, that bind one to Saṁsāra.

An average person is bound to get tempted by these alluring objects of sense. Lack of self-control results in the inevitable arising of passions. This Hindrance is inhibited by One-pointedness (*Ekaggatā*), which is one of the five characteristics of Jhānas. It is attenuated on attaining Sakadāgāmi and is completely eradicated on attaining Anāgāmi.

Subtle forms of attachment such as Rūpa Rāga and Ārupa Rāga (Attachment to Realms of Form and Formless Realms) are eradicated only on attaining Arahantship.

The following six conditions tend to the eradication of sense-desires. (i) perceiving the loathsomeness of the object, (ii) constant meditation on loathsomeness, (iii) sense-restraint, (iv) moderation in food, (v) good friendship, and (vi) profitable talk.

2. *Vyāpāda* is illwill or aversion. A desirable object leads to attachment, while an undesirable one leads to aversion. These are the two great fires that burn the whole world. Aided by ignorance these two produce all sufferings in the world.

Illwill is inhibited by *Pīti* or joy which is one of the Jhāna factors. It is attenuated on attaining Sakadāgāmi and is eradicated on attaining Anāgāmi.

The following six conditions tend to the eradication of illwill. (i) perceiving the object with thoughts of goodwill, (ii) constant meditation on loving-kindness (*Mettā*), (iii) thinking that Kamma is one's own, (iv) adherence to that view, (v) good friendship, and (vi) profitable talk.

3. *Thīna* or Sloth is explained as a morbid state of the mind, and *Middha* as a morbid state of the mental states. A stolid mind is as "inert as a bat hanging to a tree, or as molasses cleaving to a stick, or as a lump of butter too stiff for

spreading". Sloth and torpor should not be understood as bodily drowsiness, because Arahants, who have destroyed these two states, also experience bodily fatigue. These two promote mental inertness and are opposed to strenuous effort (*Viriya*). They are inhibited by the Jhāna factor (*Vitakka* or Initial Application, and are eradicated on attaining Arahantship.

The following six conditions tend to the eradication of Sloth and Torpor: (i) reflection on the object of moderation in food, (ii) changing of bodily postures, (iii) contemplation on the object of light; (iv) living in the open, (v) good friendship and (vi) profitable talk.

Uddhacca is mental restlessness or excitement of the mind. It is a mental state associated with all types of immoral consciousness. As a rule an evil is done with some excitement or restlessness.

Kukkucca is worry. It is either repentance over the committed evil or over the unfulfilled good. Repentance over one's evil does not exempt one from its inevitable consequences. The best repentance is the will not to repeat that evil.

Both these hindrances are inhibited by the Jhāna factor, *Sukha* or happiness. Restlessness is eradicated on attaining Arahantship, and worry is eradicated on attaining Anāgāmi.

The following six conditions tend to the eradication of these two states: (i) erudition or learning, (ii) questioning or discussion, (iii) understanding the nature of the *Vinaya* discipline, (iv) association with senior monks, (v) good friendship and (vi) profitable talk.

5. *Vicikicchā* is doubt or indecision. That which is devoid of the remedy of wisdom is *vicikicchā* (*vi-* = devoid; *cikicchā* = wisdom). It is also explained as vexation due to perplexed thinking (*vici* = seeking; *kicchā* = vexation).

Here it is not used in the sense of doubt with regard to the Buddha etc., for even non-Buddhists inhibit *vicikicchā* and gain *Jhānas*. As a Fetter *vicikicchā* is that doubt about Buddha etc., but as a Hindrance it denotes unsteadiness in one particular thing that is being done. The commentarial explanation of *vicikicchā* is the inability to decide anything definitely that it is so. In other words it is indecision.

This state is inhibited by the *Jhāna* factor-*Vicāra*, Sustained Application. It is eradicated on attaining *Sotāpatti*.

The following six conditions tend to its eradication: (i) knowledge of the Dhamma and *Vinaya*, (ii) discussion or questioning, (iii) understanding of the nature of the *Vinaya Discipline*, (iv) excessive confidence, (v) good friendship, and (vi) profitable talk.

CHAPTER 38

THE WAY TO NIBBĀNA

(III)

"Transient are all conditioned things,
Sorrowful are all conditioned things,
Soulless are all conditioned and non-conditioned.
                                    DHAMMAPADA*

Insight (*Vipassanā*)

When the Jhānas are developed by temporarily inhibiting the Hindrances (*Nīvarana*), the mind is so purified that it resembles a polished mirror, where everything is clearly reflected in true perspective. Still there is not complete freedom from unwholesome thoughts, for by concentration the evil tendencies are only temporarily inhibited. They may rise to the surface at quite unexpected moments.

Discipline regulates words and deeds; concentration controls the mind; but it is Insight (*paññā*), the third and the final stage, that enables the aspirant to Sainthood to eradicate wholly the defilements inhibited by Samādhi.

At the outset he cultivates 'Purity of Vision' (*ditthi visuddhi*)[1] in order to see things as they truly are. With one-pointed mind he analyses and examines this so-called being. This searching examination shows what he has called "I",

---

1. The third stage of the Path of Purity.

personality, to be merely a complex compound of mind and matter which are in a state of constant flux.

Having thus gained a correct view of the real nature of this so-called being, freed from the false notion of a permanent soul, he searches for the causes of this "I" personality. He realizes that there is nothing in the world but is conditioned by some cause or causes, past or present, and that his present existence is due to past ignorance (*avijjā*), craving (*taṇhā*) grasping (*upādāna*), Kamma, and physical food of the present life. On account of these five causes this so-called being has arisen, and as past causes have conditioned the present, so the present will condition the future. Meditating thus, he transcends all doubts with regard to past, present and future.[1]

Thereupon he contemplates the truth that all conditioned things are transient (*anicca*), subject to suffering (*dukkha*), and devoid of an immortal soul (*anatta*). Wherever he turns his eyes he sees naught but these three characteristics standing out in bold relief. He realizes that life is a mere flux conditioned by internal and external causes. Nowhere does he find any genuine happiness, for everything is fleeting.

As he thus contemplates the real nature of life and is absorbed in meditation, a day comes

---

1. *Kaṅkhāvitaraṇavisuddhi,* the fourth stage of the Path of Purity.

when, to his surprise, he witnesses an aura (*obhāsa*) emitted by his body. He experiences an unprecedented pleasure, happiness, and quietude. He becomes even-minded, religious fervour increases, mindfulness becomes clear and insight keen. Mistaking this advanced state of moral progress for Sainthood, chiefly owing to the presence of the aura, he develops a liking for this mental state. Soon the realization comes that these new developments are impediments to moral progress, and he cultivates the purity of knowledge with regard to the Path and Not-Path.

Perceiving the right path, he resumes his meditation on the arising (*udaya ñāṇa*) and passing away (*vaya ñāṇa*) of all conditioned things. Of these two states the latter becomes more impressed on his mind since change is more conspicuous than becoming. Therefore he directs his attention to contemplation of the dissolution of things (*bhaṅga ñāṇa*). He perceives that both mind and matter which constitute this so-called being are in a state of constant flux, not remaining for two consecutive moments the same. To him then comes the knowledge that all dissolving things are fearful (*bhaya ñāṇa*). The whole world appears to him as a pit of burning embers—a source of danger. Subsequently he reflects on the wretchedness and vanity (*ādīnava ñāṇa*) of the fearful and deluded

---

1. *Maggāmaggañāṇadassanavisuddhi*, the fifth stage of the Path of Purity.

world, and gets a feeling of disgust (*nibbidā ñāṇa*) followed by a strong will for deliverance from it (*muñcitukamyatā ñāṇa*).

With this object in view, he resumes his meditations on the three characteristics of transiency, sorrow, and soullessness (*patisaṅkhā ñāṇa*). and thereafter develops complete equanimity towards all conditioned things—having neither attachment nor aversion for any worldly object (*upekkhā ñāṇa*)[1]

Reaching this point of spiritual culture, he chooses one of the three characteristics for his object of special endeavour and intently cultivates insight in that particular direction until the glorious day when he first realizes Nibbāna[2], his ultimate goal.

"As the traveller by night sees the landscape around him by a flash of lightning and the picture so obtained swims long thereafter before his dazzled eyes, so the individual seeker, by the flashing light of insight, glimpses Nibbāna with

---

1. These nine kinds of insight-namely, *udaya, vaya, bhaṅga, bhaya, ādīnava, nibbidā, muñcitukamyatā, paṭisaṁkhā,* and *upekkhā, ñāṇas* are collectively termed *Paṭipadāñāṇadassanavisuddhi*—Purity of vision as regards knowledge of progress, the sixth stage of the Path of Purity.

2. Insight found in this supramundane Path Consciousness is known as *Nāṇadassana visuddhi*—Purity of Vision which is Knowledge, the seventh member of the Path of Purity.

such clearness that the after-picture never more fades from his mind.[1]"

When the spiritual pilgrim realizes Nibbāna for the first time, he is called a *Sotāpanna*, one who has entered the stream that leads to Nibbāna for the first time.

The stream represents the noble Eightfold Path.

A Stream-Winner is no more a worldling (*puthujjana*), but an Ariya (Noble).

On attaining this first stage of Sainthood, he eradicates the following three Fetters (*saṁyojana*) that bind him to existence—namely,

i *Sakkāya—diṭṭhi* = *sati* + *kāye* + *diṭṭhi*–literally, view, when a group or compound exists. Here *kāya* refers to the five Aggregates of matter, feeling, perception, mental states, and consciousness. The view that there exists an unchanging entity, a permanent soul, when there is a complex-compound of psycho-physical aggregates, is termed *sakkāyadiṭṭhi*. Dhammasangani enumerates twenty kinds of such soul-theories.[2] *Sakkāya-diṭṭhi* is usually rendered as self-illusion, theory of individuality, or illusion of individualism.

---

1. Dr. Dahlke.
2. See Dhammasangani Translation, p. 259.

ii *Vicikicchā*-Doubts. They are doubts about
(i) the Buddha, (ii) the Dhamma, (iii) the
Sangha, (iv) the disciplinary rules (*sikkhā*),
(v) the past, (vi) the future, (vii) both the
past and the future, and (viii) Dependent
Origination (*Paṭicca-Samuppāda*).

iii *Sīlabbataparāmāsa*—Adherence to (wrongful) rites and ceremonies.

Dhammasangani explains it thus: "It is the
theory held by ascetics and brahmins outside this
doctrine that purification is obtained by rules of
moral conduct, or by rites, or by both rules of
moral conduct and rites."[1]

For the eradication of the remaining seven
Fetters a *Sotāpanna* is reborn seven times at the
most. He gains implicit confidence in the Buddha,
the Dhamma, and the Sangha. He would not for
any reason violate any of the five precepts. He
is not subject to rebirth in states of woe as he is
destined to Enlightenment.

With fresh courage as a result of this distant
glimpse of Nibbāna, the noble pilgrim makes a
rapid progress, and perfecting his insight becomes
a *Sakadāgāmi* (Once-Returner), the second stage of
Sainthood, by attenuating two other Fetters—namely, sense-desires (*kāmarāga*) and illwill (*paṭigha*.)

Now he is called a Once-Returner because he
is born in the human realm only once, should he

---

1. Section, 1005.

not attain Arahantship in that birth itself. It is interesting to note that the Ariya Saint who has attained the second stage of Sainthood can only weaken these two powerful Fetters with which he is bound from a beginningless past. At times, though to a slight extent, he may harbour thoughts of lust and anger.

It is by attaining the third stage of Sainthood, that of the *Anāgāmi* (Never-Returner), that he completely eradicates those two Fetters. Thereafter he neither returns to this world nor is he born in the celestial realms, since he has rooted out the desire for sensual gratification. After death he is reborn in the Pure Abodes (*Suddhāvāsa*), an environment reserved for Anāgāmis. There he attains Arahantship and lives till the end of his life.

When a layman becomes an Anāgāmi, he leads a celibate life.

The Anāgāmi Saint now makes his final advance and destroying the remaining five Fetters— namely, attachment to Realms of Form (*rūparāga*), attachment to Formless Realms (*arūparāga*), pride (*māna*), restlessness (*uddhacca*), and ignorance (*avijjā*)—attains Arahantship, the final stage of *Sainthood*.

Stream-Winners, Once-Returners, Never-Returners are called *Sekhas* because they have yet to undergo a training. Arahants are called *Asekhas* (Adepts) because they no more undergo any training.

An Arahant, literally, a Worthy One, is not subject to rebirth because he does not accumulate fresh Kammic activities. The seeds of his reproduction have all been destroyed.

The Arahant realizes that what was to be accomplished has been done, a heavy burden of sorrow has finally been relinquished, and all forms of craving and all shades or ignorance are totally annihilated. The happy pilgrim now stands on heights more than celestial, far removed from uncontrolled passions and the defilements of the world, experiencing the unutterable bliss of Nibbāna.

Rebirth can no longer affect him since no more reproductive seeds are formed by fresh kammic activities.

Though an Arahant he is not wholly free from physical suffering, as this experience of the bliss of Deliverance is only intermittent nor has he yet cast off his material body.

An Arahant is called an *Asekha*, one who does not undergo training, as he has lived the Holy Life and has accomplished his object. The other Saints from the *Sotāpatti* stage to the Arahant Path Stage are called *Sekhas* because they still undergo training.

It may be mentioned in this connection that Anāgāmis and Arahants who have developed the Rūpa and Arūpa Jhānas could experience the Nibbānic bliss uninterruptedly for as long as seven days even in this life. This, in Pāli, is known as *Nirodha-Samāpatti.*[1]   An Ariya, in this state, is wholly free from pain, and his mental activities are all suspended.   His stream of consciousness temporarily ceases to flow.

With regard to the difference between one who has attained *Nirodha-Samāpatti* and a dead man, the *Visuddhi Magga* states: "In the corpse, not only are the plastic forces of the body (i.e., respiration), speech and mind stilled and quiescent, but also vitality is exhausted, heat is quenched, and the faculties of sense broken up, whereas in the Bhikkhu in ecstasy vitality persists, heart abides, and the faculties are clear, although respiration, observation, and perception are stilled and quiescent."[2]

According to Buddhism, in conventional terms, this is the highest form of bliss possible in this life.

Why does an Arahant continue to live when he has already attained Nibbāna?

It is because the Kammic force which produced his birth is still not spent.   To quote Schopenhauer, it is like the potter's wheel from which the hand of the potter has been lifted, or, to cite a better illustration from our own books—an Arahant is like a branch that is severed from the tree. It puts forth no more fresh leaves, flowers and fruits, as it is no longer supported by the sap of the tree.

---

1. Literally, 'attainment to cessation.'
   See *A Manual of Abhidhamma* by Nārada Thera pp. 227,435.
2. *The Path of Purity*, part ii, p. 872.

Those which already existed however last till the death of that particular branch.

The Arahant lives out his life-span adding no more fresh Kamma to his store, and utterly indifferent to death.

Like Venerable Sāriputta he would say:

"*Not fain am I to die nor yet to live.*
I shall lay down this mortal frame anon
With mind alert, with consciousness controlled.
With thought of death I dally not, nor yet
Delight in living. I await the hour
Like any hireling who hath done his task.[1]"

What happens to the Arahant after his passing away?

As a flame blown to and fro by the wind goes out and cannot be registered, so says the Buddha, an Arahant, set free from mind and matter, has disappeared and cannot be registered.

Has such an Arahant then merely disappeared, or does he indeed no longer exist?

For him who has disappeared, states the Sutta Nipāta, there exists no form by which they could say, 'he is'. When all conditions are cut off, all matter for discussion is also cut off.

The *Udāna*, explains this intricate point thus:

"*As the fiery sparks from a forge are one by one extinguished.*
And no one knows where they have gone—
So it is with those who have attained to complete emancipation,

---

1. *Psalms of the Brethren*, p. 346.

Who have crossed the flood of desire,
Who have entered the calm delight, of those no
trace remains."[1]

The Majjhima Nikāya also relates an interesting discussion between the Buddha and Vacchagotta concerning this very question.[2]

Vacchagotta, a wandering ascetic, approached the Buddha and questioned.:

"But, Gotama, where is the Bhikkhu who is delivered of mind reborn?

He was of course referring to the Arahant.

The Buddha replied:—"Vaccha, to say that he is reborn would not fit the case.

"Then, Gotama, he is not reborn.

"Vaccha, to say that he is not reborn would not fit the case.

"Then, Gotama, he is both reborn and not reborn.

"Vaccha, to say that he is both reborn and not reborn would not fit the case.

"Then, Gotama, he is neither reborn nor not reborn.

"Vaccha, to say that he is neither reborn nor not reborn would not fit the case.

Vaccha was baffled on hearing these seemingly inconsistent answers, and, in his confusion, exclaimed:

"Gotama, I am at a loss to think in this matter, and I have become greatly confused.

"Enough, O Vaccha. Be not at a loss to think in this matter, and be not greatly confused. Profound, O Vaccha, is this doctrine, recondite and difficult of comprehension, good,

---

1. See Woodward, *Verses of Uplift,* p. 114.
2. *Aggivacchagotta Sutta,* No. 72.

excellent, and not to be reached by mere reasoning, subtle and intelligible only to the wise and it is a hard doctrine for you to learn, who belong to another sect, to another faith, to another persuasion, to another discipline, and who sit at the feet of another teacher. Therefore, O Vaccha, I shall now question you, and do you make answer as may seem to you good. What think you, Vaccha? Suppose a fire were to burn in front of you, would you be aware that fire was burning in front of you?

"Gotama, if a fire were to burn in front of me, I should be aware that a fire was burning in front of me.

"But suppose, Vaccha, someone were to ask you: 'On what does this fire that is burning in front of you depend?' What would you answer, Vaccha?

"I would answer, O Gotama, "it is on fuel of grass and wood that this fire burning in front of me depends.'

"But Vaccha, if the fire in front of you were to become extinct, would you be aware that the fire in front of you had become extinct?

"Gotama, if the fire in front of me were to become extinct, I should be aware that the fire in front of me had become extinct.

"But, Vaccha, if someone were to ask you—'In what direction has that fire gone, East or West, North or South?' What would you say, Vaccha?

"The question would not fit the case, Gotama, for the fire depended on fuel of grass and wood, and when that fuel has all gone, and it can get no other, being thus without nutriment, it is said to be extinct.

"In exactly the same way, Vaccha, all forms, sensations, perceptions, mental activities, and consciousness have been abandoned, uprooted, made like a palmyra stump, become extinct, and not liable to spring up in the future.

"The Saint, O Vaccha, who has been released from what are styled the Five Aggregates, is deep, immeasurable like the mighty ocean. To say that he is reborn would not fit the case. To say that he is not reborn would not fit the case. To say that he is neither reborn nor not reborn would not fit the case."

One cannot say that the Arahant is reborn as all passions that condition rebirth are eradicated, nor can one say that the Arahant is annihilated, for there is nothing to annihilate.

Robert Oppenheimer, a scientist, writes:—

"If we ask, for instance, whether the position of the electron remains the same, we must say 'no', if we ask whether the electron's position changes with time, we must say 'no'; if we ask whether it is in motion, we must say 'no.'

"The Buddha has given such answers when interrogated as to the condition of man's self after death.[1] But they are not familiar answers from the tradition of the 17th and 18th century science."

Nibbāna, it may safely be concluded, is obtained by the complete cessation of the defilements (*kilesa*), but the real nature of this Supreme State (Dhamma) cannot be expressed in words.

From a metaphysical standpoint Nibbāna is complete deliverance from suffering. From a psychological standpoint Nibbāna is the eradication of egoism. From an ethical standpoint Nibbāna is the destruction of lust, hatred and ignorance.

---

1. Evidently the writer is referring to the state of an Arahant after death.

CHAPTER 39

THE STATE OF AN ARAHANT

"Though little he recites the Sacred Texts, but acts in accordance with the teaching, forsaking lust, hatred and ignorance, truly knowing, with mind well freed, clinging to naught here and hereafter, he shares the fruits of the Holy Life."

DHAMMAPADA.

The Tipitaka abounds with interesting and self-elevating sayings that describe the peaceful and happy state of an Arahant, who abides in the world, till the end of his life, serving other seekers of truth by example and by precept.

In the Dhammapada the Buddha states:

For him who has completed the journey,[1] for him who is sorrowless,[2] for him who from everything[3] is wholly free, for him who has destroyed all Ties,[4] the fever (of passion) exists not.[5] 90.

---

1. Of life in the round of existence, i.e., an Arahant.
2. One gives up sorrow by attaining Anāgāmi, the third stage of Sainthood. It is at this stage one eradicates completely attachment to sense-desires and illwill or aversion.
3. *Sabbadhi,* the five Aggregates etc.
4. There are four kinds of *ganthas* (Ties)—namely,
   1. covetousness (*abhijjhā*), 2. ill-will (*vyāpāda*), 3. indulgence in (wrongful) rites and ceremonies (*sīlabbataparāmāsa*), and 4. adherence to one's preconceptions as truth (*idaṁ saccābhinivesa*).
5. This verse refers to the ethical state of an Arahant. Heat is both physical and mental. An Arahant experiences bodily heat as long as he is alive, but is not thereby worried. Mental heat of passions he experiences not.

The mindful exert themselves. To no abode
are they attached. Like swans that quit their
pools, home after home they abandon (and go).[1] 91.

They for whom there is no accumulation,[2]
who reflect well over their food,[3] who have Deliverance,[4] which is Void and Signless, as their
object, their course like that of birds in the air
cannot be traced.   92.

He whose corruptions are destroyed, he who
is not attached to food, he who has Deliverance,
which is Void and Signless, as his object, his path,
like that of birds in the air, cannot he traced. 93.

---

1. Arahants wander whithersoever they like without any
    attachment to any particular place as they are free from
    the conception of "I" and "mine".
2. There are two kinds of accumulation—namely, kammic
    activities and the four necessaries of life.
    The former tend to prolong life in Saṁsāra and the
    latter, though essential, may prove an obstacle to spiri-
    tual progress,
3. To get rid of the desire for food.
4. Nibbāna is Deliverance from suffering (vimokkha). It
    is called Void because it is void of lust, hatred and ig-
    norance, not because it is nothingness or annihilation.
    Nibbāna is a positive supramundane state which cannot
    be expressed in mundane words. It is Signless because
    it is free from the signs of lust etc. Arahants experience
    Nibbānic bliss while alive. It is not correct to say that
    Arahants exist after death, or do not exist after death,
    for Nibbāna is neither eternalism nor nihilism. In
    Nibbāna nothing is eternalized nor is anything, except
    passions, annihilated.
    Arahants experience Nibbānic bliss by attaining to the
    fruit of Arahantship in this life itself.

He whose senses are subdued, like steeds well
trained by a charioteer, he whose pride is destroyed
and is free from the corruptions,— such a steadfast one even the gods hold dear.   94.

Like the earth, a balanced and well-disciplined
person resents not. He is comparable to an Inda-
khīla.¹ Like a pool, unsullied by mud, is he, —to
such a balanced one² life's wanderings do not
arise.³   95.

Calm is his mind, calm is his speech, calm is
his action, who, rightly knowing, is wholly freed⁴
perfectly peaceful,⁵ and equipoised.   96.

---

1. By indakhīla is meant either a column as firm and high
   as that of Sakka's or the chief column that stands at the
   entrance to a city.

   Commentators state that these indakhīlas are firm posts
   which are erected either inside or outside the city as
   an embellishment. Usually they are made of bricks
   or of durable wood and are octagonal in shape. Half
   of the post is embedded in the earth. hence the metaphor as firm and steady as an indakhīla.

2. *Tādi* is one who has neither attachment to desirable
   objects nor aversion to undesirable objects. Nor does
   he cling to anything. Amidst the eight worldly conditions—gain and loss, fame and infamy, blame and praise,
   happiness and pain—an Arahant remains unperturbed,
   manifesting neither attachment nor aversion, neither
   elation nor depression.

3. As they are not subject to birth and death.

4. From all defilements.

5. Since his mind is absolutely pure.

The[1] man who is not credulous,[2] who understands the Uncreate[3] (*Nibbāna*), who has cut off
the links,[4] who has put an end to occasion[5] (of
good and evil), who has eschewed[6] all desires[7] he,
indeed, is a supreme man. 97.

Whether in village or in forest, in vale or on
hill,[8] wherever Arahants dwell, delightful, indeed,
is that spot. 98.

Delightful are the forests where worldlings
delight not; the passionless[9] will rejoice (therein),
(for) they seek no sensual pleasures. 99.

Ah, happily do we live without hate amongst
the hateful; amidst hateful men we dwell un-
hating. 197.

---

1. The pun in the original Pāli is lost in the translation.
2. *Assaddho*—lit., unfaithful. He does not merely accept
   from other sources because he himself knows from
   personal experience.
3. *Akata*, Nibbāna. It is so called because it is not created
   by anyone. *Akataññū* can also be interpreted as ungrateful.
4. The links of existence and rebirth. *Sandhicchedo* also
   means a house-breaker that is, a burglar.
5. *Hata+avakāso* = he who has destroyed the opportunity
6. *Vanta+āso* = he who eats vomit is another meaning.
7. By means of the four paths of Sainthood. Gross forms
   of desire are eradicated at the first three stages, the
   subtle forms at the last stage.
8. *Ninna* and *thala*, lit., low-lying and elevated grounds.
9. The passionless Arahants rejoice in secluded forests
   which have no attraction for worldlings.

Ah, happily do we live in good health¹ amongst the ailing; amidst ailing men we dwell in good health.   198.

Ah, happily do we live without yearning (for sensual pleasures) amongst those who yearn (for them); amidst those who yearn (for them) we dwell without yearning.   199.

Ah, happily do we live, we who have no impediments.² Feeders of joy shall we be even as the gods of the Radiant Realm.   200.

For whom there exists neither the hither³ nor the farther shore,⁴ nor both the hither and the farther shore, he who is undistressed and unbound⁵ —him I call a brāhmaṇa.   385.

He who is meditative,⁶ stainless and secluded,⁷ he who has done his duty and is free from corruptions,⁸ he who has attained the Highest Goal⁹, him I call a brāhmaṇa.   386.

---

1. Free from the disease of passions.
2. *Kiñcana*, such as lust, hatred, and delusion which are hindrances to spiritual progress.
3. *Pāraṁ* the six personal sense-fields.
4. *Apāraṁ* the six external sense-fields.
5. Not grasping anything as "me" and "mine."
6. He who practises concentration (*samatha*) and insight (*vipassanā*).
7. *Āsīnaṁ*, living alone in the forest.
8. By realizing the four Truths and eradicating the fetters.
9. That is, Nibbāna.

He that does no evil through body, speech, or mind, who is restrained in these three respects,— him I call a brāhmaṇa. 391.

He who has cut off all fetters, who trembles not, who has gone beyond ties, who is unbound,— him I call a brāhmaṇa. 397.

He who has cut the strap (hatred), the thong (craving), and the rope (heresies), together with the appendages (latent tendencies), who has thrown up the cross-bar (ignorance), who is en-lightened[1] (Buddha),— him I call a brāhmaṇa. 398.

He who, without anger, endures reproach, flogg-ing and punishments, whose power—the potent army—is patience,—him I call a brāhmaṇa. 399.

He who is not wrathful, but is dutiful,[2] virtuous, free from craving, self-controlled and bears his final body,[3]—him I call a brāhmaṇa. 400.

Like water on a lotus leaf, like a mustard seed on the point of a needle, he who clings not to sensual pleasures,—him I call a brāhmaṇa. 401.

He who realizes here in this world the destruc-tion of his sorrow, who has laid the burden[4]

---

1. Who has understood the four Noble Truths.
2.. Devoted to religious austerity.
3. Because he, having destroyed the passions, would be reborn no more.
4. The burden of the Aggregates.

aside and is emancipated,—him I call a brāhmaṇa.
402.

He whose knowledge is deep, who is wise,
who is skilled in the right and wrong way,[1] who
has reached the highest goal,—him I call a brāh-
maṇa.   403.

He who is not intimate either with householders or with the homeless ones, who wanders
without an abode, who is without desires,—him I
call a brāhmaṇa.   404.

He who has laid aside the cudgel in his dealings with beings,[2] whether feeble or strong, who
neither harms nor kills,—him I call a brāhmaṇa.
405.

He who is friendly amongst the hostile, who
is peaceful amongst the violent, who is unattached
amongst the attached,[3]—him I call a brāhmaṇa. 406.

In whom lust, hatred, pride, and detraction are
fallen off like a mustard seed from the point of a
needle,—him I call a brāhmaṇa.   407.

He who utters gentle, instructive, true words,
who by his speech gives offence to none,—him I
call a brāhamaṇa.   408.

He who has no desires, whether pertaining to

---

1. Who knows the way to the woeful states, to the blissful
   states, and to Nibbāna.
2. Literally, towards beings.
3. Those who are attached to the Aggregates.

this world or to the next, who is desireless and
emancipated,—him I call a brāhmaṇa.   410.

Herein he who has transcended both good and
bad and the ties[1] as well, who is sorrowless,
stainless, and pure,—him I call a brāhmaṇa.   412.

He who is spotless as the moon, who is pure,
serene, and unperturbed, who has destroyed craving for becoming,—him I call a brāhmaṇa.   413.

He who, discarding human ties and transcending
celestial ties, is completely delivered from all
ties,—him I call a brāhmaṇa.   417.

He who has given up likes[3] and dislikes,[4] who
is cooled and is without defilements,[5] who has
conquered the world,[6] and is strenuous,—him I
call a brāhmaṇa.   418.

He who has no clinging to aggregates that are
past, future, or present, who is without clinging
and grasping,—him I call a brāhmaṇa,   421.

The fearless,[7] the noble, the hero, the great

---

1. Lust, hatred, delusion, pride and false views.
2. Undisturbed by defilements.
3. That is, attachment to sense-desires.
4. *Arati* = dislike for forest life (commentary).
5. *Upadhi*. There are four kinds of *upadhi*,—namely, the aggregates (*khandha*), the passions (*kilesa*), volitional activities (*abhisaṁkhāra*), and sense-desires (*kāma*).
6. That is, the world of Aggregates
7. *Usabhaṁ,* fearless as a bull.

sage,[1] the conqueror,[2] the desireless, the cleanser[3] (of defilements), the enlightened,[4]—him I call a brāhmaṇa.   422.

That sage who knows his former abodes, who sees the blissful[5] and the woeful states,[6] who has reached the end of births,[7] who, with superior wisdom, has perfected himself[8] who has completed[9] (the holy life), and reached the end of all passions,—him I call a brāhmaṇa.   423.

---

1. *Mahesiṁ*, seeker of higher morality, concentration, and wisdom.
2. *Vijitāvinaṁ*, the conqueror of passions.
3. *Nahātakaṁ*, he who has washed away all impurities.
4. *Buddhaṁ*, he who has understood the four Noble Truths.
5. *Sagga*, the six heavenly Realms, the sixteen Rūpa Realms, and the four Arūpa Realms.
6. *Apāya* the four woeful states.
7. *Jātikkhayaṁ*, i.e. Arahantship.
8. *Abhiññāvosito*, i.e., reached the culmination by comprehending that which should be comprehended, by discarding that which should be discarded, by realizing that which should be realized, and by developing that which should be developed (commentary).
9. *Sabbavositavosānaṁ*, i.e., having lived the Holy Life which culminates in wisdom pertaining to the Path of Arahantship, the end of all passions.

CHAPTER 40

THE BODHISATTA IDEAL

"This body of flesh and blood I bear
Just for the world's good and welfare."

SRI SANGABODHI

In the teachings of the Buddha, for the realization of the ultimate Goal, there are three modes of Enlightenment (*Bodhi*) one of which an aspirant may choose in accordance with his particular temperament. They are *Sāvaka*[1] *Bodhi, Pacceka-Bodhi* and the *Sammā-Sambodhi*.

Sāvaka-Bodhi is the Enlightenment of a disciple. This is known as the Arahant[2] ideal. He who aspires to become an Arahant usually seeks the guidance of a superior enlightened instructor. A slight indication from an understanding teacher would alone be sufficient for a morally advanced aspirant to progress on the upward path of Enlightenment. Venerable Sāriputta, for instance, attained the first stage of Sainthood, hearing only half a stanza from the Arahant Assaji. The sorrow-afflicted Paṭācāra, who lost all those dear to her under tragic circumstances, attained Arahantship by watching the water that washed her feet. The child-like Kisāgotamī who implored

---

1. Literally, a hearer.
2. Literally, a Worthy or Passionless One.

the Buddha for a cure for her dead infant, attained
Sainthood by watching a lamp that was being
extinguished.   Cūla Panthaka, who could . not
memorize a verse for four months, attained Arahantship by meditating on impermanence while
handling a clean piece of white cloth in his hand,
gazing at the sun.

After achieving his goal, an Arahant devotes
the remainder of his life to serving other seekers of
peace by example and by precept.   First he purifies himself, and then he tries to purify others by
expounding to them the teachings which he
himself has followed.   An Arahant is more
qualified to teach the Dhamma than ordinary
worldling teachers, who have no realization of
Truth, since he speaks from personal experience.

There is nothing selfish in the noble ideal of
Arahantship, for Arahantship is gained only by
eradicating all forms of selfishness.   Self-illusion
and Egoism are some of the fetters that have to
be discarded in order to attain Arahantship.   The
wise men and women who lived in the time of the
Buddha, and others later, benefited by the golden
opportunity offered by Him to gain their enlightenment in this present life itself.

Pacceka-Bodhi is the independent Enlightenment of a highly evolved person who achieves his
goal by his own efforts without seeking any
external aid.   Such a holy person is termed a
Pacceka (Private) Buddha because he lacks the

power to purify and serve others by expounding
the Dhamma which he himself has discovered.
Nevertheless he teaches morality.

Pacceka Buddhas arise only during those
periods when the Teaching does not exist. Their
number is not limited only to one at a particular
time as in the case of Sammā-Sambuddhas.
Although the Buddha Gotama of the present era
has passed away we are still living in a Buddha-
cycle, for the Teaching still exists in its pristine
purity. Accordingly no Pacceka Buddhas arise
during this period. In the Khaggavisāna Sutta of
the Sutta Nipāta are treasured some beautiful
sayings of Pacceka Buddhas. A few of their wise
utterances are quoted below:—

1. Leaving aside the cudgel towards all beings,
harming none of them, let him not yearn for sons
or friends, but wander alone like a rhinocerous.

2. Affection arises from intimacy, and sorrow
results thereby. Realizing the evil born of affection wander alone like a rhinocerous.

3. We certainly praise the value of comrade-
ship. One should associate with superiors or
equals. Failing them, lead a blameless life and
wander alone like a rhinocerous.

4. Variegated, sweet, and enchanting are sensual pleasures. In diverse forms they seduce the
heart. Recognizing their menace, wander alone
like a rhinocerous.

5.   Cold and heat, hunger, thirst, wind, sun,
mosquitoes and snakes—overcome them all, and
wander alone like a rhinocerous.

6.   Like a lion that does not tremble at every
sound, like the wind that does not cling to the
meshes of a net, like the lotus that is unsoiled by
the mud, wander alone like a rhinocerous.

7.   In due season cultivate loving-kindness,
equanimity, compassion, release, appreciative joy,
and unthwarted by the world, wander alone like
a rhinocerous.

*   *   *

Sammā-Sambodhi is the supreme Enlightenment
of a most developed, most compassionate, most
loving, all-knowing perfect being.   He who attains
this Bodhi is called a *Sammā-Sambuddha*, literally,
a fully self-enlightened One.   He is so called
because he not only comprehends the Dhamma by
his own efforts and wisdom but also expounds the
doctrine to seekers of truth to purify and save
them from this ever-recurring cycle of birth and
death.   Unlike the Private Buddhas, only one Supreme Buddha arises at a particular time, just as on
certain trees one flower alone blooms.

He who aspires to attain Sammā-Sambuddha-
hood is called a Bodhisatta.   This Bodhisatta ideal
is the most refined and the most beautiful that
could ever, in this ego-centric world, be conceived

for what is nobler than a life of service and purity?

Those who, in the course of their wanderings in Saṁsāra, wish to serve others and reach ultimate perfection, are free to pursue the Bodhisatta ideal, but there is no compulsion that all must strive to attain Buddhahood, which, to say the least, is practically impossible. Critics who contend that the Bodhisatta ideal was evolved to counteract the tendency to a cloistered, placid and inert monastic life, only reveal ignorance of the pure Buddha-Dhamma.

The Abhisamayālankāra-Āloka, a later Saṁskrit work, a sub-commentary to the Prajnā Pāramitā, states:—

"The great disciples (Srāvakas), having attained the two kinds of Enlightenment (i.e., of the Srāvaka proper and the Pratyeka Buddha) with and without residue, remain with their *minds full of fear,* since they are deprived of great compassion and highest wisdom (*uru karuṇā prajnā vaikal-yena*) Owing to the cessation of the force of life, produced by the previous Biotic force, the attainment of Nirvāna becomes possible. But in reality (*the Hinayānist* saints) are possessed only of that seeming Nirvāna which is called the Nirvāna resembling an extinguished light. The births in the three spheres of existence have ceased, but, after their worldly existence has taken an end, the Arahants are born in the most pure sphere of Buddhist activity in the unaffected plane (*anāsravadhātu*), in state of perpetual trance and abiding within the petals of lotus flowers (*padmaphuṭesu jāyante*). Thereafter the Buddha Amitābhā and other Buddhas

resembling the sun arouse them in order to remove the
undefiled ignorance (*akilishṭa ñāṇa*). Thereupon the Arahants make their creative effort for Supreme Enlightenment
and, though they abide in a state of deliverance, they act (in
the phenomenal world) as if they were making a descent to
hell. And gradually, having accumulated all the factors for
the attainment of Enlightenment, they become teachers
of living beings (i.e., Buddhas)."

This is an absolutely fantastic view completely
foreign to the spirit of the original teachings of
the Buddha.

It is argued that Arahantship is selfish and that
all must strive to attain Buddhahood to save
others. Well, one might ask:—What is the object
of attaining Buddhahood? Is it to make others
attain Arahantship and save them? If so, the
logical conclusion is that Buddhahood itself fosters
selfishness which is absurd.

Buddhahood is indisputably the best and the
noblest of all the three ideals, but all are not
capable of achieving this highest ideal. Surely all
scientists cannot be Einsteins and Newtons.
There must also be lesser scientists who help the
world according to their capabilities.

The Pāli term Bodhisatta is composed of
Bodhi which means 'wisdom' or 'enlightenment',
and *Satta* which means 'devoted to' or 'intent on.'
A Bodhisatta, therefore, means one who is devoted
to, or intent on, wisdom or enlightenment. The
Saṁskritised form should be Bodhishakta but the
popular term is Bodhisattva which means 'wisdom being' or a being aspiring to become a Buddha.

This term is generally applied to anyone who is striving for Enlightenment, but, in the strictest sense of the term, should be applied only to those who are destined to become supremely Enlightened Ones.[1]

In one sense all are potential Buddhas, for Buddhahood is not the special prerogative of specially graced persons.

It should be noted that Buddhists do not believe that there lies dormant in us all a divine spark that needs development, for they deny the existence of a Creator, but they are conscious of the innate possibilities and the creative power of man.

Buddhism denies too the existence of a permanent soul that transmigrates from life to life, acquiring all experiences. Instead of an unchanging soul, the so-called essence of man, it posits a

---

1. Prof. Rhys Davids writes in his Buddhist Birth Stories (p. xxxiv):—"There is a religious romance called Barlaam and Joasaph, giving the history of an Indian prince who was converted by Barlaam and became a hermit. This history, the reader will be surprised to hear, is taken from the life of the Buddha; and Joasaph is merely the Buddha under another name, the word Joasaph, or, Josaphat, being simply a corruption of the word Bodisat." "Joasaph is in Arabic written also Yudasatf; and this, through a confusion between the Arabic letters Y and B, is for Bodisat". See *Encyclopaedia of Religion and Ethics,* vol. 6, p. 567.

dynamic life-flux where there is an identity in process.

As a man Prince *Siddhārta,* by his own will, wisdom and love, attained Buddhahood, the highest state of perfection any being could aspire to, and He revealed to mankind the only path that leads thereto. A singular characteristic of Buddhism is that anyone may aspire to the state of the teacher himself if only he makes the necessary exertion. The Buddha did not claim any monopoly of Buddhahood. It is not a sort of evolutionary process. It may be achieved by one's own effort without the help of another. The Buddha does not condemn men by calling them wretched sinners, but, on the contrary, encourages them saying that they are pure in heart at conception. Instead of disheartening followers, creating an inferiority complex, and reserving the exalted state of Buddha to Himself, He encourages them and inspires them to emulate Him.

A Bodhisatta need not necessarily be a Buddhist. We may find everloving Bodhisattas among Buddhists today, though they may be unaware of their lofty aspirations, and Bodhisattas may also be found among other religionists as well.

Three Types of Bodhisattas

According to Buddhism there are three types of Bodhisattas—namely, Intellectual Bodhisattas (*Paññādhika*). Devotional Bodhisattas (*Saddhā-*

dhika) and Energetic Bodhisattas (*Viriyādhika*). These three kinds of Bodhisattas correspond to *Nāna Yogi, Bhakti Yogi* and *Karma Yogi* of the Hindus.

Intellectual Bodhisattas are less devotional and more energetic; devotional ones are less energetic and more intellectual; energetic ones are less intellectual and more devotional. Seldom, if ever, are these three characteristics harmoniously combined in one person. The Buddha Gotama is cited as one of the intellectual group.

According to the Books the intellectual ones attain Buddhahood within a short period, devotional ones take a longer time, and energetic ones take longer still.

Intellectual Bodhisattas concentrate more on the development of wisdom and on the practice of meditation than on the observance of external forms of homage. They are always guided by reason and accept nothing on blind belief. They make no self-surrender, and are not slaves either to a book or to an individual. They prefer lonely meditation. With their silent but powerful thoughts of peace radiating from their solitary retreats they render moral help to suffering humanity.

The element of piety—*Saddhā* or Trustful Confidence—is predominant in the Devotional Bodhisattas. With *Saddhā* as their companion they achieve their goal.

These Bodhisattas take a keen interest in all forms of homage. The image of the Buddha is a great inspiration to them.

It should be understood that Buddhists do not worship an image. They pay homage to what it represents and reflect on the virtues of the Buddha. The more they think of the Buddha the more they love Him. This is the reason why Buddhism does not denounce these external forms of homage (*āmisa pūjā*) though undoubtedly practice (*paṭipatti pūjā*) is more commendable and indisputably superior. But dry intellect has to be flavoured with *Saddhā* (faith) to obtain satisfactory results. As excessive *Saddhā* might also sometimes be detrimental, it has to be restrained by wisdom.

The energetic ones always seek opportunities to be of service to others. Nothing gives them greater delight than active service. "For them work is happiness, and happiness is work." They are not happy unless they are active. As King *Sanghabodhi* of Sri Lanka said they "bear this body of flesh and blood for the good and happiness of the world." They live not only for themselves but for others as well.

This spirit of selfless service is one of the chief characteristics of all Bodhisattas.

With relentless energy they work not as slaves but as masters. They crave for neither fame nor name. They are interested only in service. It is immaterial to them whether others recognize their

selfless service or not. They are utterly indifferent
to praise or blame.

They forget themselves in their disinterested
service to others. They would sacrifice even life
itself could such action save another fellow-being.

A Bodhisatta who forgets himself in the service
of others should practise *Karuṇā* and *Mettā* (compassion and loving-kindness) to an exceptionally
high degree.

A Bodhisatta desires the good and welfare of
the world. He loves all beings as a mother loves
her only child. He identifies himself with all. To
him nothing gives more delight than to think that
all are his brothers and sisters. He is like a
mother, a father, a friend, a teacher, to all beings.

"The compassion of a Bodhisatta consists in
realizing the equality of oneself with others (*para-
ātma-samatā*) and also the substitution of others
for oneself (*para-ātma-parivartana*)." When he
does so he loses his I-notion and finds no difference
between himself and others. He returns good for
evil, and helps even unasked the very persons
who have wronged him, for he knows that "the
strength of a religious teacher is his patience."

"Being reviled, he reviles not; being beaten,
he beats not; being annoyed, he annoys not. His
forgiveness is unfailing even as the mother earth
suffers in silence all that may be done to her."

CHAPTER 41

PĀRAMI
—
PERFECTIONS
————

"Work for the welfare of others."

SUTTA NIPĀTA

There are ten transcendental virtues, which, in Pāli, are termed *Pāramī*[1] that every Bodhisatta practises in order to gain Supreme Enlightenment-Sammā-Sambuddhahood. They are Generosity (*Dāna*), Morality (*Sīla*), Renunciation (*Nekkhamma*), Wisdom (*Paññā*), Energy (*Viriya*), Patience (*Khanti*), Truthfulness (*Sacca*), Determination (*Adhiṭṭhāna*), Loving-Kindness (*Mettā*), and Equanimity (*Upekkhā*).

According to the Cariyā Pitaka Commentary, *Pāramī* are those virtues which are cultivated with compassion, guided by reason, uninfluenced by selfish motives, and unsullied by misbelief and all feelings of self-conceit.

The actions of a Bodhisatta are absolutely selfless, being prompted solely by compassion towards all beings. so boundless is his love and so pervasive is his infinite compassion that unceasingly throughout the series of his countless lives he strives to diminish suffering, to elevate to

---

1. *Pārami-Pāraṁ* beyond, i.e., Bodhi or Enlightenment + *i*, to go. Literally, it means that which enables one to go to the Further Shore.
   The Pāli term *Pāramitā* is also used in the same sense.

greater honour the poor and the lowly, and to help the needy in every possible way.

He seeks no delight in self-indulgence while his less fortunate brethren and sisters are steeped in misery. To alleviate suffering he would not hesitate to sacrifice his most cherished possessions —not excepting life itself as illustrated in the story in the Vyāghri-Jātaka.

With heart full of compassion he works for the weal and happiness of all beings; though always guided by reason. He is generously endowed with all the essential qualities of both head and heart in their full development which are dedicated to the service of the world at large.

In serving others a Bodhisatta is not actuated by a desire for power or worldly possessions. Knowing as he does that fame comes unsought to him who is worthy of it, why should he pursue it?

He is completely altruistic in his motives and egoism plays no part in his disinterested activities.

"Let laymen and monks both think that this was done by myself. In every work great or small, let them refer to me. Such is the aspiration of the fool. His desires and pride increase.'", states the Dhammapada. Such narrow and selfish aspirations do not enter into the mind of a Bodhisatta.

*   *   *

Dāna

Dāna or Generosity is the first Pāramī. It con-

---

1. V. 74.

fers upon the giver the double blessing of inhibiting immoral thoughts of selfishness, while developing pure thoughts of selflessness. "It blesseth him that gives and him that takes."

A Bodhisatta is not concerned as to whether the recipient is truly in need or not, for his one object in practising generosity, as he does, is to eliminate craving that lies dormant within himself. The joy of service, its attendant happiness, and the alleviation of suffering are other blessings of generosity.

In extending his love with supernormal generosity, he makes no distinction between one being and another, but he uses judicious discrimination in this generosity. If, for instance, a drunkard were to seek his help, and, if he were convinced that the drunkard would misuse his gift, the Bodhisatta without hesitation would refuse it, for such misplaced generosity would not constitute a Pārami.

Should anyone seek his help for a worthy purpose, then instead of assuming a forced air of dignity or making false pretensions, he would simply express his deep obligation for the opportunity afforded, and willingly and humbly render every possible aid. Yet, he would never set it down to his own credit as a favour conferred upon another, nor would he ever regard the man as his debtor for the service rendered. He is interested only in the good act, but in nothing else springing from it. He expects no reward in return, nor even does he crave enhancement of reputation from it.

A Bodhisatta, though always ready to confer a favour, seldom, if ever, stoops to ask one. The Brahma Jātaka (No. 323) relates that once the Bodhisatta was leading an ascetic life in the park of a certain king who used to visit him daily and minister to his needs. Yet, for twelve long years he refrained from asking the boon of a pair of sandals and a leaf-parasol, trifling as they were.

When questioned as to his strange, but modest attitude, he replied to the king:—

"Who beg, *Pañcāla*, Lord, to weep are fain
They who refuse are apt to weep again"

In abundance he gives to others, irrespective of caste, creed, or colour, though seeking nothing for himself in return. A characteristic of his mind is perfect contentment such as the poet Edward Dyer contemplated.

"*Some have too much, yet still do crave,*
I little have and seek no more,
They are but poor though much they have,
And I am rich with little store."

In the Kaṇha Jātaka (No. 440) it is related that *Sakka*, attracted by the exemplary, virtuous life of the Bodhisatta, approached him and offered him a boon. Acceding to Sakka's kindly request, he wished for the following:

1.   May I harbour no malice or hatred against my neighbour!

2.   May I not covet my neighbour's possessions!

3.   May I cherish no personal affection towards others!

4.   May I possess *equanimity*!

Greatly disappointed, though full of admiration for the disinterest shown, Sakka entreated him to choose yet another boon. He replied:—

> *"Where in the woods I ever dwell,*
> *Where all alone dwell I,*
> *Grant no disease may mar my peace,*
> *Or break my ecstasy"*

Hearing this, *Sakka* thought—"Wise *Kaṇha*, in choosing a boon, chooses nothing connected with food.   All he chooses pertain to the ascetic life!"

Yet again *Sakka* said, "Choose a boon!"

The Bodhisatta responded:

> *"O Sakka, Lord of the world, a choice thou doest declare:*
>
> *No creature be aught harmed for me, O Sakka, anywhere,*
>
> *Neither in body nor in mind, this, Sakka, is my prayer."*[1]

A Bodhisatta exercises this virtue of generosity to such an extent that he is prepared to give away not only wealth and other cherished posses-

---

1.   Jātaka   Stories,   No.   440.

sions, but also his kingdom, his limbs and even his children and wife; and he is ever ready to sacrifice his own life wherever such sacrifice would benefit humanity.

The Vessantara Jātaka (No. 547) relates how, when Prince *Vessantara* was a child of only eight years, he thought with all sincerity: 'If one should need my heart, I would cut open my breast, tear it out and give it; if one should need my eyes, I would gouge them out and give them; if one should need my flesh, I would cut off what he needed.'

The Vyāghrī Jātaka depicts, in glowing terms, an incident in which he willingly and joyfully sacrificed his life for the good and happiness of others. In the Jātakamālā the story runs as follows:—

"On one occasion when the Bodhisatta was passing through a forest, accompanied by his disciple, he saw a tigress and her three cubs near death from starvation. Moved to compassion, he asked his disciple to secure some food for them. This was but a pretext to send him away, for the Bodhisatta thought:—

"Why should I search after meat from the body of another while the whole of my own body is available? Finding other meat is a matter of chance, and I may well lose the opportunity of doing my duty.

"This body being foul and a source of suffering, he is not wise who would not rejoice at its being spent for the benefit of another. There are but two things that make one disregard the grief of another-attachment to one's own pleasure

and the absence of the power of helping.   But I cannot take my
pleasure while another grieves, as long as I am able to help
him.   Why should I, therefore, be indifferent?

"By casting myself down this precipice, I sacrifice my
miserable body which will feed the tigress, thus preventing
her from killing the young ones and saving the young ones
from dying by the teeth of their mother.

"Furthermore, by so doing I set an example to those
whose longings are for the good of the world.   I encourage
the feeble; I gladden those who understand the meaning of
charity; and I inspire the virtuous.   And finally that opportunity I yearned for, when may I have the opportunity of
benefiting others by offering them my own limbs, I shall
obtain it now, and acquire before long the Sammā Sam-
buddhahood-Supreme Enlightenment."

Thinking thus, he cast himself down the precipice sacrificing his life for the welfare of those
helpless beings.

The Nevari (Nepāla Bhāshā) version of this interesting
and pitiful story is as follows:—

In the remote past there lived a devout and powerful
king named Mahāraṭṛha.   He had three sons by name, Mahā
Prashāda, Mahā Deva, and Mahāsattva, all good and
obedient.

One bright day the king, accompanied by the princes and
attendants, went on an excursion to a forest park.   The
young princes, admiring the enchanting beauty of the flowers
and trees, gradually penetrated far into the thick forest.

The attendants noticed their absence and reported the
matter to the king.   He ordered his ministers to go in search
of them and returned to his palace.

The three princes, wandering through the forest, reached
a mountain top. From there the eldest saw a starving tigress

with five cubs almost on the verge of death. For seven days since her delivery she had been without food. The cubs approached the mother to suck milk, but she had nothing to satisfy their hunger, and the tigress, driven by starvation, was clearly at the point of unnaturally devouring her own cubs.

The eldest brother was the first to see this pathetic spectacle. He showed the tigress to his brothers and said:—"Behold that pitiful sight, O brothers! That starving tigress is about to devour her cubs. How wretched is their condition!"

"What is their staple food, brother?" inquired Mahāsattva.

"Flesh and blood is the staple food of tigers and lions." replied Mahā Prashāda.

"The tigress seems to be very weak. Evidently she is without food for some days. How noble if one could sacrifice one's body for their sake!

"But, who is willing to make such great sacrifice!" remarked Mahā Deva.

"Surely, no one would be able to do so," stated Mahā Prashāda.

"I lack intelligence. Ignorant persons like us would not be able to sacrifice their bodies for the sake of another. But there may be selfless men of boundless compassion who would willingly do so," said Mahāsattva in a merciful tone.

Thus they discussed amongst themselves and casting a last glance at the helpless tigress, they departed.

Mahāsattva thought to himself:

'Sacrifice I must this fleeting body for the sake of this starving tigress. Foul is this body, and is subject to decay and death. One may adorn and perfume it, but soon it will stink and perish.'

Reflecting thus, he requested his brothers to proceed as he would be retiring to the forest for some reason or other.

He retraced his steps to the place where the tigress was resting. Hanging his garments and ornaments on a tree, again he thought:—

'Work I must for the weal of others. Compassionate we must be towards all beings. To serve those who need our succour is our paramount duty. This foul body of mine will I sacrifice and thus save the tigress and her five cubs. By this meritorious act may I gain Sammā Sambuddhahood and save all beings from the ocean of Saṁsāra! May all beings be well and happy!"

Moved by compassion and inspired by the spirit of selfless service, dauntlessly he jumped off the precipice towards the tigress.

The fall did not result in an instantaneous death. The tigress, though ruthless by nature, pitied the Bodhisattva and would not even touch his body.

The Bodhisattva thought otherwise: 'Obviously the poor animal is too weak to devour me!'

So he went in search of a weapon. He came across a bamboo splinter, and drawing near the tigress, he cut off his neck and fell dead on the ground in a pool of blood.

The hungry tigress greedily drank the blood and devoured the flesh leaving mere bones.

The story adds that, at the moment the Bodhisattva sacrificed his body, the earth quaked, the waters of the ocean were disturbed, the sun's rays dimmed, eye-sight was temporarily blurred, Devas gave cries of Sādhu, and Pārijāta flowers came down as rain from heaven.

Affected by the earthquake, the two elder brothers rightly guessed that their younger brother must have become a prey to the tigress.

"Surely, Mahāsattva must have sacrificed his life, for he spoke in a very merciful tone," said Mahā Deva.

Both of them turned back and went to the spot. They were horrified and awe-struck at the unexpected spectacle. What they saw was not their beloved brother but a mass of bones besmeared with blood. On a tree close by they saw the hanging garments.

They wept and fainted and on regaining consciousness, they returned home with a heavy heart.

On the very day the Bodhisattva sacrificed his life the mother-queen dreamt that she was dead, that her teeth had fallen out, and that she experienced a pain as if her body were cut by a sharp weapon. Furthermore, she dreamt that a hawk came drooping down and carried one of the three beautiful pigeons that were perched on the roof.

The queen was frightened, and on waking she remembered that her princes had gone for an airing in the forest. She hastened to the king and related the inauspicious dreams.

On being informed that the princes were missing, she entreated the king to send messengers in search of them.

Some ministers who had gone earlier to search for them returned to the palace with the sad news of the lamentable death of the youngest prince. Hearing it, nobody was able to refrain from weeping. The king, however, comforted the queen and, mounting an elephant, speedily proceeded to the forest with his attendants and brought back the other two grieving sons.

So great was their grief that at first they were speechless. Later summoning up courage, they explained to their bereaved mother the heroic deed of their noble brother.

Soon the order was given by the king to make necessary arrangements for them all to visit the memorable scene of the incident.

All reached the spot in due course. At the mere sight of the blood-smeared bones of the dearest son scattered here and there, both the king and queen fainted. The Purohita Brahmin instantly poured sandal wood water over them, and they regained consciousness.

Thereupon the king ordered his ministers to gather all the hair, bones, and garments and, heaping them together, worshipped them. Advising them to erect a golden Cetiya enshrining the relics, with a grieving heart, he departed to his palace.

The Cetiya was afterwards named 'Om Namo Buddhā.'

At the end of the Jātaka it is stated that the Cetiya is at present called 'Namurā.'

In spite of differences in the two versions, the central point in both is the self-sacrifice of the Bodhisatta. It is immaterial whether the Bodhisatta sacrificed his life as an ascetic or as a prince.

As in the other Jātakas the Nidāna or the occasion for the Jātaka appears in this one too. But the identification of the personages found at the end of all Jātakas is absent here.

The Nevāri Jātaka is obviously more descriptive than the Saṁskrit version. The origin of the Nevāri is uncertain.

*   *   *

Dealing with the Bodhisatta's mode of practising Dāna, an interesting account appears in an important text of the Cariyā Piṭaka Commentary.

In giving food the Bodhisatta intends thereby to endow the recipient with long life, beauty, happiness, strength, wisdom, and the Highest Fruit, Nibbāna. He gives thirsty beings to drink with the object of quenching the thirst of passion; garments to acquire moral shame and moral dread; conveyances to cultivate psychic powers; odours for the scent of Sīla (Morality); garlands and unguents to gain the glory pertaining to the Buddha's virtues; seats to win the seat of Enlightenment; lodging with the hope of serving as a refuge to the world; lights to obtain the five kinds of eyes-namely, the physical eye, the eye of wisdom, the Divine Eye, the Buddha Eye, and the Eye of Omniscience; forms to possess the Buddha aura; sounds to cultivate a voice as sweet as Brahma's; tastes so that he may be pleasing to all; contacts to gain the delicate organism of a Buddha; medicine for the sake of deathlessness (Nibbāna). He emancipates slaves in order to deliver men from the thraldom of passions; renounces children to develop the paternal feeling towards all; renounces wives to become the master of the world; renounces kingdoms to inherit the kingdom of righteousness.

Besides revealing the altruistic attitude of a Bodhisatta, these lofty aspirations disclose his disinterested efforts for the amelioration of mankind.

Sīla

Combined with this supernormal generosity of a Bodhisatta is his virtuous conduct (*Sīla*). The meaning of the Pāli term is discipline. It consists of duties that one should perform (*Cāritta*) and abstinences which one should practise (*Vāritta*). These duties towards parents, children, husband, wife, teachers, pupils, friends, monks, subordinates, etc., are described in detail in the Sigālovāda Sutta.

The duties of a layman are described in a series of relationships, each for mnemonic reasons of five items!

1. A child should minister to his parents by:—
   i. supporting them, ii. doing their duties, iii. keeping the family lineage, iv. acting in such a way as to be worthy of his inheritance and furthermore, v. offering alms in honour of his departed relatives.

2. Parents, who are thus ministered to by their children, should i. dissuade them from evil, ii. persuade them to do good, iii. teach them an art, iv. give them in marriage to a suitable wife, and v. hand over to them their inheritance at the proper time.

3. A pupil should minister to a teacher by:—
   i. rising. ii. attending on him, iii. attentive hearing, iv. personal service, and v. respectfully receiving instructions.

4. Teachers thus ministered to by pupils should:—
   i. train them in the best discipline, ii. make them receive that which is well held by them, iii. teach them every suitable art and science, iv. introduce them to their friends and associates, and v. provide for their safety in every quarter.

5. A husband should minister to his wife by:–
   i. courtesy, ii. not despising her, iii. faithfulness, iv. handing over authority to her, and v. providing her with ornaments.

6. The wife, who is thus ministered to by her husband, should:
   i. perform her duties in perfect order, ii. be hospitable to the people around, iii. be faithful, iv. protect what he brings, and v. be industrious and not lazy in discharging her duties.

7. A noble scion should minister to his friends and associates by:
   i. generosity, ii. courteous speech, iii. promoting their good, iv. equality, and v. truthfulness.

8. The friends and associates, who are thus ministered to by a noble scion, should:
   i. protect him when he is heedless, ii. protect his property when he is heedless, iii. become a refuge when he is afraid, iv. not forsake him when in danger, and v. be considerate towards his progeny.

9. A master should minister to servants and employees by: i. assigning them work according to their strength, ii. supplying them with food and wages, iii. tending them in sickness, iv. sharing with them extraordinary delicacies, and v. relieving them at times.

10. The servants and employees, who are thus ministered to by their master, should:
    i. rise before him, ii. go to sleep after him, iii. take only what is given, iv. perform their duties satisfactorily, and v. spread his good name and fame.

11. A noble scion should minister to ascetics and brahmins by:
    i. lovable deeds, ii. lovable words, iii. lovable thoughts, iv. not closing the doors against them, and v. supplying their material needs.

12. The ascetics and brahmins, who are thus ministered
    to by a noble scion, should:
    i. dissuade him from evil, ii. persuade him to do good,
    iii. love him with a kind heart, iv. make him hear
    what he has not heard and clarify what he has already
    heard, and v. point out the path to a heavenly state.

A Bodhisatta who fulfils all these household
duties (*Cāritta Sīla*) becomes truly a refined gentle-
man in the strictest sense of the term.

Apart fom these obligatory duties he endeavours his best to observe the other rules relating
to Vāritta Sīla (morality) and thus lead an ideal
Buddhist life.

Rightly discerning the law of action and reaction, of his own accord, he refrains from evil and
does good to the best of his ability.   He considers
it his duty to be a blessing to himself and others,
and not a curse to any, whether man or animal.

As life is precious to all and as no man has the
right to take away the life of another, he extends
his compassion and loving-kindness towards every
living being, even to the tiniest creature that crawls
at his feet, and refrains from killing or causing
injury to any living creature.   It is the animal
instinct in man that prompts him mercilessly to
kill the weak and feast on their flesh.   Whether to
appease one's appetite or as a pastime it is not
justifiable to kill or cause a helpless animal to be
killed by any method whether cruel or humane.
And if it is wrong to kill an animal, what must be
said of slaying human beings, however noble the
motive may at first sight appear.

Furthermore, a Bodhisatta abstains from all forms of stealing, direct or indirect, and thus develops honesty, trustworthiness and uprightness. Abstaining from misconduct, which debases the exalted nature of man, he tries to be pure and chaste in his sex life. He avoids false speech, harsh language, slander, and frivolous talk and utters only words which are true, sweet, peaceable and helpful. He avoids intoxicating liquors which tend to mental distraction and confusion, and cultivates heedfulness and clarity of vision.

A Bodhisatta would adhere to these five principles which tend to control deeds and words, whether against his own interests or not. On a proper occasion he will sacrifice not only possessions and wealth but life itself for the sake of his principles.[1]

It should not be understood that a Bodhisatta is perfect in his dealings in the course of his wanderings in Saṁsāra. Being a worldling, he possesses his own failings and limitations. Certain Jātakas like the Kanavera Jātaka (No. 318) depict him as a very desperate highway robber. This, however, is the exception rather than the rule.

---

1. "One who to save a limb rich treasures gave
   Would sacrifice a limb, his life to save
   Yea, wealth, limb, life and all away would fling,
   Right and its claims alone remembering."

The great importance attached by an aspirant to Buddhahood to morality is evident from the Sīlavīmaṁsa Jātaka (No. 362) where the Bodhisatta says: "Apart from virtue wisdom has no worth."[1]

In praise of Sīla (morality), the foundation of all other higher virtues, Venerable Buddhaghosa writes in the Visuddhi Magga.

> *"What scent else blows with   and against the wind?*
> *What stairway leads like her to heaven's gate?*
> *What door into Nibbāna's city opens?*
> *The sage whose virtue is his ornament*
> *Outshines the pomp and pearls of jewelled kings.*
> *In virtuous men virtue destroys self-blame,*
> *Begetting joy and praise.   Thus should be known*
> *The sum of all the discourse on the power*
> *Of virtue, root of merits, slayer of faults."[2]*

Nekkhamma

Still keener is the enthusiasm a Bodhisatta exhibits towards *Nekkhamma* (Renunciation), for by nature he is a lover of solitude. *Nekkhamma* implies both renunciation of worldly pleasures by adopting the ascetic life and the temporary inhibition of Hindrances (*Nīvaraṇa*) by Jhānas (Ecstasies).

A Bodhisatta is neither selfish nor self-possessive but is selfless in his activities.   He is ever ready to sacrifice his happiness for the sake of others.

Though he may sit in the lap of luxury, immersed in worldly pleasures, he may comprehend their transitoriness and the value of renunciation.

---

1. *Silena n'anupetassa sutena' ttho na vijjati.*
2. The Path of Purity, vol. i. p. 12.

Realizing thus the vanity of fleeting material pleasures, he voluntarily leaves his earthly possessions, and donning the simple ascetic garb, tries to lead the Holy Life in all its purity.   Here he practices the higher morality to such an extent that he becomes practically selfless in all his actions.   No inducement whether fame, wealth, honour, or worldly gain, could induce him to do anything contrary to his principles.

Sometimes, the first grey hair, as in the case of the Makhādeva Jātaka (No. 9), is alone a sufficient call to a Bodhisatta to abandon the uncongenial atmosphere of the palace for the independent solitary life of a hermit. At times a dew-drop or a withered leaf may induce him to adopt the ascetic life.

As a rule, however, the practice of renunciation is not observed by a Bodhisatta.

In the Kusa Jātaka (No. 531), for instance, the Bodhisatta was subjected to much humiliation owing to his unrestrained desire to win the hand of the beautiful princess Pabhāvati.

Again in the Darīmukha Jātaka (No. 373) it is mentioned that a Pacceka Buddha, quondam friend of the Bodhisatta, approached him and said:

"Pleasures of sense are but morass and mire,
The triply-rooted terror them I call.
Vapour and dust I have proclaimed them, Sire.
Become a brother and forsake them all."

He promptly replied:

"Infatuate, bound and deeply stained am I,
Brahmin, with pleasures, fearful, they may be.
But I love life, and cannot them deny;
Good works I undertake continually."[1]

In the period of a Buddhaless Cycle a Bodhisatta would adopt the life of an ascetic and lead the holy celibate life in solitude. If born in a Buddha Cycle, he would lead the life of a Bhikkhu in strict accordance with the rules that pertain thereto. An ideal Bhikkhu who leads an exemplary life is a blessing to himself and others. He teaches both by example and by precept. Within he is pure, without he purifies.

He is very strenuous in working for his inner spiritual development, catering at the same time for the spiritual needs of those lesser brethren and sisters. He is no burden to society because he gives no trouble to any. He is like the bee that extracts honey from the flower without damaging it. He possesses no property, for he has renounced everything worldly. His needs are few, and contentment is his wealth. He repents not for the past, nor is he worried about the future. He lives in the present, free from all responsibilities and trammels of the world. He is ready to wander wherever he chooses for the good and happiness of others, without clinging to any abode. Under all vicissitudes of life he maintains a balanced mind, His free services are always at the disposal of others.

---

1. Jātaka Stories, vol. iii, p. 158.

Non-Buddhist ascetics are invariably called Paribbājakas, Ajīvakas, Sanyāsins, etc. Bhikkhu (Saṁskrit, Bhikshu) has now become exclusively Buddhistic.

The rules laid down for a Bhikkhu[1] do not permit him to beg anything from another. He may accept the four requisites—robes, alms, lodging, medicine—presented to him. If in need of any requisite, he is allowed to ask it from his parents, close relatives, or from professed supporters.

A Bhikkhu is not bound to life-long vows. Of his own accord he enters the Order in order to lead the Holy Life until he chooses to leave it. Once he dons the yellow robe, the emblem of Arahants, he is bound to observe the rules that pertain thereto.

To lead a life of perfect purity and selfless service, to control and purify the mind with ease, to see things as they truly are, to think rightly and deeply, to develop the higher nature of man, to appreciate fully the higher spiritual values, no other mode of life affords such facilities and such great opportunities as the life of a Bhikkhu.

A Bhikkhu may lead either a contemplative or a studious life. The former is more in harmony with the ideal of a Bhikkhu, for the ultimate object in donning the yellow robe, the emblem of

---

1. Derived from the root 'bhikkha,' to beg. Bhikkhu, literally, means 'one who begs."
   See p. 516.

sanctity and humility, is to eradicate passions and realize Nibbāna.

Paññā

Nekkhamma is followed by *Paññā* (Wisdom or Knowledge). It is the right understanding of the nature of the world in the light of transiency (*anicca*), sorrowfulness (*dukkha*) and soullessness (*anattā*). A Bodhisatta meditates on these three characteristics but not to such an extent as to attain Arahantship, for to do this would be deviating from his Goal.

At the same time he does not disparage worldly wisdom. He tries to acquire knowledge even from his servants. Never does he show any desire to display his knowledge. nor is he ashamed to plead ignorance even in public, for under no circumstances does he ever prove to be a charlatan. What he knows is always at the disposal of others, and that he imparts to them unreservedly. He tries his best to lead others from darkness to light.

Knowledge is of three kinds. The first is knowledge acquired orally (*sutamaya paññā*). In the ancient days when printing was not in vogue knowledge was acquired by hearing-hence a learned man was then called *bahussuta* (=he who has heard much), corresponding to English erudition. The second kind of knowledge is acquired by thought (*cintāmaya paññā*). The practical scientific knowledge of the West is the direct outcome of this kind of knowledge. The third is a superior kind of knowledge acquired by meditation and contemplation (*bhāvanāmaya paññā*). It is by such meditation that one realizes intuitive truths which are beyond logical reasoning. *Bhāvanā* or meditation is not a passive reverie, but an energetic striving. It leads to self-elevation, self-discipline, self-control, and self-illumination. It is a heart-tonic as well.

Wisdom is the apex of Buddhism. It is the first factor in the Noble Eightfold Path (*sammā diṭṭhi*). It is one of the seven Factors of Enlightenment (*Dhamma Vicaya Sambojjhanga*). It is one of the four means of Accomplishment (*Vīmaṇsā Iddhipāda.*) It is one of the five Powers (*Paññābala*) and one of the five controlling Faculties (*Paññindriya*). It is wisdom that leads to purification and to final Deliverance.

Viriya

Closely allied with *Paññā* (wisdom) is *Viriya* (Energy or Perseverance). Here *Viriya* does not mean physical strength though this is an asset, but mental vigour or strength of character, which is far superior. It is defined as the persistent effort to work for the welfare of others both in thought and deed. Firmly establishing himself in this virtue, the Bodhisatta develops self-reliance and makes it one of his prominent characteristics.

In the words of Dr. Tagore a Bodhisatta, relying on his own resources, would form his mind thus:—

*"Let me not pray to be sheltered from dangers,
but to be fearless in facing them.*

*Let me not beg for the stilling of my pain,
but for the heart to conquer it.*

*Let me not crave in anxious fear to be saved.
but hope for the patience to win my freedom."*

The Viriya of a Bodhisatta is clearly depicted in the Mahājanaka Jātaka (No. 539). Shipwrecked in the open sea for seven days he struggled on without once giving up hope until he was finally rescued.

Failures he views as steps to success, opposition causes him to double his exertion, dangers increase his courage. Cutting his way through difficulties, which impair the enthusiasm of the feeble, surmounting obstacles, which dishearten the ordinary, he looks straight towards his goal. Nor does he ever stop until his goal is reached.

To Māra who advised the Bodhisatta to abandon his quest, he said:—"Death in battle with passions to me seems more honourable than a life of defeat."

Just as his wisdom is always directed to the service of others, so also is his fund of energy. Instead of confining it to the narrow course leading to the realization of personal ends, he directs it into the open channel of activities that tend to universal happiness. Ceaselessly and untiringly he works for others, expecting no remuneration in return or reward. He is ever ready to serve others to the best of his ability.

In certain respects *Viriya* plays an even greater part than *Paññā* in the achievement of the goal. In one who treads the Noble Eightfold Path, Right Effort (*Sammā Vāyāma* or *Viriya*) suppresses the arising of evil states, eradicates those which have arisen, stimulates good states, and perfects those good states which have already arisen. It serves as one of the seven Factors of Enlightenment (*Viriya Sambojjhaṅga*). It is one of the four Means of Accomplishment (*Viriyiddhipāda*). It is *Viriya* that performs the function of the four modes of Right Endeavour (*Sammappadhāna*). It is one of the five Powers (*Viriya Bala*) and one of the five controlling Faculties (*Viriyindriya*).

Viriya therefore may be regarded as an officer that performs nine functions. It is effort coupled with wisdom that serves as a powerful hand to achieve all ends.[1]

Khanti

As important as *Viriya* is *Khanti*. It is the patient endurance of suffering inflicted upon oneself by others, and the forbearance of others' wrongs.

A Bodhisatta practises patience to such an extent that he is not provoked even when his

---

1. *Paññānuyātaṁ viriyaṁ vadanti*
   Sabbattha siddhiggahanaggahatthaṁ.

hands and feet are cut off. In the Khantivādi
Jātaka, (No. 313) it appears that not only did the
Bodhisatta cheerfully endure the tortures inflicted
by the drunkard king, who mercilessly ordered
his hands and feet, nose and ears to be cut off, but
requited those injuries with a blessing.

Lying on the ground, in a deep pool of his own
blood, with mutilated limbs, the Bodhisatta said:—

"Long live the king, whose cruel hand my
body thus has marred.

Pure souls like mine such deeds as these with
anger ne'er regard."[1]

Of his forbearance it is said that whenever he
is harmed he thinks of the aggressor:—

'This person is a fellow-being of mine. Inten-
tionally or unintentionally I myself must have
been the source of provocation, or it may be due
to a past evil Kamma of mine. As it is the outcome
of my own action, why should I harbour ill-will
towards him'?

It may be mentioned that a Bodhisatta is not
irritated by any man's shameless conduct either.

Admonishing His disciples to practise forbearance, the Buddha says in the Kakacūpama Sutta:

"Though robbers, who are highway men, should
sever your limbs with a two-handled saw yet if
you thereby defile your mind, you would be no
follower of my teaching.

---

1.   Jātaka Stories, vol. iii. p. 28.

"Thus should you train yourselves: Unsullied shall our hearts remain. No evil word shall escape our lips. Kind and compassionate with loving-heart, harbouring no ill-will shall we abide, enfolding even these bandits with thoughts of loving-kindness. And forth from them proceeding, we shall abide radiating the whole world with thoughts of loving-kindness, vast, expansive, measureless, benevolent and unified."

Practising patience and tolerance, instead of seeing the ugliness in others, a Bodhisatta tries to seek the good and beautiful in all.

Sacca

Truthfulness or *Sacca* is the seventh Perfection. By *Sacca* is here meant the fulfilment of one's promise. This is one of the salient characteristics of a Bodhisatta, for he is no breaker of his word. He acts as he speaks, he speaks as he acts (*yathā-vādī tathākārī yathākārī tathāvādī*).

According to the Hārita Jātaka (No. 431) a Bodhisatta, in the course of his life's wanderings, never utters an untruth although at times he may violate the other four precepts.

Truth he hides not even to be polite.

He makes truth his guide, and holds it his bounden duty to keep his word. He ponders well before he makes his promise, but once made the promise is fulfilled at any cost, even that of his life.

In the Hiri Jātaka (No. 363) the Bodhisatta advises:

"Be thou in deed to every promise true,
Refuse to promise what thou canst not do;
Wise men on empty braggarts look askew."[1]

Again, the Mahā Sutasoma Jātaka (No. 537) recounts that to fulfill a promise the Bodhisatta was prepared even to sacrifice his life.

"Just as the morning star on high
In balanced course doth ever keep,
And through all seasons, times, and years,
Doth never from its pathway swerve,
So likewise he in all wise speech
Swerves never from the path of truth."[2]

A Bodhisatta is trustworthy, sincere and honest. What he thinks, he speaks. There is perfect harmony in his thoughts, words and deeds.

He is consistent and straightforward in all his dealings. He is no hypocrite since he strictly adheres to his high principles. There is no difference between his inner self and his outward utterance. His private life accords with his public life.

He does not use flattery to win the hearts of others, does not exalt himself to win their admiration, does not hide his defects or vainly exhibit his virtues. The praiseworthy he praises without malice, the blameworthy he blames judiciously, not with contempt but out of compassion.

---

1. Jātaka Stories, vol. iii, p. 130.
2. Warren, *Buddhism in Translations.*

Even the truth he does not always utter.
Should such utterance not be conducive to the
good and happiness of others, then he remains
silent. If any truth seems beneficial to others, he
utters it, however detrimental to himself it may
be. And he honours the word of others as he
honours his own.

Adhiṭṭhāna

Truthfulness is followed by *Adhiṭṭhāna* which
may be translated as resolute determination.
Without this firm determination the other perfections cannot be fulfilled.   It is compared to the
foundation of a building. This will-power forces
all obstructions out of the Bodhisatta's path, and
no matter what may come to him, sickness, grief,
or disaster—he never turns his eyes away from his
goal.

For instance, the Bodhisatta Gotama made a
firm determination to renounce his royal pleasures
and gain Enlightenment. For six long years his
was a superhuman struggle. He had to endure
manifold hardships and face innumerable difficulties. At a crucial moment when he most
needed their help, his five favourite disciples
deserted him. Yet he did not give up his effort.
His enthusiasm was redoubled. He strove on
alone and eventually achieved the goal.

"Just as a rocky mountain peak,
Unmoved stands, firm established.
Unshaken by the boisterous gale,
And always in its place abides.

So likewise he must ever be
In resolution firm entrenched."[1]

A Bodhisatta is a man of iron determination whose high principles cannot be shaken. Easily persuaded to do good, none could tempt him to do anything contrary to those principles. As occasion demands he is as soft as a flower and as firm as a rock.

Mettā

The most important of all Pāramis is *Mettā* (Saṁskrit *Maitri*). There is no graceful English equivalent for Mettā. It may be rendered as benevolence, goodwill, friendliness, or loving-kindness, and is defined as the wish for the happiness of all beings without exception. It is this Mettā that prompts a Bodhisatta to renounce personal deliverence for the sake of others. He is permeated with boundless goodwill towards all beings irrespective of caste, creed, colour, or sex. Since he is the embodiment of universal love he fears none, nor is he feared by any. Wild beasts in lonely jungles are his loving friends. His very presence amongst them fosters their mutual friendliness. He ever cherishes in his heart boundless goodwill towards all that lives.

Mettā, in Buddhism, should be differentiated from personal affection (*pema*) or ordinary carnal love. From affection come fear and grief, but not from *Mettā*.

---

1. Warren, *Buddhism in Translations.*

In exercising this loving-kindness one should not ignore oneself. *Mettā* should be extended towards oneself equally with others. Metta of a Buddhist embraces the whole world, including himself.

In the Mahā-Dhammapāla Jātaka (No. 385), it appears that the young Bodhisatta, extended his loving-kindness, in equal measure, towards his cruel father who ordered him to be tortured and killed, the wicked executioner, his loving, weeping mother, and his humble self.

Loving-kindness possesses a mystic power, which can easily influence beings far and near. A pure heart that radiates this beneficent force is capable of transforming wild beasts into tame ones, murderers into saints.

This mystic power lies within the reach of all. Only a slight exertion is necessary to make it our own.

"Dwelling on the mountain slopes." says the Buddha, "I drew to me lions and tigers, by the power of loving-kindness. Surrounded by lions and tigers, by panthers and buffaloes, by antelopes, stags and boars, I dwelt in the forest. No creature was terrified of me, and neither was I afraid of any creature. The power of loving-kindness was my support. Thus I dwelt upon the mountain side."

As one loves others, so is one loved by them. No apposing forces, no hostile vibrations, no

negative thoughts can affect one who is so protected by this aura of loving-kindness. With mind
at peace, he will live in a heaven of his own creation. Even those who contact him will also
experience that bliss. When one habitually feels
loving-kindness and demonstrates it in words
and deeds, water-tight compartments dissolve
away. Distinctions gradually disappear, and the
'I' is absorbed in the 'all'. Nay, there will be no
'I' at all. Finally one will be able to identify
oneself with all (*sabbattatā*), the culmination of
Mettā.

A Bodhisatta extends this Mettā towards every
living being and identifies himself with all, making
no distinction whatsoever of caste, creed, colour,
or sex. It is this Buddhist Mettā that attempts to
break all the barriers which separate one from
another. To a Bodhisatta there is no far and near,
no enemy or foreigner, no renegade or untouchable,
since universal love, realized through understanding, has established the brotherhood of all living
beings. A Bodhisatta is a true citizen of the
world, ever kind, friendly, and compassionate.

Upekkhā

The tenth *Pārami* is *Upekkhā* or equanimity.

The Pāli term *Upekkhā* is composed of *upa*,
which means justly, impartially or rightly (*yuttito*)
and *ikkha*, to see, discern or view. The etymological meaning of the term is discerning rightly,
viewing justly, or looking impartially, that is, with-

out attachment or aversion, without favour or disfavour.

Here the term is not used in the sense of indifference or neutral feeling.

The most difficult and the most essential of all perfections is this equanimity, especially for a layman who has to live in an ill-balanced world with fluctuating fortunes.

Slights and insults are the common lot of humanity. So are praise and blame, loss and gain, pain and happiness. Amidst all such vicissitudes of life a Bodhisatta tries to stand unmoved like a firm rock, exercising perfect equanimity.

In times of happiness and adversity, amidst praise and blame, he is even-balanced. Like a lion that does not tremble at any sound, he is not perturbed by the poisoned darts of uncurbed tongues. Like the wind that does not cling to the meshes of a net, he is not attached to the illusory pleasures of this changing world. Like a lotus that is unsoiled by the mud from which it springs, he lives unaffected by worldly temptations, ever calm, serene and peaceful.

"Just as the earth whate'er is thrown
Upon her, whether sweet or foul,
Indifferent is to all alike,
Nor hatred shows, nor amity,
So likewise he in good or ill,
Must even-balanced ever be."[1]

---

1. Warren, *Buddhism in Translations.*

"As no waves break the calm of ocean's depths, unruffled should his mind be."[1]

Furthermore, a Bodhisatta who practises Upek-khā metes out justice to all without being influenced by desire (*chanda*), hatred (*dosa*), fear (*bhaya*), and ignorance (*moha*).

It will be seen from the above Perfections that Bodhisattahood is, in its entirety, a course of self-sacrifice, discipline, renunciation, deep insight, energy, forbearance, truthfulness, determination, boundless love, and perfect mental equilibrium.

*   *   *

In addition to these ten Pāramis a Bodhisatta has to practise three modes of conduct (*cariyā*), namely, *Buddhi Cariyā*, doing good with wisdom, not ignoring self-development, *Nātyattha Cariyā*, working for the betterment of relatives, and *Lokattha Cariyā*, working for the amelioration of the whole world.

By the second mode of conduct is not meant nepotism, but work to promote the well-being of one's kinsfolk without any favouritism.

Thus practising the ten Pāramis to the highest pitch of perfection, while developing the three modes of conduct, he traverses the tempest-tossed sea of Saṁsāra, driven hither and thither by the irresistible force of Kamma, manifesting himself at different times in multifarious births.

---

1. See Chalmers, *Buddha's Teachings*, p. 221.

Now he comes into being as a mighty Sakka, or as a radiant Deva, at another time as a human being, high or low, again as an animal and so on until finally he seeks birth in the Tusita Heaven, having consummated the Pāramis. There he abides, awaiting the opportune moment to appear on earth as a Sammā Sambuddha.

It is not correct to think that a Bodhisatta purposely manifests himself in such various forms in order to acquire universal experience. No person is exempt from the inexorable law of Kamma which alone determines the future birth of individuals, except Arahants and Buddhas who have put an end to all life in a fresh existence.

Due to his intrinsic merit, A Bodhisatta, however, possesses some special powers. If, for instance, he is born in a Brahma Realm where the span of life extends for countless aeons, by exercise of his will-power, he ceases to live in that sphere, and is reborn in another congenial place where he may serve the world and practise Pāramis.

Apart from this kind of voluntary death (*adhi-mutti-kālakiriyā*), the Jātaka Commentary states that there are eighteen states in which a Bodhisatta, as the result of his potential Kammic. force accumulated in the course of his wanderings in Saṁsāra, is never reborn. For instance, he is never born blind or deaf, nor does he become an absolute misbeliever (*niyata micchādiṭṭhi*), who denies Kamma and its effects.　He is born in the animal kingdom, but not larger than an elephant or smaller than a snipe.　He may suffer in the ordinary states of misery (*apāya*), but is never destined to the nethermost states of woe (*avīci*). Also a Bodhisatta does not seek birth in the Pure Abodes (*Suddhāvāsa*), where Anāgāmis are reborn, nor in the Formless Realms where one is deprived of the opportunity to be of service to others.

It might be asked: Is a Bodhisatta aware that he is aspiring to Buddhahood in the course of his births?

Sometimes, he is, and at times he is not.

According to certain Jātakas it appears that on some occasions the Bodhisatta *Gotama* was fully conscious of his striving for Buddhahood.　Visayha Seṭṭhi Jātaka (No. 340) may be cited as an example.　In this particular story *Sakka* questioned the Bodhisatta as to why he was exceptionally generous.　He replied that it was not for the sake of any worldly power, but for the sole purpose of attaining Supreme Buddhahood.　In certain births as in the case of Jotipāla,[1] he was not only unaware of his high aspiration, but also abused the noble Teacher Buddha *Kassapa* at the mere utterance of the sacred word—Buddha.　It may be mentioned that it was from this very Buddha that he obtained his last revelation (*Vivaraṇa*).

1.　Majjhima Nikāya, Ghaṭikāra Sutta, No. 81.

We ourselves may be Bodhisattas who have dedicated our lives to the noble purpose of serving the world. One need not think that the Bodhisatta Ideal is reserved only for supermen. What one has done another can do, given the necessary effort and enthusiasm. Let us too endeavour to work disinterestedly for the good of ourselves and all others, having for our object in life—the noble ideal of service and perfection.

Serve to be perfect; be perfect to serve.

CHAPTER 42

BRAHMAVIHĀRA

THE SUBLIME STATES

"Rare is birth as a human being.
Hard is the life of mortals."
"Do not let slip this opportunity."

DHAMMAPADA

Man is a mysterious being with inconceivable potentialities. Latent in him are both saintly characteristics and criminal tendencies. They may rise to the surface at unexpected moments in disconcerting strength. How they originated we know not. We only know that they are dormant in man in varying degree.

Within the powerful mind in this complex machinery of man are also found a storehouse of virtue and a rubbish heap of evil. With the development of the respective characteristics man may become either a blessing or a curse to humanity.

Those who wish to be great, noble and serviceable, who wish to sublimate themselves and serve humanity both by example and by precept, and who wish to avail themselves of this golden opportunity as human beings, endeavour their best to remove the latent vices and to cultivate the dormant virtues.

To dig up precious gems embedded in the earth men spend enormous sums of money and make laborious efforts, and sometimes even sacrifice their lives. But to dig up the valuable treasures latent in man, only persistent effort and enduring patience are necessary. Even the poorest man or woman can accomplish this task, for wealth is not an essential prerequisite to the accumulation of transcendental treasures.

It is strange that the vices latent in man seem to be almost natural and spontaneous. It is equally strange that every vice possesses its opposite sterling virtue, which does not however appear to be so normal and automatic, though still within the range of all.

One powerful destructive vice in man is anger (*dosa*). The sweet virtue that subdues this evil force and sublimes man is loving-kindness (*mettā*).

Cruelty (*hiṁsā*) is another vice that is responsible for many horrors and atrocities prevalent in the world. Compassion (*karuṇā*) is its antidote.

Jealousy (*issā*) is another vice that poisons one's system and leads to unhealthy rivalries and dangerous competitions. The most effective remedy for this poisonous drug is appreciative joy (*muditā*).

There are two other universal characteristics that upset the mental equipoise of man. They are attachment to the pleasurable and aversion to the non-pleasurable. These two opposite forces can be eliminated by developing equanimity (*upekkhā*).

These four sterling virtues are collectively termed in Pāli 'Brahmavihāra' which may be rendered by Modes of Sublime Conduct, Sublime States, or Divine Abodes.

These virtues tend to elevate man. They make one divine in this life itself. They can transform man into a superman. If all try to cultivate them, irrespective of creed, colour, race, or sex, the earth can be transformed into a paradise where all can live in perfect peace and harmony as ideal citizens of one world.

The four sublime virtues are also termed illimitables (*appamaññā*). They are so called because they find no barrier or limit and should be extended towards all beings without exception. They embrace all living beings including animals.

Irrespective of religious beliefs, one can cultivate these sweet virtues and be a blessing to oneself and all others.

Mettā

The first Sublime State is Mettā (*Saṁskrit-Maitri*). It means that which softens one's heart, or the state of a true friend. It is defined as the sincere wish for the welfare and genuine happiness of all living beings without exception. It is also explained as the friendly disposition, for a genuine friend sincerely wishes for the welfare of his friend.

"Just as a mother protects her only child even at the risk of her life, even so one should cultivate boundless loving-kindness towards all living beings" is the advice of the Buddha.

It is not the passionate love of the mother towards her child that is stressed here but her sincere wish for the genuine welfare of her child.

Mettā is neither carnal love nor personal affection, for grief inevitably arises from both.

Mettā is not mere neighbourliness, for it makes no distinction between neighbours and others.

Mettā is not mere universal brotherhood, for it embraces all living beings including animals, our lesser brethren and sisters that need greater compassion as they are helpless.

Mettā is not political brotherhood or racial brotherhood, or national brotherhood, or even religious brotherhood.

Political brotherhood is confined only to those who share similar political views, such as the partial brotherhood of Democrats, Socialists, Communists, and so forth.

Racial brotherhood and national brotherhood are restricted only to those of the same race and nation. Some nationalists love their race so much that sometimes they ruthlessly kill innocent men, women and children because they unfortunately are not blessed with blond hair and blue eyes. The white races have particular love for the white skin, the black for the black, the yellow for the yellow, the brown for the brown, the pale for the pale, the red for the red. Others of a different complexion are at times viewed with suspicion and fear. Very often to assert their racial superiority they resort to brutal warfare, killing millions by mercilessly raining bombs from the sky above. The pathetic incidents of the Second World War are striking examples which can never be forgotten by mankind.

Amongst some narrow-minded peoples, within the wider circle of their ancient nations, there exist minor circles of caste and class where the so-called brotherhood of the powerful oppressors is so limited that the oppressed are not even permitted to enjoy bare human rights merely because of the accidents of birth or class. These oppressors are to be pitied because they are confined to their water-tight compartments.

Mettā is not religious brotherhood either. Owing to the sad limitations of so-called religious brotherhood human heads have been severed without the least compunction, sincere outspoken men and women have been roasted and burnt alive; many atrocities have been perpetrated which baffle description; cruel wars have been waged which mar the pages of world history. Even in this supposedly enlightened twentieth century the followers of one religion hate or ruthlessly persecute and even kill those of other faiths merely

because they cannot force them to think as they
do or because they have a different label.

If, on account of religious views, people of
different faiths cannot meet on a common platform
like brothers and sisters, then surely the missions
of compassionate world teachers have pitifully
failed.

Sweet *mettā* transcends all these kinds of
narrow brotherhood. It is limitless in scope and
range. Barriers it has none. Discrimination it
makes not. Mettā enables one to regard the
whole world as one's motherland and all as fellow-
beings.

Just as the sun sheds its rays on all without
any distinction, even so sublime *mettā* bestows
its sweet blessings equally on the pleasant and the
unpleasant, on the rich and the poor, on the high
and the low, on the vicious and the virtuous, on
man and woman, and on human and animal.

Such was the boundless *Mettā* of the Buddha
who worked for the welfare and happiness of those
who loved Him as well as of those who hated
Him and even attempted to harm and kill Him.

The Buddha exercised *mettā* equally towards
His own son Rāhula, His adversary Devadatta,
His attendant Ānanda, His admirers and His
opponents.

This loving-kindness should be extended in
equal measure towards oneself as towards friend,

foe and neutral alike. Suppose a bandit were to
approach a person travelling through a forest
with an intimate friend, a neutral person and an
enemy, and suppose he were to demand that one
of them be offered as a victim. If the traveller
were to say that he himself should be taken, then
he would have no *mettā* towards himself. If he
were to say that anyone of the other three persons should be taken, then he would have no
mettā towards them.

Such is the characteristic of real *mettā*. In
exercising this boundless loving-kindness oneself
should not be ignored. This subtle point should
not be misunderstood, for self-sacrifice is another
sweet virtue and egolessness is yet another higher
virtue. The culmination of this *mettā* is the identification of oneself with all beings (*sabbattatā*),
making no difference between oneself and others.
The so-called 'I' is lost in the whole. Separatism
evaporates. Oneness is realized.

There is no proper English equivalent for this
graceful Pāli term *Mettā*. Goodwill, loving-
kindness, benevolence and universal love are
suggested as the best renderings.

The antithesis of *mettā* is anger, ill-will, hatred,
or aversion. *Mettā* cannot co-exist with anger or
vengeful conduct.

The Buddha states:

"Hatreds do not cease through hatreds: through love alone they cease."[1]

Mettā not only tends to conquer anger but also does not tolerate hateful thoughts towards others. He who has *mettā* never thinks of harming others, nor does he disparage or condemn others. Such a person is neither afraid of others nor does he instil fear into any.

A subtle indirect enemy assails *mettā* in the guise of a friend. It is selfish affection (*pema*), for unguarded *mettā* may sometimes be assailed by lust. This indirect enemy resembles a person who lurks afar in the jungles or hills to cause harm to another. Grief springs from affection but not from *mettā*.

This delicate point should not be misunderstood. Parents surely cannot avoid having affection towards their children and children towards their parents; husbands towards their wives and wives towards their husbands. Such affection is quite natural. The world cannot exist without mutual affection. The point to be clarified here is that unselfish *mettā* is not synonymous with ordinary affection.

A benevolent attitude is the chief characteristic of *mettā*. He who practises *mettā* is constantly interested in promoting the welfare of others. He seeks the good and beautiful in all but not the ugliness in others.

---

1. Dhammapada, v. 5.

Attendant blessings of Mettā

1. He who practises *mettā* sleeps happily. As he goes to sleep with a light heart free from hatred he naturally falls asleep at once. This fact is clearly demonstrated by those who are full of loving-kindness. They are fast asleep immediately on closing their eyes.

2. As he goes to sleep with a loving heart he awakes with an equally loving heart. Benevolent and compassionate persons often rise from bed with smiling faces.

3. Even in sleep loving persons are not perturbed by bad dreams. As they are full of love during their waking hours, they are peaceful in their sleeping hours too. Either they fall into deep sleep or have pleasant dreams.

4. He becomes dear to human beings. As he loves others, so do others love him.

When a persons looks at a mirror with a smiling face, a similar face will greet him. If, on the contrary, he looks with a wry face, he will see a similar reflection. The outside world reacts on one in the same way that one acts towards the world. One full of faults himself is apt to see the evil in others. The good he ignores. An English poet (Bolton Hall) has put it beautifully:

"I looked at my brother with the Microscope of Criticism.

And I said 'How coarse my brother is!'
I looked at him through the Telescope of Scorn

And I said, 'How small my brother is!'
Then I looked in the Mirror of Truth
And I said, 'How like me my brother is!' "

Why should we see the ugliness in others when there is evil in the best of us and good in the worst of us? It would be a source of pleasure to all if we could see the good and beautiful in all.

5. He who practises *mettā* is dear to non-humans as well. Animals are also attracted to him. Radiating their loving-kindness, ascetics live in wild forests amidst ferocious beasts without being harmed by them.

6. Owing to his power of *mettā* he becomes immune from poison and so forth unless he is subject to some inexorable Kamma.

As *mettā* is a constructive healthy force it has the power to counteract hostile influence. Just as hateful thoughts can produce toxic effects in the system, even so loving thoughts can produce healthy physical effects. It is stated that a very generous and devout woman named Suppiyā, who had a wound in her thigh, was healed on seeing the Buddha. The peaceful thought vibrations of the Buddha and the woman combined to produce this salutary effect.

When the Buddha visited His birthplace for the first time, His son Rāhula, who was only seven years of age, approached Him and spontaneously remarked: "O ascetic, even your shadow is

pleasing to me." The child was so much dominated by the Buddha's *mettā* that he deeply felt its
magnetic power.

7.   Invisible deities protect him because of the
power of his *mettā*.

8.   *Mettā* leads to quick mental concentration.
As the mind is not perturbed by hostile vibrations
one-pointedness can be gained with ease.   With
mind at peace he will live in a heaven of his own
creation.   Even those who come in contact with
him will also experience that bliss.

9.   *Mettā* tends to beautify one's facial expression.   The face as a rule reflects the state of the
mind.   When one gets angry, the heart pumps
blood twice or three times faster than the normal
rate.   Heated blood rushes up to the face, which
then turns red or black.   At times the face becomes repulsive to sight. Loving thoughts on the
contrary, gladden the heart and clarify the blood.
The face then presents a lovable appearance.

It is stated that when the Buddha, after Enlightenment, reflected on the Causal Relations
(*Paṭṭhāna*), His heart was so pacified and His
blood so clarified that rays of different hue such
as blue, yellow, red, white, orange, and a mixture
of these emanated from His body.

10.   A person imbued with *mettā* dies peacefully as he harbours no thoughts of hatred towards

any. Even after death his serene face reflects his peaceful death.

11. Since a person with *mettā* dies happily, he will subsequently be born in a blissful state. If he has gained the Jhānas (ecstasies), he will be born in a Brahma realm.

Power of Mettā

Besides these inevitable worldly blessings *mettā* possesses a magnetic power. It can produce a good influence on others even at a distance and can attract others to oneself.

Once when the Buddha visited a certain city, many distinguished nobles came to welcome Him, amongst whom was a nobleman named *Roja*, who was a friend of Venerable *Ānanda*. Seeing him, Venerable *Ānanda* said: "It is very kind of you, Roja, to have come to welcome the Buddha."

"No, Venerable Sir, it is not out of any reverence towards the Buddha that I have come to greet Him. We agreed amongst ourselves that whoever would not go to greet the Buddha would be fined 500 gold coins. It is through fear of the fine that I have come here to welcome the Buddha", replied Roja.

Venerable *Ānanda* was slightly displeased. He approached the Buddha and implored Him to preach the Dhamma to Roja.

The Buddha instantly radiated *mettā* towards Roja and retired to His chamber.

Roja's body was saturated with the *mettā* of the Buddha. He was electrified, so to say, with the magnetic power of Buddha's irresistible love. Just as a calf would run after its mother he ran from cell to cell in the monastery inquiring where the Buddha was. The monks directed him to the Buddha's chamber. He knocked at the door. The Buddha opened it. In he went, saluted the Buddha, heard the doctrine, and became a convert.

Such is the magnetic power of *mettā* which everyone can exercise according to his ability.

On another occasion an intoxicated elephant was driven towards the Buddha in an effort to kill Him. The Buddha calmly radiated His love towards the elephant and subdued it.

A beautiful story may be cited to show how the Bodhisatta as a boy extended his boundless *mettā* when his own father ordered him to be killed. Young though he was, the Bodhisatta thought to himself:—

"Here is a golden opportunity for me to practise my *mettā*. My father stands before me, my good mother is weeping, the executioner is ready to chop off my hands and feet. I, the victim, am in the centre. Love I must all the four in equal measure without any distinction. May my good father not incur any suffering because of this ruthless act! May I become a Buddha in the future!"

In one of his previous births the Bodhisatta was once practising the virtue of patience in a royal park. The king, a drunkard, meaning to test his patience, ordered the executioner to beat him and cut off his hands and feet. Still he practised patience. The impatient king kicked him in the chest. Lying in a pool of blood, almost on the verge of death, the Bodhisatta blessed the king and wished him long life saying that men like himself never get angry.[1]

A Bhikkhu is expected to practise *mettā* to such an extent that he is forbidden to dig or cause to dig the ground lest insects and other minute creatures die.

The high standard of *mettā* expected from a Bhikkhu can be understood by the following admonition of the Buddha:—

"If bandits sever your limbs with a two-handled saw, and if you entertain hate in your heart, you will not be a follower of my teaching."

Such enduring patience is extremely difficult. But, that is the lofty ethical standard the Buddha expects from His followers.

The Buddha Himself has set the noble example:

"As an elephant in the battlefield withstands arrows shot from a bow," says the Buddha, "even

---

1. See p. 600.

so will I endure abuse; verily most people are undisciplined."[1]

This chaotic, war-weary, restless world of today, where the nations are arming themselves to their teeth, frightened of one another, where human life is endangered by nuclear weapons which may be released at any moment, is sorely in need of this universal loving-kindness so that all may live in one world in perfect peace and harmony like brothers and sisters.

Is it practically possible to exercise *mettā* when one is threatened with devastating bombs and other destructive weapons?

Well, what can powerless people do when bombs rain from above? Can they avert such a catastrophe?

Buddhist *mettā* is the only answer to such deadly bombs when one is faced with inexorable death.

If all warlike nations could be prevailed upon to substitute this spiritual *mettā* for the destructive weapons of materialism and rule the world not with might and force but with right and love, then only would there be genuine peace and happiness in this world.

Leaving the almost unpractical major issues aside, it is advisable to be concerned with oneself

---

1. Dhammapada v. 320.

and the rest of mankind in cultivating this sweet virtue of *mettā* to the best of one's ability.

How to Practise Mettā

A few practical hints are given below to practise this meditation on loving-kindness.

Mettā should be practised first towards oneself. In doing so a person should charge his mind and body with positive thoughts of peace and happiness. He should think how he could be peaceful, happy, free from suffering, worry and anger. He then becomes the embodiment of loving-kindness. Shielded by loving kindness, he cuts off all hostile vibrations and negative thoughts. He returns good for evil, love for anger. He becomes ever tolerant and tries his best not to give occasion for anger to any. Himself beaming with happiness, he injects happiness into others not only inwardly but also outwardly by putting his *mettā* into practice in the course of his daily life.

When he is full of peace and is free from thoughts of hatred, it is easy for him to radiate loving-kindness towards others. What he does not possess he cannot give to others. Before he tries to make others happy he should first be happy himself. He should know the ways and means to make himself happy.

He now radiates his loving-kindness towards all his near and dear ones individually and collectively, wishing them peace and happiness and freedom from suffering, disease, worry and anger.

Diffusing his thoughts of loving-kindness towards his relatives and friends, he radiates them also towards neutrals. Just as he wishes for the peace and happiness of himself and of his near and dear ones, even so he sincerely wishes for the peace and happiness of those who are neutral to him, wishing them freedom from suffering, disease, worry and anger. Finally, though this is somewhat difficult, he should radiate his *mettā* in the same way towards those (if any) who are inimical to him. If, by practising *mettā*, he could adopt a friendly attitude towards those thought to be inimical towards him, his achievement would be more heroic and commendable. As the Buddha advises—"Amidst those who hate let him live free from hatred."

Starting from himself he should gradually extend his *mettā* towards all beings, irrespective of creed, race, colour, or sex, including dumb animals, until he has identified himself with all, making no distinction whatever. He merges himself in the whole universe and is one with all. He is no more dominated by egoistic feelings. He transcends all forms of separatism. No longer confining himself to water-tight compartments, no longer influenced by caste, class, national, racial, or religious prejudices, he can regard the whole world as his motherland and all as fellow-beings in the ocean of life.

Karunā

The second virtue that sublimes man is compassion (*karunā*). It is defined as that which makes the hearts of the good quiver when others are subject to suffering, or that which dissipates the sufferings of others. Its chief characteristic is the wish to remove the woes of others.

The hearts of compassionate persons are even softer than flowers. They do not and cannot rest satisfied until they relieve the sufferings of others. At times they even go to the extent of sacrificing their lives so as to alleviate the sufferings of others. The story of the Vyāghri Jātaka[1] where the Bodhisatta sacrificed his life to save a starving tigress and her cubs may be cited as an example.

It is compassion that compels one to serve others with altruistic motives. A truly compassionate person lives not for himself but for others. He seeks opportunities to serve others expecting nothing in return, not even gratitude.

Who needs compassion?

Many amidst us deserve our compassion. The poor and the needy the sick and the helpless, the lonely and the destitute, the ignorant and the vicious, the impure and the undisciplined are some that demand the compassion of kind-hearted, noble-minded men and women, to whatever religion or to whatever race they belong.

1. See p.550.

Some countries are materially rich but spiritually poor, while some others are spiritually rich but materially poor. Both these pathetic conditions have to be taken into consideration by the materially rich and the spiritually rich.

It is the paramount duty of the wealthy to come to the succour of the poor, who unfortunately lack most of the necessaries of life. Surely those who have in abundance can give to the poor and the needy their surplus without inconveniencing themselves.

Once a young student removed the door curtain in his house and gave it to a poor person telling his good mother that the door does not feel the cold but the poor certainly do. Such a kind-hearted attitude in young men and women is highly commendable.

It is gratifying to note that some wealthy countries have formed themselves into various philanthropic bodies to help under-developed countries, especially in Asia, in every possible way. Charitable organizations have also been established in all countries by men, women and students to give every possible assistance to the poor and the needy. Religious bodies also perform their respective duties in this connection in their own humble way. Homes for the Aged, Orphanages and other similar charitable institutions are needed in under-developed countries.

The beggar problem has still to be solved in some countries where begging has become a profession. Out of compassion for the unfortunate beggars this problem has to be solved satisfactorily by the respective Governments as the existence of beggars is an insult to any self-respecting nation.

As the materially rich should have compassion on the materially poor and try to elevate them, it is the duty of the spiritually rich, too, to have compassion on the spiritually poor and sublime them though they may be materially rich. Wealth alone cannot give genuine happiness. Peace of mind can be gained not by material treasures but by spiritual treasures. Many in this world are badly in need of substantial spiritual food, which is not easily obtained, as the spiritually poor far exceed the materially poor numerically, as they are found both amongst the rich and the poor.

Even more than poverty sickness prevails throughout the world. Many are physically sick, some are mentally sick. Science provides effective medicine for the former but not for the latter, who very often languish in mental hospitals.

There are causes for these two kinds of diseases. Compassionate men and women must try to remove the causes if they wish to produce an effective cure.

Effective measures have been employed by various nations to prevent and cure diseases not only of mankind but also of animals.

The Buddha set a noble example by attending
on the sick Himself and exhorting His disciples
with the memorable words:

*"He who ministers unto the sick ministers unto
me.*

Some selfless doctors render free services towards the alleviation of suffering. Some ex-
pend their whole time and energy in ministering
to the poor patients even at the risk of their lives.

Hospitals and free dispensaries have become
a blessing to humanity but more are needed so
that the poor may benefit by them. In under-
developed countries the poor suffer through lack
of medical facilities. The sick have to be carried
for miles with great inconvenience to the nearest
hospital or dispensary for medical treatment.
Sometimes they die on the way. Pregnant mothers
suffer most. Hospitals, dispensaries, maternity
homes, etc. are essential needs in backward
village areas.

The lowly and the destitute deserve the compassion of wealthy men and women. Sometimes
servants and workers are not well paid, well fed,
well clothed and more often than not they are
illtreated. Justice is not meted out to them. They
are neglected and are powerless as there is nobody to plead for them. Glaring cases of inhuman
cruelty receive publicity in some exceptional
cases. Many such cases are not known. These
unfortunate ones have no other alternative but

to suffer meekly even as Mother Earth suffers everything in silence. When the grief is unbearable, they commit suicide in utter desperation.

The vicious, the wicked, and the ignorant deserve compassion even more than those who suffer physically as they are mentally and spiritually sick. They should not be condemned and despised but sympathised with for their failings and defects. Though a mother has equal compassion towards all her children still she may have more compassion towards a sick child. Even so, greater compassion should be exercised towards the spiritually sick as their sickness ruins their character.

The Buddha, for instance, had great compassion towards the courtesan Ambapāli, and towards Angulimāla the murderer. Both of them later became His converts and underwent a complete reformation in character.

We must understand that greatness is latent in all however wicked they may be. Perhaps one appropriate word at the right moment may change the whole outlook of a person.

The Emperor Asoka perpetrated many crimes, so much so that he was stigmatized Asoka the Wicked. Later the words from a young novice— "Diligence is the path to the deathless"—produced such a great change in him that he became Asoka the Righteous (*Dharmāsoka*).

The Buddha's advice is to shun the company of the foolish. That does not mean that the good should not associate with them so as to reform them. People avoid those who suffer from contagious diseases. But compassionate physicians, attend on them so as to heal them. Otherwise they might die. In the same way the wicked may die spiritually if the good are not tolerant and compassionate towards them.

As a rule the Buddha went in search of the poor, the ignorant and the vicious, but the good and the virtuous came in search of the Buddha.

Like *mettā* (loving-kindness), *karunā* (compassion) should also be extended without limit towards all suffering and helpless beings, including dumb animals and fertile eggs.

To deny the rights and privileges of mankind on account of caste, colour, or race is inhuman and cruel. To feast on the flesh of animals by killing or causing them to be killed is not human compassion. To rain bombs from above and ruthlessly destroy millions of men, women and children is the worst form of cruelty that deluded man has ever perpetrated.

Today this pitiless, vengeful world has sacrificed the most precious thing on earth—life—at the altar of brute force. Whither has compassion fled?

The world needs today compassionate men and women to banish violence and cruelty from the face of the earth.

Buddhist compassion, it should be noted, does not consist in mere shedding of tears and the like, for the indirect enemy of compassion is passionate grief (*domanassa*).

Compassion embraces all sorrow-stricken beings, while loving-kindness embraces all living beings, happy or sorrowful.

Muditā

The third sublime virtue is *muditā*. It is not mere sympathy but sympathetic or appreciative joy which tends to destroy jealousy, its direct enemy.

One devastating force that endangers our whole constitution is jealousy. Very often some cannot bear to see or hear the successful achievements of others. They rejoice over their failures but cannot tolerate their successes. Instead of praising and congratulating the successful, they try to ruin, condemn and vilify them. In one way *muditā* is concerned more with oneself than with others as it tends to eradicate jealousy which ruins oneself. On the other hand it aids others as well since one who practises *muditā* will not try to hinder the progress and welfare of others.

It is quite easy to rejoice over the success of one's near and dear ones, but rather difficult to do so over the success of one's adversaries. Yes, the majority not only find it difficult but also do not and cannot rejoice. They seek delight in creating every possible obstacle so as to ruin their adversaries. They even go to the extent of poisoning, crucifying, and assassinating the good and the virtuous.

Socrates was poisoned, Christ was crucified, Gandhi was shot. Such is the nature of the wicked and deluded world.

The practice of *mettā* and *karuṇā* is easier than the practice of *muditā* which demands great personal effort and strong will-power.

Do the Western nations rejoice over the prosperity of the Eastern and the Eastern over the prosperity of the Western? Does one nation rejoice over the welfare of another nation? Is one race happy over the growing prosperity of another race? Does even one religious sect, which stands for the cultivation of morals, rejoice over the spiritual influence of another sect?

One religion is jealous of another religion, one part of the globe is jealous of another part of the globe, one institution is jealous of another institution, one business firm is jealous of another business firm, one family is jealous of another family, unsuccessful pupils are jealous of successful pupils, sometimes even one brother or sister is jealous of another brother or sister.

This is the very reason why individuals and groups should practise appreciative joy if they wish to sublime themselves and be internally happy.

The chief characteristic of *muditā* is happy acquiescence in others' prosperity and success (*anumodanā*). Laughter and the like are not the characteristics of *muditā* as exhilaration (*pahasa*) is regarded as its indirect enemy.

Muditā embraces all prosperous beings and is the congratulatory attitude of a person. It tends to eliminate any dislike (*arati*) towards a successful person.

Upekkhā

The fourth sublime state is the most difficult and the most essential. It is *upekkhā* or equanimity. The etymological meaning of the term *upekkhā* is 'discerning rightly,' 'viewing justly' or 'looking impartially,' that is, without attachment or aversion, without favour or disfavour.[1]

Equanimity is necessary especially for laymen who have to live in an ill-balanced world amidst fluctuating circumstances.

Slights and insults are the common lot of mankind. The world is so constituted that the good and the virtuous are often subject to unjust criticism and attack. It is heroic to maintain a balanced mind in such circumstances.

Loss and gain, fame and infamy, praise and blame, pain and happiness are eight worldly conditions[2] that affect all humanity. Most people

1. See pp. 536, 537, 605, 606.
2. See Chapter 43.

are perturbed when affected by such favourable or unfavourable states. One is elated when one is praised, and depressed when blamed and reviled. He is wise, says the Buddha, who, amidst such vicissitudes of life, stands unmoved like unto a firm rock, exercising perfect equanimity.

The Buddha's exemplary life offers us worldlings an excellent example of equanimity.

There was no religious teacher in the world who was so severely critcised, attacked, insulted and reviled as the Buddha, and yet none so highly praised, honoured and revered as the Buddha.

Once when He went in quest of alms, He was called an outcast by an impertinent brahmin. He calmly endured the insult and explained to him that it is not birth that makes one an outcast but an ignoble character. The brahmin was converted.

Inviting him to a house for alms, a certain man entertained the Buddha with the filthiest language, current in His time. He was called 'swine', 'brute', 'ox', etc. But He was not offended. He did not retaliate. Calmly He questioned His host what he would do when guests visited his house. He replied that he would prepare a feast to entertain them.

"Well, what would you do if they did not partake of it?" questioned the Buddha.

"In that case we ourselves would partake of the feast."

"Well, good brother, you have invited me to
your house for alms. You have entertained me
with a torrent of abuse. I do not accept it.
Please take it back," calmly replied the Buddha.

The offender's character was completely transformed.

"Retaliate not. Be silent as a cracked gong
when you are abused by others. If you do so, I
deem that you have already attained Nibbāna
although you have not realized Nibbāna."[1] Such
is the advice of the Buddha.

These are golden words that should be given
heed to in this ill-disciplined world of today.

Once a lady of the court induced some drunkards to revile the Buddha so much that Venerable
Ānanda, His attendant disciple, implored the
Buddha to leave the city and go elsewhere. But
the Buddha was unperturbed.

Another woman feigned pregnancy and publicly
accused the Buddha of having placed her in
that condition. A woman was killed by His rivals
and the Buddha was accused of murder. His
own cousin and disciple Devadatta made an
unsuccessful attempt to crush Him to death by
hurling a rock from a cliff. Some of His own
disciples accused Him of jealousy, partiality,
favouritism, etc.

---

1. See Dhammapada v. 124.

On the other hand many sang the praises of the Buddha. Kings prostrated themselves before His feet and paid the highest reverence.

Like the Mother Earth the Buddha suffered everything in silence with perfect equanimity.

Like a lion that does not tremble at every sound, one should not be perturbed by the poisoned darts of uncurbed tongues. Like the wind that does not cling to the meshes of a net, one should not be attached to the illusory pleasures of this changing world. Like the lotus that is unsoiled by the mud from which it springs, one should live unaffected by worldly temptations, ever calm, serene and peaceful.

As with the first three virtues so also *upekkhā* has for its direct enemy attachment (*rāga*) and for its indirect enemy callousness or unintelligent indifference.

Upekkhā discards clinging and aversion. An impartial attitude is its chief characteristic. He who practises equanimity is neither attracted by desirable objects nor is averse to undesirable objects.

His attitude towards the sinner and saint will be the same, for he makes no distinction.

Mettā embraces all beings, *karuṇā* embraces sufferers, *muditā* embraces the prosperous, and *upekkhā* embraces the good and the bad, the loved and the unloved, the pleasant and the unpleasant.

He who wishes to be divine in this life itself may daily cultivate these four sublime virtues which are dormant in all.

He who wishes to perfect himself and compassionately work for the welfare of all beings in the course of his countless births in Saṃsāra may strenuously develop the ten Perfections (*Pāramī*) and ultimately become a Sammā Sambuddha, a Supremely Enlightened One.

He who wishes to eradicate his passions and put an end to suffering by realizing Nibbāna at the earliest possible opportunity may diligently follow the unique Noble Eightfold Path which still exists in its pristine purity.

The Buddha exhorts:

"Suppose O, monks, this mighty earth were one mass of water and a man were to throw down thereon a yoke with one hole. Then comes a wind from the east and wafts it west, and a wind from the west wafts it east; a north wind wafts it south, and a south wind wafts it north. Then once at the end of a hundred years a blind turtle push his neck through that yoke with one hole whenever he popped up to the surface at the end of a hundred years?

"It is unlikely, lord, that the blind turtle would do that.

"It is just as unlikely, O monks, that one will get birth in human form; just as unlikely that a Tathāgata should arise in the world, an Arahant, a Fully Enlightened One; just as unlikely that the Norm (*Dhamma*) and Discipline (*Vinaya*) proclaimed by a Tathāgata should be shown in the world.

"But now indeed, O monks, this state of human birth is won, and a Tathāgata has arisen in the world, and the Norm and Discipline proclaimed by the Tathāgata is shown in the world.

"Wherefore, O monks, ye must make an effort to realize: This is ill, this is the cause of ill, this is the cessation of ill, this is the way leading to the cessation of ill."[1]

---

1. Kindred Sayings, v. p. 334.

CHAPTER 43

EIGHT WORLDLY CONDITIONS

Vicissitudes of Life

(*Aṭṭhalokadhamma*)

This ill—balanced world is not absolutely rosy. Nor is it totally thorny. The rose is soft, beautiful and fragrant. But the stem on which it grows is full of thorns. What is rosy is rosy; what is thorny is thorny. Because of the rose one will not meddle with the thorns nor will one disparage the rose on account of the thorns.

To an optimist this world is absolutely rosy; to a pessimist this world is absolutely thorny. But to a realist this world is neither absolutely rosy nor absolutely thorny. It abounds with beautiful roses and prickly thorns as well, from a realistic standpoint.

An understanding person will not be infatuated by the beauty of the rose but will view it as it is. Knowing well the nature of the thorns, he will view them as they are and will take the precaution not to be wounded.

Like the pendulum that perpetually turns to the right and left, four desirable and undesirable conditions prevail in this world which everyone, without exception, must perforce face in the course of one's lifetime.

They are gain (*lābha*) and loss (*alābha*), fame (*yasa*) and defame (*ayasa*), praise (*pasaṁsā*) and blame (*nindā*), happiness (*sukha*) and pain (*dukkha*).

GAIN AND LOSS

Business men, as a rule, are subject to both gain and loss. It is quite natural to be complacent in obtaining a gain or a profit. In itself there is nothing wrong. Such righteous or unrighteous profits produce some pleasure which average men seek. Without pleasurable moments, though temporary, life would not be worth living. In this competitive and chaotic world rarely do people enjoy some kind of happiness which gladdens their hearts. Such happiness, though material, does conduce to health and longevity.

The problem arises in case of loss. Profits one can bear smilingly but not so the losses. More often than not they lead to mental derangement and sometimes to suicide when the losses are unbearable. It is under such adverse circumstances that one should exhibit moral courage and maintain a balanced mind. All have ups and downs while battling with life. One should always be prepared for the losses in particular. Then there will be less disappointment.

When something is stolen naturally one feels sad. But by becoming sad one would not be able to retrieve the loss. One should think that someone had benefited thereby though unrighteously. May he be well and happy!.

Or one can console oneself thinking—"it's only a minor loss." One may even adopt a highly philosophical attitude— "there is nothing to be called Me or Mine."

In the time of the Buddha once a noble lady was offering food to the Venerable Sāriputta and some monks. While serving them she received a note stating that her husband and all her sons who had gone to settle a dispute were way-laid and killed. Without getting upset, calmly she kept the note in her waist-pouch and served the monks as if nothing had happened. A maid, who was carrying a pot of ghee to offer to the monks, inadvertently slipped and broke the pot of ghee. Thinking that the lady would naturally feel sorry over the loss, Venerable Sāriputta consoled her, saying that all breakable things are bound to break. The wise lady unperturbly remarked—"Bhante, what is this trivial loss? I have just received a note stating that my husband and sons were killed by some assassins. I placed it in my pouch without losing my balance. I am serving you all despite the loss."

Such valour on the part of courageous women is highly commendable.

Once the Buddha went seeking alms in a village. Owing to the intervention of Māra the Evil One, the Buddha did not obtain any food. When Māra questioned the Buddha rather sarcastically whether He was hungry or not, the Buddha solemnly explained the mental attitude of those who are free from Impediments, and replied:—"Ah, happily do we live, we who have no Impediments. Feeders of joy shall we be even as the gods of the Radiant Realm."

On another occasion the Buddha and His disciples observed *vassa* (rainy period) in a village at the invitation of a brahmin, who, however, completely forgot his duty to attend to the needs of the Buddha and the Sangha. Throughout a period of three months, although Venerable Moggallāna volunteered to obtain food by his psychic powers, the Buddha, making no complaint, was contented with the fodder of horses offered by a horse-dealer.

Visākhā, the Buddha's chief female lay disciple, used to frequent the monastery to attend to the needs of the Buddha and the Sangha decked with a very valuable outer garment. On entering the monastery, she used to remove it and give it to the maid for safe custody. Once the maid inadvertently left it in the temple and returned home. Venerable Ānanda, noticing it, kept it in a safe place to be given to Visākhā when she visited the monastery. Visākhā discovering the loss, advised the maid to look for it but not to take it back in case any Bhikkhu had touched it. On inquiry the maid understood that Venerable Ānanda had kept it in safe custody. Returning home, she reported the matter. Viskāhā visited the monastery and inquired of the Buddha what meritorious act should she perform with the money obtained by selling the costly garment. The Buddha advised her to build a monastery for the benefit of the Sangha. As there was nobody to buy the garment because of its high cost, she herself bought it and built a monastery and offered it to the Sangha. After the offering, she expressed her gratitude to the maid, saying:—"If you had not inadvertently left my garment, I would not have got an opportunity to perform this meritorious act. Please share the merit."

Instead of grieving over the temporary loss and reprimanding the maid for her carelessnes, she thanked her for granting an opportunity for service.

The exemplary attitude of cultured Visākhā is a memorable lesson to all those who are quickly irritated over the misdoings of helpless servants.

Losses one must try to bear cheerfully with manly vigour. Unexpectedly one confronts them, very often in groups and not singly. One must face them with equanimity (*upekkhā*) and think it is an opportunity to practise that sublime virtue.

FAME (*yasa*) and DEFAME (*ayasa*)

Fame and defame are another pair of inevitable worldly conditions that confront us in the course of our daily lives.

Fame we welcome, defame we dislike. Fame gladdens our mind, defame disheartens us. We desire to become famous. We long to see our names and pictures appear in the papers. We are greatly pleased when our activities, however insignificant, are given publicity. Sometimes we seek undue publicity too.

To see their picture in a magazine some are ready to pay any amount. To obtain an honour some are prepared to offer any bribe or give a fat donation to the party in power. For the sake of publicity some exhibit their generosity by giving alms to one hundred monks and even more, but they may be totally indifferent to the sufferings of the poor and the needy in the neighbourhood. One may charge and punish a starving person who, to appease his hunger, were to steal a coconut in his garden, but would not hesitate to present thousand coconuts to get a good name.

These are human frailties. Most people do even a good action with an ulterior motive. Selfless persons who act disinterestedly are rare in this world. Even if the motive is not very praiseworthy, those who do any good are to be congratulated on having done a beneficial act. Most world-lings have something up their sleeves. Well, who is 100% good? How many are perfectly pure in their motives? How many are absolutely altruistic?

We need not hunt after fame. If we are worthy of fame, it will come to us unsought. The bee will be attracted to the flower, laden with honey. The flower however, does not invite the bee.

True indeed, we feel naturally happy, nay extremely happy, when our fame is spread far and wide. But we must realize that fame, honour and glory only lead to the grave. They vanish in thin air. Empty words are they, though pleasing to the ear.

What about defame? It is not palatable either to the ear or mind. We are undoubtedly perturbed when unkind de-famatory words pierce our ears. The pain of mind is still greater when the so-called report is unjust and absolutely false.

Normally it takes years to erect a magnificent building. In a minute or two, with modern devastating weapons, it could easily be demolished. Sometimes it takes years or a lifetime to build up a good reputation. In no long time the hard-earned good name can be ruined. Nobody is exempt from the devasting remark beginning with the infamous "but". Yes, he is very good, he does this and that, but......His whole good record is blackened by the so-called "but". You may live the life of a Buddha, but you will not be exempt from cri-ticism, attacks and insults.

The Buddha was the most famous and the most maligned religious teacher in His time.

Great men are often not known; even if they are known, they are misknown.

Some antagonists of the Buddha spread a rumour that a woman used to spend the night in the monastery. Foiled in this base attempt, they spread a false rumour amongst the populace that the Buddha and His disciples murdered that very woman and hid her corpse in the rubbish-heap of withered flowers within the monastery. When His historic mission met with success and when many sought ordination under Him, His adversaries maligned Him, saying that He was robbing the mothers of their sons,depriving wives of their husbands, and that He was obstructing the progress of the nation.

Failing in all these attempts to ruin His noble character, His own cousin and a jealous disciple of His, attempted to kill him by hurling a rock from above.

Being a Buddha, He could not be killed.

If such be the sad fate of faultless, pure Buddhas, what can be the state of ordinary mortals?

The higher you climb a hill, the more conspicuous you become and much smaller in the eyes of others. Your back is revealed but your front is hidden. The fault-finding world exhibits your short–comings and misdoings but hides your salient virtues. The winnowing fan ejects the husks but retains the grains: the strainer, on the contrary, retains the gross remnants but drains out the sweet juice. The cultured take the subtle and remove the gross; the uncultured retain the gross and reject the subtle.

When you are misrepresented, deliberately or undeliberately unjustly reported, as Epictetus advises, it is wise to think or say—"O, by his slight acquaintanceship and little knowledge of myself I am slightly criticised. But if I am known better, more serious and much greater would be the accusations against me."

It is needless to waste time in correcting the false reports unless circumstances compel you to necessitate a clarification. The enemy is gratified when he sees that you are hurt. That is what he actually expects. If you are indifferent, such misrepresentations will fall on deaf ears.

> In seeing the faults of others, we should behave like a blind person.

> In hearing unjust criticism of others, we should behave like a deaf person.

> In speaking ill of others, we should behave like a dumb person.
> It is not possible to put a stop to false accusations, reports and rumours.

The world is full of thorns and pebbles. It is impossible to remove them. But if we have to walk in spite of such obstacles, instead of trying to remove them, which is impossible, it is advisable to wear a pair of slippers and walk harmlessly.

The Dhamma teaches:

> Be like a lion that trembles not at sounds.
> Be like the wind that does not cling to the meshes of a net.
> Be like a lotus that is not contaminated by the mud from which it springs up.
> Wander alone like a rhinoceros.

Being the king of the forest, lions are fearless. By nature they are not frightened by the roaring of other animals. In this world we may hear adverse reports, false accusations, degrading remarks of uncurbed tongues. Like a lion, we should not even listen to them. Like the boomerang they will end where they began.

Dogs bark, caravans peacefully move on.

We are living in a muddy world. Numerous are the lotuses that spring therefrom. Without being contaminated by the mud, they adorn the world. Like lotuses we should try to lead blameless noble lives unmindful of the mud that may be thrown at us.

We should expect mud to be thrown at us instead of roses. Then there will be no disappointment.

Though difficult we should try to cultivate non-attachment.

> Alone we come, alone we go.
> Non-attachment is happiness in this world.

Unmindful of the poisonous darts of uncurbed tongues alone we should wander serving others to the best of our ability.

It is rather strange that great men have been slandered, vilified, poisoned, crucified, or shot.

Great Socrates was poisoned. Noble Jesus Christ was ruthlessly crucified. Harmless Mahatma Gandhi was shot.

Well, is it dangerous to be too good?

Yes, during their lifetime they are criticised, attacked and killed. After death they are deified and honoured.

Great men are indifferent to fame or defame. They are not upset when they are criticised or maligned for they work not for fame or name. They are indifferent whether others recognise their services or not. "To work they have the right but not to the fruit thereof."

●

PRAISE (*pasaṁsā* and BLAME (*nindā*)

Praise and blame are two more worldly conditions that affect mankind. It is natural to be elated when praised and to be depressed when blamed.

Amidst praise and blame, the Buddha says, the wise do not exhibit either elation or depression. Like a solid rock that is not shaken by the wind they remain unmoved.

Praise, if worthy, is pleasing to the ears; if unworthy, as in the case of flattery, though pleasing, it is deceptive. But they are all sounds which have no effect if they do not reach our ears.

From a wordly standpoint a word of praise goes a long way. By praising a little a favour can easily be obtained. One word of merited praise is sufficient to attract an audience before one speaks. If, at the outset, a speaker praises the audience, he will have attentive ears. If he criticises the audience at the outset, the response will not be satisfactory.

The cultured do not resort to flattery nor do they wish to be flattered by others. The praiseworthy they praise without any jealousy. The blameworthy they blame not contemptuously but out of compassion with the object of reforming them.

Great men are highly praised by the great and small who know them well though they are utterly indifferent to such praise.

Many who knew the Buddha intimately extolled the virtues of the Buddha in their own way. One Upāli, a millionaire, a new convert, praised the Buddha, enumerating hundred virtues *ex tempore*. Nine sterling virtues of the Buddha that were current in His time are still being recited by His followers, looking at His image. They are a subject of meditation to the devout. Those well-merited virtues are still a great inspiration to His followers.

What about blame?

The Buddha says. "They who speak much are blamed. They who speak a little are blamed. They who are silent are also blamed. In this world there is none who is not blamed."

Blame seems to be a universal legacy to mankind.

The majority of the people in the world, remarks the Buddha, are ill–disciplined. Like an elephant in the battle-field that endures all arrows shot at him, even so, the Buddha says, do I suffer all insults.

The deluded and the wicked are prone to seek only the ugliness in others but not the good and beautiful.

None, except the Buddha, is hundred percent good. No-body is hundred percent bad either. There is evil in the best of us. There is good in the worst of us. He who silences himself like a cracked gong when attacked, insulted and abused, he, I say, the Buddha exhorts, is in the presence of Nibbāna although he has not yet attained Nibbāna.

One may work with the best of motives. But the outside world very often misconstrues him and will impute motives never even dreamt of.

One may serve and help others to the best of one's ability sometimes by incurring debt or selling one's articles or pro-perty to save a friend in trouble. But later, the deluded world is so constituted that those very persons whom one has helped will find fault with him, blackmail him, blemish his good character and will rejoice in his downfall.

In the Jātaka stories it is stated that Guttila the musician taught everything he knew to his pupil without a closed fist, but the ungrateful man he was, he unsuccessfully tried to compete with his teacher and ruin him.

Devadatta, a pupil and cousin of the Buddha who had developed psychic powers, not only tried to discredit the Buddha but also made an unsuccessful attempt to crush Him to death by hurling a rock from above while He was pacing up and down below.

On one occasion the Buddha was invited by a brahmin for alms to his house. As He was invited, the Buddha visited his house. Instead of entertaining Him, he poured forth a torrent of abuse with the filthiest of words.

The Buddha politely inquired:—

"Do visitors come to your house good brahmin?"

"Yes", he replied.

"What do you do when they come?"

"Oh, we prepare a sumptuous feast."

"If they fail to turn up, please?"

"Why, we gladly partake of it."

"Well, good brahmin, you have invited me for alms and entertained me with abuse. I accept nothing. Please take it back."

The Buddha did not retaliate, but politely gave back what the brahmin gave Him. Retaliate not, the Buddha exhorts. Vengeance will be met with vengeance, Force will be met with force. Bombs will be met with bombs. "Hatreds do not cease through hatreds, but through love alone they cease." is a noble utterance of the Buddha.

There was no religious teacher so highly praised and so severely criticised, reviled and blamed like the Buddha. Such is the fate of great men.

In a public assembly a vile woman named Cincā feigning pregnancy, maligned the Buddha. With a smiling face the Buddha patiently endured the insult and the Buddha's innocence was proved.

The Buddha was accused of murdering a woman assisted by His disciples. Non-Buddhists severely criticised the Buddha and His Disciples to such an extent that the Venerable Ānanda appealed to the Buddha to leave for another village.

—"How, Ānanda, if those villagers also abuse us?"

—"Well then, Lord, we will proceed to another village."

—"Then Ānanda, the whole of India will have no place for us. Be patient. These abuses will automatically cease."

Māgandiyā, a lady of the harem, had a grudge against the Buddha for speaking ill of her attractive figure when her father, through ignorance, wished to give her in marriage to the Buddha. She hired drunkards to insult the Buddha in public. With perfect equanimity the Buddha endured the insults. But Māgandiyā had to suffer for her misdemeanour.

Insults are the common lot of humanity. The more you work and the greater you become, the more are you subject to insult and humiliation.

Jesus Christ was insulted, humiliated and crucified.

Socrates was insulted by his own wife. Whenever he went out to help others his intolerant wife used to scold him. One day as she was unwell she failed to perform her unruly task. Socrates left home on that day with a sad face. His friends inquired why he was sad. He replied that his wife did not scold him on that day as she was unwell.

"Well, you ought to be happy for not getting that unwelcome scolding," remarked his friends.

"Oh no! When she scolds me I get an opportunity to practise patience. Today I missed it. That is the reason why I am sad," answered the philosopher.

These are memorable lessons for all.

When insulted we should think that we are being given an opportunity to practise patience. Instead of being offended, we should be grateful to our adversaries.

●

HAPPINESS (*sukha*) and PAIN (*dukkha*)

Happiness and pain are the last pair of opposites. They are the most powerful factors that affect mankind.

What can be endured with ease is *sukha* (happiness), what is difficult to bear is *dukkha* (pain). Ordinary happiness is the gratification of a desire. No sooner is the desired thing gained than we desire some other kind of happiness. So insatiate are our selfish desires. The enjoyment of sensual pleasures is the highest and only happiness to an average person. There is no doubt a momentary happiness in the anticipation, gratification and recollection of such material pleasures highly priced by the sensualist, but they are illusory and temporary.

Can material possessions give one genuine happiness? If so, millionaires would not think of committing suicide. In a certain country which has reached the zenith of material progress about ten percent suffer from mental diseases. Why should it be so if material possessions alone can give genuine happiness?

Can dominion over the whole world produce true happiness? Alexander, who triumphantly marched to India, conquering the lands on the way, sighed for not having more pieces of earth to conquer.

Are Emperors and Kings who wear crowns always happy?

Very often the lives of statesmen who wield power are at stake. The pathetic cases of Mahatma Gandhi and Kennedy are illustrative examples.

Real happiness is found within, and is not to be defined in terms of wealth, power, honours or conquests.

If such worldly possessions are forcibly or unjustly obtained, or are misdirected, or even viewed with attachment, they will be a source of pain and sorrow for the possessors. What is happiness to one may not be happiness to another. What is meat and drink to one may be poison to another.

The Buddha enumerates four kinds of happiness for a layman. They are the happiness of possession (*atthi sukha*)- namely, health, wealth, longevity, beauty, joy, property, strength, children, etc.

The second source of happiness is derived by the enjoyment of such possessions (*bhoga sukha*). Ordinary men and women wish to enjoy themselves. The Buddha does not advise all to renounce their worldly pleasures and retire to solitude.

The enjoyment of wealth lies not only in using it for ourselves but also in giving it for the welfare of others. What we eat is only temporary. What we preserve we leave and go. What we give we take with us. We are remembered for ever by the good deeds we have done with our worldly possessions.

Not falling into debt (*ananasukha*) is another source of happiness. If we are contented with what we have and if we are economical, we need not be in debt to any one. Debtors live in mental agony and are under obligation to their creditors. Though poor, when debt free, you feel relieved and are mentally happy.

Leading a blameless life (*anavajjasukha*) is one of the best sources of happiness for a layman. A blameless person is a blessing to himself and to others. He is admired by all and feels happier, being affected by the peaceful vibrations of others. It should be stated however that it is very, very difficult to get a good name from all. The noble-minded persons are concerned only with a blameless life and are indifferent to external approbation. The majority in this world delight themselves in enjoying pleasures while some others seek delight in renouncing them. Non-attachment or the transcending of material pleasures is happiness to the spiritual. Nibbānic bliss, which is a bliss of relief from suffering, is the highest form of happiness.

Ordinary happiness we welcome, but not its opposite—pain, which is rather difficult to endure.

Pain or suffering comes in different guises.

We suffer when we are subject to old age which is natural. With equanimity we have to bear the sufferings of old age.

More painful than sufferings due to old age are sufferings caused by disease, which, if chronic, we feel that death is preferable. Even the slightest toothache or headache is sometimes unbearable.

When we are subject to disease, without being worried, we should be able to bear it at any cost. Well, we must console ourselves thinking that we have escaped from a still more serious disease.

Very often we are separated from our near and dear ones. Such separation causes great pain of mind. We should understand that all association must end with separation. Here is a good opportunity to practise equanimity.

More often than not we are compelled to be united with the unpleasant which we detest. We should be able to bear them. Perhaps we are reaping the effects of our own Kamma, past or present. We should try to accommodate ourselves to the new situation or try to overcome the obstacle by some means or other.

Even the Buddha, a perfect being, who has destroyed all defilements, had to endure physical suffering caused by disease and accidents.

The Buddha was constantly subject to headache. His last illness caused Him much physical suffering. As a result of Devadatta's hurling a rock to kill Him, His foot was wounded by a splinter which necessitated an operation. Sometimes He was compelled to starve. At times He had to be contented with horse-fodder. Due to the disobedience of His own pupils, He was compelled to retire to a forest for three months. In the forest, on a couch of leaves spread on rough ground, facing piercing cool winds, He slept with perfect equanimity. Amidst pain and happiness He lived with a balanced mind. Death is the greatest sorrow we are compelled to face in the course of our wanderings in *samsāra*. Sometimes, death comes not singly but in numbers which may even cause insanity.

Patācārā lost her near and dear ones—parents, husband, brother and two children—and she went mad. The Buddha consoled her.

Kisā Gotami lost her only infant, and she went in search of a remedy for her dead son, carrying the corpse. She approached the Buddha and asked for a remedy.

"Well, sister, can you bring some mustard seed?"

"Certainly, Lord!"

"But, sister, it should be from a house where no one has died."

Mustard seeds she found, but not a place where death had not visited.

She understood the nature of life.

When a mother was questioned why she did not weep over the tragic death of her only son, she replied; "Uninvited he came, uninformed he went. As he came, so he went. Why should we weep? What avails weeping?"

As fruits fall from a tree—tender, ripe or old—even so we die in our infancy, in the prime of manhood or even in old age.

The sun rises in the East only to set in the West.

Flowers bloom in the morning to fade in the evening.

Inevitable death, which comes to all without exception, we have to face with perfect equanimity.

> "Just as the earth whate'er is thrown
> Upon her, whether sweet or foul,
> Indifferent is to all alike,
> No hatred shows, nor amity,
> So likewise he in good or ill,
> Must even—balanced ever be."

The Buddha says—

> When touched by worldly conditions the mind of an Arahant never wavers.

> Amidst gain and loss, fame and defame, praise and blame, happiness and pain, let us try to maintain a balanced mind.

CHAPTER 44

THE PROBLEMS OF LIFE

Who? Whence? Whither? Why? What? are some important porblems that affect all humanity.

Who is man? is our first question.

Let us proceed with what is self-evident and perceptible to all.

Man possesses a body which is seen either by our senses or by means of apparatus. This material body consists of forces and qualities which are in a state of constant flux.

Scientists find it difficult to define what matter is. Certain philosophers define "matter as that in which proceed the changes called motion and motion as those changes which proceed in matter."[1]

The Pali term for matter is *Rūpa*. It is explained as that which changes or disintegrates. That which manifests itself is also another explanation.

According to Buddhism there are four fundamental material elements. They are *Paṭhavi, Āpo, Tejo,* and *Vāyo.*

Paṭhavi means the element of extension, the substratum of matter. Without it objects cannot occupy space. The qualities of hardness and softness which are purely relative are two conditions of this element. This element of extension is present in earth, water, fire and air. For instance, the water above is supported by water below. It is this element of extension in conjunction with the element of motion (*Vāyo*) that produces the upward pressure. Heat or cold is the *Tejo* element, while fluidity is the *Āpo* element.

Āpo is the element of cohesion. Unlike *Paṭhavi* it is intangible. It is this element which enables the scattered atoms of matter to cohere and thus gives us the idea of body.

---

1. Ouspensky—*Tertium Organum* p. 8.

Tejo is the element of heat. Cold is also a form of *Tejo*. Both heat and cold are included in *Tejo* because they possess the power of maturing bodies, or, in other words, the vitalizing energy. Preservation and decay are due to this element.

Vāyo is the element of motion. The movements are caused by this element. Motion is regarded as the force or the generator of heat. Both motion and heat in the material realm correspond respectively to consciousness and Kamma in the mental.

These four powerful forces are inseparable and interrelated, but one element may preponderate over another, as, for instance, the element of extension preponderates in earth; cohesion, in water; heat, in fire; and motion, in air.

Thus, matter consists of forces and qualities which constantly change not remaining the same even for two consecutive moments. According to Buddhism matter endures only for 17 thought-moments.[1]

At the moment of birth, according to biology, man inherits from his parents an infinitesimally minute cell 30 millionth part of an inch across. "In the course of nine months this speck grows to a living bulk 15,000 million times greater than it was at outset."[2] This tiny chemico-physical cell is the physical foundation of man.

According to Buddhism sex is also determined at the moment of conception.

Combined with matter there is another important factor in this complex machinery of man. It is the mind. As such it pleases some learned writers to say that man is not Mind plus Body, but is a Mind-Body. Scientists declare that life emerges from matter and mind from life. But they do not give us a satisfactory explanation with regard to the development of the mind.

---

1. During the time occupied by a flash of lightning billions and billions of thought-moments may arise.
2. Sir Charles Sherrington—*Life's Unfolding*, p. 32.

Unlike the material body immaterial mind is invisible, but it could be sensed directly. An old couplet runs:—

"What is mind? No matter.
What is matter? Never mind."

We are aware of our thoughts and feelings and so forth by direct sensation, and we infer their existence in others by analogy.

There are several Pāli terms for mind. *Mana, Citta, Viññāṇa* are the most noteworthy of them. Compare the Pali root *man,* to think, with the English word man and the Pali word *Manussa* which means he who has a developed consciousness.

In Buddhism no distinction is made between mind and consciousness. Both are used as synonymous terms. Mind may be defined as simply the awareness of an object since there is no agent or a soul that directs all activities. It consists of fleeting mental states which constantly arise and perish with lightning rapidity. "With birth for its source and death for its mouth it persistently flows on like a river receiving from the tributary streams of sense constant accretions to its flood." Each momentary consciousness of this ever-changing life-stream, on passing away, transmits its whole energy. all the indelibly recorded impressions, to its successor. Every fresh consciousness therefore consists of the potentialities of its predecessors and something more. As all impressions are indelibly recorded in this ever-changing palimpsest-like mind, and as all potentialities are transmitted from life to life, irrespective of temporary physical disintegrations, reminiscence of past births or past incidents becomes a possibility. If memory depends solely on brain cells, it becomes an impossibility.

Like electricity mind is both a constructive and destructive powerful force. It is like a double-edged weapon that can equally be used either for good or evil. One single thought that arises in this invisible mind can even save or destroy the world. One such thought can either populate or depopulate a whole country. It is mind that creates one's heaven. It is mind that creates one's hell.

Ouspensky writes:—"Concerning the latent energy contained in the phenomena of consciousness, *i.e.* in thoughts, feelings, desires, we discover that its potentiality is even more immeasurable, more boundless. From personal experience, from observation, from history, we know that ideas, feelings, desires, manifesting themselves, can liberate enormous quantities of energy, and create infinite series of phenomena. An idea can act for centuries and milleniums and only grow and deepen, evoking ever new series of phenomena, liberating ever fresh energy. We know that thoughts continue to live and act when even the very name of the man who created them has been converted into a myth, like the names of the founders of ancient religions, the creators of the immortal poetical works of antiquity, heroes, leaders, and prophets. Their words are repeated by innumerable lips, their ideas are studied and commented upon.

"Undoubtedly each thought of a poet contains enormous potential force, like the power confined in a piece of coal or in a living cell, but infinitely more subtle, imponderable and potent."[1]

Observe, for instance, the potential force that lies in the following significant words of the Buddha:—

Mano-pubbaṅgamā dhammā—mano—seṭṭhā—manomayā.
Mind fore-runs deeds; mind is chief, and mind-made are they.

Mind or consciousness, according to Buddhism, arises at the very moment of conception, together with matter. Consciousness is therefore present in the foetus. This initial consciousness, technically known as rebirth-consciousness or

---

1. Ouspensky—*Tertium Organum* p. 125.

relinking consciousness (*Paṭisandhi viññāṇa*), is conditioned by past kamma of the person concerned. The subtle mental, intellectual, and moral differences that exist amongst mankind are due to this Kamma conditioned consciousness, the second factor of man.

To complete the trio that constitutes man there is a third factor, the phenomenon of life that vitalizes both mind and matter. Due to the presence of life reproduction becomes possible. Life manifests itself both in physical and mental phenomena. In Pāli the two forms of life are termed *Nāma jivitindriya* and *Rūpajivitindriya*—psychic and physical life.

Matter, mind, and life are therefore the three distinct factors that constitute man. With their combination a powerful force known as man with inconceivable possibilities comes into being. He becomes his own creator and destroyer. In him are found a rubbish-heap of evil and a storehouse of virtue. In him are found the worm, the brute, the man, the superman, the deva, the Brahma. Both criminal tendencies and saintly characteristics are dormant in him. He may either be a blessing or a curse to himself and others. In fact man is a world by himself.

Whence? is our second question.

How did man originate?

Either there must be a beginning for man or there cannot be a beginning. Those who belong to the first school postulate a first cause, whether as a cosmic force or as an Almighty Being. Those who belong to the second school deny a first cause for, in common experience, the cause ever becomes the effect and the effect becomes the cause. In a circle of cause and effect a first cause is inconceivable. According to the former life has had a beginning; while according to the latter it is beginningless. In the opinion of some the conception of a first cause is as ridiculous as a round triangle.

According to the scientific standpoint, man is the direct product of the sperm and ovum cells provided by his parents. Scientists while asserting 'Omne vivum ex vivo'—all life from life, maintain, that mind and life evolved from the lifeless.

Now, from the scientific standpoint, man is absolutely parent-born. As such life precedes life. With regard to the origin of the first protoplasm of life, or 'colloid' (whichever we please to call it), scientists plead ignorance.

According to Buddhism man is born from the matrix of action (kammayoni). Parents merely provide man with a material layer. As such being precedes being. At the moment of conception, it is Kamma that conditions the initial consciousness that vitalizes the foetus. It is this invisible Kammic energy generated from the past birth that produces mental phenomena and the phenomenon of life in an already extant physical phenomenon, to complete the trio that constitutes man.

Dealing with the conception of beings the Buddha states:—

"Where three are found in combination, there a germ of life is planted. If mother and father come together, but it is not the mother's period, and the 'being-to-be born' (gandhabba) is not present, then no germ of life is planted. If mother and father come together, and it is the mother's period, but the 'being-to-be-born' is not present, then again no germ of life is planted. If mother and father come together, and it is the mother's period, and the 'being-to-be-born' is also present, then, by the combination of these three, a germ of life is there planted."

Here Gandhabba (= gantabba) refers to a suitable being ready to be born in that particular womb. This term is used only in this particular connection, and must not be mistaken for a permanent soul.

For a being to be born here a being must die somewhere. The birth of a being corresponds to the death of a being in a past life; just as, in conventional terms, the rising of the sun in one place means the setting of the sun in another place.

The Buddha states—"a first beginning of beings who, obstructed by ignorance and fettered by craving, wander and fare on, is not to be percieved."

This life-stream flows *ad infinitum* as long as it is fed with the muddy waters of ignorance and craving. When these two are completely cut off, then only does the life-stream cease to flow; rebirth ends as in the case of Buddhas and Arahants. An ultimate beginning of this life-stream cannot be determined, as a stage cannot be perceived when this life force was not fraught with ignorance and craving.

The Buddha has here referred merely to the beginning of the life-stream of living beings. It is left to scientists to speculate on the origin and the evolution of the universe.

Whither? is our third question.
Where goes man?

According to ancient materialism which, in Pali and Saṁskrit, is known as *Lokāyata*, man is annihilated after death, leaving behind him any force generated by him. 'Man is composed of four elements. When man dies the earthy element returns and relapses into the earth; the watery element returns into the water; the fiery element returns into the fire; the airy element returns into the air, the senses pass into space. Wise and fools alike, when the body dissolves, are cut off, perish, do not exist any longer. There is no other world. Death is the end of all. This present world alone is real. The so-called eternal heaven and hell are the inventions of imposters."[1]

---

1. Sri Radhakrishna—*Indian Philosophy* Vol. 1. p. 278.

Materialists believe only in what is cognizable by the senses. As such matter alone is real. The ultimate principles are the four elements—earth, water, fire and air. The self-conscious life mysteriously springs forth from them, just as the genie makes its appearance when Aladdin rubs his lamp. The brain secretes thought just as liver secretes bile.

In the view of materialists the belief in the other world, as Sri Radhakrishna states, "is a sign of mendaciousness, feminism, weakness, cowardice and dishonesty."

According to Christianity there is no past for man. The present is only a preparation for two eternities of heaven and hell. Whether they are viewed as places or states man has for his future endless felicity in heaven or endless suffering in hell. Man is therefore not annihilated after death, but his essence goes to eternity.

"Whoever," as Schopenhaeur says, "regards himself as having become out of nothing must also think that he will again become nothing; or that an eternity has passed before he was, and then a second eternity had begun, through which he will never cease to be, is a monstrous thought."

The adherents of Hinduism who believe in a past and present do not state that man is annihilated after death. Nor do they say that man is eternalized after death. They believe in an endless series of past and future births. In their opinion the life-stream of man flows *ad infinitum* as long as it is pro-pelled by the force of Kamma, one's actions. In due course the essence of man may be reabsorbed into Ultimate Reality (*Paramātma*) from which his soul emanated.

Buddhism believes in the present. With the present as the basis it argues the past and future. Just as an electric light is the outward manifestation of invisible electric energy even so man is merely the outward manifestation of an in-visible energy known as Kamma. The bulb may break, and the light may be extinguished, but the current remains and the light may be reproduced in another bulb. In the same way the Kammic force remains undisturbed by the disintegration of the physical body, and the passing away of the present consciousness leads to the arising of a fresh one in another birth. Here the electric current is like the Kammic force, and the bulb may be compared to the egg-cell provided by the parents.

Past Kamma conditions the present birth; and present Kamma, in combination with past Kamma, conditions the future. The present is the offspring of the past, and becomes in turn the parent of the future.

Death is therefore not the complete annihilation of man, for though that particular life span ended, the force which hitherto actuated it is not destroyed.

After death the life-flux of man continues *ad infinitum* as long as it is fed with the waters of ignorance and craving. In conventional terms man need not necessarily be born as a man because humans are not the only living beings. Moreover, earth, an almost insignificant speck in the universe, is not the only place in which he will seek rebirth. He may be born in other habitable planes as well.[1]

If man wishes to put and end to this repeated series of births, he can do so as the Buddha and Arahants have done by realizing Nibbāna, the complete cessation of all forms of craving.

Where does man go? He can go wherever he wills or likes if he is fit for it. If, with no particular wish, he leaves his path to be prepared by the course of events, he will go to the place or state he fully deserves in accordance with his Kamma.

Why? is our last question.
Why is man? Is there a purpose in life?
This is rather a controversial question.
What is the materialistic standpoint?

---

1. "There are about 1,000,000 planetary systems in the Milky Way in which life may exist."
See Fred Hoyle, *The Nature of the Universe* pp. 87-89.

Scientists answer:—

> *"Has life purpose? What, or where, or when?*
> *Out of space came universe, came Sun,*
> *Came Earth, came Life, came Man, and more must come.*
> *But as to Purpose: whose or whence? Why, None."*

As materialists confine themselves purely to sense-data and the present material welfare ignoring all spiritual values, they hold a view diametrically opposite to that of moralists. In their opinion there is no purposer—hence there cannot be a purpose. Non-theists, to which category belong Buddhists as well, do not believe in a creative purposer.

"Who colours wonderfully the peacocks, or who makes the cuckoos coo so well?" This is one of the chief arguments of the materialists to attribute everything to the natural order of things.

"Eat, drink, and be merry, for death comes to all, closing our lives," appears to be the ethical ideal of their system. In their opinion, as Sri Radhakrishna writes—"Virtue is a delusion and enjoyment is the only reality. Death is the end of life. Religion is a foolish aberration, a mental disease. There was a distrust of everything good, high, pure, and compassionate. The theory stands for sensualism and selfishness and the gross affirmation of the loud will. There is no need to control passion and instinct, since they are nature's legacy to men."[1]

Sarvadarsana Sangraha says:—

> "While life is yours, live joyously,
> None can escape Death's searching eye;
> When once this frame of ours they burn,
> How shall it e'er again return?"[2]

---

1. Indian Philosophy Vol. I., p. 201.
2. P. 2.

"While life remains let a man live happily, let him feed on ghee even though he runs in debt."

Now let us turn towards science to get a solution to the question "why."

It should be noted that "science is a study of things, a study of what is and that religion is a study of ideals, a study of what should be."

Sir J. Arthur Thompson maintains that science is incomplete because it cannot answer the question why.

Dealing with cosmic Purpose, Bertrand Russell states three kinds of views—theistic, pantheistic, and emergent. "The first", he writes, "holds that God created the world and decreed the laws of nature because he foresaw that in time some good would be evolved. In this view purpose exists consciously in the mind of the Creator, who remains external to His creation.

"In the 'pantheistic' form, God is not external to the universe, but is merely the universe considered as a whole. There cannot therefore be an act of creation, but there is a kind of creative force in the universe, which causes it to develop according to a plan which this creative force may be said to have had in mind throughout the process.

"In the 'emergent' form the purpose is more blind. At an earlier stage, nothing in the universe foresees a later stage, but a kind of blind impulsion leads to those changes which bring more developed forms into existence, so that, in some rather obscure sense, the end is implicit in the beginning."[1]

We offer no comments. These are merely the views of different religionists and great thinkers.

Whether there is a cosmic purpose or not a question arises as to the usefulness of the tapeworm, snakes, mosquitoes and so forth, and for the existence of rabies. How does one account for the problem of evil? Are earthquakes, floods pestilences, and wars designed?

1.   Bertrand Russell, *Religion and Science.* p. 191.

Expressing his own view about Cosmic Purpose, Russell boldly declares:—"Why in any case, this glorification of man? How about lions and tigers? They destroy fewer animals or human lives than we do, and they are much more beautiful than we are. How about ants? They manage the Corporate State much better than any Fascist. Would not a world of nightingales and larks and deer be better than our human world of cruelty and injustice and war? The believers in cosmic purpose make much of our supposed intelligence, but their writings make one doubt it. If I were granted omnipotence, and millions of years to experiment in, I should not think Man much to boast of as the final result of all my efforts."[1]

What is the purpose of life according to different religions?

According to Hinduism the purpose of life is "to be one with Brahma" or "to be re-absorbed in the Divine Essence from which his soul emanated."

According to Judaism, Christianity and Islam, it is "to glorify God and to enjoy Him for ever."

Will an average person of any religion be prepared to give up his earthly life, to which he tenaciously clings, for immortality in their ultimate havens of peace?

Very doubtful, indeed!

Now, how does Buddhism answer the question "why?"

Buddhism denies the existence of a Creator. As such from a Buddhist standpoint there cannot be a fore-ordained purpose. Nor does Buddhism advocate fatalism, determinism, or pre-destination which controls man's future independent of his free actions. In such a case freewill becomes an absolute farce and life becomes purely mechanistic.

To a large extent man's actions are more or less mechanistic, being influenced by his own doings, upbringing, environment and so forth. But to a certain extent man can exercise his

---

1. Bertrand Russell, *Religion and Science*, p. 221.

freewill. A person, for instance, falling from a cliff will be attracted to the ground just as an inanimate stone would. In this case he cannot use his freewill although he has a mind unlike the stone. If he were to climb a cliff, he could certainly use his freewill and act as he likes. A stone, on the contrary, is not free to do so of its own accord. Man has the power to choose between right and wrong, good and bad. Man can either be hostile or friendly to himself and others. It all depends on his mind and its development.

Although there is no specific purpose in man's existence, yet man is free to have some purpose in life.

What, therefore, is the purpose of life?

Ouspensky writes:—"Some say that the meaning of life is in service, in the surrender of self, in self-sacrifice, in the sacrifice of everything, even life itself. Others declare that the meaning of life is in the delight of it, relieved against 'the expectation of the final horror of death.' Some say that the meaning of life is in perfection, and the creation of a better future beyond the grave, or in future life for ourselves. Others say that the meaning of life is in the approach to non-existence; still others, that the meaning of life is in the perfection of the race, in the organization of life on earth; while there are those who deny the possibility of even attempting to know its meaning."

Criticising all these views the learned writer says:—"The fault of all these explanations consists in the fact that they all attempt to discover the meaning of life outside of itself, either in the nature of humanity, or in some problematical existence beyond the grave, or again in the evolution of the Ego throughout many successive incarnations—always in something outside of the present life of man. But if instead of thus speculating about it, men would simply look within themselves, then they would see that in reality the meaning of life is not after all so obscure. It consists in knowledge."[1]

---

1. Tertium Organum, p. 192.

In the opinion of a Buddhist, the purpose of life is Supreme Enlightenment (*Sambodhi*), *i.e.* understanding of oneself as one really is. This may be achieved through sublime conduct, mental culture, and penetrative insight; or in other words, through service and perfection.

In service are included boundless loving-kindness, compassion, and absolute selflessness which prompt man to be of service to others. Perfection embraces absolute purity and absolute wisdom.

MANGALA SUTTA[1]

BLESSINGS

Thus have I heard:—

On one occasion the Exalted One was dwelling at the monastery of Anāthapindika[1], in Jeta's Grove[2], near Sāvatthi,[3] Now when the night was far spent, a certain deity, whose surpassing splendour illuminated the entire Jeta Grove, came to the presence of the Exalted One and, drawing near, respectfully saluted Him and stood at one side. Standing thus, he addressed the Exalted One in verse[4]:—

1. Many deities and men, yearning after good, have pondered on blessings. Pray, tell me the Highest Blessing.[5]

2. Not to associate with fools, to associate with the wise, and to honour those who are worthy of honour—this is the highest Blessing.

3. To reside in a suitable locality,[6] to have done meritorious actions in the past, and to set oneself in the right course[7]—this is the Highest Blessing.

4. Vast-learning[8], perfect handicraft[9], a highly trained discipline,[10] and pleasant speech—this is the Highest Blessing.

5. The support of father and mother, the cherishing of wife and children, and peaceful occupations—this is the Highest Blessing.

6. Liberality, righteous conduct, the helping of relatives, and blameless actions—this is the Highest Blessing.

7. To cease and abstain from evil[11], forbearance with respect to intoxicants, and steadfastness in virtue—this is the Highest Blessing.

8. Reverence[12], humility, contentment, gratitude and opportune hearing of the Dhamma[13]—this is the Highest Blessing.

9. Patience, obedience, sight of the Samanas[14] and religious discussions at due season—this is the Highest Blessing.

10. Self-control, Holy life, perception of the Noble Truths, and the realisation of Nibbāna—this is the Highest Blessing.

11. He whose mind does not flutter by contact with worldly contingencies[15], Sorrowless, Stainless, and Secure[16]— this is the Highest Blessing.

12. To them, fulfilling matters such as these[17], everywhere invincible, in every way moving happily—these are the Highest Blessings[18].

Notes on Mangala Sutta

1. Compare Mahāmangala Jātaka (No. 453). This Sutta appears in the Sutta Nipāta and Khuddaka Nikāya.

2. Lit., "He who gives alms to the helpless" or "Feeder of the Forlorn." His former name was *Sudatta.* After his conversion to Buddhism, he bought the pleasant grove, belonging to Prince Jeta, and erected a monastery which was subsequently named Jetavanārāma.

It was in this monastery that the Buddha spent the greater part of His life.

For a detailed account of the conversion of Sudatta see Kindred Sayings, Part 1, p. 27; and Vinaya Text, vol. iii. p. 179,

3. Identified with modern Sahet-Mahet.

4. The commentary states that one day an interesting discussion arose in the "Public Hall" as to what constituted a Blessing (Mangala). People naturally held diverse views. One declared that auspicious sights in the early morning (such as a woman with child, little boys, white bulls, etc) should be considered a Mangala; another, auspicious sounds, such as

"Full", "Luck", etc., and yet another, favourable experiences such as the odour of fragrant flowers, the touching of the earth, etc.

Men were so divided in their opinions that it resulted in the formation of three groups; and this partizanship ultimately extended, so the story goes, even as far as the Deva world. The Devas who would not rest satisfied until the controversial point was finally settled, appealed to the superior wisdom of their acknowledged leader, Sakka, who discreet as he was, ordered a certain Deva to approach the Buddha and obtain His trustworthy opinion. It was this particular Deva that drew near the presence of the Exalted One and addressed Him in verse.

5. According to the commentary *Mangala* means that which is conducive to happiness and prosperity. Etymologists derive the term from three syllables "*Man*" (woeful state). "*ga*" (going) and "*la*" (cut) and it is explained as "that which obstructs the way to states of misery."

6. I.e., any place where Bhikkhus, Bhikkhunis, Upāsakas and Upāsikās continually reside, where pious people are bent on the performance of the ten meritorious deeds, and where the Dhamma exists as a living principle. (Comy.)

7. I.e., setting one's immorality in morality, faithlessness in faith, and selfishness in generosity. (Comy.)

8. *Bahussutta*, literally, means "Much-hearing". This term conveys the same idea as connoted by the word "erudition" in English. In the ancient days one's education was judged by what one had memorised from oral teaching. Here "much hearing" refers to the knowledge of the Dhamma.

9. The commentary mentions that handicrafts are of two kinds, namely—the harmless crafts of householders, such as those of jewellers, goldsmiths, etc., and the crafts of homeless ones, such as stitching of robes etc.

10. *Vinaya,* i.e., discipline in thought, word and deed. The commentary speaks of two kinds of discipline—the discipline of the householder, which is abstinence from the ten immoral actions, and that of the homeless one, which is either the non-transgression of the seven kinds of offences, enumerated in the Pātimokkha, or the observance of the four divisions of Sīla (morality).

11. I.e., total abstinence and not merely temperance.

12. I.e., to Buddha, Disciples, teachers, parents, elders, etc. (Comy.)

13. For instance, when one is obsessed with evil thoughts. (Comy.)

14. Those who have calmed down their passions.

15. The eight Lokadhammas constitute gain and loss, honour and dishonour, praise and blame, pain and happiness.

16. *Asokaṁ, Virajaṁ* and *Khemaṁ.* Each of these three expressions refers to the mind of the Arahant. *Asoka* is freedom from sorrow. *Virajaṁ* is freedom from the stains of lust, hatred, and ignorance. *Khema* is security from the bonds of sense-desires (*Kāma*), becoming (*Bhava*), false views (*Diṭṭhi*), and ignorance (*Avijjā*).

17. I.e., the above-mentioned thirty-eight Blessings. (Comy.)

18. Compare Prof. Rhys David's "Buddhism", p. 125, and Woodward's "Some Sayings of the Buddha". p. 56.

PARĀBHAVA SUTTA[1]

DOWNFALL

Thus have I heard:—

On one occasion the Exalted One was dwelling at the monastery of Anāthapiṇḍika, in Jeta's Grove, near Sāvatthi.

Now when the night was far spent a certain deity whose surpassing splendour illuminated the whole Jeta Grove, came to the presence of the Exalted One, and, drawing near, respectfully saluted Him and stood at one side. Standing thus, he addressed the Exalted One in verse:—

1. Having come to interrogate the Exalted One, we ask thee, O Gotama, about the falling man. Pray, tell us the cause of one's downfall.

2. Easily known is the progressive one, easily known is the declining one. A lover of the Dhamma is the progressive one. A hater of the Dhamma is the declining one.

3. This then we learn is the first cause of one's downfall. Pray, O Exalted One, tell us the second cause of one's downfall.

4. The vicious are dear to him, in the virtuous he finds nothing pleasing,[1] he favours the creeds of the vicious-this is the cause of one's downfall.

5. This then we learn is the second cause of one's downfall. Pray, O Exalted One, tell us the third cause of one's downfall.

---

1. After hearing the Mangala Sutta which deals with things that tends to one's happiness and prosperity, the Devas were desirous of hearing from the Buddha Himself things that tend to one's downfall. Accordingly the Devas came to the Buddha and asked these questions.

6. The man who is drowsy, fond of society, not industrious, indolent, and who manifests anger—this is the cause of one's downfall.

7. This then we learn is the third cause of one's downfall. Pray, O Exalted One, tell us the fourth cause of one's downfall.

8. Whosoever, being rich, does not support his aged mother and father, who have passed their youth—this is the cause of one's downfall.

9. This then we learn is the fourth cause of one's downfall. Pray, O Exalted One, tell us the fifth cause of one's downfall.

10. He who, by falsehood, deceives a Brahmana or an ascetic or any other mendicant—this is the cause of one's downfall.

11. This then we learn is the fifth cause of one's downfall. Pray, O Exalted One, tell us the sixth cause of one's downfall.

12. The man who owns much property, who has gold and food, but alone enjoys his delicacies—this is the cause of one's downfall.

13. This then we learn is the sixth cause of one's downfall. Pray, O Exalted One, tell us the seventh cause of one's downfall.

14. The man who prides in birth or wealth or clan, and despises his own kinsmen—this is the cause of one's downfall.

15. This then we learn is the seventh cause of one's downfall. Pray, O Exalted One, tell us the eighth cause of one's downfall.

16. The man who is a debauchee, a drunkard, a gambler, and who squanders whatever he possesses—this is the cause of one's downfall.

17. This then we learn is the eighth cause of one's downfall. Pray, O Exalted One, tell us the ninth cause of one's downfall.

18. Not contented with one's own wives if one is seen amongst courtesans and the wives of others—this is the cause of one's downfall.

19. This then we learn is the ninth cause of one's downfall. Pray, O Exalted One, tell us the tenth cause of one's downfall.

20. The man who, past his youth, brings a very young wife and sleeps not for jealousy of her—this is the cause of one's downfall.

21. This then we learn is the tenth cause of one's downfall. Pray, O Exalted One, tell us the eleventh cause of one's downfall.

22. He who places in authority an intemperate spendthrift woman, or a man of similar nature—this is the cause of one's downfall.

23. This then we learn is the eleventh cause of one's downfall. Pray O Exalted One, tell us the twelfth cause of one's downfall.

24. He who, of slender means, but vast ambition, of warrior birth, aspires to sovereignty—this is the cause of one's downfall.

25. Knowing well these causes of downfall in the world, the Noble Sage, endowed with insight shares a happy realm.

VASALA SUTTA

OUTCAST

Thus have I heard:—

On one occasion the Exalted One was staying at the monastery of Anāthapiṇḍika in Jeta's Grove, near Sāvatthi. Thereupon the Exalted One, having garbed Himself in the forenoon, took His bowl and robe, and entered Sāvatthi for alms.

Now at that time, in the house of the brahmin *Aggika Bhāradvāja* a fire was burning and an offering was prepared. Then the Exalted One, going for alms from house to house in Sāvatthi approached the house of the brahmin. *Aggika Bhāradvāja*. The brahmin, seeing the Exalted One coming at a distance, said:—Stay there, O shaveling! Stay there, O wretched monk: Stay there, O miserable outcast![1]

When he spoke thus the Exalted One addressed him as follows: Do you know, O brahmin, who an outcast is, or the things that make an outcast?

Nay, indeed, O Venerable Gotama:[1] I do not know who an outcast is, or the things that make an outcast. Will the Venerable Gotama be so good as to declare the Doctrine to me so that I may know who an outcast is and what things make an outcast?

Hear then, O brahmin! Bear it well in mind; I shall speak.

Very good, Venerable One, the brahmin responded.

The Exalted One spoke as follows[2].

1. The man who is irritable, rancorous, vicious, detractive,[3] perverted in views, and deceitful—know him as an outcast.

2. Whosoever in this world harms living beings-once-born or twice-born[4] in whom there is no compassion for living beings—know him as an outcast.

3. Whosoever destroys and besieges villages and hamlets, and is known as an oppressor—know him as an outcast.

4. Whether in the village or in the forest whosoever appropriates by theft what belongs to others, or what is not given—know him as an outcast.

5. Whosoever, having really taken a debt, flees, when pressed, saying—"There is no debt to you,"—know him as an outcast.

6. Whosoever, desiring some trifle, kills a man going along on the road, and pillages something—know him as an outcast.

7. Who, for his own sake, or for the sake of others, or for the sake of wealth, utters lies when asked as a witness—know such a man as an outcast.

8. Whosoever by force or with consent is seen transgressing with the wives of relatives or friends—know him as an outcast.

9. Whosoever, being rich, does not support his aged mother and father who have passed their youth—know him as an outcast.

10. Whosoever strikes or, by speech, annoys mother, father, brother, sister, or mother-in-law—know him as an outcast.

11. Whosoever, when questioned about what is good, counsels what is wrong and teaches in a concealing way—know him as an outcast.

12. Whosoever, having done an evil deed, wishes that it may not be known to others, and is concealed in actions—know him as an outcast.

13. Whosoever, having gone to another's house, and partaken of choice food, does not honour him in return, when he comes—know him as an outcast.

14. Whosoever, deceives by falsehood, a Brahmana[5] or ascetic or any other mendicant—know him as an outcast.

15. Whosoever, by speech annoys a Brahmana or ascetic, when meal-time has come, and does not give (alms) know him as an outcast.

16. Whosoever in this world, shrouded in ignorance, predicts what is not, expecting something—know him as an outcast.

17. Whosoever exalts himself and despises others, and is debased by his pride—know him as an outcast.

18. Whosoever is annoying, avaricious, of base desires, selfish, deceitful, shameless and fearless (in evil action)—know him as an outcast.

19. Whosoever reviles the Buddha or a disciple of His—be he a recluse or a householder—know him as an outcast.

20. Whosoever, without being an Arahant, claims to be an Arahant is a thief in the whole universe[6]—he is the lowest outcast.

    Those whom I have described to you are indeed called outcasts.[7]

21. Not[8] by birth is one an outcast,[9] not by birth is one a Brahmana.   By deeds is one an outcast, by deeds is one a Brahmana. [10]

22. Know it as such by this[11] illustration:—There was the son of an outcast, known as Mātanga, a "dog-cooker".[12]

23. This Mātanga attained to highest glory, difficult to obtain.   Many warriors and brahmins came to minister unto him.

24. Mounting the celestial vehicle[13], along the passionless highway[14], he soared[15] the Brahma realm, having discarded sense-desires.   Birth did not prevent him from being reborn in the Brahma realm.

25.   There are brahmins born in the family of preceptors,[16] kinsmen of (Veda) hymns. They too are frequently seen addicted to evil deeds.

26.   In this life itself they are despised, in the next they get a woeful state. Birth does not preclude them either from a woeful state or from condemnation.

27.   By birth one is not an outcast, by birth one is not a Brahmana. By deeds is one an outcast, by deeds is one a Brahmana.

When this was spoken the brahmin *Aggika Bhāradvāja* addressed the Exalted one as follows:—

Excellent, O Venerable Gotama, Excellent! It is as if, O Venerable Gotama, a man were to set upright that which was overturned or were to reveal that which was hidden, or were to point out the way to one who has gone astray, or were to hold a lamp amidst the darkness, so that whoever has eyes may see, even so has the Doctrine been expounded in various ways by the Venerable Gotama.

And I seek refuge in the Venerable Gotama, the Doctrine, and the Order of Disciples. May the Venerable Gotama receive me as a follower who has taken refuge from this very day to life's end.

Notes on Vasala Sutta

1.   "The contrast in the brahmin's abusive terms here, and respectful address when he next speaks merits a word of explanation. The commentary states that the Buddha, that morning, looking over the world with divine power, saw that this brahmin was ripe for taking Refuges and Precepts. So the Teacher set out specially to encounter him. The brahmin who has just made his Brahma-Pūjā, turned to look for a sign of fortune. His eyes fell on a "shaveling" and a "Samana", both unlucky signs according to brahmin superstition. His dismay and anger found vent in words of abuse.

But on hearing the Buddha's quiet words in a kindly voice, and seeing the unruffled compassion in the Master's expression, the brahmin was ashamed, and his subsequent words reflect his repentance." (Kassapa Thero).

2. The brahmin was inflamed at the seemingly inauspicious sight of the Buddha and spoke discourteously to Him. The Buddha, who would never retaliate, replied curteously and calmly without either disparaging the brahmin or exalting Himself, that one who gives vent to anger, harbours ill-will, etc. is in the strictest sense of the term, an outcast—*Vasala*—although one may be born on the head of Brahma. By His reply the brahmin was compelled to infer that the Buddha was really a Brahmana whilst he—a so-called brahmin, —was an outcast.

3. *Makkha*—usually rendered "hypocritical", "hypocrisy", lit., erasing the good of others.

4. *Ekajaṁ-Dvijaṁ*—"Once-born",—All beings excepting those of egg-birth, like birds. "Twice-born",—beings who first appear as eggs. The second birth is when the eggs hatch over. The Master's humour is evident here, for brahmins styled themselves the "twice-born."

5. A perfect saint who has destroyed all passions. (Kilesa)

6. *Sabrahmake loke* lit.—in the world together with the Brahma, i.e., the whole universe. (Comy.)

7. In these 20 verses the Buddha has enumerated thirty-four kinds of conditions that make an outcast.

The first verse deals with six, such as anger etc., the second, with harmfulness; the third, with oppression, the fourth, with theft; the fifth, with defrauding creditors; the sixth, with pillage; the seventh, with false evidence; the eighth with perfidious conduct; the ninth, with ingratitude towards parents; the tenth, with striking and annoyance; the eleventh with self-deception; the twelfth, with doing evil and concealing it; the thirteenth, with ungratefulness; the fourteenth, with deception; the fifteenth, with annoying religious persons; the sixteenth, with fraud; the seventeenth, with self-exaltation and condemnation of others; the eighteenth, with seven conditions such as annoying etc; the nineteenth, with reproaching the Buddha and His disciples; the twentieth, with false claim to Saintship. Judging not by birth but by deeds, these thirty four kinds of persons are called outcasts by the Ariyas.

8. This verse was uttered by the Buddha to eradicate the erroneous view to which the brahmin was clinging.

9. According to the commentary—*Vasala* is one who rains (*vassanto*) impure deeds, and a Brahmana is one who wards off (*bāhento*)) impurity by pure deeds.

In this translation the term "Brahmana" is applied to an Arahant, whilst "brahmin" is used to denote a person of that particular caste.

10. Comp.
"Birth makes Brahmin, nor non-Brahmin makes;
'Tis life and doing that mould the Brahmana true.
Their lives mould farmers, tradesmen, merchants, serfs;
Their lives mould robbers, soldiers, chaplains kings."
(*Vāseṭṭha Sutta*)

11. The Buddha was alluding to a past birth of His, when, as an outcast, he led an exceptionally virtuous life, commanding the respect of all, and was born in the Brahma realm. See Mātanga Jātaka—No. 497.

12. *Caṇḍāla*—outcast-signifies his low cast; *Sopāka*, which means one who cooks corpses of dogs for self-consumption, indicates his degrading livelihood; and Mātanga was the name by which he was known. (Comy.)

13. That is the Noble Eightfold Path which is capable of conveying one to the Brahma realm.

14. Being the path followed by great personages such as Buddha etc.

15. After the dissolution of the body.

16. Those who are engaged in the learning of the Veda.

RATANA SUTTA[1]

JEWELS

1. Whatsoever beings are here assembled, whether terrestrial or celestial, may every being be happy! Moreover may they attentively listen to my words!

2. Accordingly give good heed, all ye beings; show your
   love to the humans who, day and night, bring offerings to you.[2] Wherefore guard them zealously.

3. Whatsoever treasure there be either here or in the
   world beyond, or whatever precious jewel[3] in the
   heavens[4] yet there is none comparable with the
   Accomplished One.
   Verily, in the Buddha is this precious jewel.
   By this truth may there be happiness!

4. The tranquil Sage[5] of the Sakyas realised that Cessation, Passion-Free, Immortality Supreme. There is
   nought comparable with that Dhamma.
   Verily, in the Dhamma is this precious jewel.
   By this truth may there be happiness!

5. That Sanctity praised by the Buddha Supreme, is
   described as "concentration without interruption"[6]
   There is nought like that concentration.
   Verily, in the Dhamma is this precious jewel.
   By this truth may there be happiness!

6. Those Eight Individuals[7] praised by the virtuous;
   they constitute four pairs. They, the worthy of offerings, the disciples of the Welcome One—to these gifts
   given yield abundant fruit.
   Verily, in the Sangha is this precious jewel.
   By this truth may there be happiness!

7. With steadfast mind, applying themselves thoroughly
   in the Dispensation of Gotama, exempt (from passion),
   they have attained to that which should be attained,[8]

and, plunging into the Deathless, they enjoy the Peace obtained without price.
Verily, in the Sangha is this precious jewel.
By this truth may there be happiness!

8. Just as a firm post[9] sunk in the earth, cannot be shaken by the four winds; even so do I declare him to be a righteous person who thoroughly perceives the Noble Truths.
Verily, in the Sangha is this precious jewel.
By this truth may there be happiness!

9. Those who comprehend clearly the Noble Truths, well taught by Him of wisdom deep, do not, however exceeding heedless they may be, undergo an eighth birth.[10]
Verily, in the Sangha is this precious jewel.
By this truth may there be happiness!

10. For him with the acquisition of Insight[11], three conditions[12] come to nought, namely—illusion,[13] doubt[14] and indulgence in (wrong) rites and ceremonies, should there be any.
From the four states of misery,[15] he is absolutely freed, and is incapable of committing the six heinous crimes.[16]
Verily, in the Sangha is this precious jewel.
By this truth may there be happiness!

11. Whatever evil deed he does, whether by deed, word or thought, he is incapable of hiding it: for it hath been said that such an act is impossible for one who has seen the Path.
Verily, in the Sangha is this precious jewel.
By this truth may there be happiness!

12. Like unto the woodland groves[17] with blossomed tree-tops[18] in the first heat of the summer season,[19] hath

the Sublime Doctrine, that leads to Nibbāna, been
taught for the Highest Good.
Verily, in the Buddha is this precious jewel.
By this truth may there be happiness!

13. The unrivalled Excellent One, the Knower, the Giver,
and Bringer of the Excellent has expounded the excellent Doctrine.
Verily, in the Buddha is this precious jewel.
By this truth may there be happiness!

14. Their past is extinct, a fresh becoming there is not,
their minds are not attached to a future birth, their
desires grow not[20]—those wise ones go out even as
this lamp.[21]
Verily, in the Sangha is this precious jewel.
By this truth may there be happiness!

15. We beings here assembled, whether terrestrial or
celestial, salute the Accomplished Buddha, honoured,
by gods and humans. May there be happiness!

16. We beings here assembled, whether terrestrial or
celestial, salute the Accomplished Dhamma, honoured
by gods and humans. May there be happiness!

17. We beings here assembled, whether terrestrial or
celestial, salute the Accomplished Sangha, honoured
by gods and humans. May there be happiness.[22]

Notes on Ratana Sutta

1. The commentary gives a graphic description of the
origin of this important discourse.

It states that on one occasion the inhabitants of the prosperous city of Vesāli were oppressed with three dangers—
famine, evil spirits, and pestilence. Famine visited them
first, causing several deaths amongst the poor folk. Attracted
by the nauseating smell emanating from the decaying corpses,

evil spirits were attracted to the place. Finally there broke out a pestilence resulting in many more deaths.

Faced with these dangers, driven to the limits of endurance they were in utter despair, not knowing what they should do to avert a final catastrophe. It was at this critical moment that they suddenly conceived the idea of inviting the Buddha, who was then temporarily residing at Rājagaha, to visit the panic-stricken city of theirs.

Two Licchavi Nobles, accompanied by a powerful retinue, immediately set out for Rājagaha. When the object of their embassy had been explained, the Buddha, divining the great benefits they would derive by His visit, accepted their invitation. Surrounded by a large company of Bhikkhus, including the Venerable Ānanda Thera, the Buddha left Rājagaha, and crossing the river Ganges, arrived at the city of Vesāli.

No sooner the Buddha reached Vesāli a torrential downpour occurred—the rain descending in such volume that all the putrefying corpses were swept away and the polluted air was completely purified. Thereupon the Buddha expounded this Ratana Sutta to the Venerable Ānanda and instructed him to tour through the city with the Licchavi Nobles, reciting the Sutta as a mark of protection for the inhabitants. Accordingly the Venerable Ānanda paraded the streets, reciting this Sutta, and, at the same time, sprinkling sacred water from the Buddha's own bowl. The commentator mentions that on the immediate utterance of the words—*yaṁ kiñci*—by the Thera, all the evil spirits fled in terror from the city. The pestilence also subsided. The Thera, after touring the city and protecting the citizens in the foregoing manner, returned to the Public Hall where the Buddha and His disciples had assembled awaiting his arrival.

On this occasion the Buddha expounded the Ratana Sutta again to the whole assembly.

2. The commentary mentions that people draw pictures of Devatās (deities) or carve their figures on wood, and hanging them on trees and shrines, make offerings in their name.

3. *Ratana* means a precious jewel. Here the term *Ratana* is applied to the Buddha, Dhamma, and the Sangha. According to Etymologists *Ratana* is composed of the three syllables— *ra, ta,* and *na. Ra* means to attract, *ta,* to cross and *na,* to lead. Buddha, Dhamma and Sangha are collectively called *Ratana,* because they possess virtues that attract the minds of the wise, because they act as a means to cross the ocean of Saṃsāra, and because they lead to heavens and Nibbāna those who seek refuge in them.

4. This includes all the realms from the lowest to the highest Brahma realm—Akaniṭṭha. (Comy.)

5. So called because all passions are completely rooted out. (Comy.)

6. The Path (*Magga*) is termed *Ānantarika Samādhi* because the *Phala* (Fruit) follows immediately without any intervening stage.

7. Namely: (i) he who has attained the *Sotāpatti Path* and (ii) Fruit (iii) he who has attained the *Sakadāgami Path* and (iv) Fruit (v) he who has attained the (*Anāgāmi Path* and (vi) Fruit, (vii) he who has attained the *Arahant Path* and (viii) Fruit. Thus these eight Individuals constitute four Pairs.

8. I.e. the fruit of Arahantship.

9. *Indakhīla*—*Inda* means Sakka, the king of the Devas or chief. By *Indakhīla* is meant either a post as firm and high as that of Sakkha's or the chief post.

Commentaries mention that these *Indakhīlas* are firm posts which are erected either inside the city as an embellishment or outside the city as a means of protection. Usually they are made of bricks or durable wood in octangular shapes. Half of the post is embedded in the earth—hence the metaphor, as firm and steady as an Indakhīla.

"Indra's post; the post, stake or column of Indra, at or before the city gate; also a large slab of stone let into the ground at the entrance of a house." P.T.S. Dict.

10. One who has attained the first stage of Sainthood. (*Sotāpatti*) is born at the most only seven times.

11. That is the first glimpse of Nibbāna.

12. The first three of the ten *Saṁyojanas* (*Fetters*).

13. *Sakkāyadiṭṭhi*—the belief that arises when a body exists, i.e. the conception of a permanent soul or self. This is one of the three *Maññanās* or notions that arise with respect to the body. The other two are craving (*Tanhā*) and pride (*Māna*). (Comy.) *Buddhist Psychology*, p. 257.

14. Doubt with regard to (i) Buddha, (ii) Dhamma, (iii) Sangha, (iv) Discipline, (v) a past, (vi) a future, (vii) a past and future, (viii) *Paṭicca Samuppāda*, the Law of Dependent Origination. See Buddhist Psychology, p. 260.

15. Namely—the woeful states (*niraya*), the animal kingdom, the Peta realm, and the Asura realm.

16. *Abhiṭhānāni;* (i) matricide, (ii) parricide, (iii) the murder of Arahants, (iv) the shedding of Buddha's blood, (v) causing schism in the Sangha, and (vi) permanent pernicious false beliefs (*Niyata Micchā Diṭṭhi*).

17. *Vanappagumbe.* Commentary explains this compound as *Vane pagumbo,* thicket or bush in the forest. Here the locative is used in the sense of the nominative.

18. Here too the locative is used in the sense of the nominative.

19. The forests and groves look glorious with blossomed tree tops in the first month of the summer season. Likewise the Dhamma expounded appears glorious with its manifold teachings.

20.   An Arahant is not born again on account of his past actions.   The acts he performs during his lifetime are termed ineffective (*Kiriya*) since they are freed from all taints of craving.

21.   Pointing to a lamp which was kept burning in honour of the tutelary deities of the city, and which, at that very moment, got extinguished.

22.   When the Buddha concluded His sermon conferring peace and happiness upon the inhabitants of Vesāli, Sakka, the king of Devas, recited the last three verses and took leave of the Buddha with his retinue.

The commentary states that the Buddha expounded this Sutta successively for seven days in Vesāli.

METTA SUTTA[1]

LOVING-KINDNESS

1. He who is skilled in his good and who wishes to attain that state of Calm[2] should act (thus):
   He should be efficient, upright, yea, perfectly upright[3], obedient, gentle and humble.

2. Contented, easily supportable, with few duties, of light livelihood, controlled in senses, discreet, not impudent, not be greedily attached to families.

3. He should not commit any slight wrong such that other wise men might censure him.
   May all beings be happy and secure! May their hearts be wholesome!

4. Whatsoever living beings there be:—feeble or strong, long, stout or medium, short, small or large, seen or unseen, those dwelling far or near, those who are born and those who are to be born—may all beings, without exception, be happy minded!

5. Let none deceive another nor despise any person whatsoever in any place. In anger or ill-will let him not wish any harm to another.

6. Just as a mother would protect her only child at the risk of her own life, even so let him cultivate a boundless heart towards all beings.

7. Let his thoughts of boundless love pervade the whole world—above, below and across—without any obstruction, without any hatred, without any enmity.

8. Whether he stands, walks, sits, or lies down, as long as he is awake, he should develop this mindfulness, This they say, is the Highest Conduct[4] here.

9. Not falling into Error[5], virtuous, and endowed with insight[6], he discards attachment to sense-desires. Of a truth, he does not come again for conception in a womb.

Notes on Metta Sutta

1. As the rainy (*Vassāna*) season was drawing near, several Bhikkhus received instructions from the Buddha about meditation and went in search of a suitable place. In the course of their wanderings they came to a secluded spot with secenic beauty, and decided to stay there and meditate to gain their Deliverance.

The Devas who were dwelling on tree tops resented their unwelcome presence and wanted to drive them away. At night they disturbed them in their meditations and succeeded in their attempt.

The Bhikkhus, finding it difficult to concentrate their minds amidst such uncongenial surroundings, returned to the Buddha and informed Him of their nocturnal adventures.

Thereupon the Buddha taught this Sutta and advised them to go to the very spot and act accordingly.

The Devas were now pleased as they were pervading the whole atmosphere with their radiant thoughts of love, and instead of obstructing their spiritual progress, they gave them every possible help.

Within the Vassāna period itself all the Bhikkhus gained Arahantship.

This discourse serves both as a mark of protection and as a subject of meditation. In the first part of the discourse are found virtues that should be practised by anyone who desires one's welfare, and in the latter part, the method of practising Mettā or goodwill is explained in detail.

Mettā (Sans. Maitri). It is difficult to give a graceful English equivalent to this term. Sometimes it is rendered by "benevolence" which is exactly what Mettā signifies, but it is too flaccid a word to convey the rapture of Buddhist Mettā. See "The Blessing." p. 194.

2. I.e., Nibbāna.

3. *Uju* and *Sūjū*. The first term refers to uprightness in word and deed, the second term refers to uprightness in mind. (Comy.)

4. *Brahma-Vihāra*.

5. Here error means self-illusion (*Sakkāyadiṭṭhi*).

6. I.e., the first glimpse of Nibbāna.

7. When one attains the stage of Anāgāmi one is born in the Pure Abodes (*Suddhāvāsa*), and is not born in the human realm.

INTRODUCTION

Satipaṭṭhāna Sutta is a very important discourse as it mainly deals with different subjects of contemplation to develop Concentration (*Samatha*) and Insight (*Vipassanā*).

The Pāli term *Satipaṭṭhāna* is composed of *sati* and *Paṭṭhāna* or *sati* and *upaṭṭhāna*.

Sati means mindfulness, awareness, attentiveness. *Paṭṭhāna* means establishment, foundations, bases, subjects, application.

Satipaṭṭhāna, therefore, means 'The Foundations of Mindfulness' or 'The Chief Objects of Mindfulness.'

Satipaṭṭhāna may also be derived from *Sati+upaṭṭhāna*, arousing or application. *Satipaṭṭhāna*, therefore, means 'The Application of Mindfulness' or 'The Arousing of Mindfulness.'

Satipaṭṭhāna may simply be interpreted as 'The Foundations of Mindfulness' or 'The Chief Objects for the Application of Mindfulness.'

In this discourse are found four objects of contemplation (*anupassanā*) to suit the different temperaments of individuals.

The first is the contemplation as regards the body (*kāyānupassanā*) in order to get rid of the misconception of so-called beauty or desirableness (*subhavipallāsa*). This contemplation enables one to understand that there is no doer but just doing, no actor but just action. One realises that there is no "I".

The body-contemplation begins with concentration on inhalation and exhalation (*ānāpānasati*) to gain the one-pointedness of the mind (*ekaggatā*) which leads to ecstacies (*Jhānas*) and ultimately to *Arahantship*.

The invisible mind, the most important factor in this complex machinery of man, is not easily controllable. It wanders hither and thither. To focus one's mind on a particular object even for a few seconds is as difficult as to place a mustard seed on the tip of a needle. Though difficult it is possible to gain one-pointedness of the mind by constant practice because it is a common mental state latent in all. When this one-pointedness is present in an immoral consciousness (*akusala citta*) it is evil. When it is present in a moral consciousness (*kusala citta*) it is good. This one-pointedness can be developed into a Jhāna factor. The same one-pointedness can be elevated into a Factor of Enlightenment (*bojjhanga*) and to a factor of the Noble Eight-fold Path (*magganga*). This is the reason why Buddhism states that greatness or goodness is innate in all. Within us are found "a rubbish heap of evil and a store-house of virtue".

Gaining *Jhānas* by means of this concentration, one tries to attain Arahantship, Emerging from the *Jhāna* state, one meditates on the three characteristics—impermanence (*anicca*), sorrow (*dukkha*) and no-soul (*anattā*). After a great endeavour, on attaining Arahantship, one lives completely emancipated from craving (*taṇhā*) and ignorance (*avijjā*), clinging to naught in this world.

The section on bodily postures—sitting, standing, walking, and lying down—also leads to concentration and self-awareness and also to understand that there is no agent but causally conditioned movements.

The section on loathsomeness of the thirty-two bodily parts and the four elements that comprise this so-called body and the ten corpses—namely, i. bloated (*uddhumātaka*), ii. discoloured (*vinīlaka*), iii. festering (*vipubbaka*), iv. dissected (*vicchiddaka*), v. gnawed-to-pieces (*vikkhāyika*), vi. scattered in-pieces (*vikkhittaka*), vii. mutilated and scattered-in-pieces (*hatavikkhittaka*), viii. bloody (*lohitaka*), ix. worm-infested (*pulavaka*) and x. skeleton (*aṭṭhika*) tend to remove selfish desires one may entertain towards this evanescent body.

The second contemplation with regard to feelings (*ve danānupassanā*) of any kind—worldly or spiritual—that may arise in oneself, enables one to get rid of the false notion of ephemeral happiness (*sukhavipallāsa*).

In the course of one's lifetime one experiences pleasurable, displeasurable or neutral feelings. All are transitory. Hence there is no genuine happinesss in them. Nibbāna is bliss supreme. It is a bliss of relief from suffering.

The third contemplation with regard to different states of consciousness (*cittānupassanā*) one experiences, tends to dissipate the false notion of permanence (*niccavipallāsa*).

Mind or consciousness arises and perishes every moment with lightning rapidity. It changes even faster than fundamental units of matter. Every moment we experience a moral or immoral thought. Different types of consciousness are enumerated in this section in pairs.

The fourth is the contemplation on the *dhammas*, (*dhammānupassanā*) a difficult Pali term to be translated in this context. Here *dhammas* embrace the five Hindrances (*nīvaraṇa*), the seven Factors of Enlightenment (*bojjhanga*), the five Aggregates of Attachment (*upādānakkhandha*), the six Sense-Bases (*salāyatana*), and the four Noble Truths (*ariyasacca*). Hence it is advisable to retain the Pali term.

This contemplation (*Dhammānupassanā*) tends to get rid of the false notion of an unchanging immortal soul (*attabhāvavipallāsa*).

One is free to choose any of the four subjects according to one's temperament and cultivate it until one attains Arahantship or, for practical purposes, all the four alternately. To develop the *Jhānas* it is advisable to adhere to one suitable subject.

To those of lustful temperament the contemplation on the loathsomeness of the body, the composite elements and the ten corpses are suitable. No hard and fast rule can be laid with regard to the selection of suitable subject for contemplation.

Oneself is the best judge.

A quiet secluded spot is congenial for these contemplations. A forest is extremely congenial but it is not essential to retire to a forest. One can contemplate even in one's own room, provided there are no external distractions. Solitude is in one's heart.

If our minds are not settled, even a quiet forest would not be a congenial place. But if our minds are settled, even the heart of a busy town may be congenial. The atmosphere in which we live acts as an indirect aid to tranquillize our minds.

Early in the morning when the mind is fresh and active, or before bedtime, if one is not over-tired, is generally the most appropriate time for meditation. But, whatever the time selected, it is advisable daily to keep to that particular hour, for our minds then become conditioned to the practice.

The meditation posture, too, serves as a powerful aid to concentration.

Easterners generally sit crosslegged, with the body erect. They sit placing the right foot on the left thigh and the left foot on the right thigh. This is the full position, If this posture is difficult, as it certainly is to many, the half position may be adopted, that is, simply placing the right foot on the left thigh or the left foot on the right thigh.

When this triangular position is assumed, the whole body is well balanced.

The right hand should be placed on the left hand, the neck straightened so that the nose is in a perpendicular line with the navel. The tongue should rest on the upper palate. The belt should be loosened, and clothes neatly adjusted. Some prefer closed eyes to shut out all unnecessary light and external sights.

Although there are certain advantages in closing the eyes, it is not always recommended as it tends to drowsiness. Then the mind gets out of control and wanders aimlessly, vagrant thoughts arise, the body loses its erectness, quite unconsciously the mouth opens itself, saliva drivels, and the head nods.

The Buddhas usually sit with half closed eyes looking through the tip of the nose not more than a distance of four feet away.

Those who find the crosslegged posture too difficult may sit comfortably in a chair or any other support, sufficiently high to rest the feet on the ground.

It is of no great importance what posture one adopts provided it is easy and relaxed.

Persistent effort to subdue passions like lust and hatred should be made to succeed in this practice. Quick results should not be expected. It might take months and years or even one day to achieve any notable result, but one should not be discouraged. Constant practice is essential. Effort should be combined with a clear comprehension of things as they truly are. Wisdom, the apex of Buddhism, is absolutely necessary for one's purification. Secular education is an asset, but what is of importance is right understanding of one self as one really is. As such petitional prayers play no part in Buddhism for Deliverance from suffering. Constant mindfulness is as essential as both effort and wisdom. Equipped with these three pre-requisites, he should try to give up temporarily the five Hindrances that obstruct his spiritual progress. He should try to overcome attachment to sense-pleasures. This does not mean that one must wholly give up all material pleasures, but one should not be slaves to them.

An equally powerful destructive force like lust is anger or hatred. Both lust and hatred are ravaging fires that consume oneself and others.

It is true that until one attains Anāgāmi, the third stage of Sainthood, one is subject to lust and hatred, but one should try to overcome them to the best of one's ability.

Mental alertness, freedom from useless worry, mental equipoise and certainty as to the desired goal are equally necessary for success in this unparalleled contemplation.

The ultimate object of these contemplations is complete deliverance from ignorance (*avijjā*) and craving (*tanhā*) by attaining Arahantship. Thereafter he clings to naught in this world.

In concluding this profound discourse the Buddha assures the aspirant of definite success in his noble attempt not in seven years but even in seven days.

SATIPAṬṬHĀNA SUTTA[1]

Thus have I heard:—

The Buddha spoke thus:—

There is this unique way[2] for the purification of beings, for the destruction of suffering,[3] for the attainment of wisdom (i.e., the Noble Eightfold Path), and for the realization of Nibbāna—namely, the Four Foundations of Mindfulness.

What are the four?

Herein (in this Teaching) a disciple [4] lives:

(i) contemplating the body (*kāyānupassanā*) in the body,[5] energetic (*ātāpi*), clearly comprehending (*sampajāno,*) mindful (*satimā*), giving up [6] (temporarily) covetousness (*abhijjhā*) and grief (*domanassa*)[7] in this world (*loke = the* five aggregates);

(ii) contemplating the feelings (*vedanānupassanā*);

(iii) contemplating the states of mind (*cittānupassanā*);

(iv) contemplating the *dhammas* (*dhammānupassanā*).

*   *   *   *   *

(1) The Contemplation of the Body (*kāyānupassanā*)

How does a disciple live contemplating the body?

Mindfulness on Breathing (ānāpāna sati).

A disciple, having retired to the forest[8], or to the foot of a tree, or to a lonely place, sits with legs crossed, [9] the body held erect, intent on mindfulness.

Consciously (*sato*) he inhales; consciously he exhales. Inhaling a long breath, he knows, —'I am inhaling a long breath'. Exhaling a long breath, he knows —I am exhaling a long breath.'

Inhaling a short breath, he knows—'I am inhaling a short breath'.

Exhaling a short breath, he knows—'I am exhaling a short breath.'

Experiencing the entire (breathing) process [10] (*sabbakā-yapaṭisaṁvedī*) 'I will inhale', thus he trains himself.

Experiencing the entire (breathing) process 'I will exhale'—thus he trains himself.

Calming the body of respirations (*passambhayam kāya-samkhāram*), 'I will inhale'—thus he trains himself.

Calming the body of respirations, 'I will exhale'—thus he trains himself.

Just as a skilful turner or a turner's apprentice, making a long turn, knows—'I am making a long turn', making a short turn, knows—'I am making a short turn'; even so a disciple inhaling a long breath, knows—'I am inhaling a long breath', inhaling a short breath, knows—'I am inhaling a short breath'. ......as above......thus he trains himself.

Thus he lives contemplating the body internally or externally[11] or both internally and externally.

He lives contemplating the rising nature [12] (*samuda-yadhamma*) of the body of respirations, the perishing nature[13] (*vayadhammas,*) the arising and perishing nature of the body of respirations.

Now there arises in him the mindfulness—'there exists only a body [14] to the extent necessary for the growth of wisdom, for the growth of mindfulness.' Independent [15] (*anissito*) he lives, clinging to naught in this world. [16]

Thus a disciple lives contemplating the body.

*　　*　　*　　*　　*　　*

Section on Bodily Postures
(*Iriyāpatha*)

A disciple while walking [17] understands—'I am walking'; while standing, understands—'I am standing'; while sitting, he understands—'I am sitting;' while lying down, he understands—'I am lying down'. He understands every position his body assumes.

Thus he lives contemplating the body internally or externally or both internally and externally.

He lives contemplating the arising nature of the body, or the perishing nature of the body or both the arising and perishing nature of the body. Now there arises in him the mindfulness—there exists only a body ....as above....in this world.

*　　*　　*　　*　　*　　*

Section on Awareness
(*Catusampajaññā*)

A disciple is fully aware of his going forwards or backwards, in looking ahead or around, in bending (his limbs) or stretching, in using robes and bowl, in eating, drinking, chewing, tasting, in answering a call of nature, in going, standing, sitting, sleeping, keeping awake, speaking, and keeping silence.

Thus he lives contemplating the body....as above.... in this world.

* * * * * *

Reflection on Loathsomeness[18]
(*Paṭikkūlamanasikāra*)

———

A disciple reflects on this body upwards from the soles of his feet and downwards from his crown, enclosed in skin, and abounding with diverse kinds of filth.

In this body are—hair of the head, hair of the body, nails, teeth, skin, flesh, sinews, bones, marrow, kidneys, heart, liver, diaphragm, spleen, lungs, stomach, intestines, mesentery, excrement, bile, phlegm, pus, blood, sweat, fat, tears, grease, spittle, snot, oil of the joints, and urine.

Just as if there were a double-mouthed bag, full of different kinds of grain, such as rice, paddy, green-gram, cow-pea, sesamum, and husked rice; and a person with sight should open it and reflect thus—this is rice, this is paddy, this is green-gram, this is cow-pea, this is sesamum, this is husked rice. Even so a disciple reflects on the different kinds of impurities of the body.

Thus he lives contemplating the body....as above.... clinging to naught in this world.

Reflection on Elements[19]
(*Dhātumanasikāra*)

A disciple reflects upon this very body according as it is placed or disposed, with regard to body elements. There are in this body earth-element (–the element of extension), water-element (–the element of cohesion), fire-element (–the element of heat), air-element (–the element of motion.)

Just as a skilful butcher or a butcher's apprentice, having slaughtered an ox and dividing it into portions, were to sit at a junction, even so a disciple contemplates the body with regard to elements.

Thus he lives contemplating the body....as above.... clinging to naught in this world.

*   *   *   *   *   *

Reflection on the nine kinds of corpses
(*Navasīvathikāpabba*)

(i) A disciple would see the body, thrown in the charnel-ground, one day dead, or two days dead, or three days dead, swollen, blue and festering. He then applies (this perception) to his own body thus: 'Truly this body, too, is of the same nature, such it will become, it has not escaped that state.

Thus he lives contemplating the body..as above.... clinging to naught in this world.

(2) A disciple would see the body, thrown in the charnel-ground, being devoured by crows, or hawks, or vultures, or dogs, or jackals, or by various kinds of worms. He then

applies (this perception) to his own body thus: "Truly this body; too, is of the same nature, such it will become, it has not escaped that state.'

Thus he lives contemplating the body....as above.... clinging to naught in this world.

(3) A disciple would see the body, thrown in the charnel-ground, reduced to a skeleton, held together by sinews, with some flesh and blood adhering to it....

(4) A disciple would see the body thrown in the charnel-ground, reduced to a skeleton, held together by sinews, without flesh, besmeared with blood....

(5) A disciple would see the body thrown in the charnel-ground, reduced to a skeleton, held together with sinews, without flesh and blood....

(6) A disciple would see the body thrown in the charnel-ground, reduced to loose bones scattered in various directions—bones of the hand, bones of the foot, shin bones, thigh bones, pelvis, spine and skull.

(7) A disciple would see the body thrown in the charnel-ground, reduced to white bones of shell-like colour....

(8) A disciple would see the body thrown in the charnel-ground, reduced to a heap of bones, more than a year old....

(9) A disciple would see the body thrown in the charnel-ground, reduced to rotten bones, crumbling to dust. He then applies (this perception) to his own body thus: 'Truly, this body, too, is of the same nature, such it will become, it will not escape that state.

Thus he lives contemplating the body....as above.... clinging to naught in this world.

(2) Contemplation on Feelings
(*Vedanānupassanā*)

A disciple, when experiencing a pleasant feeling, understands—

'I am experiencing a pleasant feeling'.

A disciple, when experiencing a painful feeling, understands—
'I am experiencing a painful feeling'.

A disciple, when experiencing a neutral feeling, understands—
'I am experiencing a neutral feeling.'

A disciple, when experiencing a pleasant worldly feeling (*Sāmisa*), understands—
'I am experiencing a pleasant worldly feeling.'

A disciple, when experiencing a painful worldly feeling, understands—
'I am experiencing a painful worldly feeling.'

A disciple, when experiencing a neutral worldly feeling, understands—
'I am experiencing a neutral worldly feeling.'

A disciple, when experiencing a pleasant unworldly (*nirāmisa*) feeling understands—
'I am experiencing a pleasant unworldly feeling'.

A disciple, when experiencing a painful unworldly feeling, understands—
'I am experiencing a painful unworldly feeling.'

A disciple, when experiencing a neutral unworldly feeling, understands—
'I experience a neutral unworldly feeling'.

Thus he lives contemplating the feelings internally or externally, or both internally and externally.

He lives contemplating the arising nature of feelings, the perishing nature of feelings, the arising and perishing nature of feelings.

Now there arises in him the mindfulness—there exist only feelings to the extent necessary ....as above....in this world.

*   *   *   *   *   *

(3) Contemplation on States of mind
(*Cittānupassanā*)

A disciple knows the mind with lust (*rāga*) as with lust, knows the mind without lust as lust-free. He knows the mind with hate (*dosa*) as with hate. He knows the mind without hate as hate-free. He knows the mind with ignorance (*moha*) as with ignorance, the mind without ignorance as without ignorance. He knows the shrunken state of mind as shrunken (*samkhitta*, i.e. associated with sloth and torpor) the distracted mind as distracted (*vikkhitta*—associated with restlessness —*uddhacca*). He knows the elevated mind (*mahaggata*) as elevated, the non-elevated mind as non-elevated (*amahaggata*—*kāmāvacara,* sentient). He knows the surpassable [20] mind as surpassable (*sauttara*)—either *kāmāvacara* or *rupāvacara*), the unsurpassable mind (*anuttara*) as unsurpassable. He knows the concentrated mind (*samāhita*) as concentrated, the unconcentrated mind as unconcentrated (*asmāhita*) He knows the freed mind (*vimutta*) as (temporarily) freed, the non-freed mind as non-freed (*avimutta*).

Thus he lives contemplating the states of mind internally or externally, or both internally and externally.

He lives contemplating the arising nature of the states of mind, the perishing nature of the states of mind, the arising and perishing nature of the states of mind.

Now there arises in him the mindfulness—there exist only states of mind to the extent necessary....as above.... in this world.

*   *   *   *   *   *

(4)   Contemplation on the dhammas[21]
(Dhammānupassanā)

(1)   *The Five Hindrances* (*Nīvaraṇa*)

A disciple lives contemplating the dhammas with respect to the Five Hindrances.

When *sense-desire* (*kāmacchanda*) is present a disciple knows well—I have sense-desire, or when sense-desire is not present he knows well—I have no sense-desire. He knows well how the arising of the non-arisen sense-desire comes to be; he knows well how the abandoning of the arisen sense-desire comes to be; he knows well how the non-arising in the future of the abandoned sense-desire comes to be.

When *anger* (*vyāpāda*) is present he knows well—'I have anger', or when anger is not present he knows well—'I have no anger'. He knows well how the arising of the non-arisen anger comes to be; he knows well how the abandoning of the arisen anger comes to be; he knows well how the non-arising in the future of the abandoned anger comes to be.

When *sloth and torpor* (*thīnamiddha*) are present he knows well—'I have sloth and torpor,' or when sloth and torpor are not present the knows well—'I have no sloth and torpor'. He

knows well how the arising of the non-arisen sloth and torpor comes to be; he knows well how the abandoning of the
arisen sloth and torpor comes to be; he knows well how the
non-arising in the future of the abandoned sloth and torpor
comes to be.

When *restlessness and brooding* (*uddhacca kukkucca*)
are present he knows well—'I have restlessness and brooding,'
or when prestlessness and brooding are not presen the knows
well—'I have no restlessness and brooding.' He knows well
how the arising of the non-arisen restlessness and brooding
comes to be; he knows well how the abandoning of the arisen
restlessnes and brooding comes to be; he knows well how the
non-arising in the future of the abandoned restlessness and
brooding comes to be.

When *indecision* (*vicikicchā*) is present he knows well—
'I have indecision' or when indecision is not present he knows
well—'I have no indecision.' He knows well how the arising
of the non-arisen indecision comes to be; he knows well how
the abandoning of the arisen indecision comes to be; he knows
well how the non arising in the future of the abandoned indecision comes to be.

Thus a disciple lives contemplating the *dhammas* with
respect to the Five Hindrances.

*   *   *   *   *   *

2. The Five Aggregates of Grasping

A disciple thinks: 'Thus is material form (*rūpa*), thus
is the arising of material form, thus is the perishing of material
form.   Thus is feeling (*vedanā*). thus is the arising of feeling,
thus is the perishing of feeling.   Thus is perception (*saññā*),
thus is the arising of perception, thus is the perishing of per-

ception. Thus are mental states (*sankhāra*), thus is the arising of mental states, thus is the perishing of mental states.
Thus is consciousness (*viññāṇa*), thus is the arising of consciousness, thus is the perishing of consciousness.

Thus a disciple lives contemplating the dhammas with
respect to the Five Aggregates of Grasping.'

*   *   *   *   *   *

(3) The six internal and the six external sense-bases
(*Salāyatana*)

A disciple knows well the eye and material forms and the
fetter that arises dependent on both. He knows well how the
arising of the non-arisen fetter comes to be, how the abandoning of the arisen fetter comes to be, how the non-arising
in the future of the abandoned fetter comes to be.

Similarly he knows well the ear and sounds, the nose and
the odours, the tongue and the tastes, the body and the contacts, the mind and the mental objects and the fetters that
arise dependent on both (respectively). He knows well how
the arising of the non-arisen fetters comes to be, how the
abandoning of the arisen fetters comes to be, how the non-
arising in the future of the abandoned fetters comes to be.

Thus a disciple lives contemplating the dhammas with
respect to the six internal and external sense-bases.

*   *   *   *   *   *

(4) The Factors of Enlightenment
(*Bojjhanga*)

When the enlightenment factor of '*Mindfulness*' (*sati*)
is present he knows well—'I have the enlightenment factor
of mindfulness', or when it is not present —he knows well
that it is absent; he knows well how the arising of the non-

arisen enlightenment factor of mindfulness comes to be and how the fulfilment by meditation of the arisen enlightenment factor of mindfulness comes to be.

When the enlightenment factor of *'Investigation of reality'* (*Dhammavicaya*) is present he knows well —'I have the enlightenment factor of investigation of reality;' when it is not present he knows well that it is absent; he knows well how the arising of the Enlightenment factor of investigation of reality comes to be and how the fulfilment by meditation of the arisen enlightenment factor of investigation of reality comes to be.

When the enlightenment factor of *'Energy'* (*Viriya*) is present he knows well—'I have the enlightenment factor of energy,' or when it is not present, he knows well that it is absent; he knows well how the arising of the non-arisen enlightenment factor of energy comes to be and how the fulfilment by meditation of the arisen enlightenment factor of energy comes to be.

When the enlightenment factor of *'Joy'* (*Pīti*) is present he knows well—'I have the enlightenment factor of joy' or when it is not present he knows well that it is absent; he knows well how the raising of the non-arising enlightenment factor of joy comes to be, and how the fulfilment by meditation of the arisen enlightenment factor of joy come to be.

When the enlightenment factor of *'Tranquillity'* (*Passaddhi*) is present he knows well—'I have the enlightenment factor of tranquillity' or when it is not present he knows well that it is absent; he knows well how the arising of the non-arisen enlightenment factor of tranquillity comes to be, and how the fulfilment by meditation of the arisen enlightenment factor of tranquillity comes to be.

When the enlightenment factor of *'Concentration'* (*Samādhi*) is present he knows well—'I have the enlightenment factor of concentration,' or when it is not present he knows well that it is absent, he knows well how the arising of the non-arisen enlightenment factor of concentration comes to be, and how the fulfilment by meditation of the arisen enlightenment factor of concentration comes to be.

When the enlightenment factor of *'Equanimity'* (*upekkhā*) is present he knows well—'I have the enlightenment factor of equanimity,' or when it is not present he knows well that it is absent; he knows well how the arising of the non-arisen enlightenment factor of equanimity comes to be, and how the fulfilment by meditation of the arisen enlightenment factor of equanimity comes to be.

Thus he lives contemplating the *dhammas* . . . . as above . . . clinging to naught in this world.

Thus a disciple lives contemplating the *dhammas* with respect to the seven factors of enlightenment.

(5) Contemplation on the Four Truths

A disciple is fully aware, as it really is—'This is suffering' 'this is the cause of suffering', 'this is the cessation of suffering', 'this is the way leading to the cessation of suffering'.

Thus he lives contemplating the *dhammas* internally, or externally or both internally and externally, He lives contemplating the arising nature of dhammas, or their perishing nature, or both the arising and perishing nature of dhammas.

Now there arises in him the mindfulness—'There exist only dhammas to the extent necessary for the growth of wisdom, for the growth of mindfulness.' Independent he lives, clinging to naught in this world.

Thus he lives contemplating the dhammas with respect to the four Noble Truths.

Verily, should any person develop these four Foundations of Mindfulness in this way for seven years, he would either become an Arahant here and now or a Never-Returner (*Anā-gāmi*) if there still be any attachment.

Nay, should he develop them for six years....five years.. four years.. three years.. two years.. one year.. seven months.. six months.. five months.. four months.. three months.. two months.. a month.. half a-month.. a week.. he would become an Arahant or an *Anagāmi* (Never-Returner) if there still be any attachment in this very life.

Because of this it was said—

There is a unique way for the destruction of suffering, for the purification of beings, for the attainment of Wisdom, and for the realization of Nibbāna.

Thus spoke the Exalted One. The disciples were delighted.

NOTES

1. *Sati* = mindfulness; *paṭṭhāna* = establishment, foundations, bases, objects, applications

    Sati — mindfulness; *upaṭṭhāna* = arousing, application. Chief objects for the application of mindfulness.

2. *Ekāyana* = sole way, only way, one way, etc.

3. Text states—grief, lamentation, pain and displeasure.
    Suffering embraces all four.

4. Any person whether a member of the Sangha or a lay-
    follower who wishes to get rid of suffering can practise
    these meditations.

5. *Kāye kāyanupassanā* = Lit., body-contemplation in the
    body–i.e. to restrict this contemplation only to the body
    and not to feelings, consciousness and the dham-
    mas. The other contemplations should be similarly
    understood.

6: Giving up temporarily at the time of the practice.
    Strictly speaking, they are temporarily inhibited by gain-
    ing the *Jhānas* and totally eradicated by attaining Ara-
    hantship.

7. All the five Hindrances are understood by mentioning
    the two chief ones.

8. Any quiet place, even at home.

9. This is the ideal posture for this practice. One
    may adopt a convenient posture, if the sitting posture
    is inconvenient. One may even sit upon a chair.

10. *Sabbakāyapaṭisaṁvedī* = Here *kāya* means the whole
    'body' of breathing process. He inhales and exhales,
    making known, making clear to himself the beginning,
    middle and end of the whole 'body' of respiration.

11. As a rule one does this concentration internally.

12. Breathing occurs on account of the body, nostrils and consciousness.

13. Breathing perishes with the perishing of these three.

14. That is, no being, no individual, no man, no woman, no soul, no "I" or no "me".

15. *Anissito*—Not being supported by craving (*Tanhā*) and false view (*Ditthi*).

16. As he thus concentrates on inhalation and exhalation a stage might come when he temporarily inhibits the five Hindrances and gains the first *Jhāna*, replete with the *Jhānas* factors—initial application (*vitakka*), sustained application (*vicāra*), joy (*pīti*), happiness (*sukha*) and onepointedness (*ekaggatā*). *Jhāna* literally means either the close meditation on the object or the burning up of adverse hindrances. There is no appropriate English equivalent for this term. It is not a state of trance but a moral state, a religious experience. Emerging from Jhāna, he meditates on the three characteristics–impermanence (*anicca*), suffering (*dukkha*) and soullessness (*anattā*) –and attains Sainthood. Thereafter he lives "emancipated" (*anissito*) being delivered from craving and false views, clinging to naught in this world. After attaining Arahantship he clings not to anything in this world as he does not erroneously think in terms of me and mine.

The final object of *Anāpāna sati* is first to gain the *Jhānas* and then to develop the four Supramundane Paths and Fruits.

This is the reason why at the outset it was stated—for the purification of beings, for the destruction of suffering, for the attainment of the Noble Eightfold Path and for the realization of Nibbāna.

17. Even an animal is aware of bodily movements. The object herein implied is not mere awareness. While walking, he should rightly understand that there is merely a walking but strictly no agent or person to walk. In other words, there is just an action, no actor, just a deed but no doer. By such awareness no misconception about an eternal soul arises.

18. This meditation on the impurities of the body is invariably practised by most bhikkhus. This was the favourite subject of meditation of Venerable Ānanda.

This subject is suitable to those of a lustful temperament as it leads to non-attachment to the so-called beautiful body. Some may prefer to meditate on the dormant possibilities of man.

19. The four elements are *Paṭhavi, Āpo, Tejo,* and *Vāyo.* One must not understand that these elements are earth, water, fire and air.

Paṭhavi is the element of extension, the substratum of matter. Without it objects cannot occupy space. The qualities of hardness and softness, which are purely relative, are two conditions of this particular element.

Āpo is the element of cohesion. Unlike *Paṭhavi* it is intangible. It is this element that makes scattered particles of matter cohere and gives rise to the idea of 'body'. When some bodies are melted this element becomes more prominent in the resulting fluid. The element of extension and cohesion are so closely inter-related that when cohesion ceases extension disappears.

Tejo is the element of heat. Cold is also a form of *tejo*. Both heat and cold are included in *tejo* because they possess the power of maturing bodies. *Tejo*, in other words, is the vitalizing energy. Preservation and decay are also due to this element. Unlike the other three essentials of matter, this element has the power to regenerate matter by itself.

Inseparably connected with heat is *vāyo*, the element of motion. Movements are caused by this element. Motion is regarded as the force or the generator of heat. "Motion and heat in the material realm correspond respectively to consciousness and Kamma in the mental."

These four elements co-exist and are inseparable, but one may preponderate over another as, for instance *pathavi,* in earth, *āpo* in water, *tejo* in fire, and *vāyo* in air.

20. Both types of consciousness pertaining to the Sense-sphere (*kāmāvacara*) and Form-sphere (*rūpāvacara*), are surpassable, while types of consciousness pertaining to the Formless-sphere are unsurpassable (*anuttara*), as here Supramundane consciousness is not taken into account.

21. *Dhammānupassanā*—Here *dhamma* does not mean the doctrine. It is a general term applied to both mundane and supramundane .things. It resembles the broad meaning of the English term—thing. *Dhamma* in this connection is applied to *Nīvaraṇa* (Hindrances), *Bojjhaṅga* (Factors of Enlightenment) Five Aggregates of Grasping (*Upādānakkhandha*), *Āyatana* (Sense-spheres) and the Four Noble Truths (*Ariyasacca*).

It is advisable to retain the Pāli term here.

—:::—

INDEX

INDEX

INDEX

INDEX

I vow that when my life approaches its end,
All obstructions will be swept away;
I will see Amitabha Buddha,
And be born in His Western Pure Land of
Ultimate Bliss and Peace.

When reborn in the Western Pure Land,
I will perfect and completely fulfill
Without exception these Great Vows,
To delight and benefit all beings.

~The Vows of Samantabhadra
Avatamsaka Sutra~

PUBLISHER'S NOTE

HE BUDDHA AND HIS TEACHINGS provides a good source of information for those who wish to understand the life of the Buddha and his fundamental teachings.

The Book was first published in 1942. The present edition has been revised and expanded. Though primarily intended for the students and beginners rather than scholars, the reader will find it an extremely valuable handbook, offering a sound foundation to the basic tenets of Buddhism as found in its original Pali tradition.

Besides providing a comprehensive account of the Life of the Buddha and His chief disciples, the moral and ethical code of conduct, culminating in the Ten Perfections, a considerable portion of the book deals with current issues in Buddhist studies regarding KARMA, REBIRTH and NIBBANA. It also includes an introduction to Buddhist Meditation with particular reference to the practice of the Four Sublime States (or Brahma Viharas) namely METTA (loving-kindness), KARUNA (Compassion), MUDITA (Sympathetic Joy), and UPEKKHA (Equanimity).

The Author, the Venerable Narada Maha Thera is a wellknown Buddhist Missionary from Sri Lanka. He is also the author of many other Buddhist publications – well-used among students of Buddhism. We are grateful to him for his kind permission, enabling this reprint to be effected in Malaysia.

Buddhist Missionary Society
Malaysia.   ISBN: 967-9920-44-5

DEDICATION OF MERIT

May the merit and virtue
accrued from this work
adorn the Buddha's Pure Land,
repay the four great kindnesses above,
and relieve the suffering of
those on the three paths below.

May those who see or hear of these efforts
generate Bodhi-mind,
spend their lives devoted to the Buddha Dharma,
and finally be reborn together in
the Land of Ultimate Bliss.
Homage to Amita Buddha!

NAMO AMITABHA

南無阿彌陀佛

Printed for free distribution by
The Corporate Body of the Buddha Educational Foundation
11F., 55 Hang Chow South Road Sec 1, Taipei, Taiwan, R.O.C.
Tel: 886-2-23951198 , Fax: 886-2-23913415
Email: overseas@budaedu.org.tw
Website: http: //www.budaedu.org.tw
This book is strictly for free distribution, it is not to be sold.
Printed in Taiwan
6000 copies; July 2001
EN096-2539